MW01038366

REAL ESTATE INVESTMENT TRUSTS

REAL ESTATE INVESTMENT TRUSTS

Structure, Analysis, and Strategy

RICHARD T. GARRIGAN
JOHN F. C. PARSONS, Editors

McGraw-Hill

New York San Francisco Washington, D.C. Auckland Bogatá
Caracas Lisbon London Madrid Mexico City Milan
Montreal New Delhi San Juan Singapore
Sydney Tokyo Toronto

Library of Congress Cataloging-in-Publication Data

Garrigan, Richard T., John F. C. Parsons, editors.
Real estate investment trusts: structure, analysis, and strategy / Richard T. Garrigan, John F. C. Parsons.
p. cm.
ISBN 0-7863-0002-7
1. Real estate investment trusts—United States. I. Garrigan, Richard T. II. Parsons, John F. C.
KF1079.R437 1997
346.7304'3—cc21 97-25325
CIP

McGraw-Hill

A Division of The ***McGraw-Hill*** *Companies*

6 7 8 9 0 DOC/DOC 0 2

ISBN 0-7863-0002-7

The sponsoring editor for this book was *Steven Sheehan* and the production supervisor was *Suzanne W. B. Rapcavage.* It was set in Times Roman by *Judy Brown.*

Printed and bound by R. R. Donnelley & Sons Company.

This publication is designed to provide accurate and authoritative information in regard to the subject matter covered. It is sold with the understanding that neither the author nor the publisher is engaged in rendering legal, accounting, or other professional service. If legal advice or other expert assistance is required, the services of a competent professional person should be sought.

—From a Declaration of Principles jointly adopted by a Committee of the American Bar Association and a Committee of Publishers.

This book is printed on recycled, acid-free paper containing a minimum of 50% recycled de-inked fiber.

RTG's corner

To Ralph A. Rieves,
Friend and editor
extraordinaire

JFCP's corner

For Larry Miller,
In memory of
our dear friend

CONTENTS

FOREWORD

Real Estate Investment Trusts (REITs) were created in 1960 for the purpose of providing the public with a vehicle to participate in the equity ownership of commercial real estate. Their tax structure, which avoided corporate taxation as long as 95 percent of the income was passed through to the owners of the beneficial interests, envisioned large operating companies with diverse properties. Although various iterations were created in the interim 30-year period, such as short-term mortgage trusts, finite life structures, and variations on these themes, the industry never became an investment factor until the early 1990s.

The severe liquidity crisis of the early 1990s and the dramatic reduction in valuation of existing properties opened the door for the creation of REITs as originally envisioned in the 1960's legislation. Although there are many reasons why it took 30 years for this to occur, no single reason is more important than the fact that the private market was much more attractive to the real estate practitioner than the public market. As in every element of the economic spectrum, events occur when the incentives match up.

The REIT as a form of ownership of commercial real estate is very much in its infancy. Despite growth by a factor of 10 in the first half of the 1990s to about $70 billion, the size and scope of the equitization process to come dwarfs what has already occurred. I envision a REIT industry in the first decade of the next century being well in excess of $250 billion. Even with this goal achieved, it will still represent significantly less than 20 percent of all the commercial real estate in the United States.

The success of REITs in the 1990s can be directly attributed to the differences between these entities and their predecessors.

MANAGEMENT

Prior to the 1990s most of the publicly held REITs had an independent management company. These companies were generally owned by the sponsor and, often times, conflicts of interest occurred between the managers and the REITs. Today, in excess of 90 percent of the REITs are 100 percent self-managed. This not only avoids potential conflicts of interest, it also directly connects employees of the trust with the performance of the trust.

OWNERSHIP

The "new" REITs were created by the major players in the commercial real estate arena at the time by using an UPREIT structure. The principals were able to defer tax on their existing properties, contributing them to a partnership that shared ownership prorata with the public shareholder. As a result, the REIT industry has vested owner management in excess of most other industries. In the prior 30 years most management was employed and incentivized but had no downside risk. The new REITs' governance and management is much more closely aligned with shareholders.

INFORMATION

The proliferation of REITs and the scope of capital committed has resulted in a very active analytical community following these companies. Analysts are regularly providing investors and participants in the industry with extensive current information on individual companies, individual markets, and general trends within the industry. The plethora of information not only answers the questions but provides a growing level of confidence to the investment community. In the past, with a very small amount of capital allocated to this industry, information was sparse and the typical analyst covered steel, oil, and REITs (when they had a chance).

LEVERAGE

Historically, 75 percent loans to value were the standard in the real estate industry. This standard was predicated on the underlying assumption that real estate only goes up in value. Therefore, highly leveraged real estate became an investment whose focus was on capital gains as opposed to recurrent income. Although this method of real estate investment proved extraordinarily profitable in the nonpublic arena, the public arena looks for and values companies based on recurrent and predictable income. The new REITs no longer represent warrants on assets but instead reflect operating companies with predictable and repetitive operating income. Consequently, much lower ratios of leverage produce distributable income and materially reduce the risk of debt. Understanding the importance of lower fixed charges and the benefits the market bestows on a conservative balance sheet, the new REITs have sought and acquired credit ratings and have maintained commensurate leverage.

The structural changes described above and the contrast with the past created an environment in which REITs have become the preferred methodology for real estate investment. This continued growth is occurring because of many changing factors in investment conditions in this asset class.

REAL ESTATE INDUSTRY DYNAMICS

The Availability of Properties

The 1990s will go down in history as experiencing the greatest change of ownership of commercial real estate of all time. This dramatic change in ownership has resulted from the confluence of a number of factors, all of which insure a steady flow of appropriate investment opportunities for REITs.

1. The 1980s saw the creation of $200 billion of publicly sold limited partnership interests. These limited partnerships, by unwinding in the 1990s, have provided a flow of apartments, self-storage facilities, and strip shopping center properties for inclusion in REITs.
2. In January 1994, the National Association of Insurance Commissioners altered the reserve requirements on real estate equity owned by insurance companies. The reserve requirement changes dramatically increased the cost to the insurance industry of holding any real estate directly. Consequently, the major insurance companies that previously had as much as 50 percent of their real estate asset allocation in equities are spending the 1990s reducing these holdings through sale or stock swaps with existing REITs. The insurance companies, with a heavy preponderance of investments in office and hotel properties, became a major source of such properties.
3. The Resolution Trust Corporation (RTC), which was a government entity created to liquidate the savings and loans, did so to a large extent by bulk sales. These bulk sales were largely made to intermediaries who bought the properties or the debt. Over a period of time, these properties were liquidated, adding

primarily apartments, self-storage facilities, and mobile home parks to the supply of property available for acquisition.

4. The liquidity crunch of the early 1990s and the material drop in values and demand left the domestic and foreign banking systems awash in foreclosed or non-performing real estate assets. As the banking system reliquified, it also provided supplies of all forms of real estate assets, particularly office and hotel properties.
5. Foreign investors, especially the Japanese, were very large real estate owners and lenders in the 1980s. These investors liquidated pools of loans and properties and continued to do so throughout the decade. Their general preference for office and hotel properties slowly brought further supply of these properties into the marketplace.
6. Pension funds in the 1980s increased their real estate asset allocation from about 1 percent to about 6 percent. The premise for this massive movement of capital was inflation protection and the strong growth in values of the late 1970s and early 1980s. The very disappointing returns from this allocation led to a significant disgorgement of properties and the conversion from direct ownership to the REIT intermediary form. This has further increased the potential availability of quality commercial properties with particular emphasis on offices and hotels.

Direct Investment versus Indirect Investment

During the 1980s, direct real estate investments were made on the basis of recommendations by consultants and appraisals of the properties. When the crunch came in the 1990s investors quickly discovered that appraisals often reflected "made as instructed" and that the perceived liquidity was nonexistent. The most significant issue within the investment community in the 1990s was direct versus indirect investment. Prior to the creation of the new REITs there were no indirect real estate investment options that encompassed management, ownership, information, and leverage. The growth of the new REITs provided all of the above including the discipline of "mark to market" valuations as reflected on the New York Stock Exchange. This growth has been fueled by institutional investors electing the indirect investment approach.

The characteristics of the new REIT environment reflect the impact of the abovementioned changes and the methodology of doing business. The REIT industry is still very much in its infancy. REITs are no longer different from any other industry that is dependent on access to capital markets. Whereas, historically, the argument has been made that real estate is non-correlative and functions differently than the rest of the capital markets, this is no longer an acceptable premise. The new REITs have introduced the real estate business to the benefits and pitfalls of the capital markets. This introduction has also reinforced the recognition that capital availability to the real estate industry will be governed by the rules that apply to all other participants in the capital markets. Real estate will find that in order to access capital, it will have to compete and earn its allocation of capital based on performance, not on its asset class. Liquidity is the single most important factor encouraging the equitization of real estate. The experiences of the early 1990s defined value as liquidity. REITs have continued to define the "haves" and the "have nots" by liquidity. Thus, the market multiples for large liquid companies are 30 to 40 percent higher than the smaller illiquid examples.

The new REITs represent an asset class in the capital markets that has permanently changed institutional investment in real estate and simultaneously created appropriate opportunities for the individual investor to participate in commercial real estate. As in any embryonic market, one can expect constant alteration as the participants begin to realize the advantages and limitations of the public REIT format. Mergers and consolidations are likely to follow as the players are confronted with the responsibilities of running a public company and operating it in a fashion that will attract capital. The successful REITs are the ones that can be characterized as operating companies versus a collection of properties.

Real estate as an asset class has seen many attempts in the past 40 years to create both availability of real estate equity options and liquidity for investors. Previous attempts to do so have not been successful, primarily because of the failure to create true liquidity. The new REIT creation of the 1990s has, in fact, achieved that objective and truly represents the envy of the rest of the world. The creation and growth of these new REITs will provide investors worldwide with the opportunity to participate in the ownership of equity real estate and that, in turn, will accelerate the equitization process within the United States by drawing capital worldwide.

Sam Zell

PREFACE

Real Estate Investment Trusts is a unique reference book. It is written by leading industry experts who are active in the rapidly growing segment of the commercial real property market that is owned by investors through publicly traded real estate securities. *Real Estate Investment Trusts* is specifically designed to serve the needs of executives, investors, and other interested parties who are actively involved with REITs and public real estate operating companies. The focus of the book is on practical knowledge, perspectives, and industry insights that address the rapid shift in commercial real estate from private format ownership to publicly traded REITs.

As noted in the foreword by Sam Zell, the U.S. real estate market has experienced an enormous positive change as real estate operators and capital sources adjust to recent market cycles by transitioning toward the ownership of real estate through public real estate operating companies. This ownership transition presents real estate executives and investors with increasingly diverse and complicated challenges. Against this background, *Real Estate Investment Trusts* is a highly useful source for executives and investors involved with REITs to start a search for relevant concepts on a particular topic. *Real Estate Investment Trusts* provides comprehensive coverage of the major topics on which there is a need to be informed.

Topics have been treated narrowly enough to permit users who have a specific idea of what they are looking for to be able to turn directly to a chapter on that topic. Other users may wish to read *Real Estate Investment Trusts* from cover to cover. The chapters appear in a logical sequence so that each chapter relates to all the others. Each chapter has been written specifically for this book and provides extensive insights into critical aspects of the real estate investment trust industry.

Real Estate Investment Trusts consists of 18 chapters organized within five major divisions. Part One: The Emergence of REITs in the U.S. Real Estate Market focuses on the evolution of REITs into the modern real estate investment trust industry as well as the process through which a REIT goes public. Part Two: REITs and the Regulatory Environment provides an overview of how REIT activities are shaped by legal and tax considerations.

Part Three: Business and Financial Strategies of REITs deals with these firms' strategic managerial policies and practices. Part Four: Investment Analyses of REITs considers REITs from capital market, real estate, securities, and asset allocation perspectives. Part Five: Institutional Investor Strategies considers REITs from several different institutional investment points of view.

The editors would like to express their deep gratitude to the 27 contributing authors, who are identified in the individual chapters. Without their talents, dedication, and willingness to make time available, *Real Estate Investment Trusts* would remain only an idea.

Richard T. Garrigan
John F. C. Parsons

ACKNOWLEDGMENTS

In acknowledging the contributions of the many individuals who helped make *Real Estate Investment Trusts* a reality, it is appropriate that we first recognize the many thoughtful contributions of Daniel P. Guenther, Lansdowne Research, whose early research and editorial work helped lay the groundwork for the development of this book.

We also especially wish to thank Mark Decker, Victoria Baker, David Brandon, and Chris Lucas, all of whom were officers at the National Association of Real Estate Investment Trusts in December 1992, when *Real Estate Investment Trusts* went under contract with the publisher. Their early review of the book's proposed contents and many suggestions as to prospective contributing authors were of great assistance as work commenced on the book. Willis Andersen, Jr., REIT Consulting Services, also very generously gave his time in providing us with an extensive list of prospective authors having the qualifications to write individual chapters.

Many other persons also offered advice on the book's contents, suggestions as to contributors, and general encouragement. We therefore wish to thank Joseph L. Pagliari, Jr., Citadel Realty; H. Patrick Hackett, Jr., RREEF Capital; Tim Getz, Glimcher Realty (a true pioneer of the REIT industry while he served as real estate director with the Public Employees' Retirement System of Ohio); Marianne Dunn, Bradley Real Estate; Jeff Johnson, The Equity Group; Ted Pincus, The Financial Relations Board; Roger Franz, California Public Employees Retirement System; Anne Mengden, European Investors; Adam Metz, Urban Shopping Centers; Diane Rohlin, The Financial Relations Board; Leonard Sahling, Merrill Lynch; Larry Lettow, Old Kent Bank; J. Kurt Freundlich, First National Bank of Chicago; Donald Fortunato, Canterbury Partners; J. Grayson Sanders, Koll Investment Management; Violetta Kapsalis Buhler, Federal National Mortgage Association; and Jon Haahr, EVEREN Securities.

Several other people deserve special recognition. At DePaul University, Geoffrey Hirt, Finance Department Chair, provided not only needed departmental funds, but of much greater importance, gave us strong encouragement at every step in the book's development. Also at DePaul, Dana Berry, our project assistant, spent countless hours on such tasks as tracking due dates, handling correspondence, and typing manuscripts. His work was always first class. At MacGregor Associates, Brad Hunter kindly coordinated our frequent meetings with contributing authors.

We especially value Irwin editor Ralph A. Rieves' willingness to support this project from the idea stage to its near completion. At McGraw-Hill, we greatly benefited from both the advice and editorial skills of Steven J. Sheehan and Kevin Thornton who took over the book project as the last chapter manuscripts were being completed. We also want to thank both Pam Sourelis for her outstanding work as copy editor and Judy Brown for her superior services in preparing the book's composition.

As any editor knows, a book project like ours is truly a team effort with one's family. For their continued enthusiasm, encouragement, and generous support, we wish to thank Robin Parsons and Kris Garrigan, our wives, as well as Mac and Charlotte Parsons and Matt Garrigan, our children.

PART I

THE EMERGENCE OF REITs IN THE U.S. REAL ESTATE MARKET

CHAPTER

I

THE MODERN REAL ESTATE INVESTMENT TRUST INDUSTRY

An Overview

Mark O. Decker, *Managing Director, Friedman Billings Ramsey & Co., Inc.*

An extraordinary change has taken place in the United States that has rechanneled and restructured the flow of capital into commercial real estate. The change is fundamental to commercial real estate and is ushering in a return to basic real estate economics that has deeply altered the way investors—large and small—will own commercial real estate in the future. The vehicle called the real estate investment trust, or REIT, has been both the U.S. commercial real estate market leader and the beneficiary of this change.

The REIT concept has always been a good one. As Congress enunciated in the Committee Report accompanying the legislation creating the REIT tax vehicle in 1960:

> Your committee believes that equality of tax treatment between the beneficiaries of real estate investment trusts and the shareholders of regulated investment companies is desirable since in both cases the methods of investment constitute pooling arrangements whereby small investors can secure advantages normally available only to those with large resources. These advantages include the spreading of risk of loss by the greater diversification of investment which can be secured through the pooling arrangements; the

> opportunity to secure the benefits of expert investment counsel; and the means of collectively financing projects which the investors could not undertake singly.

In the early 1970s, the REIT concept, with some noticeable exceptions, was misused just as it began its maiden voyage into U.S. capital markets. However, the successful REITs that survived the 1970s were conservatively managed, with low leverage, and produced spectacular total returns for investors. The equity REIT group of companies established a stellar 20-year performance record, posting an average annual total return to shareholders of 16.01 percent between August 1975 and August 1995. During this 20-year period, equity REITs consistently outperformed the S&P 500, the Dow Jones Industrials, utilities, bonds, and direct real estate owned by U.S. institutions as measured by the Frank Russell index. This was no fluke. The REIT industry, like the mythical Phoenix, reformed itself through self-regulation and some painful lessons of the early 1970s.

Unfortunately for the REIT industry, which had begun to strongly rebound in the late 1970s, real estate tax shelter partnerships came along in the early 1990s. In 1981, with congressional blessing of real estate tax shelters, the real estate marketplace was converted from an industry largely disciplined by basic supply and demand, to a real estate marketplace where tax shelters drove the investment and overdevelopment of commercial real estate. It's easy to see why investors getting as much as a $4 tax deduction for every $1 invested in a real estate partnership would pour tens of billions of dollars into real estate partnerships. Nobody cared that real estate tax shelters were creating the largest explosion of overbuilt, nonviable real estate development activity in the history of the United States, or that fundamental supply/demand disciplines, both in properties built and capital flows to real estate, had reached a preposterous disequilibrium. But to their credit, in the 1986 Tax Reform Act, Congress rapidly, albeit callously, changed the ground rules.

The 1986 tax legislation was important to creating a halt in construction, a shakeout, and a healing period for a then mostly overbuilt commercial real estate marketplace. This legislation forever changed the fundamental forces of U.S. commercial real estate investments, development, and ownership. Following the 1986 tax reform agenda, investors began seeking current income and long-term growth as real estate investment performance characteristics. Investors began turning to the REIT industry for this income and growth.

In 1985, the REIT industry, although small at $16.6 billion in assets and $7.71 billion in market capitalization, anticipated this investor interest and was ready to step into the painful void. The REIT industry knew that the impending "death" of real estate tax shelters meant that REITs would play a much more significant role. The industry, led by NAREIT and a dedicated group of mentor REIT companies and associated law and accounting firms, successfully convinced Congress to include a package of REIT "modernization" amendments in the 1986 tax reform legislation. Among these amendments was the most important change to take place in the REIT tax regimen since the 1970s. A NAREIT amendment to the "independent contractor" requirement permitted a REIT, for the first time in the REIT industry's history, to manage its own properties. There were a number of other important amendments as well, which allowed for changes such as REIT subsidiaries, expansion of the prohibited transaction safe harbor for REITs that needed to sell or dispose of properties, and greater flexibility by REIT managements to make short-term investments of newly raised capital.

Of the 13 new amendments, none was more important than the amendment that altered the independent contractor requirement, permitting REITs to perform property management services that were "usual and customary" for their tenants. This still relatively unheralded amendment has been a significant catalyst in the exciting evolution of real estate securitization through the REIT tax election.

A more obvious explanation of the current REIT revolution/evolution is based on many limitations associated with private-format real estate investment vehicles, such as partnerships and commingled funds, which previously attracted capital from banks, S&Ls, insurance companies, pension funds, and individual investors. During the early 1990s, private-format real estate vehicles and their relative poor performance, absence of liquidity, infrequent valuation, lack of management's interests being aligned with investors', and relative costly fee- and transaction-based compensation arrangements, encouraged institutional capital sources to reconsider their alternatives for public-format investments.

Commercial real estate investment is management- and capital-intensive. The withdrawal of traditional private capital sources created a capital crisis, or what the real estate industry termed a "credit crunch," in the mid-to-late 1980s. Private capital disappeared. Tens of billions of investors' dollars were lost or severely devalued, and investor dollars that remained from the massive devaluation of commercial real estate were often frozen in liquid positions. Investors stopped investing in commercial real estate. If they were to return to real estate in the future, they wanted to see corporate governance and other corporate-type attributes in their investment vehicles. They wanted management to be fairly rewarded, with incentive compensation for excellent performance. They wanted management's interests to be more aligned with the interests of investors, with managers sharing the risk rather than behaving as disinterested managers/advisers. They wanted more accountability of managers who served as fiduciaries to investors; a more reliable valuation system to clarify the performance of real estate; and a liquidity mechanism enabling them to more efficiently enter or exit their real estate investments. In effect, they wanted the real estate investment trust.

Capital markets have responded with a thriving expansion of public and nonpublic corporate REIT offerings to serve these investment needs. The modern REIT industry will fill much of the void caused by the excesses of the 1980s. Although the REIT is not a panacea, it is a tax vehicle that is highly attractive for both real estate investors and owner/operators. It is an efficient corporation that receives a dividends-paid deduction and thus can avoid a corporate entity level tax, resulting in a single tax on the income stream at the shareholder level. This publicly traded real estate corporation has brought real estate to investors in the same vehicle they currently use to access auto, technology, energy, and other business sectors. The modern REITs have become operating businesses with visionary managements and the ability to add value through their management expertise.

The REIT industry that survived the 1970s had learned its lesson well. As the non-REIT real estate industry was crumbling in the mid-to-late 1980s and early 1990s, the REIT industry was experiencing record growth and unparalleled access to inexpensive equity capital. It was also postured with healthy, low-leveraged balance sheets. The KIMCO initial public offering in November 1991 proved to be the deal that ignited the rapid expansion of new REIT IPOs and secondary offerings by existing REITs.

The pre-1991 REIT industry showed impressive strength and size in the retail sector, e.g., neighborhood shopping centers, as well as health care properties and diversified portfolios. Since 1991, we have seen major expansion of the traditional REIT company niches and the emergence of strong REIT company presence in multifamily, industrial, office, enclosed mall, factory outlet center, manufactured home community, mini-warehouse, triple net lease, and hotel sectors—virtually the full panoply of "core" commercial real estate. More importantly, some of the biggest and best names in the real estate industry are now operating as REITs. Well-known real estate entrepreneurs and giants in the real estate industry, such as Sam Zell, Bill Sanders, David Simon, and Robert Taubman, have emerged as leaders of a massive $3 to $4 trillion commercial real estate market. Their entry into the REIT world is not by chance; it portends a different future for real estate, a different way of doing business—as a corporate entity operating a business instead of deals and transactions driving the markets. These individuals, and many others, are leaders of an evolution as fundamental as any change that has occurred in the real estate industry in the past 50 years.

What is most exciting about the REIT industry, however, is not its current status but its long-term growth potential. Today, the REIT industry is, by virtually all expert opinions, a young growth industry at the front end of its growth cycle. The REIT industry in 1996 had a market capitalization of $89 billion. Over the next 30 years, this industry should easily hold 29 to 30 percent of this $3 to $4 trillion market and achieve a market capitalization of approximately $400 to $600 billion. REITs are driving private market vehicles to adapt REIT-like characteristics. Investors like the REIT profile of management accountability to shareholders, ongoing operating corporations, management putting their own equity at risk by coinvesting with the public, low-leverage real estate ownership, and liquidity. REITs are revolutionizing property valuation, both those properties held in existing portfolios and those that will be involved in future transactions.

This is good news for the U.S. economy and for investors, for the corporate, tax-efficient REIT vehicle is creating much greater efficiency in the heretofore inefficient commercial real estate market—efficiency in capital flowing to real estate, efficiency in valuation of commercial real estate portfolios, and efficiency in valuing the management that operates commercial real estate.

An introduction to the modern REIT industry would not be complete without some mention of the important role of private, non-trading REITs. The role of the private REIT has an important history and an even more important future.

Historically, a small number of generally large private REITs have existed to benefit a relatively small number of large institutional investors. Private, non-trading REITs must abide by the full panoply of REIT rules and regulations. They are not, however, traded on public stock exchanges and are not required to meet public REIT disclosure and reporting with the Securities and Exchange Commission. The private REIT will be used by the larger U.S. pension funds because of corporate governance, management structure, and the tax-efficient nature of the REIT vehicle. The private REIT also offers an exit strategy, as does the public REIT, in a manner more familiar to historic patterns of investment by U.S. pension funds in U.S. equities. The private REIT can also be used to incubate a future public REIT.

Use of the private REIT by large institutional investors, particularly pension funds, has just begun. Public REITs will also attract more institutional capital. As the REIT industry grows in size, depth, and quality as the analytical infrastructure matures through more experienced buy- and sell-side analysts as well as independent analysts, and as REIT companies become more accessible to investors through market acceptance and growth of actively managed real estate securities funds, large flows of capital seeking stable, attractive current yields and long-term growth in cash flow from real estate investments will become commonplace.

The real estate market is cyclical; the stock market is cyclical; the economy is cyclical. Whatever the environment, REITs have historically proven their ability to perform. Capital will flow to proven REIT companies whose managements have performed well.

The economics of supply and demand for real estate and real estate capital is alive and well in the United States. This environment is breeding a strong, diverse commercial real estate industry in the United States. REITs have proven that, contrary to historical thought, real estate is not different from other economic sectors. It will increasingly become clear to investors that owning a liquid real estate security has tremendous appeal relative to owning brick-and-mortar buildings. For most investors, owning a commercial real estate property, instead of an equivalent stock in a company whose business is owning and operating such properties, will be as incomprehensible as deciding to buy a car dealership in order to make an investment in the auto industry.

The REIT vehicle brings capital-intensive and management-intensive commercial real estate in a liquid corporate security to the small and large investor, just as Congress envisioned in 1960 when the vehicle was created.

CHAPTER

2

GOING PUBLIC

The Formation of a REIT

W. Blake Baird, *Principal, Morgan Stanley Realty Incorporated*

REASONS FOR GOING PUBLIC

Conversation overheard on Wall Street:

> *Investment banker:* So, you want to go public. How come?
>
> *REIT wanna-be:* Lots of reasons, but I really want access to capital.
>
> *Investment banker (with dollar signs in eyes):* Sure, no problem!

Of course, it's not so easy. Thousands of such conversations occurred between bankers and prospective issuers during the REIT IPO frenzy of 1993–1994. The three most common reasons prospective issuers gave for going public were access to capital (usually for post-IPO growth), debt reduction, and estate planning.

Access to capital was by far the most common reason given. It was also the area in which investment bankers did the worst job explaining market realities to prospective issuers.

By the early 1990s, most sources of liquidity had abandoned private real estate companies. Insurance companies and banks were not lending or were requiring low loan-to-value ratios. Private equity was not available to bridge the lending gap. Commingled funds were dramatically reducing their property purchases. Private real estate companies desperately needed access to equity capital to roll over their debt and to take advantage of market opportunities. Of course, investment bankers did not explain to these private companies that being public does not *guarantee* access to capital, it only provides the *opportunity* to access capital. (We will explore this distinction further at the end of the chapter.)

The second reason for going public was debt reduction, which represents the flip side of the access-to-capital coin. Many loans made to real estate companies in the building boom of the mid-to-late 1980s were five- to seven-year maturity "mini-perms." These loans were also called (in retrospect, prophetically) five- to seven-year "bullets." Most private real estate owners who had borrowed 90 to 110 percent of the cost of an asset did not have the equity to refinance at 60 to 70 percent loan-to-value based on lower valuations than original cost. Compounding the problem was the banks' desire to grab collateral to secure their previous unsecured borrowings. This need for debt reduction led to the "go broke or go public" status of many private real estate companies by the early 1990s.

The third common reason for wanting to go public was estate planning. Even though most real estate developers believe they are immortal, a generation of developers that came of age in the late 1950s to mid-1960s were reaching the age of at least contemplating their estate problems. Many of these developers concluded that the tax bill triggered at their death might require a partial or total liquidation of assets to satisfy the liability. Owning shares in a public REIT as opposed to individual assets allows for liquidity without the company having to make real estate asset sales. This proved compelling for two reasons. First, it was tax efficient, and second, it allowed these entities to enter a form in which a company could outlive its founder.

RECENT HISTORY OF REIT IPOs

On November 22, 1991, an event occurred that would prove a watershed in REIT history. Kimco Realty completed its $128 million initial public offering through Merrill Lynch, Dean Witter, and Smith Barney. This was a seminal event for many reasons. It had been 26 months since the REIT industry had raised as much equity in a month as Kimco had raised in one offering. Moreover, there had not been a significant REIT IPO in three years since the Koger Equity IPO of 1988. REIT investment bankers in

1988–1991 felt a little like the Maytag repairman—ready for action but with not much to do.

Kimco was a well-known, established, fully integrated, credible shopping center company, unlike the generally externally advised, mostly passive REITs that had preceded it. But Kimco was so important to the development of the REIT IPO market because they were willing to "leave a little on the table" at the IPO, a wonderful philosophy of "underpromise and overperform." In other words, Kimco had enough foresight not to try to maximize value at the time of the IPO by pricing their IPO at the highest achievable price. By structuring and pricing the IPO in an "investor-friendly" way, they positioned themselves well for future capital raising. Even though Kimco was well-known in the real estate world, many public market investors were seeing them for the first time; how they conducted themselves during the IPO left deep, and favorable, impressions. Of course, five years later Kimco has more than recouped anything left on the table, as the share price has more than doubled and the dividend has been raised consistently.

If Kimco had failed in its IPO, it would have been disastrous for the REIT market. The success of Kimco and the rewards to its investors and employees showed that a REIT IPO could be completed and be profitable.

The second event that helped open the REIT IPO floodgates of 1993–1994 occurred almost exactly one year after Kimco. The IPO of Taubman Centers (managed by Morgan Stanley, Dean Witter, and Alex Brown) ushered in the era of the UPREIT and, as a result, unquestionably "high quality" real estate. Even though Taubman has not been as successful, so far, for its investors as Kimco has, the UPREIT (which will be discussed later) was instrumental in softening the tax burden of going public.

Table 2–1 illustrates the explosion of equity capital raised for REIT IPOs in 1993 and 1994.

What about the performance of the REIT IPOs in Table 2–1? As of December 31, 1995, three of the IPOs had merged with other companies. These three did not prove to be stellar performers. At the point of delisting, Holly Residential Properties, McArthur/Glen Realty, and Crocker Realty Investors were trading on an average at 29.3 percent below their IPO price. Of the remaining 92 IPOs, 58 (63 percent) were trading above their IPO price, and 34 (37 percent) were trading below their IPO price. The average price change for the group showed a 3.6 percent increase from IPO date to December 31, 1995. Given that most investors expect one-half of their

TABLE 2–1

REIT IPOs: 1987–1996 (dollars in millions)

	Number of Offerings	Dollars Raised	Average Offering Size
1987	3	$ 29.6	$ 99.5
1988	1	160.0	160.0
1989	0	0	0
1990	0	0	0
1991	1	128.0	128.0
1992	4	637.9	159.5
1993	43	8,304.0	193.1
1994	38	6,330.1	166.6
1995	5	832.3	166.5
1996	5	1,090.0	218.0
	100	$17,511.9	$175.1

return from investing in REITs from price appreciation and one-half from dividends (which averaged 8.1 percent on offer price for the 89 IPOs), REITs have proven to be a stock picker's market, not a sector buyer's one.

FRAMEWORK FOR ANALYZING REIT IPOs

We have developed an analytical framework for reviewing REIT IPOs based on the concept of the three-legged stool. If all three legs of the stool are strong, it will stand up well. If one or more legs are not strong, a wobbly stool may result. The three legs of the REIT stool are assets, management, and structure. If these three legs are strong and balanced, the REIT will stand up well in the market. If one leg is deficient, accidents could occur.

Assets underlay every analysis of a REIT. The questions one needs to ask are legion: How are the properties constructed and maintained? How are they located and managed? What rental growth exists? What competition exists or could exist? Are the assets concentrated in one sector (multifamily or retail for example)? Can the assets be altered to meet market demands (expansion, reconfiguration, and so on), or might they become functionally obsolete? and so on. Asset classes represented within REITs have changed over the years. Before 1990, the majority of REIT invest-

TABLE 2–2

The 100 Largest REIT Market Values by Asset Class

	Number of Companies	Market Value of Equity[1]
Multifamily	21	$ 20,694,877,621
Office	12	15,259,022,779
Shopping center	17	13,445,062,678
Regional mall	6	11,965,565,779
Health care	11	10,314,545,056
Industrial	8	9,591,593,675
Hotel	8	8,970,091,150
Self-storage	5	5,788,406,052
Factory outlets	3	2,106,566,746
Manufactured homes	3	2,098,420,758
Mixed	3	2,049,514,669
Other	3	2,395,807,776
	100	$104,679,474,739

[1] Implied market value: sum of market value of common shares plus value of partnership units in UPREIT structures, prices as of June 30, 1997.

ments were in either neighborhood and community shopping centers, and to a lesser extent, small office and multifamily assets. REITs were not large enough to own regional malls or CBD offices. Today, all income-producing real estate asset classes are represented, as is illustrated in Table 2–2.

Much discussion has centered on the quality of REIT assets. We believe, in addition to quality being in the eye of the beholder, that a quality asset in the right hands can (and will) produce superior risk-adjusted returns. Much of the quality (for example, trophy) real estate of the 1980s significantly underperformed the so-called poorer-quality real estate held by REITs during the decade.

Management is the second leg of our stool. All of the legs are important, but management is "first among equals." Any analysis of any company (REIT or not) must begin and end with management. Appropriate questions to ask are: Is management knowledgeable and capable of producing good returns from their real estate? Are they motivated and interested in working for the shareholders? Do they understand that the "right side" of the balance sheet is just as important as the left side (in other words, are they financially savvy in addition to being real estate savvy)? Do they have a strategic vision and a plan to reach it? and finally, Are they good "students of the market"? The last point is important; many good real estate companies have performed poorly in the public market because they did not learn what the market wanted and what it would reward with a higher share price.

The third leg is structure. Simply put, the structure of a REIT should be one in which shareholders can most likely (and most efficiently) take advantage of the other two legs: assets and management. Let's review a few of the critical elements of structure, all of which should be considered in the formation, and ongoing evaluation, of a REIT.

The first structural issue is the balance sheet. Historically, real estate was financed on a deal-by-deal basis, generally using floating-rate construction loans and fixed-rate mortgage debt. In the future, the most successful REITs will finance more like traditional corporations, by using an appropriate mix of unsecured corporate debt; convertible debt; and convertible preferred, nonconvertible preferred, and common equity. Let's discuss each of these in more detail.

In the formation of a REIT, one must balance the constraints of the existing capital structure, the desire to maximize initial cash flow to hopefully (not always) maximize "equity value," and the ultimate goal of the "perfect balance sheet."

Unsecured debt ultimately can provide more financial flexibility at a lower cost than secured debt. Even if unsecured debt carried the same cost as secured, it would be preferable because of the elimination of consents, lender approvals, mortgage taxes, and so on. Of course, unsecured debt is generally unavailable at the time of the IPO. So it is generally best to attempt to start REIT life with medium- to long-term fixed-rate financing, leaving as many properties unencumbered as possible. As the debt is repaid and the equity base grows, it is then possible to obtain an investment-grade credit rating.

It is tempting for a prospective IPO candidate to increase its cash flow via shorter-term, cross-collateralized, variable-rate financing. This is ultimately detrimental. Many investors will afford a lower multiple to the company's cash flow due to the risky nature of the debt. Investors may also assume the debt is refinanced at a medium-term, fixed rate in valuing the company, also lowering valuations. Encumbering assets in this way (as stated previously) makes the rating agency process more difficult.

What about debt levels? Generally, a debt-to-total-market capitalization (market value of equity plus debt) of 50 percent or less is required for a REIT IPO. (Of course, debt-to-market capitalization is not the best way to analyze debt levels. Coverage ratios, maturity schedules, and so on are more important. However, debt-to-market capitalization is a widely used, convenient measure.) Ratios of less than 35 percent are more desirable in that a company has room to grow by taking on modest amounts of additional debt after the IPO with the more conservative balance sheet.

Many investment bankers made the critical mistake of bringing REITs public with excessive debt in order to create equity for the insiders. This proved shortsighted. They argued that debt could be reduced, and growth funded, with additional equity sales (at presumably higher than IPO prices). Many of these REITs were DOA (dead on arrival). Equity markets are cyclical, and REITs without financial flexibility that "had to raise equity" were precisely those companies to which the market would afford the lowest valuation. We call this phenomenon "being in the capital box." In other words, a company needs to raise equity to reduce debt and grow. However, because it has too much debt, the stock trades poorly and makes selling equity prohibitively expensive.

Let's assume a REIT believes in medium- to long-term fixed-rate debt but believes that secured debt is cheaper and so doesn't (or can't) obtain an investment-grade rating. Such a course prohibits the issuance of a very important part of the "perfect balance sheet." This piece is nonconvertible perpetual preferred stock. This security is so attractive to a REIT issuer because it carries a perpetually fixed dividend (at a lower rate than the expected total return of common equity). The preferred dividend is more expensive than debt, but the preferred has the advantage of having *no maturity* and the ability to refinance *at the company's option* after five years with other capital stock issues (that is, common stock or new preferred issues). Also, and this shouldn't matter to most REITs, not repaying debt can put one in bankruptcy; preferred has no such penalty. Finally, perpetual preferred investors offer a different source of capital, one that may not buy a REIT's common equity or debt securities.

Therefore, in forming a REIT, it is important to keep one's goals in mind. A good place to start would be the "perfect balance sheet." Approximately 30 percent of the capital structure would be medium- to long-term fixed-rate debt. The maturities should be staggered, which in effect makes the debt self-amortizing. A layer of fixed-rate, nonconvertible perpetual preferred would make up 10 percent of the capital structure. And finally, common equity would constitute the remaining 60 percent. This structure, if implemented appropriately, should allow coverage ratios that could support a strong triple-B rating. Enough debt and fixed-rate preferred exists to leverage the returns to the common shareholders but not so much that the debt becomes too expensive due to credit concerns. Of course, sometimes within market cycles other securities (convertible debt and preferred, variable-rate debt, mortgage debt, and so on) may be appropriate, but this will most likely be an intermediate deviation, not a permanent change to the capital structure.

The next structural issue considered is conflict of interest. Again, many investors have agonized over the minutiae of conflicts. The issue boils down to this: Do the structure and policies of the company create a framework in which management's interests are aligned as closely as possible with those of the shareholders? For example, does management own a significant amount of stock; and did they earn such stock, or was it given to them? Also, does the stock constitute a meaningful portion of management's net worth? Why is this important? For years, Bill Newman (CEO of New Plan, thc first REIT to reach the $1 billion market-value level) explained that a one-eighth point rise in New Plan stock was worth more than his annual salary, and that his family (which founded the company) had never sold a share of New Plan stock. This compelling argument showed a great alignment of management and shareholder interests.

Of course, the opposing argument points out that when a conflict involves, for example, a related-party transaction, the economics may overwhelm management's shareholdings interest. If a manager owns 5 percent of a REIT and sells a property (wholly owned by him) to the REIT for an excessive amount, it is possible that since other shareholders shoulder some of the overpayment, the ownership interest didn't cure the conflict. I believe that while management ownership of stock doesn't cure all evils, it certainly helps.

Policies should be adopted to minimize conflicts. Self-dealing should be eliminated or severely restricted. Senior management should devote substantially all of their business time to the company. Compensation should be heavily weighted with incentives (short, intermediate, and long) to reward improving shareholder value. Incentives should generally be based on per-share results, not aggregate ones. Management should have the opportunity to be *extremely* well paid if the results produced for shareholders have been extraordinary. In summary, the issue of conflicts boils down to a simple premise: Align the interests of management and shareholders through structural policy and financial methods and hold management accountable for results. Superior returns and superior rewards for management should go hand in hand.

A third structural issue (following capital structure and conflicts) is whether or not an umbrella partnership (UPREIT) structure is used. The UPREIT, first used in the 1992 Taubman Centers IPO, is a structure in which a partnership owns the assets of the company. The partnership in turn is owned by the REIT and existing investors in the company that is going public. The REIT is then owned by its shareholders (largely new public individual and institutional investors). Primarily, using the structure at worst defers and at best eliminates serious tax liabilities for owners of "low tax basis" properties. An additional reason for using an UPREIT structure is the future possibility of using UPREIT equity interests as currency in tax-deferred acquisitions. In fact, several UPREITs have used UPREIT units in this way.

The debate over the UPREIT has been heated and emotional, but the issues are, in essence, simple. The UPREIT structure does create conflict in that, because of differing tax liabilities, owners of UPREIT units and common shareholders may come to different conclusions when deciding whether to sell a property or merge the company. In addition, some UPREITs have corporate governance structures in which unit holders have a greater proportional say in governance than their economic ownership would dictate.

Reasoned observers should make the following observations regarding the UPREIT:

- Adding a structural layer (the UPREIT) between the shareholder and the investor is a negative.
- The UPREIT as currency advantage can be accomplished by forming a DownREIT (a subsidiary UPREIT) with fewer conflicts than the UPREIT (albeit with somewhat more tax uncertainty).
- The UPREIT structure could conceivably be challenged by tax authorities, although most think this is unlikely.
- More inherent conflicts reside in the UPREIT structure than in a "clean" corporate structure.

Therefore, if given a choice, many investors prefer to not have an UPREIT structure. *However,* one very compelling argument exists for the UPREIT. A number of very high-quality real estate companies could not (or would not) have come public without the UPREIT. The REIT market and REIT investors are much better off having the opportunity to invest in many of these companies as public entities. As a matter of fact, of the 100 largest REITs, 52 are organized using the UPREIT format. So, while understanding the clear negatives of the structure, one must remember the bigger issue of the ultimate investment opportunity provided.

A fourth structural issue to consider is a REIT's board of directors. Historically, board members for REITs were selected for two reasons: Either they were friends of management or they were real estate experts. These should be the least important qualifications of a director. A board's responsibility is corporate governance. Experience in public company environments, in dealing with conflicts and shareholder obligations, in setting broad strategic direction, in making business decisions, and so on are what board members' experiences should prepare them for and allow them to provide. Real estate expertise is relatively unimportant. Management has real estate expertise. Obviously, board members must have, or obtain, a working knowledge of real estate, but that knowledge should not replace that of management. Most importantly, board members must not be beholden to management. In potential merger situations, for example, a decision in the best interest of shareholders may not represent the best personal interest of management. A board must be independent and able to make tough, possibly antimanagement decisions to fulfill their fiduciary obligations. In the future, investors will increasingly reward companies that have selected independent directors with the role of corporate governance in mind.

A fifth structural issue, or decision, in going public, is setting a payout ratio. *Payout ratio* is generally defined as the percentage of a REIT's funds from operations (FFO) that is paid as a dividend. Once again, the "right thing" and the "real-world thing" diverge. REITs are required to pay out 95 percent of their "REIT taxable income" to maintain their REIT status and generally desire to pay out at least 100 percent of taxable income to avoid any negative tax ramifications. Due to noncash expenses however, a REIT's funds from operations generally exceeds taxable income, sometimes greatly. Generally, given the high cost of raising additional equity and the potential to profitably reinvest excess cash flow in the REIT's business, it would be desirable to maintain a "low" payout ratio. In other words, in most cases, a dividend of 100 percent of taxable income is the "right" dividend. For most REITs, this would translate into a payout substantially below the 80 to 90 percent of FFO maintained by most REITs today.

However, as always, a practical argument countervails the "right" payout. REITs are capital-intensive businesses. Obviously, anything that affects a REIT's stock price will affect its short-term cost of capital. (Long-term cost of capital is a different issue, which albeit fascinating, is beyond the scope of this chapter.) Some REIT investors purchase REIT shares for the dividend. In these investors' minds, the more dollars paid as dividends, the higher the stock price should be. Even if a rational valuation would be based on an FFO multiple, with higher multiples awarded companies with higher risk-adjusted return expectations, as long as dividends matter, REIT managements face a dilemma: Keep it or pay it. I believe a balanced approach is warranted. Generally, REIT managers should consider setting their payouts toward the lower end of their asset-class peer group at IPO. Post-IPO management should share some of their FFO growth with investors in the form of increased dividends. However, growing the dividend at a rate slower than FFO growth (which will lower the payout ratio over time) should balance the divergent desires of investors. Until the day of "rational REIT valuations," this is the only practical approach.

The sixth, and final, issue to consider in analyzing the structure of an IPO is valuation. Valuation is the product of FFO and the multiple applied to such FFO. Investors will debate, and ultimately decide, the multiple. Therefore, management must present what its FFO is (or more recently, what it is expected to be).

At the time of the Kimco IPO, the initial dividend level was set with the knowledge that, due to certain special circumstances and events subsequent to the time period covered in the historical financial statements, cash flow in the period immediately following the IPO was highly likely to exceed historical levels. However, the SEC commented during their review prior to marketing the IPO that it did not appear that earnings supported the dividend. Our response to the SEC became known as "the road map." It was a quantification of known events subsequent to the historical financials that were intended to show the investor a conservative guide in calculating "in-place" funds from operations. The Kimco road map was conservatively prepared, and Kimco "underpromised and overperformed," reporting actual results significantly better than the road map indicated.

An unfortunate trend developed. REITs began to be more and more aggressive in "projecting" FFO on the road map. This led market pundits (cynics?) to recharacterize the road map as "the magic page." Issuers hoped that if investors were convinced by the magic page that FFO was higher (which supported higher dividends) than was otherwise anticipated, a higher IPO price could result.

As with many market excesses, some companies subsequently failed to meet the expectations raised by the magic page. The market predictably punished those that "overpromised and underperformed."

The prudent path appears clear. It is fine in connection with an IPO to give guidance to potential investors regarding the real "in-place" earnings potential of a company. A road map is therefore appropriate and helpful. On the other hand, issuers (and some investment bankers) need reminding that not all investors believe in "magic."

THE PROCESS

The first part of the IPO process is "the mating dance." The prospective issuer must choose its IPO team: the lawyers, accountants, and investment bankers who will undertake what will likely turn out to be the biggest step the company has ever made.

Choosing accountants is often the easiest step since most private real estate companies have outside auditors. It is important that the accounting firm chosen has an SEC practice and it's helpful if the firm has public REIT experience. This will ease the preparation and presentation of the new public entity's financial statements.

Choosing a law firm to act as issuer's counsel comes next. Again, it is very helpful to have a law firm with SEC experience and, preferably, REIT experience. Often, private real estate companies have real estate counsel only and often retain a new firm to represent the issuer. Investment bankers, accountants, and other public REITs can give guidance to a prospective issuer if choosing a new law firm. A new law firm may work in tandem with existing counsel or on its own.

Next comes the "Wall Street Bake-Off" in which a lead, and then comanager(s) are chosen to manage the underwriting. Typically, a prospective issuer will interview four to six possible managers to lead the underwriting team. Sometimes, one or more of these firms will either have a prior banking relationship or some knowledge of the company. What should an

TABLE 2–3

Best Performers	Lead Manager	Comanagers
1. Kimco Realty	Merrill Lynch	Dean Witter, Smith Barney
2. RFS Hotel Investors	Morgan Keegan	—
3. Storage USA	Morgan Keegan	Kemper Securities
4. Crescent Real Estate	Merrill Lynch	Bear Sterns, Dean Witter, PaineWebber, Prudential
5. Developers Diversified	Dean Witter	Alex. Brown, Prudential, McDonald

issuer look for? Of course, every banker will represent his or her firm as the best choice. Consider the following qualifications:

- **Knowledge/capabilities of the investment banker.** This should include knowing the market preferences and dislikes, having the ability to coordinate the team, having credibility, and having a long-term commitment to financing the REIT industry. Track record of previous managed offerings is a good indication. Table 2–3 shows at year-end 1995 the five best performing REIT IPOs since the 1991 Kimco IPO and the lead and comanagers of each.
- **Distribution strength.** This should include both retail (individual investor) and institutional distribution. A successful IPO for a REIT manages to attract both retail and institutional investors. A well-run REIT IPO is typically sold between 40 and 60 percent to institutions and 40 to 60 percent to retail.
- **Research.** Sell-side research analysts are typically involved in helping structure and market a good REIT IPO. They also follow up with research coverage to keep investors informed. The most widely followed ranking of REIT research analysts is published annually by *Institutional Investor* magazine.

A prospective issuer should choose his lead manager with three criteria in mind: banking expertise, distribution, and research. Comanaging underwriters are typically chosen after a lead manager is selected. The team, typically consisting of four managers, should be chosen to compliment the strengths and weaknesses of the lead manager and other comanagers.

Occasionally larger IPOs (greater than $300 million) will use five or more managers in order to assure adequate distribution. When considering the addition of managers, an issuer must balance the potential for additional strength against the potential dilution of the other manager(s).

Once the team is in place, it's time to make the last, and most important, structural decisions: what's in and what's out. This is the consolidation phase of the transaction. A private real estate entrepreneur faces two competing criteria when embarking on an IPO. First, typically the public market likes a focused, logical story, whereas a private company may pursue various strategies to make money. For example, a company may have both a shopping center company and a commercial brokerage operation, or both a multifamily operation and a home builder; or possibly a company might have assets that don't fit the new public focus of the company or that simply cannot be "profitably" put into the REIT. In general, as discussed earlier, the market does not like conflicts. Therefore, the prospective issuer must balance a third factor: a skeptical market questioning every aspect of any preformation transaction. The best advice is to try and take the company public. In other words, to the extent that thc REIT rules allow and it fits the strategy of the company, an asset or operation should be in the REIT. The market has shown that in instances where assets were included in the REIT "for nothing" (that is, the assets did not generate current cash flow), the market has been fairly efficient in rewarding companies in the aftermarket for real value. Occasionally, certain people or assets cannot be included in the public entity. On these occasions, the reason for exclusion should be easily explainable, should be accomplished with no actual or perceived conflicts, and should be biased in favor of the new public shareholders.

Next in the IPO process comes the preparation of the registration statement. The registration statement (filed with the SEC to "register" the securities to be sold) is the document that describes the company (its history, people, assets, structure), the offering, the industry, conflicts or risks, and financial condition and discussion. The prospectus (a part of the registration statement) is the document that offers the company' s security to the public. The prospectus must "tell the story" and must disclose all material facts that a reasonable investor would expect to know in order to make an informed investment decision. The prospectus is prepared by the issuer's counsel with input from the investment bankers and their counsel and the company. The financial statements are prepared by the company working closely with the independent accountants and are, of course, reviewed by issuer's counsel, and the bankers and their counsel.

As part of the preparation of the registration statement, due diligence is conducted. In this process, the bankers and counsel investigate the company to make sure that all material facts affecting an investment in the company have been disclosed. Due diligence, broadly speaking, focuses on four areas: properties, legal, environmental, and financial. Each is briefly discussed below.

Due diligence on the properties involves site inspections, market reviews, lease terms, rental and expense histories, and so on. A property tour (sometimes lasting several days) will be undertaken by the bankers early in the process with additional visits (including those for analysts) occurring later in the process. Legal due diligence involves a review of corporate records, litigation review, incorporation requirements and logistics, property title review, material lease review, and so on. Environmental review, which is part of both asset and legal due diligence, is an increasingly important aspect of due diligence. Given the potential liability of property owners for environmental contamination, this process is time-consuming and often expensive. Environmental assessments (so-called Phase I's) are often required, and disclosure on potential and actual problems is extensive. Finally, financial due diligence involves reviewing the financial statements and pro formas and their preparation, projections, review of accounting policies controls and procedures, and other items deemed material.

Once due diligence has been completed, the registration statement is finalized and filed with the SEC. After a typical 30-day review, the SEC comments on the filing. Once comments are responded to appropriately, the amended registration statement is filed. A preliminary prospectus (known as a "red herring" because of the required red-colored legend on the cover page) is printed and distributed to potential investors, and marketing begins.

Most management teams that have lived through a road show will relate stories of long days, stressful travel, even more stressful meetings, not enough sleep, and bad chicken for lunch at 10 different venues. All of this, of course, is made more stressful by the uncertainty of whether the offering will be successful or whether the transaction can even be completed at all. The IPO road show lasts two to three weeks, during which managers tell their story, generally using a 20-minute slide show. A typical day generally includes breakfast and lunch group meetings, meetings in retail brokerage offices for groups of brokers, and institutional one-on-ones. The one-on-ones generally consist of 60- minute sessions with large institutional buyers who can be critically important to the offering's success. Management is accompanied by an investment banker and often a sell-side analyst from the lead manager. Days almost always begin and end in different cities, and a visit to Europe is not uncommon.

While the road show proceeds, the syndicate desk of each comanager collects orders and reflects them to the lead (or book-running) manager. Some orders will be "good in the range." That is, a buyer is willing to purchase within the expected price range on the cover of the red herring (usually a 10 percent or so spread, for example, \$20 to \$22 per share). Some orders will have a limit. At the end of the road show, the book-running manager will assemble the orders he or she has received directly from comanagers and from a syndicate of underwriters assembled by the lead manager.

A pricing proposal is then presented to the management of the issuer. This represents a firm commitment by the underwriters to purchase a certain number of shares at a certain price. The underwriters in turn sell those shares to the public at a public offering price. The price paid to the issuer is generally 93 percent of the public offering price. The 7 percent difference, or gross spread, is compensation to the underwriters and is used to pay salespeople, cover expenses, and compensate the managers for preparing the offering. Table 2–4 outlines a sample summary IPO timetable for the public-offering process. If the process is successfully completed, the company is ready to begin life as a publicly traded entity.

ALTERNATIVES TO THE IPO

The process just described illustrates the most common way to undertake an initial public offering. There are alternative ways to "go public," outlined briefly below.

A company may choose to merge with an existing public company, generally in one of three forms. A private company can "sell out" to a larger company and give up most, or all, of its control over the business. This may get the best price for a seller since the buyer might be willing to pay a control premium. A second alternative would be a "merger of equals," where similar-size public and private companies would merge and subsequently share management. This "strategic merger" has great potential but can be

TABLE 2–4

Sample Summary of IPO Timetable

Date	Action
Week 1	Lead manager selected Due diligence begins Accountants begin working on financials Issuers counsel begins drafting S-11
Week 3	Rough first draft of S-11 circulated to working group
Week 4	Initial drafting session
Week 5	Second draft of S-11 circulated Comanagers invited Accountants circulate first draft of financials
Week 6	Third draft of S-11 circulated (with draft financials)
Week 8	Final draft of S-11 circulated Underwriters finish committee process
Week 9	File S-11 with SEC
Week 12	First draft of road show presentation circulated
Week 13	Second draft of road show presentation circulated
Week 14	Receive SEC comments
Week 15	File amendment with SEC Begin printing red herrings Finalize slide/road show presentation Road show rehearsals, internal presentations
Weeks 16–17	Road show
Week 18	Price and offer Closing

hampered by cultural differences or conflicts over control (the "who sits in what chair" phenomenon). In the last merger alternative, a larger private company merges with a relatively small public company. This "backdoor merger" would cede control generally to the larger private company. This merger makes sense in theory, but it occurs rarely, primarily because managements of smaller companies want to keep their jobs even if the merger might be in the shareholders' best interest.

An extreme form of the merger just discussed is the "shell REIT." In this merger, a private company merges with a public company that has little or no assets or management. Again, this makes sense in theory, but in practice, the few "shell REITs" available may be hindered by unwanted legal or financial liabilities, which caused them to become shell REITs in the first place.

Another form of IPO can be called the "incubator REIT." In this alternative, the private company takes the intermediate step of forming a private REIT, often using new private capital to fix the balance sheet on an interim basis. This alternative has the advantage of allowing the formation transactions to occur and an operating history in to-be-public form to be built prior to the IPO. The only significant negative to this alternative could be the higher returns often demanded by private capital sources as opposed to the public market. At certain times in the public market IPO cycle, the incubator REIT may indeed be a more attractive alternative.

AFTER THE IPO, THEN WHAT?

Remember how this chapter began? Companies go public to obtain access to capital. However, as stated earlier, public status does not guarantee access to capital, it only provides the *opportunity* to access capital. The single best way for a REIT to assure access to attractively priced capital over the long term is to perform for its investors. Investors will always come back for more if they have received, and expect to receive in the future, attractive returns on the capital they provide. By "underpromising and overperforming," management can assure friendly providers of capital.

Many new public companies focus on investor relations (IR) early in public life. The method of investor relations is relatively unimportant (that is, dedicated IR person or not, outside PR firm or not, regular analyst meetings or not, glossy quarterly reports or not). More important (maybe critical) to an investor relations effort is consistent, detailed disclosure of results, actions, strategies, and policies. Investors do not like surprises (which are, more often than not, negative). Detailed financial and nonfinancial disclosure is critical. The communication media could include annual and quarterly reports; press releases on acquisitions, dispositions, and capital market transactions; regular analyst meetings and property tours; internet disclosure; conference presentations; and so on. It isn't just a matter of doing what you do; it's making sure the investing community knows what you do and why you do it.

Does size matter? Full debate of this question extends beyond the scope of this chapter. However, in the REIT world, size generally does matter. With the caveat that size for size sake is a poor objective and that per-share results matter much more to investors than aggregate results, size does convey certain advantages. Size allows for greater share liquidity and therefore the ability to attract large investors. Size, at least approximately \$200 million of equity, is almost a necessity to achieve investment-grade credit ratings. Some critical mass is necessary to take advantage of operating efficiencies and to afford management talent. Finally, larger REITs generally trade at higher multiples of cash flow than smaller REITs. There may be a legitimate "chicken or egg" question over why this is true, but the quantitative result is unrefutable. Given this, REIT managers should keep in mind the advantages of size; while managements should not pursue "bigger is better," pursuing profitable growth is very worthwhile.

SUMMARY

The modern era for REIT IPOs is only five years old. In 1975, the total market value of REITs was less than \$1 billion. In 1990, it was \$8 billion; today it's approximately \$100 billion. Almost half of all public REITs were not public five years ago. In such a rapidly changing environment, no discussion of REIT IPOs or what the market wants should be taken as doctrine. When things change, the best approach is to study the market. One can try to educate the REIT market but should not single-handedly try to change it.

W. Blake Baird, a student of the REIT market, is a Principal of Morgan Stanley Realty Incorporated. Mr. Baird joined Morgan Stanley in 1997 in connection with the merger of Morgan Stanley and Dean Witter. Prior to the merger, Mr. Baird was Managing Director and Co-Head of Real Estate Investment Banking at Dean Witter, where he began focusing on REITs in 1988.

PART

II

REITs AND THE REGULATORY ENVIRONMENT

CHAPTER

3

REITs AS LEGAL ENTITIES

William B. King, *President of William B. King, PC*
Partner, Goodwin, Procter & Hoar, L.L.P.

INTRODUCTION

The paradigm of today's successful publicly owned real estate investment trust is a fully integrated operating company that owns, manages, and develops real properties with which it and its management have had years of successful experience. The company typically focuses its ownership on a distinct type of property, frequently in a distinct geographical area.

By definition, the principal source of income of the company, because it is a REIT, will be rents (or, if a financing vehicle such as the health care REITs, mortgage interest). So, in addition to being familiar with property type and geographic area, today's successful REIT management is also likely to have significant experience with its tenants or tenant types who will pay the rent. Notwithstanding the original concept that a qualified REIT needs to be a passive investor, typically one thinks of today's publicly owned REIT as an operating business rather than a portfolio of individual properties. Indeed, the franchise value of this business, or the value added by experienced management, is what justifies the aggregate market capitalization of many REITs exceeding the net aggregate values of their individual portfolio properties.

Because a real estate investment trust is a creature of the Internal Revenue Code (the Code), it must be either a domestic corporation or some other "corporation, trust or association . . . taxable as a domestic corporation."[1] Entities that are partnerships under the Code or trusts without transferable shares cannot qualify as REITs (although the new "check-the-box" Treasury regulation effective January 1, 1997, permits certain noncorporate entities to elect whether to be taxed as a corporation or a partnership and could theoretically result in entities organized as partnerships or limited liability companies under state law electing to be taxed as a corporation and thereby also becoming eligible to elect REIT status for federal tax purposes).[2]

Today's model REIT clearly contemplates capital-raising activities primarily on a companywide basis, rather than the asset-by-asset or portfolio-by-portfolio basis that was the model for the partnership syndications of individual properties in the early 1980s. However, because of the existing partnership status of most of the properties combined during the formation process of the many REITs organized in the early 1990s and of so many other properties that have subsequently been consolidated into existing REITs, and because of the heavy tax cost to the existing partner owners of those properties that would be occasioned upon a taxable disposition of such property directly into a REIT taxable as a corporation, title to many of the properties that are now treated as being "owned" by REITs are actually owned by operating partnerships (OPs) controlled by the REIT as general partner. Such REITs that own all of their properties through a single operating partnership are sometimes generically referred to as UPREITs, and REITs that own some but not all of their properties through one or more partnerships have more recently been dubbed DownREITs.

Many of the management teams that today operate and manage the real estate owned by the REIT (or its operating partnership) have experience and skills in, and before becoming a part of a REIT management team had a track record of generating income from, providing the same property management, development, leasing, or other real estate-related services to third parties. But because of the income requirements and asset limitations for REIT qualification under the Code, a REIT itself may receive only a nominal amount of its gross income from third-party services. As a result, many of today's REITs also have established non-REIT affiliates to engage in these nonqualifying activities.

Accordingly, while one tends to think of today's REIT as a unified operating business, like many single unified businesses in other industries, the legal entity comprising that business may actually consist of a parent corporation with a variety of subsidiaries, affiliates, joint ventures, or other strategic partners as a part of the unified venture. Like many other unified business entities doing business in the United States, today's REIT may actually consist of a public (that is, having at least 100 shareholders) corporate (or business trust) parent company qualifying as a REIT with a variety of other types of entities affiliated or subsidiary to it.

THE EFFECTS OF TAX QUALIFICATION REQUIREMENTS ON ORGANIZING THE REIT

Organizational Requirements

The first six of the seven enumerated requirements for meeting the definition of a "real estate investment trust" under the Code relate to the organization and governance of the entity seeking REIT status:

> For purposes of this title, the term "real estate investment trust" means a *corporation, trust,* or *association*—
>
> 1. which is managed by one or more trustees or directors;
> 2. the beneficial ownership of which is evidenced by transferable shares or by transferable certificates of beneficial interest;
> 3. which (but for the provisions of this part) would be taxable as a domestic corporation;
> 4. which is neither (A) a financial institution referred to in section 582(c)(5), nor (B) an insurance company to which subchapter L applies;
> 5. the beneficial ownership of which is held by 100 or more persons;
> 6. which is not closely held (as determined under subsection (h)); and
> 7. which meets the requirements of subsection (c). [emphasis added][3]

Whether organized as a corporation or a business trust, a company planning REIT status should have little trouble meeting the first six of these qualification requirements.

An entity organized in corporate form probably automatically meets the requirements of clauses (1) (managed by one or more trustees or directors), (2) (ownership evidenced by transferable shares), and (3) (taxable as a corporation). Prior to 1976, the Code permitted only unincorporated trusts or associations that (but for the special REIT provisions) would be taxable as a domestic corporation to qualify as REITs. As a practical matter, therefore, the early REITs were all organized as what is referred to as a "Massachusetts trust" or a "business trust," that is, "trusts whose beneficial interest is divided into transferable certificates of participation or shares,"[4] whose definition the original REIT drafters clearly had in mind in drafting original Section 856(a) of the Code. When in 1976 the Code was amended to permit corporations to qualify as REITs, clauses (1) and (2) effectively were rendered superfluous as to corporations but were still necessary to distinguish between different types of trusts. The words "or directors" were added to clause (1), which had originally referred only to management "by one or more trustees." Clause (1) and the separate requirement in clause (2) that the beneficial ownership be evidenced by transferable shares or by transferable certificates of beneficial interest were included in the original legislation to distinguish trusts with this corporate characteristic that are eligible to be treated as REITs from partnerships and from donative probate-types of trusts that are not. Clause (4) was also added in 1976 to eliminate insurance companies, banks and other financial institutions, and finance companies from those corporations that may qualify as REITs. The financial institution and insurance company prohibitions of clause (4) are not issues for most would-be REITs.

The 100-shareholder requirement of clause (5) is merely a question of counting investors.

The not-closely-held requirement of clause (6) is sometimes also referred to as the five-or-fewer, or 5-50, rule.[5] It follows the concept in the original qualification requirement that a REIT not only be widely held, with at least 100 shareholders, but that ownership not be so closely held that five or fewer "individuals" directly or indirectly own 50 percent or more in value of the outstanding shares of the REIT. Certain domestic tax-exempt investors fall within the definition of "individual" for this purpose, thereby originally precluding control of a REIT by a small group of institutional investors as well as individuals, but a change in the law in 1993 now permits a REIT to qualify notwithstanding concentrated ownership by certain qualified pension or profit-sharing trusts.[6] Careful attention needs to be given to the 5-50, not-closely-held requirement in drafting the governing documents of a REIT. A later section of this chapter addresses the "excess shares" provisions that most REITs include in one form or another in their governing documents to prevent inadvertent failure to meet this requirement for qualification.

Historical Background

Except for the 100-shareholder and 5-50 rules, the original organizational requirements basically described what is known as a "business trust" (that is, a trust established for business purposes whose beneficial interest is represented by transferable shares) or a "Massachusetts trust" of the type that is common in that state. Not surprisingly, this type of organization was commonly used to own investment properties of the type sponsored and managed by the primarily Boston-based real estate property managers who were the principal sponsors of the original REIT legislation. This type of ownership of investment properties was common in Massachusetts and elsewhere at least back into the last quarter of the 19th century, and the business trust organization was generally believed to be exempt from federal income taxation applicable to corporations until the United States Supreme Court, in the case of *Morrissey v. Commissioner,*[7] in 1934 held otherwise.

The *Morrissey* decision not only affected the early real estate trusts organized as common law Massachusetts business trusts but also several mutual funds organized as business trusts. In 1940, the mutual fund industry was successful in sponsoring legislation adding what is now Part I of Chapter M of the Internal Revenue Code.[8] As a result, a "regulated investment company" organized in either business trust or corporate form that met certain asset, income, and ownership requirements and that distributed substantially all of its otherwise taxable income as dividends to shareholders was entitled to a deduction for dividends paid. Twenty years later in 1960, managers and sponsors of real estate trusts finally obtained essentially comparable treatment for "real estate investment trusts," with the addition of Part II of Chapter M of the then Internal Revenue Code in 1954.[9]

Various of the organizational requirements applicable to regulated investment companies ("RICs"), including the 100-shareholder and 5-50 rules were carried over to the qualification requirements for REITs in Part II of Chapter M. It is notable that corporations were not originally eligible to qualify as REITs. Early on in the REIT legislative effort, it became apparent that there were many in Congress and at the Treasury Department who viewed the ability of a corporation to elect REIT status as a potentially huge loophole through which all sorts of typical corporate business organizations that conduct their operations on real estate (for example, hotels and parking garages) might escape corporate tax. The logic may not have been there, but the paranoia was. The sponsors of the REIT legislation, used to conducting business in the business trust form, really did not care and chose not to fight the issue. So the original REIT legislation became available for business trusts only.

This proved to be an unnecessary restriction on the normal form of organization for doing business in the United States. After 16 years of no apparent REIT abuse, and comforted by the other restrictions and requirements for REIT qualification, Congress in 1976 amended the Code to permit corporations (other than banks, insurance companies, and certain other financial institutions) to qualify for REIT status.

Other requirements for qualification as a REIT under the original 1960 legislation, and the evolutionary changes in certain of such requirements, are also relevant to an understanding of the organizational structure of today's paradigm REIT.

Asset-Limitation Requirements

Limitations on Ownership of Stock and other Securities

A qualified REIT must meet certain requirements at the close of each taxable quarter relating to the composition of its assets. Basically, at least 75 percent of its assets must consist of defined "real estate assets," cash, and government securities. "Real estate assets" include debt secured by mortgages on real property and stock of other qualified REITs. Except for government securities and securities that are "real estate assets," a REIT may not own more than 10 percent of the outstanding voting securities of any single issuer, and no more than 5 percent of its total assets may be represented by securities of any one issuer (whether such securities are voting stock, nonvoting stock, debt, or some other kind of securities), and no more than 25 percent of its total assets may be represented by securities of all issuers.[10]

Subsidiaries Limited to "Qualified REIT Subsidiaries"

These asset limitations have had substantial impact on the organization and operation of REITs over the years. Because of the 10 percent limitation on voting stock of any corporation, a REIT could not operate through corporate subsidiaries until 1987, when the law was changed to permit a REIT to own a "qualified REIT subsidiary" (QRS). Basically, a QRS is defined as a corporation, 100 percent of whose stock is held by the REIT at all times during the period the corporation has been in existence. For federal income tax purposes, the QRS is ignored and not treated as a separate taxpayer, although it is a separate legal entity for state law purposes and may therefore serve to limit liability to the properties or activities held or conducted by the QRS. The QRS may be subject to separate state taxation. Because it is not deemed to exist for federal income tax purposes, all of the assets and all of the income of the QRS are deemed to be income and assets directly of the REIT. Intercorporate payments between the REIT and its QRS are ignored.[11]

Source-of-Income Requirements; Restrictions on Management Activities

A REIT must meet three separate source-of-income requirements, two of which essentially mandate that 75 percent and 95 percent, respectively, of the REIT's gross income consist of designated sources of income.[12] For an equity REIT owning real estate, the principal source of qualifying income is "rents from real property."[13] One of the major limitations on REIT activities under the original REIT legislation was the provision still in today's Code that excludes from the definition of "rents from real property" any amount of rent from a property if the REIT "furnishes or renders services to the tenants of such property, or manages or operates such property, other than through an independent contractor from whom the trust itself does not derive or receive any income."[14]

The "independent contractor" requirement was a source of irritation for REITs for years until the passage of the Tax Reform Act of 1986. The Code, as originally drafted and still today, defines "independent contractor" in terms of ownership—that is, that neither the REIT nor the independent contractor own directly or indirectly more than a 35 percent interest in the other.[15] In a series of revenue rulings, however, the Internal Revenue Service effectively imposed further restrictions against employees of the REIT also serving as employees of the independent contractor. The "independent contractor" requirement effectively mandated that a REIT engage one or more independent property management firms to provide day-to-day management of its rental properties. More than any other requirement of the Code for REIT qualification, the limitations that prevented a qualified REIT from actively managing its own properties also prevented it from becoming an integrated operating company. So ingrained was the notion that a REIT had to have an independent contractor manage its properties, in order to ensure that the rents from such properties qualified as "rents from real property" for purposes of the 75 percent and 95 percent source-of-income requirements, that prior to 1986 virtually all of the revenue rulings and private-letter rulings relating to this matter dealt with the question of whether a particular property manager would meet the definition of "independent contractor," and almost no rulings focused on what activities might constitute the "furnishing or rendering of services to tenants" or the "management or operation" of the property. The mandated separate management built cost inefficiency into the REIT structure: Wholly aside from the management fees that a REIT had to pay to an independent contractor, the arrangement resulted in lack of responsibility and accountability in the management of properties. The REIT, as a vehicle, was at a competitive disadvantage to other forms of property companies (for example, those organized in partnership form) in managing its properties. The "independent contractor" requirement also fostered the creation of many conflict-of-interest situations, as REIT officers not infrequently were the owners of the independent contractor.

Repeal of the independent contractor requirement was the major legislative priority of the National Association of Real Estate Investment Trusts (NAREIT) for years. Although sympathetic to the REIT industry arguments, several in Congress were leery about the potential effect of an outright repeal of the independent contractor provision. Finally in the Tax Reform Act of 1986, Congress took a halfway step by permitting a REIT to manage its own properties to the same extent that various tax-exempt entities such as pension funds, charities, and universities could directly manage their properties without creating "unrelated business taxable income." The 1986 Act effected this change without disturbing the original "independent contractor" language contained in the operative language of the Code (subparagraph (C) of subsection 856(d)(2) by adding the following stub sentence at the end of subsection 856(d)(2)(C): "Subparagraph (C) shall not apply with respect to any amount if such amount would be excluded from unrelated business taxable income under section 512(b)(3) if received by an organization described in section 511(a)(2)."[16]

Although few realized it at the time, the Tax Reform Act of 1986's inclusion of this stub sentence into the REIT provisions of the Code has been the single most important change in the REIT tax regime that has permitted the explosive growth of the REIT industry in the 1990s and to REITs becoming real operating companies. Initially, REITs were cautious about the effect of the change in the independent contractor rules. While the reference to the sections relating to tax-exempt entities made it clear that a REIT could now "operate" and "manage" its properties directly and need not do so through an independent contractor, because of the lack of pre-1986 letter rulings there was significant uncertainty as to what activities might constitute "furnishing or rendering services to tenants." A series of private-letter rulings in the late 1980s and early 1990s issued by an Internal Revenue Service that understood the realities of multitenant property management as well as the intent of Congress established that a REIT may now directly perform virtually all normal management services relating to multitenant property so long as such services relate to the efficient operation and enhancement of the value of the property, are customary with respect to the property type and in the market in which the property is located, and are not primarily for the benefit of the tenant. Many of the old-line REITs quickly internalized the property management services that they had previously farmed out to third-party managers. Wall Street and other investors applauded and rewarded the increased efficiency and accountability and, in the several situations in which the independent contractor had been basically owned or controlled by management of the REIT personally, the elimination of a conflict of interest.

Fully as significantly, many privately owned real estate companies with experienced management and development teams on their payrolls, that had previously developed and separately syndicated and financed a series of individual properties, could now see their way clear to combining their real properties and their management and development teams into a single unified operating business entity that could access the public capital markets through REIT formation.

COMPONENT ORGANIZATIONS OF THE REIT OPERATING "ENTITY"

Introduction

As noted in the preceding section of this chapter, the Internal Revenue Code forces a REIT to be organized as a corporation or business trust. Until qualified REIT subsidiaries were permitted to be formed commencing in 1987, the REIT could not hold its properties (or its mortgages or other "interests in real property") through a subsidiary. However, from the very beginning the Internal Revenue Service acknowledged that a REIT could hold its interests as a partner in a partnership. An original Treasury regulation, promulgated in 1962 and essentially unchanged in substance since, provides that a REIT that is a partner in a partnership "will be deemed to own its proportionate share of each of the assets of the partnership and will be deemed to be entitled to the income of the partnership attributable to such share," with "the interest of a partner in the partnership's assets . . . determined in accordance with his capital interest in the partnership;" and "the character of the various assets in the hands of the partnership and items of gross income of the partnership shall retain the same character in the hands of the partners for all purposes of section 856."[17] So, from the earliest days of the REIT industry, REITs have been able to be in partnerships. The key restraint, because of the regulation just cited, has been that the partnership could not hold assets or receive income that, if owned or received directly by the REIT, would jeopardize the tax qualification of the REIT.

Because most REITs were initially sponsored by people who made their money providing services to other investors, most early REITs were externally advised under an advisory contract with the sponsor or an affiliate of the sponsor. Over time, several of these early REITs brought their corporate management in-house, although until the effects of the Tax Reform Act of 1986 became clear, the day-to-day management of an equity REIT's properties had to be performed externally by an independent contractor. All functions necessary for the management of a real estate company were present, but the shareholders of the REIT, while effectively owning the economics of the real estate, did not also control the economics of the operation and services with respect to the company and its assets.

By contrast, the modern REIT structure places emphasis on having all, or as many as possible, of the economics related to the unified real estate operations, including from the management and the service end of the business as well as from the ownership of properties, flow directly to the shareholders of the REIT. Virtually all of the old-line, formerly externally advised and managed REITs have become fully integrated companies. When desirable for limitation of liability, tax efficiency, or other valid business purposes, the REIT may now hold all or some of its properties through one or more wholly owned qualified REIT subsidiaries. Many of the new REITs of the 1990s have been organized using the UPREIT structure, in which the actual ownership of the real estate properties are held by an operating partnership of which the REIT is the general partner and usually the holder of a majority of the outstanding OP units. Although the shareholders of the UPREIT may not own 100 percent of the interests in the unified real estate business being conducted by the OP, they do own 100 percent of their pro rata share of such interests and are no worse off than the owners of a REIT that is a joint venture partner with some other investor in a particular property or portfolio of properties. Increasingly common also are DownREIT transactions in which an existing corporate REIT may contribute one or more of its existing properties or a cash investment to a partnership to which the existing owners of one or more other properties also contribute their interests, becoming (or remaining) partners, generally in contemplation of eventually exchanging their interests in the DownREIT partnership for REIT shares—yet again another variant on the REIT's owning properties or interests in real estate through a partnership. And, finally, various structuring devices have evolved to assure that components of the unified REIT business that cannot be rendered directly by the REIT without jeopardizing its favored tax status may nevertheless be performed by taxpaying "C" corporations most of whose economic benefits, if not voting control, are held by the REIT.

The following sections of this chapter will address various of the issues and consequences involved in the form of legal organization of the various separate component entities of the unified business entity comprising today's REIT.

The Organization of the REIT Itself

Corporation or Business Trust

A qualified REIT must be either a corporation, or a trust or association (business trust) taxable as a corporation. Both types of vehicle are appropriate and suitable for engaging in for-profit operating business, although the corporation is by far the better known and more widely used form of vehicle.

A *corporation* is a legally distinct entity created under statute. Every state has a general corporation law and a simple procedure for organizing a corporation, which generally is deemed to come into existence upon filing of a certificate of incorporation or articles of incorporation with an appropriate state agency (usually the Secretary of State of the domicile state). Although the corporation laws of the various states are similar in most respects, there are differences from state to state. Because it is a distinct legal entity, the debts, obligations, and other liabilities of a corporation are the corporation's own, rather than debts, obligations, or liabilities of its shareholders, directors, officers, or other agents. Thus, a key characteristic of a corporation is that its directors and officers have no personal liability for the debts or other obligations of the corporation to other parties.

As a separate legal entity, a corporation may enter into contracts, acquire properties, issue stock, incur debt, and do virtually anything that an individual person may legally do. To be sure, a corporation, which is owned by its shareholders, run by its directors, and managed on a day-to-day basis by its officers and employees, acts through individual persons. The domicile state's corporation statute generally sets forth the respective rights and obligations of the shareholders, directors, and officers of the corporation among themselves, including rights of indemnification of directors and officers for any personal obligations incurred by such individuals during the proper conduct of their responsibilities. Corporation statutes also generally set forth the standard of fiduciary duty of the directors and officers to the corporation and to its shareholders and provide, or authorize the articles of incorporation to provide, when such individual actors may or may not be held personally liable for a breach of their duties. Within the standards set forth in the applicable corporation statute, the articles of incorporation may provide for a large number of provisions relating to the governance of the particular corporation. The articles of incorporation of a corporation, as supplemented by the corporation's bylaws, is regarded as a contract among the corporation and its shareholders; and investors buying stock of the corporation, even though not specifically named parties to the contract that is constituted by the articles of incorporation and the applicable state corporation statute, become subject to that contract.

The *business trust* in its purest form does not depend on a state statute for its existence. Rather, the rights and obligations of the shareholders and trustees arise solely from the provisions of the declaration of trust applicable to that business trust. Under the declaration of trust, named trustees, for themselves and their successor trustees, declare that they will hold and manage property contributed to the trust, in the manner provided under the declaration of trust, for the benefit of the holders of transferable shares of beneficial interest in the trust. Like articles of incorporation of a corporation, the declaration of trust of a business trust constitutes a contract between the trustees and the shareholders. However, the right to enter into such a contract and the consequences of such contract no more depend on the existence of state authorization than the right, say, of a parent to declare a trust for the benefit of their children or grandchildren, or of one or more individuals (trustees) to say to one or more others (shareholders) in effect: "If you give us your dollars, we will invest and manage them in a business and run the business in the manner provided in this declaration of trust for the benefit of you or to whomever you may subsequently assign your interest in the trust if such assignment is permitted by the declaration of trust." In brief, a business trust exists and is recognized at common law as a result of individuals' or other legal entities' right to contract among themselves.[18]

Because there is no corporation statute that dictates the parameters for governance of a common-law business trust, the details of such governance and of the relationships and respective rights between shareholders and trustees is established by the drafter of the declaration of trust. Typically, the powers of the trustees set forth in the declaration of trust are very broad, with the trustees given the same flexibility and authority to run the business of the trust as directors are afforded under state corporation statutes and articles of incorporation to run the business of corporations. While it is fundamental that the trustees of a business trust have a fiduciary duty to run the business and the affairs of the trust for the benefit of the shareholders that is at least as strong as like fiduciary duties of directors of corporations to the shareholders of the corporation, typically declarations of trust provide for standards of fiduciary care and rights of indemnification and limitations on personal liability comparable to those provided in corporation statutes. Governance features of a business trust may be tailored to the particular situation and need not necessarily include the same limitations or restrictions of a corporation statute, which normally require annual meetings of shareholders, prescribe maximum times for record dates, specify the right of a designated number of shareholders to call special meetings, impose limitations on a corporation's ability to pay dividends or redeem shares, and so on. A declaration of trust may set its own rules for such matters. It may provide that trustees serve without specified terms and have the power to appoint their successors without the need to stand for election at an annual meeting of shareholders each year (or every three years). While legally permissible, as a practical matter, however, such a provision relating to the trustees would likely preclude the business trust from raising money in the capital markets and from meeting basic shareholder rights requirements for listing shares on the major stock exchanges or trading markets.

Like articles of incorporation, the declaration of trust of a business trust should specify the authority of the trustees to issue shares. Unlike corporation statutes, which typically require that the maximum authorized capital be specified in articles of incorporation, most declarations of trust typically authorize the trustees of a business trust to issue an unlimited number of shares. The declaration of trust of a business trust needs to cover matters that may be left unsaid in articles of incorporation of a corporation because they are provided for in the applicable state corporation law (for example, authority and procedures for merger and what distributions to shareholders are permissible). In general, the creativity of a drafter of a declaration of trust is limited solely by matters of public policy: Is this provision so unusual as to be likely declared unconscionable or void as against public policy and therefore not an enforceable provision of a contract?

Common-Law Business Trusts

The fact that a common-law business trust is not a creature of statute has important implications, at least in Massachusetts, where the concept of the business trust is most developed under common law. Massachusetts courts have determined that the declaration of trust does not create a separate legal entity but instead creates a *relationship* among the trustees and shareholders.[19] Not being a distinct separate legal entity, the liabilities of the business trust to third parties are not limited to the assets of the trust. Rather, the assets are deemed to be owned by the trustees, and liabilities associated or arising in connection with the conduct of the business of the trust are likewise deemed to be liabilities of the trustees.[20] As a matter of law, and also as a matter of routine in every declaration of trust, the trustees of a business trust are entitled to be indemnified from the assets of the trust for any liabilities incurred by them in the proper conduct of their duties. But, if the liabilities of the business trust exceed the value of its assets, the trustees' personal assets may be subject to exposure. Every declaration of trust provides, and it has also become standard procedure that every contractual undertaking by a business trust will provide, that the other party contracting with the business trust shall agree to look solely to the assets of the trust. Typically, a party contracting with a business trust has no problem including such agreement in the contract because that would be the result if such party were contracting with a corporation. Also typically, trustees of a business trust provide for sufficient insurance against tort claims. Accordingly, in practice the potential personal liability of trustees of a business trust becomes more of a theoretical than actual problem.

An old line of cases in Massachusetts also provides for theoretical personal liability of the shareholders of a business trust whose assets are not sufficient to cover the trust liabilities if the shareholders have sufficient powers to "control" the affairs of the trust or the activities of the trustees, such as to make the trustees agents of the shareholders. While this doctrine of liability for shareholder control is clear under the old Massachusetts cases, there is no clear line that establishes what combination of shareholder powers do or do not constitute "control" in any particular instance.[21] Although the fact that in a modern public company, such as a REIT, that is organized as a business trust, the shareholders annually elect the trustees of the trust and may therefore have ultimate control over the trustees, nevertheless the practical powers of the trustees, in contrast to those of the shareholders, to run the business of the trust is such as to make very unlikely a determination that the shareholders "control" the trust so as to impose on them personal liability for the obligations of the trust. Since the enactment of the original REIT tax legislation in 1960, no case of which this author is aware involving any REIT or any other publicly owned business entity organized in business trust form has resulted in a shareholder being held personally responsible for debts of the trust. Nevertheless, every declaration of trust also provides for indemnification from the trust assets for any personal liability asserted against a shareholder of the trust in such capacity, and every prospectus for the offering of shares of a business trust typically recites the theoretical personal liability of the shareholder as a potential risk factor. Notwithstanding such disclosure, the remoteness of such potential liability has not affected the ability of business trusts (whether REITs, mutual funds, public utility holding companies, or others) to avail themselves of the capital markets.

Statutory Trusts

While the common-law business trust has been a familiar form of vehicle in Massachusetts and certain other states, including Illinois and Pennsylvania, a few states found it desirable to enact legislation specifically recognizing this form of business organization in order to accommodate the new form of tax-favored REIT, following enactment of the original REIT tax legislation in 1960. Examples include California[22] and, most significantly, Maryland.[23] Each of these statutes specifically limits the liability of shareholders for the obligations of the REIT, and the Maryland statute also limits the liability of trustees for such liabilities.[24]

The Maryland REIT statute specifically recognizes a real estate investment trust as a permitted form of unincorporated trust or association authorized to conduct business in Maryland in accordance with the statute. The statute states that it does not limit present law as it applies to the creation of or doing business by vehicles known as "common-law trust," "business trust," or "Massachusetts trust." The statute then sets forth specific powers and authorities of a "real estate investment trust" that are comparable to the powers and authorities specified in the Maryland statute relating to corporations. The statute requires specific provisions to be included in the declaration of trust, authorizes the classification of shares (but requires that the authorized number of shares be specified in the declaration of trust, that is, precluding the authority to issue an unlimited number of shares), sets forth specific statutory powers that the trust may exercise, and specifically authorizes statutory merger of the trust.[25] Maryland statutes also specifically make applicable to Maryland real estate investment trusts the antitakeover protections of the corporate statutes applicable to business combinations and limitations on voting rights of holders of control shares.[26] The enactment of the Maryland real estate investment trust statute was obviously intended to make Maryland a domicile of choice for REITs that had to be organized as a "trust or association" prior to the 1976 amendment to the Internal Revenue Code that also permitted corporations to elect REIT status. Subsequent to the change in the tax law, Maryland's continued emphasis on being a hospitable domicile to REITs has continued into the corporation arena and, as discussed in more detail below, has resulted in Maryland being a domicile of choice for either a corporate REIT or an unincorporated REIT for which there is no particularly germane reason to organize in some other state.

In 1988, Delaware, which has long been known as the domicile of choice for many of the country's publicly owned manufacturing and financial corporations, also enacted a statute providing for a statutory business trust organized under the laws of that state. Under the Delaware Business Trust Act, "business trust" is defined as:

> an unincorporated association which (i) is created by a trust instrument under which property is or will be held, managed, administered, controlled, invested, reinvested and/or operated, or business or professional activities for profit are carried on or will be carried on, by a trustee or trustees for the benefit of such person or persons as are or may become a beneficial interest in the trust property . . .[27]

Notably absent from the definition is the requirement that the beneficial interest in a statutory Delaware business trust be transferable. The Delaware statute specifically states that a business trust shall be a separate legal entity.28 Like the Maryland real estate investment trust statute, the Delaware business trust statute specifically limits personal liability of shareholders and trustees of the business trust.[29] The Delaware business trust statute, similar to the Maryland statute, provides a comprehensive statutory scheme of governance and of rights and obligations for business trusts organized under the laws of that state, with an obviously more expansive scope of potential business application intended than merely to REITs as in neighboring Maryland. A major limitation on the practicality of the Delaware business trust statute for public companies is its requirement that (except in the case of regulated investment companies) at least one trustee be either a person residing in, or a business entity having its principal place of business in, the State of Delaware.[30]

The Corporate Excise/Franchise Tax

In Massachusetts, at least, common-law business trusts are exempt from corporate excise and franchise taxes on constitutional grounds.[31] Since a business trust is not a separate legal entity created pursuant to state statute, the theory is that there is no "commodity" (which the court has defined to include as a franchise granted by state action) upon which the state may justify the imposition of an excise tax. Many states impose excise or franchise taxes on *corporations* doing business in those states (whether or not organized under the laws of such states), generally based on some allocation of the actual or authorized capital of the business to activities within that state. Depending on the state in which a corporation owns properties or engages in business activities, these state excise taxes can become significant costs of doing business.

One of the traditional benefits that REITs organized as *business trusts* have experienced over REITs organized as corporations is their not being subject to excise taxes. A REIT doing business in or proposing to do business in a particular state carefully needs to consider the effect of taxes in that state. The extent of the total tax burden may well depend on the form of organization. The laws of several states that do impose excise taxes limit the imposition of such taxes to corporations; in such states, there would be a clear monetary advantage to operating as a business trust.[32]

In 1991, the Massachusetts Department of Revenue issued a ruling letter involving a registered investment company organized as a common-law Massachusetts business trust proposing to reorganize as a Delaware business trust.[33] The ruling letter noted that the Delaware business trust, while not a corporation, was organized pursuant to a statute in Delaware that specifically limited the potential personal liability of trustees and shareholders and that declared such business trusts to be separate legal entities. The letter accordingly ruled that, because the business trust had been established pursuant to and with the benefits of a statute rather than by voluntary action at common law, there was a franchise upon which an excise tax could be imposed under the Massachusetts corporate excise tax that defines a "foreign corporation" to include an "association . . . established . . . under laws other than those of the commonwealth . . . which has privileges, powers, rights or immunities not possessed by individuals or partnerships." The Department of Revenue therefore concluded that the statutory Delaware business trust would be subject to the Massachusetts corporate excise tax imposed on foreign corporations doing business in Massachusetts if the Delaware business trust were to do business in Massachusetts. For this same reason, the Department of Revenue presumably would conclude that a Maryland real estate investment trust that holds property and does business in Massachusetts would be subject to the Massachusetts corporate excise tax.[34]

Although the franchise tax statutes of most states that impose this type of excise tax specifically refer to "corporations," it is not clear that such states might not be able to amend their statutes to apply to other types of noncorporate entities that enjoy the benefit of *statutory* exemption from personal liability, such as statutory business trusts and limited-liability companies.

Comparative Corporation Statutes: The Maryland Advantage

As indicated earlier, every state has a corporation statute providing for governance and other provisions relating to corporations organized under the laws of that state. The fact that a corporation may be organized (or, with shareholder approval, reorganized) under the laws of any state provides the organizers or board of a corporation significant opportunity for forum shopping. By far, the most popular state of domicile for public companies in the United States is Delaware, whose legislature is finely attuned to the desirability of refining the Delaware General Corporation Law to meet changing times and changing demands. One of the major reasons for the popularity of Delaware as a corporate domicile is its extensive and highly qualified chancery court system, which has a national reputation in regularly dealing with and resolving corporate disputes.

Yet Delaware has not proven a popular domicile for REITs for one simple reason: the Delaware franchise tax, which is based on the authorized capital of the corporation. The maximum annual franchise tax is $150,000, which is triggered by a corporation's having approximately 30 million shares of authorized capital. Because most REITs are public companies with expansive growth plans, their authorized capital frequently exceeds the 30 million shares that produces this maximum tax. While $150,000 of annual franchise tax may not be a particularly significant cost to a General Motors or a General Electric, it is indeed a heavy cost for a REIT whose stock is valued primarily by capitalizing its funds from operations (FFO). A REIT that trades at 10 times FFO and that can save $150,000 of unnecessary franchise tax each year adds $1.5 million to its market value.

Accordingly, most REITs that do not otherwise have any connection with Delaware (such as, for example, owning property there) tend to incorporate elsewhere. For the reasons outlined earlier, but particularly because of only nominal organization and annual corporate filing fees, Maryland has evolved as the domicile of choice for many corporate REITs. The investing community seems perfectly comfortable with a Maryland-domiciled REIT even though that state lacks the sophisticated and experienced chancery court system of neighboring Delaware.

Indeed, experience indicates that investors really pay little attention to either the form (corporate versus business trust) or forum (choice of domicile state) of REITs. REITs organized during the formation wave of the early 1990s as well as REITs that have been in existence for several years are organized in a broad number of states.

Some specific issues need to be considered in selecting a jurisdiction of domicile, however. And, as discussed above, the state tax regime of the domicile state needs to be carefully considered.

State incorporation laws have different provisions relating to the authority of the board of directors to make distributions to shareholders and to redeem shares. Because of the REIT distribution requirement, and more particularly because of the practice of making distributions that exceed net income determined in accordance with generally accepted accounting principles (GAAP), it is important that the applicable incorporation statute not preclude the corporation's legal authority to make distributions necessary to retain REIT status or to meet the expectations of the marketplace. Similarly, the state incorporation law should not preclude a REIT's ability to redeem "excess shares" if necessary to prevent its failing the tax-qualification requirement that it not be closely held. For example, the relatively few REITs organized as California corporations need to be concerned with limitations in the California Corporations Code that preclude distributions, unless after the distribution the corporation either (1) has a positive retained earnings account (not likely if the corporation has consistently been making distributions from FFO in amounts exceeding net income) or (2) has tangible assets whose depreciated book value is at least one and one-quarter times liabilities *and* current assets that are in excess of current liabilities.[35]

In contrast, the Maryland General Corporation Law follows the more typical approach of permitting distributions that do not render the corporation insolvent (that is, after giving effect to the distribution, [1] the corporation is able to pay its debts as they become due in the usual course of business and [2] its total assets exceed its total liabilities). The statute specifically authorizes the directors to make a determination that a distribution is not prohibited based either upon the "financial statements prepared on the basis of accounting practices and principles that are reasonable in the circumstances" *or* a "fair valuation or other method that is reasonable in the circumstances."[36] Thus, a California corporation's ability to make distributions is based on historic book value, GAAP accounting, while a Maryland corporation's authority to make distributions is based on a fair current valuation or other reasonable method. Likewise, a Maryland corporation may redeem shares unless the amounts paid would render the corporation insolvent.[37]

For some corporate managements, the ability to have the corporation protected by "business combination" and "control share" statutes and other reasonable protective devices is important. Maryland has both a "business combination"[38] and a "control-share statute"[39] equally applicable to Maryland corporations and Maryland real estate investment trusts. In 1989, the validity of both of these statutes and of a Maryland REIT's 9.8 percent "excess shares" provision were upheld by the United States District Court in Maryland in the context of an unsolicited tender offer by one REIT for majority control of another REIT.[40] In the context of successful REITs' continuing need to access the capital markets and to enjoy institutional investor support, it is important, however, that the defensive measures involved be fair to all investors and not be perceived as merely protecting an entrenched management.

"Excess-Share" Provisions

The governing documents of most public (and many private) REITs today (whether the declaration of trust of a business trust REIT or the articles of incorporation of a corporate REIT) typically contain restrictions on the number of outstanding shares of the REIT that may be owned by any one person to a number that ensures that the REIT will not fail the tax Code requirement that it not be "closely held," that is, that five or fewer individuals do not own more than 50 percent in value of the REIT's outstanding shares.[41] A typical restriction provides in effect that no single person or group of affiliated persons may own more than 9.8 percent of the outstanding shares (such number is defined as the "limit") and that any shares in excess of the limit that are acquired by the holder are deemed to be converted into a separate class of excess shares. The governing document then typically deems that excess shares are held by the holder for the benefit of a charitable beneficiary, are redeemable by the REIT without profit to the holder, are not entitled to vote, and may not receive dividends.

The rationale for establishing the limit is that it thereby becomes mathematically impossible for any five holders to own more than 50 percent in value of the outstanding shares. Having the governing REIT document include such a limit that is contractually binding on all REIT shareholders is justified because there is no other way that the board of directors and management of the REIT can enforce the Code's not-closely-held requirement for REIT qualification. Indeed, of all the various requirements contained in the Code necessary for a taxpayer to qualify as a REIT, the not-closely-held requirement is the only one that an alert and well-advised board and management cannot themselves control without a restriction in the REIT's governing document such as an excess shares provision.

A few REITs that may have, or have had, an initial owner or owners constructively owning more than 9.8 percent of the outstanding shares have provided for a limit greater than 9.8 percent in the case of such initial shareholders and a lower limit for others. If one person initially owns, say, 20 percent of the outstanding shares, then, while excepting that ownership from the limit, the operative limit in the REIT's articles of incorporation or declaration of trust would be reduced for any other shareholder to a lesser percentage (for example, 7.25 percent) so that the aggregate ownership of the five largest holders cannot mathematically exceed 49 percent.

It is important to be aware that the 5-50 rule speaks in terms of an aggregate of 50 percent *of value,* rather than of number, of outstanding shares. It therefore becomes important to consider (1) the possible impact of additional value that may be attributed to a major block (such as 20 percent or more) and (2) the effect on numbers of shares when there may be more than one class of shares (for example, common stock and preferred stock) outstanding at the same time.

A typical excess-shares provision provides authority for the board to waive or suspend the limit in cases in which it receives assurance that holdings in excess of the specified limit will not jeopardize continued REIT status. Such situations might include temporary ownership by an underwriter who will quickly distribute the shares in a public offering, or holdings by a mutual fund that provides assurance to the REIT that, as a result of the look-through rules built into the not-closely-held requirement,[42] a single holding of more than the specified limit will in fact be deemed to be held by several separate individuals, each owning significantly less than the limit. It is not uncommon for mutual fund groups to seek a waiver of a 9.8 percent limit so that the fund group as a whole may own up to, say, 13 percent of a REIT's outstanding shares. Because of the look-through nature of a fund complex's ownership, it is usually safe for a REIT to issue such a waiver with the understanding that the REIT will not sell such shares in a single block to another holder whose ownership might not be so benign.

Some excess-share provisions also provide an automatic exclusion for accumulations of ownership in excess of the limit pursuant to a tender offer made to all of the REIT's shareholders under circumstances where all shareholders will be treated fairly and may receive the benefit of a premium associated with the tender offer. The lack of an automatic exclusion for such a tender-offer scenario is justified by other REITs on the grounds that the board of the target REIT may waive the limit in the context of a tender offer that is supported by the board, just as any applicable business combination or control-share statute may be waived with respect to transactions supported by the board. The important thing is that the board or management of, or counsel for, a public REIT give thoughtful consideration to the tools both to protect the REIT's tax qualification and to provide fairness to all shareholders in the event of a potential premium offer.

The New York Stock Exchange requires as a condition of listing REIT shares that any excess-share restrictions specifically state that such restriction will not be used to prevent settlement of any trade effected on the Exchange. A carefully drafted provision should allow the settlement of all trades on the Exchange but should add that the restrictions apply to the purchaser of such shares if its ownership would thereupon exceed the limit, with such acquired shares being considered excess shares to the extent applicable in the hands of the purchaser.

UPREITs and Operating Partnerships

UPREIT is an acronym for umbrella partnership real estate investment trust. It basically refers to a REIT whose real properties are held by and operations are conducted by a single partnership, or by two or more partnerships that are under the umbrella of a single partnership, referred to as an "operating partnership" (or OP). The REIT (occasionally through a qualified REIT subsidiary) is typically the general partner of the operating partnership.

The REIT itself is, of course, an explicit creature of the Internal Revenue Code, defined in Code Section 856 and provided with its special tax provisions in immediately following sections. The UPREIT is also a creature of the Code although in a different respect. Neither the phrase "umbrella partnership real estate investment trust" nor the term *UPREIT* appears in the Code, but the structure was driven by the desire to avoid federal income tax that would result upon recognition of gain on the transfer of real estate currently owned by an individual or by a partnership to a REIT. In many cases, the federal income tax basis of an owner of property may be significantly lower than the value of that property. A transfer of property directly to a REIT—which, remember, is taxable as a corporation for federal income tax purposes—would result in recognition of gain to the individual owner or partner of the transferring partnership; however, a contribution by that individual owner or by an existing partnership owning the property to another partnership in exchange for a continuing interest in the transferee partnership, can be effected without recognition of gain.

The first public UPREIT was created in 1992 when Taubman Centers, Inc., a Michigan corporation, had an initial public offering of approximately 26.8 million shares, concurrently contributing the proceeds of the offering to and becoming general partner of the Taubman Realty Group Limited

Partnership, a Delaware limited partnership, which as a result of a concurrent restructuring became the owner of all of the interests of A. Albert Taubman and various affiliates in a portfolio of shopping centers known as the Taubman Shopping Centers as well as the owner of the management entity that operated the Taubman Shopping Centers. Taubman Centers, Inc., was expressly organized to qualify as a REIT. Virtually all of its assets consisted of its ownership of a 32.8 percent interest in the Taubman Realty Group Limited Partnership. Mr. Taubman and certain previous institutional and individual investors retained or received the remaining limited partnership units in the OP. The partnership agreement of the OP and related documents provided that interests in the OP would be represented by units initially valued at two thousand times the initial public-offering price of the REIT shares, that distributions by the OP with respect to the units (including those held by the REIT) would be at the rate of two thousand times the REIT's distribution with respect to each of its outstanding shares, and that each partner of the OP other than the REIT would have the right to sell their partnership units back to the operating partnership after a period of time pursuant to a continuing tender offer for such units at a price equal to two thousand times the then market value of the publicly traded REIT shares. If such units are tendered back to the OP, the OP may elect to deliver two thousand newly issued shares of the REIT, rather than cash, for each unit tendered by the tendering partners.

The prospectus (dated November 20, 1992) for the Taubman offering describes many other transactions and rights of the various participants in the restructuring of the ownership of the Taubman Shopping Centers and related management and development business. Basically, Taubman Centers, Inc., became the country's first public UPREIT, and the Taubman Realty Group Limited Partnership became the first OP of an UPREIT and the model in many respects for the large number of subsequent UPREIT reorganization and initial public offering (IPO) transactions involving the capital markets securitization of other previously private real estate companies, although not all of the governance arrangements described in the Taubman Prospectus have become common.

After its IPO, Taubman Centers, Inc., the UPREIT, owned only 32.8 percent of the interests in the operating partnership, with 67.2 percent of the OP ownership interests held by Mr. Taubman and previous investors in the Taubman Shopping Centers. Taubman is somewhat different from the several UPREIT formations that followed it, in that most of the later

UPREITs own more than a 50 percent interest in the affiliated OP. But each OP structure, while tailored to its own facts and formation transactions, must recognize and address certain minimal basic issues arising from the fact that the OP is a separate legal entity from the UPREIT itself.

Fiduciary Duty and Conflict of Interest

The UPREIT as general partner of the OP has a fiduciary duty to the limited partners of the OP, as well as a separate fiduciary duty to its own shareholders. Individual members of the management or the former owners of the preexisting real estate group that is the sponsor/organizer of the UPREIT who become senior officers of the UPREIT and serve on the UPREIT's board of directors typically retain their ownership interest in properties contributed to the OP on a tax-recognition deferred basis, so the decision of whether and when it is in the interests of the UPREIT to sell or mortgage (or not to sell or mortgage) the property in a transaction that would trigger recognition of taxable gain to such individual creates an obvious potential conflict for the individual whose personal interest would presumably dictate no transaction that would trigger the taxable gain. The partnership agreement of the OP needs to address how such conflict issue may be resolved as well as other fiduciary duties and governance issues. The independence of a majority of the board of directors of the UPREIT and their willingness to deal with the potential conflicts of interest, perhaps to the detriment of the company's founders and senior officers, are also important.

Separate Issuer of Securities

The operating partnership units held by the UPREIT and by the other partners of the OP are separate securities from those of the UPREIT itself, although in the view of the Securities and Exchange Commission, the offering of OP units may be integrated with the public offering of the UPREIT's shares. The issuance of such separate securities needs to be carefully analyzed under federal and state securities laws. Because the OP is a separate entity, it may issue securities that are completely different from securities of the UPREIT. Some OPs have issued preferred OP units or separate OP debt securities that create a claim against the OP rather than against the UPREIT. Although the world at large may consider properties as belonging to the UPREIT, actual title is held by the OP. Accordingly, the OP (or other actual titleholder) will be the issuer of any mortgage on the properties securing any particular issue of secured debt. (In collateralized pools of mortgage debt, such as a REMIC obligation, title to the properties is likely to be held by a subsidiary partnership of the OP, with the subsidiary partnership being the actual issuer of the collateralized debt.) The OP will obviously have to prepare separate accounts and reports for the holders of securities of which it is the issuer.

One of the advantages of the UPREIT-OP structure in the case of those previously existing real estate groups whose individual owners (such as Mr. Taubman and his affiliates) continue to hold significant ownership interests in the UPREIT-OP following the formation of the UPREIT is that such interests may be held wholly through such owners' interest in the OP or may be split between the UPREIT and the OP. Consequently, the REIT may be formed with no individual owning more than 9.8 percent (or other "limit") of the outstanding UPREIT shares. As in the Taubman transaction, the partnership agreement of the OP or other governing document typically provides that, at some point a year or more after the initial transaction, the OP partners (other than the UPREIT) will have the authority to cause such OP units to be redeemed by the OP or by the UPREIT in whole or in part. Typically, the OP may at its option either redeem the tendered units for cash or exchange them for UPREIT shares. (It will usually be important that the option to issue UPREIT shares be the option of the UPREIT rather than of the OP unitholder because, under the 5-50 attribution rules,[43] an individual is considered to own shares that he or she has an option to acquire; however, if upon full exchange no holder of OP units will be considered to own a number of UPREIT shares in excess of the applicable limit, the exchange option may be an option given to the unit holder.) The exchange ratio is typically fixed so that, initially, each OP unit would be exchanged for a fixed number (for example, 2,000-for-1, or more typically 1-for-1) of UPREIT shares. Consideration has to be given to situations in which the initial exchange ratio (as well as the partnership distribution provisions) might be appropriately adjusted to reflect subsequent securities issuances by either the OP or the REIT.

Separate Tax Returns, Accounting, and Financial Statements

As a separate entity, the OP will of course have to prepare and file separate tax returns and consider in what circumstances and for what purposes it will have to prepare separate accountings and separate financial statements with respect to its properties and operations, or with respect to its separate securityholders, in addition to financial statements that will be consolidated with those of the REIT. Each separate partnership of which the REIT or the OP is administrative partner will obviously have the same considerations.

Future Acquisitions

Because individual and partnership property owners may generally contribute their properties to a new or existing partnership without recognition of built-in gain in their partnership interests, the UPREIT-operating partnership structure has proven a very flexible and favorable structure for subsequent acquisitions, after the initial formation of the UPREIT, of additional properties from other individuals and partnership owners. Subject to the provisions of the OP partnership agreement relating to the admission of new partners, an existing OP may acquire additional properties contributed to it, or an interest in an existing partnership owning properties, for additional OP units and/or for cash, assumption of debt secured by the new properties, or other consideration. The newly issued OP units will presumably be exchangeable for newly issued UPREIT shares at the price, at the times, and on other terms negotiated in the acquisition agreement. The opportunity for the UPREIT as general partner of the OP to expand through such acquisitions will obviously be enhanced to the extent that the partnership agreement of the OP authorizes the general partner to admit new partners and create new classes of partners without the prior concurrence of the existing limited partners of the OP.

The final section of this chapter (Securities Laws Issues in Acquisitions of Additional Assets) discusses in more detail the implications of various securities laws to existing UPREITs in making acquisitions of additional properties through the issuance of OP units. Those implications are equally applicable in the context of an existing REIT that may determine to form a new operating partnership to make acquisitions.

DownREITs

The UPREIT structure was created in the context of bringing previously separately owned, though generally commonly controlled, real property partnerships and their sponsor/developer/management entities to the capital markets in an initial public offering of a new REIT. As just addressed, if permitted by the partnership agreement of its OP, an UPREIT may expand, on a tax-favored basis to the acquirees, by admitting the existing partners or owners of other acquiree partnerships or groups of partnerships in exchange for additional partnership interests in the OP.

Traditional corporate (or business trust) REITs that own their existing properties directly may make similar tax-favored acquisitions of existing individually or partnership-owned properties by forming a new partnership to acquire and own the newly acquired properties. The existing REIT may choose to contribute some of its existing properties to this new partnership, or merely cash or other consideration. The term *DownREIT,* therefore, at a minimum refers to a REIT that owns properties directly but that also holds some of its properties in a partnership having other partners. Like the existing owners of interests in properties acquired or held by an OP of an UPREIT who continue to hold an interest in such properties through their interests in the OP until it is redeemed or exchanged for cash or REIT shares, the existing owners of interests in the properties acquired by the DownREIT partnership continue to hold an interest in such properties through their interests in that DownREIT partnership.

The question in any DownREIT formation transaction becomes what other properties the new DownREIT partners acquire partnership interests in and how the respective interests of the DownREIT partners are defined. In the pure UPREIT situation, presumably newly admitted partners to the existing OP acquire interests in all of the properties associated with the UPREIT through that OP and, except for the redemption or exchange price, on substantially the same terms as the other nonREIT owners of the existing OP. If the only properties held by a new DownREIT partnership are those acquired from the existing owners, those owners are going to have an interest only in those properties, although those properties will presumably be enhanced by the REIT's cash contributions whose proceeds will probably be used to discharge debt or to improve or expand the properties.

Accordingly, in theory at least, the existing individual owners of property contributed to a DownREIT partnership will not acquire the same commonality of interest with the REIT's shareholders in the entire portfolio of the sponsoring REIT as they would have with the shareholders of an UPREIT if they had instead contributed their properties to that UPREIT's operating partnership. This may or may not be a distinction of substance for existing individual or partnership property owners seeking to affiliate with an existing public REIT, depending on the particular situation and the particular terms of both the DownREIT partnership agreement and related acquisition agreement related to the transaction.

While the term *DownREIT* contemplates a partnership of which the REIT will be the general partner and one in which the economic interests of the other partners may be defined to track distributions made by the REIT to its shareholders and may ultimately be redeemable or exchangeable for REIT shares, comparable to the rights of partners of the pure UPREIT OP, the specific terms of the REIT's control and of the distribution and other rights of the other partners may vary substantially from the pure UPREIT model.

Ultimately, the specific partnership agreement between the REIT and the existing owners of the properties contributed to the partnership could turn out to involve little more than a conventional joint venture agreement between the REIT and the existing owners of or coinvestors in the particular properties. If so, the term *DownREIT* is probably inappropriate to define the situation. But just as real estate joint venture partnership terms involving REITs have varied ever since the Treasury regulations relating to REITs were initially promulgated in 1962,[44] the REIT will in any partnership—ranging from joint venture through DownREIT partnership to UPREIT OP—be concerned and insistent that the partnership not be permitted to own assets, receive income, or be operated in a way that would disqualify the REIT if the REIT itself directly owned the same assets or received the same income.

Taxable "C" Corporation "Beneficial Subsidiaries"

As a result of the expansion effected in the Tax Reform Act of 1986 to a REIT's abilities to manage its own properties, it has become feasible for a REIT to include on its own (or its OP's) payroll the management personnel who are responsible for managing and developing its own account. When a REIT performs such services for properties in which the REIT has only a partnership interest, questions arise as to whether any compensation the REIT receives from such activities is "good" REIT income. Any fee income from performing services for real estate in which the REIT has no ownership interest is obviously "bad" income and if received by the REIT itself cannot, together with all other "bad" income, exceed 5 percent of the REIT's gross income in any year.[45]

Many of the real estate organizations that formed REITs or UPREITs in the 1990s contained integrated real estate service companies that provided development, management, leasing, and other services to third parties as well as with respect to properties that were contributed to the REIT or its operating partnership. To reconcile the objectives of (1) bringing these existing organizations into the REIT, (2) continuing to provide development, management, and other fee-based services to third parties without being limited to the 5 percent "bad" income limitation, and (3) having the economics of such third-party fee income inure to the REIT and its shareholders, several REITs (or UPREIT OPs) have placed some or all of their service operations into a separate corporation that has two classes of stock: a class of nonvoting stock owned by the REIT that is entitled to substantially all of the economic interest in the service corporation, and a class of voting stock, of which less than 10 percent is owned by the REIT. The REIT should not own more than 99 percent of the economics of the service company. The consequences of this structure are as follows:

- **Financial.** The service corporation is substantially wholly owned by the REIT, with its after-tax net income effectively passed through to the REIT in the form of dividends. Because the REIT does not control the voting of the shares of the service corporation, there may, however, be a question about the REIT's ability to consolidate the service corporation's financial results into the REIT's financial statements.
- **Tax.** The service corporation is a taxable "C" corporation. Its net income, therefore, does not receive the same shelter as the REIT's income does.
  - The dividend income paid to the REIT is "good" 95 percent income, although not "good" 75 percent income.[46]
  - The stock of the service corporation should be a "good" REIT asset, *provided* that (1) the REIT does not own more than 10 percent of the outstanding voting securities of the service corporation, (2) the value of the securities of any one such corporation does not exceed 5 percent of the value of the total assets of the REIT, and (3) the value of all securities (that are not real estate assets, cash items, and government securities) owned by the REIT does not exceed 25 percent of the value of its total assets.[47]
- **Operating.** The obvious drawback in this structure is the inability of the REIT to vote the stock of its beneficial subsidiary. Various approaches have been used to attempt to structure a commonality of interest—short of actual voting control—between the REIT and the holder(s) of the voting stock and usually involve restricting the ownership of the voting stock not held by the REIT to key management individuals as well as bylaw provisions requiring 100 percent voting stock approval of certain major corporate actions.

Because the REIT owns substantially all the economic interest in, but not the power to control the vote of, the "C" corporation, such a corporation is sometimes referred to as a "beneficial subsidiary" of the REIT. A cautionary note needs to be said about the use of beneficial subsidiaries to provide services to the REIT's own tenants. While a REIT may now generally manage its own properties, certain services to tenants that are not customary still must be furnished or rendered only through an independent contractor, lest the rents from the tenant fail to meet the definition of "rents from real property" needed to qualify as a REIT under the Code. The beneficial subsidiary service corporation will not meet the definition of independent contractor if the REIT owns more than 35 percent of the total shares of all classes of its stock. The Internal Revenue Service may not have the same view as management of the service corporation as to whether noncustomary services performed for the tenant of a REIT by the service corporation are furnished or rendered at the behest of the service corporation rather than of the REIT.

REITs UNDER THE SECURITIES LAWS

The federal securities laws are a fact of life for every REIT. Each REIT that has publicly traded securities has been through the registration process established by the Securities Act of 1933 (Securities Act) and lives with the public reporting requirements of the Securities Exchange Act of 1934 (Exchange Act) and with the formal regulations of the Securities and Exchange Commission (SEC) under these two acts, as well as the practices of the individual SEC staff personnel (principally of the Division of Corporation Finance) charged with administering these laws. Public REITs are also subject to the rules, governance, and other listing requirements of the stock exchange (for most REITs, the New York Stock Exchange) on which their securities are listed. In addition, REITs should at least be aware generally that each state has its own state securities laws (commonly referred to as blue-sky laws).

The Federal Securities Laws

Securities Act

In brief summary, the Securities Act applies to transactions involving the issuance and sale of securities. Unless the sale of securities falls within one of the specified exemptions, the Act requires that a registration statement covering the specific issue or sale transaction(s) be filed with and declared effective by the SEC before the securities may be sold. If a registration statement must be filed, its contents must conform to the requirements of the Securities Act and applicable regulations of the SEC. The SEC has prescribed different forms of registration statements for various situations and detailed the matters that must be covered in each form. For an initial public offering (IPO) of a REIT, the required registration statement is Form S-11, the instructions for which require that the prospectus for the particular offering of shares that are being registered for sale in the registration statement contain disclosures with respect to several specified areas of information. As most public REITs are keenly aware, the process of drafting, responding to comments by the SEC staff, and getting an IPO Form S-11 registration statement declared effective by the SEC takes several months. The SEC staff routinely reviews all IPO registration statements in great detail, and the registration process frequently involves amending the registration statement three, four, or more times to respond to staff comments before the staff is prepared to declare the registration statement effective.

The principal exemption from the requirement that a registration statement be in effect with respect to a particular issuance and sale of securities is that the sale is a transaction "by an issuer not involving a public offering."[48] This generally means that the sale of securities is solely to wealthy, knowledgeable, and sophisticated purchasers ("accredited investors") who do not require the benefit of the information contained in the registration statement. The SEC has prescribed a series of rules within Regulation D[49] that provide a "safe harbor" exemption from registration under the Securities Act if the provisions of such rules are satisfied. Some of these rules require that written information be furnished to the investors containing substantially the same information required for a registration statement. In general, however, substantially less work, time, and expense is involved in effecting a private placement transaction than a registered public offering.

A number of "private" REITs whose shares are not publicly held have been formed, primarily for institutional investors. Because of the REIT qualification requirement that there be at least 100 shareholders, however, most such REITs look to knowledgeable individuals who with family members can help reach the 100-shareholder goal. The provisions of Regulation D, which permit a sale of an issuer's securities solely to "accredited investors" and not more than 35 other purchasers, are typically relied on in these situations. It is critical that care be taken to assure that investors assumed to be "accredited" in fact are.

Exchange Act

While the Securities Act focuses on the particular issuance of particular securities, the focus of the Exchange Act is the regulation of the markets on which and the mechanics by which securities are bought and sold. The Act requires the registration with the SEC of persons who are brokers and dealers of securities. It regulates the conduct of the formal and informal securities exchanges. It also requires issuers of widely held or publicly traded securities to register those securities under the Act and requires that those issuers file specified types of periodic or transactional reports, comply with specified rules in soliciting shareholder proxies or consents, and attend to a variety of other matters designed to create an orderly and informed public securities market. Among other provisions in the Exchange Act, applicable to *all* purchases and sales of securities, whether of a class registered under the Act and whether or not a public or private sale, is the provision of Section 10(b) of the Act, which makes it unlawful for:

> any person, directly or indirectly . . . by the use of any means or instrumentality of interstate commerce . . . to use or employ, in connection with the purchase or sale of any sale of any security . . . any manipulative or deceptive device or contrivance in violation of such rules and regulations as the Commission may prescribe as necessary or appropriate in the public interest or for the protection of investors.

Concurrently with the effectiveness of an IPO of securities under the Securities Act, a company will register under the Exchange Act the class of securities involved with the SEC to permit trading of the security after its issuance. The New York Stock Exchange, various other stock exchanges, and the National Association of Securities Dealers Automated Quotation National Market System (NASDAQ/NMS) have their own individual criteria for listing a company's securities for trading on the particular system; and a new issuer must separately apply for listing on the particular exchange, which if it accepts such application, will certify the listing of the class of securities to the SEC. A significant number of REITs have their shares listed for trading on the New York Stock Exchange.

A company with securities registered under the Exchange Act is required to file with the SEC periodic reports of financial and other information (annual reports on Form 10-K, quarterly reports on Form 10-Q, and reports of other significant current events on Form 8-K) in order to make available to investors (whether buyers, sellers, or holders) current information with respect to the company. (The New York Stock Exchange and other exchanges have their own supplemental rules relating to press releases and disclosures of other important information concerning listed companies.) Assuming that the registrant company has filed all required reports on a timely basis for at least a year, that company may thereafter be eligible to register additional securities for sale under the Securities Act pursuant to a simplified registration statement on Form S-2 or Form S-3, each of which in effect incorporates by reference the periodic and other filings that the company has made under the Exchange Act. A company with more than $75 million of market value of stock held by investors who are not affiliated with the company is entitled to use the simpler of these forms, Form S-3, for such subsequent offers. The Form S-3 registration statement may also be used to cover the issuance of shares pursuant to a dividend reinvestment plan and for the registration of securities being sold by existing shareholders who may have acquired the securities in a previous unregistered transaction not involving a public offering.

Accordingly, a REIT that has been in existence for over a year, that has timely made all required filings under the Exchange Act, and that has at least $75 million worth of stock held by the public is likely to be able to return to the capital markets for further issuances of securities in a far more streamlined transaction than it encountered in its IPO. The SEC staff will frequently declare a follow-on registration statement on Form S-3 effective without review. However, when it does review a Form S-3 registration statement, it will scrutinize the incorporated filings that the company has made under the Exchange Act to make sure they conform to the staff's views as to the adequacy of ongoing periodic and current disclosure obligations of public companies; so it is important that a public company pay a lot of attention to its reports and filings under the Exchange Act on a regular basis.

The Exchange Act also imposes certain other obligations on companies whose securities are registered under the Act and on officers, directors, and certain shareholders of such companies. The company must conform to the Act's proxy rules (Section 14 and the rules thereunder) for solicitations of votes of shareholders and the requirements that the company send annual reports to its shareholders (Rule 14a-3). Beneficial holders of 5 percent or more of any class of the company's shares must publicly report their holdings to the SEC (Section 13d and the rules thereunder). Directors, executive officers, and beneficial owners of 10 percent or more of any class of the company's shares must file reports of their ownership and are subject to the mandatory requirement of the Act that any short-swing profits (that is, profits realized upon matching any sale against any purchase [or any purchase against any sale] of the relevant securities) within any six-month period (Section 16 and the rules thereunder).

Application of the Securities Laws to the Formation of a Multi-Entity REIT Structure

Where a REIT is to be formed by the acquisition of identified existing properties by a company that is concurrently having a public offering of its shares, or in connection with such REIT's becoming a partner in an operating partnership that will acquire such properties, a number of separate legal entities are involved. It is important to analyze the various steps in the formation process and the possible applicability of the securities laws to each such step.

In addition, the REIT formation process includes the transfer of existing property from its existing ownership to new ownership—either the REIT itself (or a qualified REIT subsidiary) or an operating partnership—in exchange for either cash, assumption of existing mortgage debt, securities of the acquiring REIT or OP, or a combination of such consideration.

If the existing owner of the property is a partnership, what is the authority to transfer the assets of that partnership? A solicitation of the existing partners may involve (1) a solicitation of a proxy that may or may not be subject to the proxy rules under Section 14 of the Exchange Act relating to solicitations of proxies and (2) the "sale" of a security (the limited partnership interest held by the solicited partner), which sale may be subject to the antimanipulation/antideception provisions of Rule 10b-5 under the Exchange Act, in each case whether the consideration to the existing partners is cash or securities. If the consideration includes securities of either the REIT or the OP, then (3) the issuing REIT or OP will need to consider whether such issue requires a registration statement to be effective under the Securities Act or is exempt from registration as an issue not involving a public offering, and (4) if the securities of the REIT or of the OP have to be or are registered under a registration statement, the special partnership roll-up rules of the SEC's Regulation S-K Subpart 900, relating to "roll-up transactions," may be applicable.

Certainly the issuance of shares of the new REIT to the public will require registration pursuant to an effective Form S-11 registration statement under the Securities Act. If, concurrently with such public offering of REIT shares, the REIT's affiliated operating partnership is issuing its OP units to existing owners of the properties being acquired by the operating partnership, it is the SEC staff's position that the issuance of OP units to the current property owner is "integrated" with the REIT's public share issue so as also to require a registration statement covering the issuance of the OP units, unless (1) the issue of the OP units would otherwise be exempt from registration because it does not involve a public offering *and* (2) the current owners are committed, *before the filing of the registration statement for the REIT shares,* to accept the OP units in exchange for their property interests.

Typically, the new REIT will want to be in a position to have its shares trade on the New York Stock Exchange. It will therefore need to file a listing application with the Exchange. Assuming that the REIT will meet the Exchange's governance, size, potential profitability, and diversity of share ownership standards for listing, the Exchange will approve such listing subject to official notice of issuance of the shares. The Exchange will so certify to the SEC, the company will file a simple Exchange Act registration form with the SEC, and the SEC will typically declare effective the company's Exchange Act registration of the class of shares concurrently with declaring effective the company's Securities Act registration statement relating to the specific numbers of shares of that class that will be issued in the IPO.

State Blue-Sky Laws

The REIT formation process may also require complying with the securities laws of the various states whose residents will be receiving any security as a result of the transaction. The National Securities Markets Improvement Act effective in October 1996 substantially preempted the authority of states to register or qualify offerings of "Covered Securities," which include securities authorized for listing on the New York or American Stock Exchanges or quoted on NASDAQ/NMS as well as securities issued in a private placement under Rule 506 of Regulation D. Accordingly, most securities offerings by REITs will not have state blue sky law implications. For those limited number of REIT formations which will involve the issuance of securities other than Covered Securities (that is, a REIT formed by a public offering requiring registration of the securities and for which no active trading market is contemplated), the organizers of the REIT will need to deal with the extremely complex and substantively restrictive

"Statement of Policy" relating to REIT securities offerings adopted by the North American Security Administrators Association that has been adopted formally by some states and that is followed, as a matter of administrative policy, by many other states. The Statement of Policy is contained in Commerce Clearing House *Blue Sky Reporter,* Volume 1.

Shelf Registration of REIT Shares for OP Unit Exchange

There will be one further registration statement under the federal Securities Act that a new REIT may anticipate filing as a result of its formation transactions if the formation has resulted in the typical UPREIT-operating partnership structure. Because the exchange feature in the typical UPREIT-OP structure that provides for a future exchange of UPREIT shares for OP units will involve an issuance of its shares by the UPREIT, the UPREIT will typically agree to file a shelf-registration statement under SEC Rule 415 that registers the issuance of such UPREIT shares to the holders of the OP units. The shelf-registration statement may typically also register the resale of the UPREIT shares by the former OP unitholders. Such shelf-registration statement will have to be on Form S-11 if filed within one year of the REIT's IPO, but may be filed on Form S-3 thereafter.

Future Offerings: The "Universal Shelf Registration"

Many seasoned REITs that expect to raise additional capital in the public markets take advantage of procedures that authorize the filing of a shelf-registration statement that registers for future sale a specified dollar amount of securities that the company may determine to be in its interest at the particular time of issuance. The "universal shelf-registration statement" will contain a base prospectus that lists and describes the various types of securities that the company may register—for example, common shares, preferred shares, various types of senior and/or subordinated debt of various maturities, depositary certificates, warrants, rights, and units of the above. Importantly, the base prospectus incorporates by reference the company's most recent annual, quarterly, and current reports filed with the SEC and all future filings with the SEC, so this information is deemed to be a part of the registration statement even if not actually appearing in the printed base prospectus. After the registration statement is declared effective, the company may issue any of the registered securities without further action of the SEC by attaching to the base prospectus a prospectus supplement identifying the specific securities and dollar amount being sold and the underwriting and pricing terms of such offering. If appropriate, the company may also update the underlying base prospectus. The filing of the prospectus supplement and updated base prospectus may be accomplished pursuant to Rule 424(b) under the Securities Act rather than as an amendment to the registration statement that requires SEC action to make it effective.

The uniform shelf-registration statement, like other Form S-3 registration statements, registers securities for sale under the Securities Act by incorporating into the prospectus and prospectus supplement relating to the securities being sold current information concerning the company and its business that has been filed with the SEC under the Exchange Act. The Securities Act imposes liability for registration statements that contain an untrue statement of a material fact or omit to state a material fact required therein or necessary to make the statements therein not misleading, not only upon the issuing company, but also on certain officers and on the directors of the issuer and on underwriters of the securities sold. Such individuals and underwriters (but not the issuer) are relieved from liability, however, if they had, after reasonable investigation, reasonable ground to believe and did believe at the time the relevant part of the registration statement became effective that it contained no untrue statement of a material fact or omissions needed to make the statements therein not misleading, they may be liable.[50] Similar liability is imposed on any person who offers or sells a security by means of a prospectus or oral statement that is untrue or contains a material omission, unless such person can prove that he or she did not know, and in the exercise of reasonable care could not have known, of such untruth or omission.[51]

While a major convenience, the shelf-registration provisions create significant issues for underwriters and other persons engaged in the distribution of securities in making sure that the registration statement and prospectus do not contain material untruths or omissions at the time of sale, thus involving a continuing "due diligence" obligation on such persons. Recent efforts further to streamline the capital-raising process have included recommendations to revise the registration procedures under the Securities Act effectively to have a one-time registration of the company issuing securities rather than one-time registration statements that relate to specific securities; and the proponents of such revisions have acknowledged the need to accommodate the potential civil liability implications by providing some new mechanism for assuring that the information available in the marketplace concerning the issuer and the effects of its capital raising have been run through an effective "gatekeeper" process.[52]

SECURITIES LAW ISSUES IN ACQUISITION OF ADDITIONAL ASSETS

Introduction

Almost by definition, today's successful REIT will continually be alert to opportunities to grow through the acquisition of additional properties or portfolios of properties from less efficient current owners of the properties. Such acquisitions may be effected by purchases for cash, assumption of existing indebtedness to which the properties are subject, and/or the issuance of securities, which may be either securities of the REIT itself or, in the case of an acquisition by an existing operating partnership of an UPREIT or by a newly formed OP in a DownREIT transaction, partnership units of the OP.

The structure of each acquisition transaction will of course depend on a variety of factors. If securities of the REIT or an OP are to be issued, then the issuance of such securities involves Securities Act implications for both the REIT and the OP, as well as likely reporting obligations under the Exchange Act.[53] If the transaction involves securities that directly or indirectly (for example, upon conversion of OP units into REIT shares) involves the issuance of 20 percent or more of the REIT's outstanding shares, then the rules of the New York Stock Exchange (and other major securities markets) will require a shareholders' meeting of the REIT to approve the transaction, or if the transaction will be pursuant to a statutory merger that under the state corporation law applicable to the REIT requires shareholder approval, in either event the proxy rules[54] will require detailed disclosure and procedural requirements in connection with the proxy material for that meeting of REIT shareholders. If the acquiree itself is a public company, it is likely that its governing documents will require its shareholders' or other owners' consent, for which a shareholders' or owners' meeting or consent will be necessary, thereby also involving compliance with the proxy rules by the acquiree.[55]

Any acquisition transaction will inevitably focus on the tax consequences of the transaction to the sellers as well as to the REIT. While a discussion of the tax-planning issues involved in acquisitions is beyond the scope of this chapter, a common form of asset acquisition by REITs involves a structure pursuant to which individual owners or partners ("contributors") of a partnership owning the subject property contribute their interest in the subject property or partnership to an operating partnership of an UPREIT or DownREIT in exchange for units in the OP that eventually become redeemable for shares of capital stock of the REIT. The remainder of this chapter discusses the Securities Act implications of this structure.

Issuance of OP Units to Acquire Assets

The REIT and the OP as Issuers

The SEC takes the position that an offer and sale of OP units that are convertible into REIT shares is deemed to be an offer and sale of both the units and the shares. Consequently, a purchase of real estate assets for OP units raises securities law issues for both the OP and the REIT. As described in more detail below, it is important to coordinate private OP unit issuances with any public or private securities offerings conducted by the REIT. Similarly, the redemption rights granted to OP unitholders and any related lockup agreements can affect the manner in which the REIT provides liquidity to contributors through the sale of registered REIT shares.

Securities Law Exemptions

Because of the time and expense associated with a public offering, issuances of OP units for real estate assets are, where possible, structured as private placements that are exempt from Securities Act registration requirements. Both state and federal securities laws impose various requirements for a sale of securities to qualify as a private placement. The federal exemption most frequently relied on is Regulation D, which is a safe harbor for satisfying Section 4(2) of the Securities Act. Many states have adopted a private placement exemption similar to Regulation D, but because each state has its own peculiar requirements, compliance with Regulation D may not be sufficient to satisfy the applicable state private placement requirements. Before definitively deciding to offer OP units in an acquisition transaction, securities counsel should be consulted regarding the applicability of any state securities law provisions in each state in which any contributor resides and whether the National Securities Markets Improvement Act of 1996 has preempted such law in whole or in part or whether the state statute itself may have an applicable exemption.

Accredited Investors

Regulation D permits sales to an unlimited number of "accredited investors" and up to 35 investors who do not qualify as accredited investors. An individual qualifies as an accredited investor if he or she has a net worth (alone or together with his or her spouse) of at least $1 million or has had an annual income of at least $200,000 (or $300,000 together with his or her spouse) for the last two years and a reasonable likelihood of the same income level for the current year. A corporation, partnership, or other entity will qualify as an accredited investor if it was not formed for the purpose of making the particular investment and has total assets in excess of $5 million. Other entities, such as banks, tax-exempt organizations, and trusts as well as employee benefit plans and other collective investment vehicles will also qualify as accredited investors under certain circumstances. For each contributor, the OP and the REIT must either reasonably believe that the contributor qualifies as an accredited investor or treat that contributor as a nonaccredited investor. The issuer's "reasonable belief" is usually based on the contributor's responses to an investor questionnaire.

Investor Information

Although Regulation D allows up to 35 nonaccredited investors, nonaccredited investors typically receive cash in acquisition transactions rather than OP units because of the information that must be delivered to them under Regulation D. Regulation D generally requires the issuer to provide to each nonaccredited investor an information memorandum that contains substantially the same information that would be included in a prospectus if the sale of OP units were a public offering. This information requirement applies even if only one contributor fails to qualify as an accredited investor. It should be noted that a public REIT structure should have much of this information already on file with the SEC and that preparing the Regulation D information memorandum would be analogous to preparing a prospectus supplement for a shelf offering. If all contributors qualify as accredited investors, Regulation D does not impose any information-delivery requirements. However, to respond to contributors' requests for information and because the OP units are convertible, at the REIT's option, into REIT shares, typically the contributors will receive copies of the REIT's most recent Form 10-K, proxy statement and annual report, all Forms 10-Q and 8-K filed since the last Form 10-K, and if applicable, any recent prospectuses on file with the SEC.

Integration of Offerings

To prohibit issuers from breaking up what would otherwise be a public offering into a number of smaller transactions that satisfy the limits on the number of investors for a private placement, the federal securities laws provide for the integration of securities offerings under certain circumstances. The integration of two or more private placements could cause them to fall outside of the applicable exemptions from registration. Similarly, the integration of a public offering and a private placement could result in both offerings violating the securities laws. Although this is more frequently an issue that arises when a REIT is engaged in a public offering (or has engaged or intends to engage in a public offering within six months) it is also important to monitor if the REIT is frequently engaging in property acquisitions for OP units.

Regulation D provides that a private placement will not be integrated with another offering or sale of securities by the same issuer that is made at least six months prior to the commencement of the current offering or six months after the completion of the current offering. The SEC has also adopted Rule 152 under the Securities Act, which establishes a safe harbor for private placements completed prior to the commencement of a public offering. Generally, under Rule 152 if the purchasers in the private placement (that is, the contributors) have entered into binding agreements to acquire the units, subject only to the satisfaction of conditions that are not within their control, prior to the initial filing of the public offering registration statement with the SEC, then the private placement and the public offering will not be integrated. If the OP and the REIT are relying on the Rule 152 safe harbor, it is important to remember that the terms for the private placement cannot change after the filing of the registration statement in a manner that is so material that it effectively results in a different investment decision for the investor.

When analyzing the integration of two or more private placements or when the requirements of Rule 152 have not been satisfied in the case of simultaneous private and public offerings, the SEC applies a five-factor test that looks at the following: (1) whether the sales are part of a single plan of financing, (2) whether the sales involve the issuance of the same class of securities, (3) whether the sales have been made at or about the same time (that is, within six months), (4) whether the same type of consideration is received for the securities, and (5) whether the sales are made for the same general purpose. Generally, the acquisition of properties for OP units will fail at least factors (1), (4), and (5) when determining whether a transaction will be integrated with a REIT securities offering for cash and therefore should not be integrated under the five-factors test. However, multiple property acquisitions may not satisfy the five-factor test, and it may be necessary to integrate these transactions for purposes of determining compliance with Regulation D.

Roll-Up Legislation

The SEC has adopted special regulations that apply to roll-up transactions.[56] Unless an exemption is otherwise applicable, a transaction will be treated as a roll-up transaction if it involves the combination or reorganization of one or more partnerships or other finite-life entities, directly or indirectly, in which some or all of the investors in any of the partnerships or other finite-life entities will receive new securities or securities in another entity (regardless of whether such other entity is a finite-life entity). Generally, if a transaction comes within the definition of a roll-up transaction, certain proxy rules and extensive disclosure requirements must be satisfied as a condition to issuing securities, including OP units. Only a few transactions have been structured in a manner that requires compliance with the roll-up rules because of the time and expense involved in satisfying the SEC's requirements.

The SEC has adopted a number of exemptions from the definition of a roll-up transaction which, in most cases, will exempt the issuance of OP units and the subsequent issuance of REIT shares. The exemption most frequently relied on in the initial public offering context and by REITs that have not been public for at least 12 months is an exemption for transactions for which a registration statement under the Securities Act is not required to be filed and is not filed[57]—that is, private placements. As noted above, there are various requirements for a transaction to qualify as a private placement. However, as an additional prerequisite for a private placement to be exempt from the roll-up provisions, the SEC requires that the OP units not be redeemable for REIT shares (that is, the OP units must be "locked up") for at least one year.

REITs that have been publicly traded for at least 12 months can rely on an exemption from the roll-up rules for transactions that involve the issuance of securities representing 20 percent or less of the total outstanding securities of the REIT.[58] This exemption is available to seasoned REITs when the contributors will not agree to the one-year lock-up that is required for the private placement roll-up exemption described above. There is also an exemption from the definition of a roll-up transaction for transactions where a nonaffiliated party succeeds to the interests of the general partner or sponsor of the contributing entity if the transaction is approved by at least two-thirds of the outstanding units of each participating partnership and, as a result of the transaction, the existing general partners will receive only compensation to which they were entitled under the preexisting terms of the applicable partnership agreements.[59]

In addition to the federal roll-up rules, California has adopted roll-up rules that apply when one or more of the contributors are residents of California. Generally, if a transaction is exempt from the federal roll-up rules, it will also be exempt from the California roll-up rules. It is likely that the application of the National Securities Markets Improvement Act of 1996 will preempt the California roll-up rules in transactions in which the securities to be issued are "Covered Securities" under that Act.

Registration and Resale of Common Stock Issued upon Redemption of OP Units

Nature of Common Stock Issued

Shares of common stock issued upon the redemption of OP units may be either registered securities, which are freely tradable unless the holder is an "affiliate" of the REIT, or privately placed securities (commonly referred to as "restricted securities"), which may only be traded pursuant to a resale registration statement or an exemption from registration. Because the contributors will usually have a tax obligation upon redemption of OP units, they will want to sell at least part of the shares they receive to satisfy that obligation. To ensure some degree of liquidity, the contributors will insist on registration rights that will require the REIT to register either the issuance of the REIT shares to the contributors or the contributors' resale of those shares. Typically, registration rights expire after some period of time, and the contributor is then left to rely on an exemption from registration for the resale of any shares subsequently received on redemption of OP units.

Original Issue and Resale Registration of Common Stock

If the OP units are not convertible into REIT shares for a period greater than one year from the date of issuance, under current SEC practice the REIT may register the issuance of the shares of REIT common stock to the contributors in exchange for their OP units. The registration statement typically would be filed and become effective prior to the expiration of the lock-up period and would remain in effect until the earlier of the redemption of all of the OP units or some outside date specified in a registration rights agreement between the REIT and the contributors.

Registering the original issuance of REIT shares to the contributors in redemption of their OP units, rather than the resale of those shares by the contributors, is preferable to the contributors who are not "affiliates" of the REIT because the shares would not be "restricted securities" and would be freely tradable. Registering the original issuance of the shares to the contributors is also advantageous for the REIT because the REIT does not have to worry about whether the issuance of the shares can be made pursuant to valid federal and state private placement exemptions.

For example, even if the OP units are originally issued in a valid private placement solely to accredited investors, between the date of issuance of the OP units and the issuance of shares in redemption of the OP units (which could be a number of years) one, or more, of the contributors may have had a change in circumstances that causes her or him to no longer qualify as an accredited investor. Under those circumstances, the REIT could be forced to redeem the investor's OP units for cash or comply with the information requirements applicable when issuing securities to nonaccredited investors.

One exception to the general preference for original issue registration applies to "affiliates" of the REIT. An "affiliate" is defined for purposes of the Securities Act to mean any person who directly or indirectly controls, is controlled by, or is under common control with the issuer. Generally, directors and key executive officers of the REIT (those in a position to control the management of the REIT) as well as stockholders with a controlling (but not necessarily a majority) interest are considered affiliates. An affiliate of a public company is always subject to certain limitations on the resale of shares of the public company even if the shares were purchased by the affiliate in the public market. As a result, an affiliate will have greater liquidity if he or she can sell the shares pursuant to a resale registration statement and will be less concerned about whether the shares were originally issued in a registered transaction.

If the REIT does not register the original issuance of the shares to the contributors, the shares issued upon the redemption of the OP units must be issued in a valid private placement and will be "restricted securities." As indicated above, the concern for the REIT is whether subsequent events will change the accredited investor status of one or more of the contributors and, therefore, the REIT's ability to issue the shares through an exempt private placement. Placing restrictions on the transfer of OP units will help limit the possibility that a nonaccredited investor will become an owner of redeemable OP units, but the REIT has no way of controlling events that can cause an existing investor to no longer meet the financial requirements for accredited investor status. The principal concern for contributors is that the shares they receive will be "restricted securities" under the Securities Act.

As holders of restricted securities, the contributors will be subject to various limitations on the resale of their shares unless a resale registration statement is in place and effective for the shares that they hold. As noted below, a REIT should negotiate the right to block the use of the resale registration statement from time to time (commonly referred to as a "black-out period") whenever certain material events are pending but have not been announced to the public or otherwise completed. In addition, because the registration rights agreement will have some outside date after which the REIT is no longer required to keep it effective, the contributors could find themselves holding restricted securities in the future. In most cases, this means that the contributors will be forced to comply with the restrictions of Rule 144 under the Securities Act unless the REIT shares have been held for at least two years. For purposes of calculating the two-year holding period under Rule 144, the contributors will not be allowed to include the period during which they held the OP units that were redeemed for REIT shares.

Rule 144

Rule 144 provides a nonexclusive safe harbor from the registration requirements of the Securities Act for specified sales of restricted securities or securities held by affiliates of the issuer, which are commonly referred to as "control securities." Rule 144 is only a safe harbor, and the actual exemption from registration to which it relates is set forth in Section 4(1) of the Securities Act. However, it is common practice to comply with Rule 144 for all transactions that are intended to be exempt pursuant to Section 4(1).[60]

Rule 144 provides an exemption from the registration requirements for the resale of restricted or control securities if the following basic conditions are met: (1) adequate current public information with respect to the issuer of the securities is available (that is, the issuer has filed all 10-Ks, 10-Qs, and other Securities Exchange Act reports); (2) if the securities are restricted securities, they must be held for at least one full year after the issuer has received the full purchase price or other consideration for such securities; (3) the securities the holder sells in any three-month period may not exceed the greater of (a) 1 percent of the outstanding securities of the same class or (b) the average weekly reported trading volume of the securities during the preceding four calendar weeks (the so-called "dribble-out" rule); (4) the securities must be sold in a brokers' transaction or in transactions directly with a market maker; and (5) concurrently with placing the sales order with the broker or the execution of a sale with the market maker, a report on Form 144 must be filed with the SEC and the applicable securities exchange if the holder's sales of securities in reliance on Rule 144 during the three-month period exceed 500 shares or $10,000 in aggregate sales price. However, if the holder is not an affiliate of the issuer and has not been an affiliate for the past three months and if the holder has held the securities for at least two years, sales may be made under Rule 144 free of the public information, volume limitation, brokers' transaction, and Form 144 requirements.

Registration Rights Agreements

Generally, the REIT will provide registration rights that commence concurrently with the issuance of the REIT shares. However, there is typically a contractual limitation on the maximum number of shares that may be sold in any three- or six-month period, which helps to manage the number of shares of common stock available for sale in the marketplace at any given time. Ordinarily, a registration rights agreement will permit the holders of restricted securities to demand that the REIT file a registration statement covering the resale of their shares (a "demand registration") and will also permit holders to participate as selling stockholders in other public offerings of the REIT's common stock (a "piggyback registration"). Demand and piggyback registration rights are generally subject to cutback to ensure that the REIT is not prevented from selling all of the shares that it desires to sell in subsequent offerings. In addition, some contributors may try to negotiate a cutback priority that will require the REIT to limit sales by other stockholders first in the event a cutback is necessary.

The registration rights agreement will provide that the REIT must use reasonable efforts to file a registration statement and maintain its effectiveness for at least 90 days and frequently as long as one year. The REIT's obligation to maintain the effectiveness of the registration statement usually terminates as soon as the shares are eligible for resale under Rule 144 without the application of the dribble-out rule. Since the registration statement remains effective for an extended period, it is important that the REIT be able to halt selling under the registration statement when there is material nonpublic information that has not been disclosed to the public or when the REIT is otherwise engaged in a transaction that could be negatively affected by the sale of a substantial block of securities by an existing stockholder. Consequently, the REIT generally should have the right to "black out" the use of the registration statement for at least two 60-day periods in any 12-month period. Additionally, the registration rights agreement should provide that the underwriters of any subsequent offering of REIT securities may restrict the sale of REIT shares under the resale registration statement for a period of time prior to and following the pricing of the REIT's offering.

Changes in the Wind

On July 24, 1996, the SEC released the final report of its Advisory Committee on the Capital Formation and Regulatory Process. The report recommends that the SEC implement a voluntary "company registration" system, initially limited to companies eligible to file Form S-3 registration statements and whose securities are listed on the New York or American Stock Exchanges or the NASDAQ National Market System, that would, for companies electing such system, substantially replace the current transactional system for registering securities transactions.[61] While the recommendations of the Advisory Committee would not affect the application of securities laws to REIT or UPREIT IPO transactions described in this chapter, new rules that the SEC may promulgate to implement the Advisory Committee report, as well as other possible reforms of the Securities Act offering process, may result in significant changes in the Securities Act implications described above of issuing OP units or other securities upon the acquisition of assets.

ENDNOTES

1. Internal Revenue Code ("IRC") Section 856(a).
2. Treasury Regulation ("Treas. Reg.") Section 301.7701-3.
3. IRC Section 856(a).
4. This is the key definition distinguishing this type of trust from other trusts, such as personal donative trusts of the probate type. See Massachusetts General Laws, chapter 182, section 1.

5. See IRC Sections 856(h) and 542(a)(2).
6. See current IRC Section 856(h)(3).
7. *Morrissey v. Commissioner,* 296 U.S. 344 (1935).
8. IRC Sections 851–855.
9. IRC Sections 856–859. In 1978, a new Part III was added to Chapter M, consisting of a single Section 860 relating to "deficiency dividend" deductions applicable both to regulated investment companies and to real estate investment trusts, but for which RICs and REITs that fail to meet various of the source-of-income tests of the Code in a prior year might thereby lose their qualification.
10. The REIT asset requirements are contained in IRC Section 856(c)(5).
11. The "qualified REIT subsidiary" provisions are contained in IRC Section 856(i).
12. The 75 percent and 95 percent source-of-income requirements are contained in IRC Sections 856(c)(3) and (2) respectively.
13. "Rents from real property" are defined in IRC Section 856(d).
14. IRC Section 856(d)(2)(C).
15. IRC Section 856(d)(3).
16. Section 511(a)(2) basically describes tax-exempt institutions (such as pension funds, charities, etc.) that are exempted from the normal income tax rules by virtue of IRC Sections 401(a) and 501(c).
17. Current Treasury Regulation Section1.856.3(g).
18. See the discussion in *State Street Trust Company v. Hall,* 311 Mass. 299 (1942). Also see the Annotation "Massachusetts or Business Trusts" in 156 ALR 22-231 (1945), which, although now over 50 years old and therefore does not deal with the use of the business trust vehicle for RICs, REITs, and in other modern business contexts, nevertheless contains a thorough discussion of the basics of the business trust vehicle.
19. *State Street Trust Company v. Hall,* supra; *Peterson v. Hopson,* 306 Mass. 597 (1940); *Commissioner of Corporations and Taxation v. Springfield,* 321 Mass. 31 (1947).
20. *Dolben v. Gleason,* 292 Mass. 511 (1935).
21. Compare *First National Bank of New Bedford v. Chartier,* 305 Mass. 316 (1940) and the cases cited therein at pages 320 and 321 (powers of shareholders recited in the applicable declarations of trust constituted "control" by the shareholders) with *Commissioner of Corporations and Taxation v. Springfield,* supra (very comparable powers of shareholders under the applicable declaration of trust did not constitute shareholder "control" over the trustees).

22. California Corporations Code ("California Code"), Section 23000.

23. General Corporations Law of Maryland ("GCL Maryland"), Title 8.

24. California Code, Section 23001; GCL Maryland, Sections 8-601(b) and 5-350.

25. GCL Maryland, Title 8 (Sections 8-101 through 8-701).

26. See GLC Maryland Title 3, Subtitles 6 and 7. For a general discussion of these business combination and control share statutory provisions, see notes 38 and 39 below.

27. Delaware Code, Title 12, Chapter 38 ("Delaware Code").

28. Delaware Code, Section 3801(a).

29. Delaware Code, Section 3803.

30. Delaware Code, Section 3807.

31. See *Gleason v. McKay,* 134 Mass. 419 (1883); *Opinion of Justices*, 266 Mass. 590 (1929).

32. Chapter seven (State Taxation of REITs) explores this matter in detail.

33. Massachusetts Department of Revenue Letter Ruling 91-2, July 1, 1991.

34. Several years ago, the author participated in a task force of the Boston Bar Association that considered recommending legislation that would eliminate the potential personal liability of shareholders and trustees of REITs and other businesses organized as business trusts in Massachusetts. The task force abandoned its efforts when advised that the Department of Revenue would take the position that such legislation, if successful, would constitute state action sufficient to no longer justify the constitutional exemption of such business trusts from an excise tax in Massachusetts. A subsequent task force in which the author also has participated has proposed an amendment to the fiduciary laws, as opposed to the business statutes, of Massachusetts that would clarify and reverse the common-law rule that trustees (including trustees under probate-type donative trusts) have personal liability for the liabilities of their trusts, so as to make it clear that all trustees of all trusts in Massachusetts that act within the express authority of the applicable declaration of trust are free from personal liability for obligations of the trust.

35. California Code, Section 500.

36. GCL Maryland, Section 2-311.

37. GCL Maryland, Section 2-310.

38. GCL Maryland Sections 3-601 through 3-604, in brief, prohibit mergers and other specified "business combination" between the corporation and any person owning more than 10 percent of its outstanding voting stock (an "Interested Stockholder") for a period of five years after the person became an Interested Stockholder and permits such business combinations thereafter only if approved by supermajority votes of the stockholders. The section does not apply, however, to business combinations that are approved or exempted by the board of directors prior to the person's becoming an Interested Stockholder.

39. GCL Maryland Sections 3-701 through 3-709 eliminate the voting rights of "control shares" in certain circumstances by the "acquirer" of such shares unless a supermajority of other shares have approved the voting of such control shares within the range specified in the following sentence. "Control shares" are shares which, when aggregated with other shares previously acquired by the acquirer, would entitle the acquirer to vote in the election of directors within one of the following ranges of voting power: (i) one-fifth up to one-third, (ii) one-third but less than a majority, and (iii) a majority of voting power. The statute permits a corporation to opt out of the foregoing restrictions by including an opt-out provision in its charter or bylaws.

40. *Realty Acquisition Corporation v. Property Trust of America,* available both in Commerce Clearing House *Federal Securities Law Reporter* at ¶95,245 and on the Westlaw system (1989 WL 21447).

41. See IRC Section 856(h).

42. See IRC Section 544, as modified by Section 856(h)(3).

43. See IRC Section 544(a)(3).

44. See Treas. Reg. Section1.856-3(g).

45. IRC Section 862(c)(2).

46. IRC Sections 856(c)(2)(A) and 856(c)(3).

47. IRC Section 856(c)(5)(B).

48. Securities Act Section 4(2).

49. See Securities Act Rules 501–508 and the Preliminary Notes thereto.

50. Securities Act, Section 11.

51. Securities Act, Section 12.

52. See the July 24, 1996, report of the SEC Advisory Committee on the Capital Formation and Regulatory Processes described in SEC Securities Act Release No. 7314, Exchange Act Release No. 37480, which Release also requests public comments on the Advisory Committee's recommendations.

53. If the acquisition by the REIT or its OP is of a "significant" amount of assets, then a Form 8-K Report will be required to be filed within 15 calendar days of the acquisition reporting under Item 2 of the Report the acquisition and under Item 7 various financial information concerning the acquired properties. The financial information will need to conform to Rule 3-14 of Regulation S-X, and pro forma financial information will be required consistent with Article 11 of Regulation S-X. If not then available, the financial information may be filed in an amendment to the Form 8-K not later than 60 days after the due date of the Form 8-K. A "significant" amount of assets is involved if the acquired assets exceed 10 percent of the total consolidated assets of the REIT at the most recent fiscal year-end or the gross income of the acquired assets exceeds 10 percent of the total consolidated gross income of the REIT during its most recent fiscal year.

54. Regulation 14A, Rules 14a-1 through 14b-2 under the Exchange Act.

55. A merger of public REIT B into public REIT A will likely involve separate shareholder meetings of both REITs and the preparation of a joint proxy statement that will form the basis of the solicitation for proxies by each REIT for its respective meeting, that will comply with the proxy rule requirements for each meeting, and that will serve as a prospectus under the Securities Act for the REIT A shares (or other securities) to be issued to REIT B's shareholders upon consummation of the merger. The joint proxy statement/prospectus will constitute a part of a registration statement on Form S-4 to be filed by REIT A to register such shares.

56. See Regulation S-K, Part 900, Items 901–915.

57. Regulation S-K, Item 901(c)(2)(ii).

58. Regulation S-K, Item 901(c)(2)(v).

59. Regulation S-K, Item 901(c)(2)(iv).

60. The exemptions provided in Sections 4(1) and 4(2) of the Securities Act from the requirement that securities be sold only pursuant to an effective registration statement under Section 5 of the Act differ depending on the identity of the seller. Section 4 provides (among other exemptions) that: "Section 5 shall not apply to: (1) Transactions by any person other than an issuer, underwriter or dealer. (2) Transactions by an issuer not involving any public offering." The effect of Rule 144 is to provide a safe-harbor determination that a person who meets its conditions is not an underwriter or a dealer of the securities involved.

61. See note 52 supra.

CHAPTER

4

FEDERAL TAXATION OF REAL ESTATE INVESTMENT TRUSTS

David L. Brandon, *Director, Coopers & Lybrand, L.L.P.*[1]

I. HISTORY OF THE REIT

The origins of the real estate investment trust, or REIT, can be traced to the 19th century when corporate entities faced statutory restrictions on acquiring and developing real property. Since corporate entities could not own real property, investors frequently used common-law business trusts, or "Massachusetts trusts," to pool real property investments. These early realty trusts are the predecessors of the modern REIT.

Although the corporate ownership restrictions eventually disappeared, the early realty trusts acquired another advantage over corporations when the first constitutional corporate tax was enacted in 1909.[2] In *Eliot v. Freeman*[3] the Supreme Court held that the trusts, unlike corporations, were exempt from the new tax because they were not "organized under the laws" as corporate entities. Although Congress eliminated this particular requirement when it enacted the broader income tax in 1913, realty trusts remained exempt from the tax for a period based on a number of judicial decisions.[4]

The realty trusts finally lost their preferred tax status as a result of the 1935 Supreme Court decision in *Morrissey v. Commissioner*.[5] In *Morrissey*, the Court established a three-part inquiry for determining whether an entity was an association taxable as a corporation. To be taxable, the undertaking must have (1) associates that have come together for a joint enterprise; (2) a business purpose; and (3) a preponderance of traditional corporate attributes, such as limited liability, centralized management, continuity of life, and freely transferable ownership interests. A few years later, in *North American Bond Trust,* the Second Circuit determined that a trust need not conduct an active business to have a business purpose under the *Morrissey* tests. Rather, the trustees of the entity need only be vested with the power to vary the investment of the beneficiaries.[6] Since all realty trusts were able to vary their investments, these two decisions foreclosed any possible avenues for them to escape the corporate income tax until Congress passed the REIT tax regime over 20 years later.

The first REIT tax legislation was passed in 1960 as an amendment to An Act to Amend the Internal Revenue Code With Respect to the Excise Tax On Cigars.[7] This legislation, which granted REITs pass-through tax treatment for federal income tax purposes, was modeled after the tax regime for regulated investment companies (RICs) and was premised on the passive nature of realty trust income. President Eisenhower had initially opposed the REIT legislation on the grounds that realty rents, unlike dividends received by RICs, are not subject to at least one level of corporate taxation. His objections were eventually overcome and he agreed to sign the legislation the second time it was presented by Congress.[8]

The original REIT tax rules retreated from the strict business purpose standard in *North American* and made a REIT's pass-through status contingent on avoiding the active conduct of a trade or business. Although these rules have been amended dozens of times to conform with the real estate marketplace, the central theme of passivity remains largely intact.[9] Perhaps the most significant relaxation of this standard occurred with the Tax Reform Act of 1986, which permitted REITs for the first time to manage directly their own properties, rather than relying on independent contractors for this purpose.[10] This commendable change deserves at least a portion of the credit for the REIT boom in the early 1990s.[11]

Interestingly, the Internal Revenue Service recently published final regulations Sections 301.7701-1 through -3, which replace the corporate classification standards first enunciated in *Morrissey* with a "check-the-box" system. In the case of privately held entities, these new regulations will allow many of them simply to elect whether to be treated as a corporation, trust, or partnership. However, the "check-the-box" system does not materially alter the classification rules for publicly traded entities, nor lessen the need for a special tax regime for REITs.

II. OVERVIEW OF THE REIT TAX PROVISIONS

Generally, a qualified corporation or business trust that elects to be taxed as a REIT is entitled to a deduction for dividends paid to shareholders, which effectively makes it a pass-through entity for tax purposes. In order to qualify as a REIT, the entity must first satisfy a number of organizational requirements found in Section 856(a) of the Internal Revenue Code. These provisions require that the REIT issue transferable shares to at least 100 persons, that the majority ownership of the shares not be closely held among five or fewer individuals, and that the REIT comply with recordkeeping requirements regarding its shareholders. In addition, the REIT must derive at least 95 percent of its gross income from real estate sources or passive interest and dividends, and at least 75 percent of its gross income from real estate sources alone. The remaining 5 percent is not restricted and is often referred to as the bad income basket. Finally, at least 75 percent of a REIT's assets must be real estate assets.

If an electing entity satisfies these requirements and, further, distributes at least 95 percent of its taxable income each year to shareholders, then it is entitled to take the dividends paid deduction for its dividend distributions. A REIT is not required to distribute up to 5 percent of its ordinary income nor its net capital gains, but it will be subject to regular corporate tax on any of these amounts that it retains.

As a result of statutory amendments over the years, REITs may be subject to tax in a variety of other circumstances in lieu of facing disqualification of REIT status. These include imposition of the highest corporate rate (currently 35 percent) under Section 11 of the Code on any gain on foreclosure property that is held for sale to customers, a 100 percent tax on the amount of a qualified income shortfall if the income tests are not satisfied, a 100 percent tax on gains from prohibited transactions (that is, nonforeclosure property that is held for sale to customers in the ordinary course of business under Section 1221(1) of the Code) and possible interest and penalties if a deficiency dividend is required under Section 860 in order to satisfy the income distribution requirement for a prior year. Finally, a REIT may also be liable for a 4 percent excise tax to the extent it fails to distribute at least 85 percent of its ordinary income and 95 percent of its capital gains before the end of the calendar year.

If a REIT is disqualified, it may be precluded from reelecting REIT status for a period of five years unless it is able to persuade the IRS that the reason for disqualification was due to reasonable cause and not willful neglect. Since the tax consequences of disqualification are potentially draconian, it is critical that a REIT establish a history of strict and methodical adherence to the REIT qualification rules. In addition to minimizing the risks of actual disqualification, evidence of a REIT's historical tax compliance efforts may help establish reasonable cause and an absence of willful neglect for purposes of requalifying as a REIT.

III. FORMING A NEW REIT

There are several tax impediments to contributing assets to a new REIT or converting a C corporation into a REIT. The following discussion does not attempt to provide a thorough analysis of these problems, but hopefully illustrates the broader issues involved in a new REIT offering.

A. Traditional REITs

Ordinarily, when organizing a new corporation, gain or loss is not recognized on the contribution of assets to the entity in exchange for shares (except to the extent that contributed liabilities exceed contributed asset bases), provided the contributor(s) possess at least 80 percent control following the transaction.[12] In the case of a REIT, however, this nonrecognition provision is unavailable if the transaction results in a diversification of the contributors' investments.[13]

Diversification is deemed to occur if two or more contributors transfer nonidentical assets in the transaction.[14] Thus, if two partnerships with different investors contribute their respective portfolios to a newly organized REIT in exchange for shares, the investments of the individual partners will become diversified as a result of the transaction and the transaction will be fully taxable. A similar diversification can occur if a single contributor transfers appreciated assets to a new REIT in conjunction with a public offering of shares.

On the other hand, a taxable diversification is avoided if a single partnership incorporates and elects REIT status without admitting new investors. However, even if there is no taxable diversification, gain must still be recognized under Section 357(c) to the extent that liabilities assumed by the new corporation exceed the bases of the transferred properties.

The conversion of an existing, taxable corporation, or C corporation, into a REIT also avoids diversification issues under Section 351(e), since there is no transfer of assets involved. However, concurrently with the repeal of the *General Utilities* doctrine, the Tax Reform Act of 1986 authorized the Treasury to issue regulations that would tax the built-in gains (that is, the appreciated value of assets) of C corporations that convert or merge into pass-through entities.[15]

In response, the IRS promulgated Notice 88-19, which provides that built-in gain regulations will be issued with a retroactive effective date of June 10, 1987.[16] According to the Notice, the regulations will permit REITs to elect to retain built-in gain assets for a period of 10 years, in lieu of paying a built-in gains tax. If assets are sold during the 10-year period, the built-in gains are taxable and are subject to rules similar to those for REIT foreclosure properties, discussed below.[17]

Finally, a REIT is also required to distribute any earnings and profits it may have inherited from a predecessor C corporation or acquired by way of merger with a C corporation. The earnings and profits must be distributed by the end of the taxable year in which it was acquired.[18]

B. Umbrella Partnership REITs

In the early 1990s, a new type of offering was created called the umbrella partnership REIT, or UPREIT, in order to avoid the many tax barriers to organizing a new REIT with existing portfolios of properties. In a nutshell, an UPREIT transaction involves transferring existing properties (or partnership interests) to a new partnership, called the operating partnership. A REIT is organized for purposes of a public offering and transfers all of the offering proceeds to the operating partnership in exchange for a general partnership interest therein.

Because the REIT has no earnings and profits and acquires no appreciated assets for shares, it avoids the built-in gain rules and E&P distribution requirements. The transfer of assets to the operating partnership generally is tax-deferred. Built-in gains on the transferred properties generally must be allocated to the transferring partners. Future depreciation deductions for the transferring partners may also be reduced under the Section 704(b) regulations.

NonREIT partners in the operating partnership may be entitled to convert their partnership units into REIT shares, or at the option of the REIT (or operating partnership) redeem their units for REIT shares or cash. Generally, in order to maintain fungibility between the units and the REIT shares, the REIT will acquire no material assets outside of its interest in the operating partnership. The IRS's recently issued partnership anti-abuse regulations appear to sanction the UPREIT structure, albeit with an example that is narrower than most practitioners would have wished.[19]

Although the UPREIT structure initially encountered criticism from analysts and investment bankers, it has since gained wide acceptance in the REIT market. In addition to deferring gain recognition on contributed assets, the structure permits tax-deferred acquisitions of partnership assets in the future on an ongoing basis. This particular feature of the UPREIT has prompted a few traditional REITs to convert to UPREITs in order to remain competitive in the property marketplace.

IV. REIT QUALIFICATION: ORGANIZATIONAL REQUIREMENTS

In order to qualify initially as a real estate investment trust, an entity must be organized as either a corporation, trust or association:

1. Which is managed by one or more trustees or directors.
2. The beneficial ownership of which is evidenced by transferable shares, or by transferable certificates of beneficial interest.
3. Which, but for the REIT provisions, would be taxable as a domestic corporation.
4. Which is neither a financial institution (within the meaning of Section 582(c)(5) of the Code), nor an insurance company to which Subchapter L of the Code applies.
5. The beneficial ownership of which is held by 100 or more persons.
6. Which is not closely held (under the personal holding company test in Section 542(a)(2)).
7. Which meets the REIT income and asset tests, described below.[20]

Under Section 856(c)(1), an entity desiring REIT status also must file an election with the IRS for the taxable year or have already made a valid election in a previous year. The election is made simply by computing taxable income as a REIT for the taxable year for which the election is desired.[21] This is done by filing Form 1120-REIT. Neither the statute nor the regulations require that the election be made by any specific date; thus, a Form 1120-REIT filed after March 15 under an extension should qualify as a valid REIT election.

The requirements in items (1) through (4) above must be met by the REIT during its entire taxable year; whereas, the 100-shareholder test in item (5) must be satisfied during 335 days of a 12-month year or a proportionate part (11/12th's) of a shorter year.[22] The closely held restriction in item (6) must be satisfied throughout the last half of a REIT's taxable year.[23] Neither the 100-shareholder restriction nor the closely held restriction apply during a REIT's first taxable year.[24]

A. Management by Trustees or Directors

In the early days of the REIT vehicle, questions sometimes arose whether the delegation of powers to an outside adviser violated the requirement that a REIT be managed by its trustees or directors. In Rev. Rul. 72-254,[25] the IRS determined that a delegation of powers to an adviser to make loans and investments within specified limits did not violate this requirement. Today, virtually all new public REITs are both internally advised and managed, so the issue of trustee management rarely arises.

In situations in which a trustee or director owns shares in an independent contractor for the REIT, questions may arise whether his or her relationship to the REIT affects the independence of the contractor. Generally, these issues are resolved in favor of independence.[26]

B. REIT Share Ownership Requirements

The REIT share ownership tests include the 100-shareholder requirement, the closely held restrictions, and the share transferability requirement. Under Section 857(a)(2) and the regulations, the tests also involve specific recordkeeping requirements, which if violated could result in REIT disqualification.

1. The 100-Shareholder Rule

The 100-shareholder rule counts most legal persons as shareholders, so that an individual, corporation, partnership, estate, or a trust are each considered a single shareholder, even when such shareholder itself is a widely held entity. On the other hand, the 100-shareholder rule is not restricted by attribution rules and most related persons may be treated as separate and distinct shareholders.

Generally, almost any level of ownership that is not purely nominal is respected for purposes of the 100-shareholder rule. Thus, a REIT whose ownership is concentrated in a few shareholders may satisfy the rule by issuing low-value shares, possibly of a second class, to enough other persons to satisfy the requirement. Sometimes this is accomplished by donating shares to a variety of charitable organizations. In private-letter ruling PLR 8342016, a parent company owned in excess of 99.9 percent in value of the outstanding shares of a newly formed REIT. In order to satisfy the 100-shareholder rule, the new REIT issued one share of nonvoting preferred stock to each of 125 employees of the adviser for $10 per share. Although the IRS approved this structure, today most practitioners would advise using a higher par value for shares (for example, $500 to $1,000) to ensure that the shares are not considered nominal.

2. The Closely Held Restriction (or Five-or-Fewer Rule)

The REIT five-or-fewer rule provides that five or fewer individuals cannot own, directly or indirectly, more than 50 percent in value of its outstanding stock at any time during the last half of its taxable year. This rule is incorporated from Section 542 (personal holding company tests) by Section 856(h), and applies beginning in a REIT's second taxable year.[27] This rule effectively limits share ownership to an average of 10 percent of outstanding shares per unrelated individual shareholder.

Unlike the 100-shareholder rule, the five-or-fewer rule applies to individuals and not to persons. Generally, corporations, partnerships, and trusts (including foreign pension plans) that invest in REITs will be counted based on the proportional interests of their respective individual shareholders, partners, or beneficiaries.[28] This treatment is called the look-through rule, since these entities are looked through to determine if the five-or-fewer rule is satisfied.

Certain entities are excluded from look-through treatment and are treated as single individuals for purposes of the five-or-fewer rule. These are qualified domestic pension, profit-sharing, and stock bonus plans under Section 401(a) of the Code, unemployment compensation plans under Section 501(c)(17), private foundations under Section 509(a) and charitable remainder trusts under Section 642(c). Beginning in 1994, certain qualified plans may be entitled to look-through treatment as discussed more fully below.

For purposes of the five-or-fewer test, the family attribution rules of Section 544(a)(2) apply to aggregate shares of family members into the hands of a single individual. In addition, holding an option to acquire REIT shares is considered equivalent to owning the shares.[29] However, there is no partner-to-partner attribution under Section 544.

3. Pension Fund Ownership of REIT Shares

REITs are especially attractive vehicles for pension investment in real estate, since their dividends are excluded from unrelated business taxable income[30] and their shares offer a more realistic exit strategy than do interests in pension commingled funds.[31] Until the Omnibus Budget and Reconciliation Act of 1993 (OBRA), however, domestic pension funds were restricted in the amount they could invest in a single REIT since they were treated as single individuals for purposes of the five-or-fewer rule. This treatment discriminated against domestic pension funds vis-a-vis their unrestricted foreign counterparts and was considered by many to be a barrier to the recovery of the distressed real estate markets.

The five-or-fewer rule restrictions were liberalized by OBRA, effective January 1, 1994, to encourage greater domestic pension investments in REITs. New Code Section 856(h)(3) permits pension funds and other Section 401(a) qualified trusts to take advantage of the look-through rule if needed to maintain the qualified status of the REIT. Under this provision, these trusts are not counted as single individuals, but are counted based on the number of their beneficiaries. The beneficiaries' interests are determined in proportion to their actuarial interests in the trust.

In order to prevent tax-exempt entities from using REITs primarily to convert unrelated business taxable income ("UBTI") into tax-exempt REIT dividends, the amendment includes a special provision for REITs that are predominantly held by a few large pension funds. Under this provision, if a pension-held REIT relies on the safe harbor, its dividend distributions to the larger pension distributees may be subject to the unrelated business income tax.[32] These dividends are characterized as unrelated business taxable income in proportion to the amount of income earned by the REIT that would be UBTI if earned by a qualified trust. Because of the constraints already imposed on REIT income sources, the most likely form of UBTI under this provision is income from debt-financed properties.[33]

4. Recordkeeping Requirements

Section 857(a)(2) requires that in order for a REIT to maintain its qualification, it must comply with regulations issued by the IRS for the purpose of determining the actual beneficial ownership of its outstanding shares. These regulations require that a REIT demand, from certain shareholders of record, written statements regarding the beneficial ownership of their shares. This demand must be made within 30 days of the close of the taxable year and the responses (or a list of those who fail to respond) must be maintained as permanent records of the REIT. Although there are no penalties imposed on shareholders for failing to respond to these demands, such shareholders are nevertheless required to provide similar information with their own tax returns.[34]

The purely administrative shareholder demand requirements create grief for noncomplying REITs that is far out of proportion to the legislative policy they serve. Fortunately, a more reasonable rule that imposes financial penalties in lieu of disqualification is being promoted by the National Association of Real Estate Investment Trusts. It was included in a REIT simplification bill recently introduced in Congress.[35]

5. Share Transfer Restrictions

In order to ensure compliance with the 100-shareholder rule and the five-or-fewer rule, REIT charters have traditionally imposed limited transfer restrictions on outstanding shares. Generally, these restrictions prohibit transfers to any persons if the transfer would result in fewer than 100 persons owning all of its shares, or would result in the transferee owning more than 9.8 percent of outstanding shares.[36] Although the REIT qualification standards require that REIT shares be transferable, the regulations have long recognized the need for certain transfer restrictions[37] and the IRS has frequently approved such restrictions in private rulings.

In the past, some share transfer restrictions provided only that a prohibited transfer was null and void. More recent provisions void the transfer as well, but also provide for an automatic creation and transfer of a second class of nonvoting shares (excess shares) to a special trust to be held for the benefit of the ultimate permissible purchaser of the shares.[38]

If an excess share trust is used, the IRS requires that the excess shares pay current dividends to a party or parties other than the REIT or the prohibited transferee. This requirement ensures that the excess shares are treated as outstanding for purposes of the five-or-fewer rule. In addition, the IRS apparently insists that the share's voting rights be exercisable and that the ownership limit be at least 5 percent (the threshold for William's Act filings) to ensure that it can be monitored via SEC filings.[39]

C. Type of Entity

The REIT organizational rules require that the entity be organized either as a trust, corporation, or association that is taxable as a domestic corporation. Prior to 1976, REITs had to be organized as business trusts, a requirement that heralded their history more than any practical tax policy concerns. One consequence of the old rule was that a C corporation that converted into a business trust could not elect REIT status in the year of the transaction, even though the reorganization qualified for tax-free treatment.[40] Recent private letter rulings now approve REIT elections under these circumstances.[41] In addition, a foreign corporation cannot make a REIT election, since it is not "taxable as a domestic corporation," notwithstanding that it may have made an election to be treated as a domestic entity under Sections 897(i), 953(d), or 1504(d).[42]

The remaining entity requirements prohibit REITs from qualifying as financial institutions or as insurance companies.

V. OPERATIONAL REQUIREMENTS: THE REIT INCOME AND ASSET TESTS

The REIT income and asset tests account for the vast majority of the REIT private-letter rulings and significantly influence the day-to-day operations and activities of REIT managers. Unfortunately, these tests have their genesis in the mutual fund rules rather than the real estate business. As they have been amended to accommodate the needs of the industry, the result often has been added layers of ambiguity and complexity. Consequently, REITs are still well advised to seek tax counsel or IRS assurances prior to undertaking new investment or management activities or offering new services to tenants.

A. Income Tests

The REIT 75 percent real estate source income test is found in Section 856(c)(3) of the Code. It provides that an entity will not be a qualified REIT unless at least 75 percent of its *gross* income (excluding prohibited transaction income) is derived from the following:

1. Rents from real property.
2. Interest on obligations secured by mortgages on real property (or on interests in real property).
3. Gain from the sale or other disposition of real property (including interests in real property and interests in mortgages), which is not "dealer property" under Section 1221(1).
4. Dividends or other distributions on, and gain from the sale of, shares (other than prohibited transactions) in other qualified REITs.
5. Abatements and refunds of real property taxes.
6. Income and gain from foreclosure property.
7. Certain amounts received as consideration to enter agreements to (i) make mortgages, or (ii) to purchase or lease real property.
8. Gains from sales of real property that are included within the prohibited transaction safe harbor.
9. Qualified temporary investment income.

The 95 percent income test mandates that at least 95 percent of a REIT's income be derived from the foregoing sources, plus dividends and interest. Thus, a REIT is permitted to earn up to 25 percent of its income from non-real estate passive sources and up to 5 percent from unrelated sources.

The REIT 30 percent gross income test provides that no more than 30 percent of a REIT's gross income may be derived from the sale or disposition of stock or securities held less than one year, real property (including mortgages) held less than four years, or from prohibited transactions (that is, property held for sale to customers in the ordinary course of business, or "dealer" sales). To the extent gain is recognized from involuntary conversions of property under Section 1033 and from foreclosure property sales, it is excluded from the 30 percent test.[43]

1. Rents From Real Property

Rents from real property are the largest source of qualified income for REITs. In defining rents, the regulations provide only that the term means the gross amounts received for the use of, or the right to use, real property of the REIT.[44] Thus, most of the guidance regarding rents is found in published rulings or in specific statutory safe harbors or exclusions.

(a) Services Rendered by Independent Contractors Section 856(d)(2)(C) excludes from rents any amounts received or accrued, directly or indirectly, with respect to real or personal property, if the REIT furnishes or renders services to tenants, or manages or operates the property, other than through an independent contractor from whom the REIT does not derive any income. A violation of the independent-contractor rule potentially disqualifies all the rents received from the property. However, Section 856(d)(1) specifically provides that the term "rents" includes special charges (whether or not separately stated) for services customarily furnished or rendered in connection with leasing real property.[45]

Read together, these provisions permit the REIT to charge and collect (and even retain a profit) for the performance of customary services, as long as the actual service is performed by an independent contractor who is adequately compensated.[46] If the service is not customary, the regulations provide that the independent contractor must separately bear the cost of the service, separately charge the tenants therefor, and retain the proceeds.[47] In effect, the REIT is prohibited from becoming financially involved in the provision of any noncustomary service at the cost of disqualifying all its rents.

In order to qualify as a customary service, the service must be customary in the geographic area for tenants in buildings of a similar class. The regulations list numerous services that are often customary, including the provision of heat, light, water, air conditioning, general maintenance janitorial service of common areas, elevators, swimming pools, watchman services, laundry facilities, and so on.[48]

In 1986, the independent-contractor rule was amended to permit REITs to perform directly certain usual and customary property management functions. However, the old rule continues to apply to noncustomary services and to personal services.

(b) Definition of Independent Contractor In order to qualify as an independent contractor, a person cannot own directly or indirectly more than 35 percent of the shares of the REIT. In addition, if the independent contractor is an entity, no more than 35 percent of its outstanding voting shares (or 35 percent of its total shares), or 35 percent of its assets or net profits, may be owned by any person or persons who collectively own more than 35 percent of the REIT.[49]

The regulations prohibit employees of the REIT from qualifying as independent contractors, but this prohibition does not prevent REIT board members or officers from owning a corporate independent contractor or from acting as directors in both entities, provided the share ownership tests are satisfied.[50] A REIT adviser, however, cannot qualify as an independent contractor because of its fiduciary relationship to the REIT, although its subsidiary may qualify.[51]

With respect to the prohibition against deriving income from an independent contractor, the receipt of dividends or mortgage interest from a contractor disqualifies its independence.[52] On the other hand, the IRS has permitted qualifying independent contractors to lease space from a REIT for their own occupancy, if it is conducive to managing the REIT's property.[53]

(c) Property Management Services Rendered by the REIT In 1986, the independent-contractor rule was amended to permit a REIT to render services to a tenant, or manage its own property, to the same extent that a tax-exempt entity could do so without generating unrelated business taxable income under Section 512(b)(3) of the Code.[54] If a service or activity qualifies under this provision, the REIT need not engage an independent contractor to avoid tainting its rental income. The determination of qualified services under this provision is factual by nature and has created a veritable cottage industry for REITs seeking private rulings from the IRS.

The IRS's regulations generally provide that amounts received for the use of space are not considered rents if services are also rendered to the occupant. Services are considered rendered to the occupant if they are primarily for his or her convenience and are other than those usually or customarily rendered in connection with the rental of space for occupancy only.[55] Notwithstanding the conjunctive test provided in the regulations, IRS representatives have on numerous occasions stated their position that disqualifying services include those that are *either* for the primary convenience of the tenant, *or* are not usual or customary in connection with the rental of space for occupancy only.[56]

In recent years, the scope of the qualified services test has been illuminated through dozens of private-letter rulings. These rulings tend to approve services that are in the nature of property management activities and are usual and customary for the type of property involved. Services that are not related to property management (such as aerobics classes in an office building gymnasium), or that are for the primary convenience of a tenant (such as repainting an apartment in the middle of a lease term) are not approved, unless an independent contractor is used.[57]

Examples of types of services that REITs are permitted to perform without using independent contractors include repairs and maintenance for common areas, HVAC systems, general lighting, electrical, entranceways, and elevators.[58] REITs also may provide snow removal, landscaping, common area painting, security systems, sprinkler systems, and trash collection.[59] Provision of free parking spaces for tenants and their customers is allowed, but parking management usually is provided by independent contractors. In addition, two private-letter rulings appear to sanction treating hourly parking fees as rents from real property, even if the fees are received from the general public, provided independent contractors perform the daily management for the lots.[60]

REITs have provided tenants with free use of conference facilities, club houses, exercise rooms (with independent contractor instructors), and washer/dryers.[61] For retail properties, REITs have provided advertising on behalf of malls and shopping centers and for special groupings of retail tenants, but generally are not allowed to advertise on behalf of individual tenants. The IRS has also shown an inclination to approve services that are more in the nature of public utilities or related to public safety and welfare, whether or not they are akin to property management services. Examples include cable television, wheelchairs, and swimming pool lifeguards when required by law.[62]

In one recent ruling, the IRS offered a new interpretation of the statutory phrase "services rendered to tenants." In PLR 9627017, the IRS determined that the operation of a marina and the provision of brokerage services to tenants and to the general public constituted "separate lines of business." As fully integrated, separate lines of business open to the public, these activities are not considered "services rendered to tenants," even though tenants may use the services. Accordingly, although the income from such activities is nonqualified, the activities themselves do not taint other rents received by the REIT.

Unfortunately, there are few bright lines in the area of permissible services, and many of the rulings that have been issued required the taxpayer to submit empirical data proving that proposed services were usual and customary. Thus, REITs should seek tax counsel advice or a ruling from the IRS regarding any services that may be questionable.

(d) Trustee Administrative Obligations Certain services or activities engaged in by the trustees or employees of a REIT are considered more akin to satisfying their fiduciary obligations to investors than rendering services to tenants. Consequently, the performance of these services will not affect the qualification of rents. The regulations recognize a variety of functions that fit within this exception, including establishing rental terms, selecting tenants, entering and renewing leases, handling taxes, interest and insurance payments, and making property acquisitions, repairs, and other capital expenditures.[63]

(e) Tenant Ownership Restrictions Real property rents may be disqualified if the REIT owns directly or indirectly more than 10 percent of the outstanding equity interests of the tenant. This rule ensures that the REIT's investment performance is based on real estate and not the underlying business of the tenant. In the case of a corporate tenant, the limitation is based on the combined voting power of all classes of shares entitled to vote, or on the total number of all outstanding shares. In the case of noncorporate entities, the limitation is based on the REIT's interest in the assets or net profits of the entity.[64]

For purposes of determining indirect ownership of a tenant, the corporate attribution rules in Section 318 of the Code apply and may create a trap for the unwary. If shareholders in a REIT are members of a partnership that includes the owner of the REIT's tenant, the attribution rules will aggregate the ownership within the partnership of both the REIT shares and the tenant's shares. Under Section 318(a)(3)(C), the REIT is then treated as owning the tenant, which disqualifies the tenant's lease payments. Thus the attribution rules merit special attention in situations where a REIT's sponsor also owns a REIT tenant(s).

(f) Lease of Personal Property The definition of qualified "rents from real property" includes payments attributable to personal property that is leased under, or in connection with, the real property lease. This preferential treatment is permitted only if the personal property lease income does not exceed 15 percent of the total lease income for the real and personal property combined. For purposes of qualifying for this *de minimis* rule, amounts attributable to personal property are determined in proportion to the relative tax bases of the two types of property. The average of the tax bases at the beginning and at the end of the taxable year is used.[65]

If rents attributable to personal property exceed the 15 percent limitation, the preferential treatment is lost and all of the rent attributable to the personal property is nonqualifying income. However, rents attributable to real property are not tainted or otherwise affected by this treatment.[66] The personal property rule is usually applied separately to each lease of property, but substantially similar leases for multiple-unit projects may be aggregated.[67]

Although the relative tax bases of the real and personal property are used to apportion rents when determining whether the *de minimis* rule applies, the statute does not impose this formula when the *de minimis* rule is inapplicable. Accordingly, the actual fair value of personal property rents and real property rents, as determined under Section 61, should be used to calculate the amount of nonqualified income when the *de minimis* rule does not apply.

The personal property limitation is particularly significant to REITs that invest in hotels, restaurants, and similar properties that have significant amounts of personalty. In some cases, it may be necessary to transfer title to the personal property to the lessee to avoid generating excessive nonqualifying income.

The statutory phrase "in connection with [a] real property lease" occasionally leads to interesting results. In one private ruling, the IRS acknowledged that renting baby strollers in a retail mall was "in connection with" the real property leases and, thus, produced "rents from real property."[68]

(g) Rents Based on Net Profits Real property rents generally do not include any amounts based on the income or net profits derived by any person from the leased property, although rents may be based on a percentage of net receipts or sales.[69] The net profits restriction parallels the tenant ownership restriction in limiting the ability of the REIT to participate in an active business through a lease arrangement.

The regulations provide that rents may be based on differing percentages for different types of gross receipts or gross sales (or for different departments), but that they cannot be renegotiated frequently or determined in a manner that has the effect of basing the rents on net profits. Percentage rents may include escalation clauses for common expenses such as taxes and insurance.

An exception to the general rule permits rents to be based on the income or net profits of a tenant that derives substantially all its income from subleasing the property, provided the sublease income itself would qualify as rents if earned directly by the REIT. In this case, the REIT's rents may be disqualified only in proportion to the amount of disqualifying income at the sublease level.[70]

Some expenses associated with rental property may clearly be borne by the REIT without causing rents to be based on the income or profits of the tenant. These include items such as mortgage interest, real estate taxes, insurance, and maintenance.[71]

2. Interest Income

(a) In General The regulations define interest income as amounts received as compensation for the use or forbearance of money.[72] Generally, interest income is qualifying income under the 95 percent income test, without regard to its source. In order to qualify as real estate source income under the 75 percent test, the underlying obligation must be secured by mortgages on real property or on interests in real property.

If a loan is secured by both real and other property, interest on the loan must be apportioned to determine how much qualifies as mortgage interest for purposes of the 75 percent test. If the value of the real property exceeds the face amount of the loan, then the entire interest income may be apportioned to the real property. However, if the amount of the loan is greater than the value of the real property, then the qualifying mortgage interest is determined based on the ratio of the real property value to the total loan amount.[73]

The proportionality rule favors the REIT if the value of all the secured property (both real and personal) exceeds that of the loan, but the rule prejudices the REIT if the loan amount exceeds the total value of the collateral. In the latter case, a better rule perhaps would have been to apportion the interest according to the ratio of the value of the real property to the value of the real and personal property combined.

(b) Interest Based on Profits and Shared Appreciation Mortgages As in the case of "rents from real property," interest income cannot be based on the income or profits of another person. Similarly, this rule does not prevent a REIT from earning contingent interest based on a percent of gross receipts or sales, or based on the net income of a debtor, substantially all of whose gross income consists of qualified rents. If a REIT can receive either a stated interest rate or an amount based on income or profits, then interest on the loan is not disqualified unless it is actually paid in whole or in part based on the income or profits contingency. If so, all of the interest for that year is disqualified, even if a portion was based on a fixed rate.[74]

In 1986, Congress added Section 856(j) to the Code, which permits a REIT to share in the gain from the sale of property on which it owns a mortgage. This provision unfortunately requires the REIT to characterize income from a shared appreciation provision based on the character of the underlying property. Thus, if the property owner sells the property in a prohibited transaction, the participation portion could be subject to a 100 percent tax. Furthermore, if the property is sold within four years, income from the participation provision may cause the REIT to violate the 30 percent gross income tests, discussed below.

By its terms, the shared appreciation provision applies only to participation in gains realized by the seller and not to participation in some form of gross receipts. At one time, the IRS apparently intended to issue a ruling extending the application of this provision to a gross receipts form of participation, but it is not presently pursuing the project.

(c) Loans Made to Partnerships For a period, the IRS was willing to rule that a loan secured by an interest in a real estate partnership qualified as a real estate asset and produced qualifying interest for purposes of the 75 percent income test. The IRS is reconsidering this position and no longer issues these rulings.[75] Therefore, it is unclear if such investments are qualified real estate assets that generate real estate source income.

(d) Commitment Fees In 1976, Congress amended Section 856 to provide that commitment fees to make loans (as well as to enter leases) is treated as qualifying income. This change nullified the holdings in several prior revenue rulings.[76]

(e) Retained Mortgage Participations Income earned by a REIT for servicing mortgages owned by others is generally nonqualified income. However, prior to the enactment of Section 1286 (coupon stripping rules), if a REIT originated and sold a mortgage pool but retained a significant participation therein (for example, 10 percent), then all of the income from the retained interest was qualifying income, even though the REIT's return exceeded that of the other participants.[77] By retaining a large interest in such pools, REITs could effectively convert servicing income into qualifying income. In addition, such REITs could avoid recognition of gain on the portion of the pool that was sold simply by allocating basis to that portion equal to the amount realized on the sale.[78] Rulings approving this tax treatment were suspended following the enactment of Section 1286.[79]

Today, a retained income interest in excess of standard servicing amounts is treated as a stripped coupon and is taxed like a bond. The amount of tax basis allocable to the retained interest is based on the relative fair market values of the stripped coupon (that is, the retained interest) and the stripped obligation. As a result, significant gains may be realized by the REIT when the pool is sold, which could be attributable either to a subordination of the REIT's interest or to a decline in interest rates. In either case, such gains usually result in bad income for purposes of the 30 percent gross income test and may represent prohibited transaction income.[80] Future income (OID) earned on the "stripped coupon," as well as income earned on retained participations in the underlying mortgages, should be qualifying income.

To the extent that a retained income interest represents servicing income, it should be qualified income in proportion to the REIT's retained participation in the underlying mortgages, although the IRS has not ruled on this issue. For purposes of determining whether a retained income interest represents servicing income, the IRS has established several safe harbors in Revenue Procedure 91-50.[81]

(f) Mortgage Pool Certificates Interest income from fixed investment trusts that hold mortgages, such as Ginnie Mae and Freddie Mac certificates, is qualifying mortgage interest for purposes of the 75 percent income test and the certificates are qualifying real estate assets.[82]

(g) REMIC Income Income from interests in real estate mortgage investment conduits is qualified income for a REIT. If less than 95 percent of the REMIC's assets are mortgages, then income from the REMIC is qualified in proportion to the mortgages held by the REMIC.[83]

(h) Repurchase Agreements Repurchase agreements (repos) are structured as a sale of a security and a simultaneous agreement to buy back the security in the near future, typically at a slightly higher price. For tax purposes, a standard repo transaction is considered a secured loan under Section 1058 of the Code; that is, the taxpayer is treated as posting the security as collateral for a short-term borrowing. A reverse repo represents the other side of the transaction, in which the taxpayer loans money and receives a security as collateral.

In Revenue Ruling 77-59, the IRS held that a REIT's loan of cash in a reverse repo of a government security is not a qualified real estate asset, although the interest income it earns is qualified income under the 95 percent income test.[84] The IRS's position in this ruling is probably outdated in view of more recent regulations issued by the Securities and Exchange Commission, which consider a reverse repo to be an investment in the underlying security.[85] Under Section 856(c)(2)(6)(F), the IRS is generally obliged to follow the SEC's interpretations of terms defined in the Investment Company Act of 1940 when the Code fails to provide a definition. Thus, following the SEC's characterization, a reverse repo on a government security should be treated as a qualified asset, notwithstanding the contrary position in Revenue Ruling 77-59.

3. Qualified Temporary Investment Income

The 1986 Act amended the Code to permit REITs to earn certain types of passive, non-real estate income for purposes of the 75 percent income test. This provision addresses the difficulty in investing newly raised capital in qualified assets over a relatively short period of time. It provides that income from stocks and certain debt instruments that are acquired with the proceeds of a stock or debt offering (minimum five-year debt) will satisfy the real estate source test for a period up to one year after the offering was completed.[86]

4. Income from Hedging Instruments

Section 856(c)(6)(G) treats income from interest rate swaps or caps as qualifying income or gain under the 95 percent income test, provided the swap was used to hedge variable rate indebtedness of the REIT. This rule also treats these instruments as securities for purposes of the 30 percent gross income test. Unfortunately, this provision does not apply to other types of hedging instruments, such as floors, collars, futures, or forward contracts. Accordingly, gross income from these types of instruments may constitute nonqualified income for a REIT.[87] In addition, since many hedges are held for less than one year, even a qualified hedge may result in bad income under the 30 percent test.

Some relief for the treatment of derivative hedges is provided in the IRS's accounting rules for these instruments and in the hedging regulations. For example, Section 1.446-3 of the Regulations provides that the gross amounts to be received and paid under notional principal contracts are first offset before arriving at a determination of gross income. Thus, if a REIT is entitled to a $1.5 million fixed-rate payment under a swap, but is obliged to pay a $1 million variable payment, the REIT is treated as receiving only $500,000 gross income rather than $1.5 million for purposes of the qualifying income tests.

In addition, Section 1.446-4 of the regulations permits the recognition of gains from most identified hedges to be amortized over the life of the hedged position. This rule may reduce the amount of nonqualified gross income that is required to be recognized in a single taxable year to a level that is acceptable for REIT qualification purposes.[88]

5. Income from Partnerships

For purposes of determining whether the gross income (and asset) tests are satisfied, a REIT that holds an interest in a partnership is deemed to own its share of the partnership's gross income (and assets) in proportion to its capital interest in the partnership. This look-through treatment applies only for purposes of Section 856 and not for purposes of calculating REIT taxable income under Section 857. When the holding period of an asset is important, for example under the 30 percent test, the REIT is deemed to have held the property for the shorter of the time during which it was a member of the partnership or during which the partnership actually held the property.[89]

The IRS has held that in the case of a REIT receiving property management fees from a partnership in which it holds a significant interest, the fees are disregarded to the extent attributable to the REIT's partnership interest, in order to avoid counting the income twice. To the extent the fees are attributable to other partners' interests, they are considered nonqualifying income.[90]

6. Option Premiums

Premiums earned on written options that lapse unexercised are not qualifying income under the 75 and 95 percent income tests, even though an option on real property is a qualified asset. On the other hand, such premiums are not taken into account as bad income under the 30 percent gross income rule.[91]

7. Liquidating Gains

Gains realized upon liquidation are not taken into account under the 30 percent gross income test, but generally should be qualifying income under the 75 and 95 percent tests to the extent attributable to qualifying assets.[92]

B. Asset Tests

1. Real Estate Assets

To maintain their qualification, REITs must satisfy certain asset tests at the close of each quarter of each taxable year. These tests require that at least 75 percent (by value) of a REIT's total assets be represented by real estate assets, cash and cash items (including receivables), and government securities. Real estate assets include real property, leaseholds, options to acquire real property, co-ownership interests, a proportionate share of real estate property held by a partnership, interests in mortgages, shares in other REITs, and qualified temporary investments. The term does not include mineral, oil, or gas royalty interests.[93]

Under the regulations, real property includes permanent structures and the structural components of a building, such as wiring, plumbing, central HVAC systems, etc., but does not include assets that are accessory to the operation of a business, such as printing presses and machinery. Characterization of an item as a fixture under local law is not controlling.[94]

Several older revenue rulings have found that railroad properties, mobile home units (permanently fixed), air rights, foreign real estate, microwave transmission facilities, condominium units, and mortgage pool certificates all constitute "real estate assets" for REIT qualification purposes.[95] The IRS has also held in a private ruling that hypothecation loans (wherein a debt is satisfied through the assignment to the REIT of an interest in a mortgage owned by the debtor) are qualified assets, as are loans secured by an interest in a real estate partnership.[96] Certificates of deposit are qualifying cash items, although repurchase agreements are not considered qualified assets by the IRS.[97]

2. Determining Value

The Regulations provide that for purposes of the asset tests, value means fair value as determined in good faith by the REIT's trustees or directors.[98] But the Regulations also provide that "total assets" means the gross assets of the company determined in accordance with generally accepted accounting principles.[99] The reference to GAAP book assets should not be interpreted as applying for purposes of determining value, since that would contradict both the statute and the regulatory definition of value. Instead, the reference to book assets should be applied solely for purposes of identifying assets that are includable in total assets.

Although REITs must satisfy the asset tests at the end of each quarter, they are not required to revalue assets for any quarter in which no new security or other property was acquired. Mere changes in the nature of cash items are not considered acquisitions for this purpose.[100]

3. Securities and Other Assets

No more than 25 percent of a REIT's assets, by value, may be represented by securities of other issuers, unless such securities qualify under the 75 percent asset test (for example, Ginnie Maes, REIT shares, government obligations). REITs are further restricted from investing more than 5 percent by value of their assets in the securities of a single other issuer, or from holding more than 10 percent of the voting securities of another issuer.[101]

The restrictions relating to the securities of any one issuer are derived almost verbatim from the diversification rules applicable to regulated investment companies under the Investment Company Act of 1940. These rules had little consequence in the REIT industry until recently, when large numbers of new REITs sought permissible ways to include third-party management operations in their initial public offerings. REITs could not engage directly in such activities without violating the income tests, nor could they control an entity that conducted the activities without violating the securities ownership tests. The solution to this problem was to place the business in a taxable management subsidiary in which the REIT held most of the economic interests through nonvoting preferred shares, while placing the voting control in the hands of a trusted director or trustee. The bulk of the profit inures to the REIT as qualified dividend income.

Although the IRS initially sanctioned taxable management subsidiaries, it no longer issues rulings approving their structure. Apparently, it is concerned that some REITs may retain effective control for purposes of the security diversification test, even though they own only nonvoting shares. Thus, when structuring a management company, it is critical that the REIT have neither *de jure* nor *de facto* voting control in the entity.[102]

A common area of confusion for some REIT managers has been whether the management subsidiary is an independent contractor. Since the REIT derives income in the form of dividends from the subsidiary, it cannot qualify as an independent contractor. Accordingly, any services performed by the subsidiary on behalf of REITs for their tenants must be qualified services under the tests set forth in the tax-exempt regulations, discussed under Part V.A.1.(c), "Property Management Services Rendered by the

REIT," above. Services performed by the subsidiary on behalf of nonREIT customers should have no impact on the REIT's qualified income.

Another area of confusion involves money market funds. REIT managers are frequently tempted to place excess cash in money market funds and often assume that such funds represent cash or cash items for purposes of the REIT asset tests. In fact, money market funds are regulated investment companies whose beneficial interests are represented by corporate shares. As such, these holdings are subject to the security diversification restrictions.

4. Qualified REIT Subsidiaries

Notwithstanding the security diversification restrictions, since 1986 a REIT has been permitted to own 100 percent of the outstanding shares of a qualified REIT subsidiary (QRS). If a REIT has a QRS, the QRS's separate tax status is ignored for federal income tax purposes and all of its assets, liabilities, and items of income, loss, deduction, or credit are considered to be those of the REIT. The purpose of a QRS is to permit a REIT to manage its properties through a bankruptcy or liability remote vehicle, as is commonly done within the real estate industry.[103]

In order to qualify as a QRS, 100 percent of the subsidiary's shares must have been held by the REIT at all times. Several years ago, the IRS ruled that when a parent corporation with a wholly owned subsidiary (that it has owned since its organization) elects REIT status, the subsidiary will be deemed to have been liquidated and reincorporated at the time of the REIT election.[104] More recently, it has approved a subsidiary as a QRS where the subsidiary was acquired by the REIT's predecessor C corporation.[105] The IRS has also ruled on the merger of a C corporation into a qualified subsidiary in exchange for REIT stock. The transaction is treated as a merger directly into the REIT.[106]

The federal tax treatment of QRSs may or may not be respected for state and local tax purposes. In some cases, a state may view a QRS as a consolidated subsidiary or as a separate taxable corporation.

5. Thirty-Day Curative Period

A REIT is not automatically disqualified for failing to satisfy an asset requirement, provided the failure is due solely to changes in value and not attributable to new acquisitions. If the discrepancy is the result of an acquisition, the REIT has 30 days following the close of the quarter to rectify the problem, or else face disqualification.[107]

VI. REIT TAXABLE INCOME AND DISTRIBUTION REQUIREMENTS

REITs generally compute their taxable income like other corporations, but rely on a dividends-paid deduction to avoid paying a corporate-level tax. In addition, REITs are generally required to make dividend distributions annually that are at least equal to 95 percent of REIT taxable income, as calculated before taking the dividend deduction. Net capital gains, certain excess noncash income, and amounts representing taxes paid by the REIT are not required to be distributed. Amounts of income or capital gains that are retained by the REIT are subject to regular corporate taxes.

A. REIT Taxable Income

In order to determine the required dividend distribution, the REIT must first calculate REIT taxable income. This is determined in the same manner as regular corporate taxable income, but with a number of special modifications.[108]

The various special deductions for dividends received from other corporations (Sections 248, *et seq.*) are not allowed, since the REIT itself is a pass-through entity. Net income from foreclosure property (that is, foreclosure taxable income, less related taxes) is computed and taxed separately from the computation of REIT taxable income, although it is subject to the income distribution requirement. Certain disqualifying income and income from prohibited transactions that are subject to 100 percent punitive taxes are excluded from REIT taxable income and, for obvious reasons, not included in the distribution requirements. In addition, REIT taxable income is computed without special adjustments as a result of a change in accounting period. Finally, the dividends-paid deduction is allowed (but as noted above, is excluded when calculating the distribution requirement).

To the extent a REIT has taxable income after taking the dividends-paid deduction, the income is subject to regular corporate tax under Section 11 of the Code.

1. Capital Gains

If a REIT chooses to retain some or all of its net capital gains, the tax thereon is computed based on the lesser of the REIT's regular tax or the alternative corporate capital gains rate (currently the same, 35 percent). The amount of retained capital gains is the difference between the net capital gains realized by a REIT and the amount of capital gain dividends.

A REIT may designate any dividend, or portion thereof, as a capital gain dividend, provided it mails a notice to its shareholders within 30 days of the close of its taxable year, or includes such notice in its annual report. In the hands of a shareholder, the amount of capital gain dividends must be in proportion to the REIT's net capital gain for the taxable year. Thus, if a REIT realizes a capital loss after declaring and distributing a capital gain dividend, a shareholder may treat only a proportionate part of the designated dividend as a capital gain. In the hands of a shareholder, a capital gain dividend is treated as a long-term capital gain.[109]

To the extent a REIT pays capital gain dividends to its shareholders, the REIT's net capital gain is excluded from REIT taxable income for purposes of determining a net operating loss or net operating loss carryover. Thus, NOLs are offset only with ordinary income rather than capital gains. This permits a higher proportion of a REIT's total taxable dividends to be treated as capital gain dividends that are entitled to the preferential capital gains rate.[110]

REITs are subject to the rules in Section 291, which recapture as ordinary income up to 20 percent of the capital gains realized on the sale or disposition of real property. This recharacterization significantly alters a REIT's required distribution and is discussed in detail under Part VI.B.2, "Corporate Gain Recapture," below.

2. Foreclosure Property Income

In the early 1970s, mortgage REITs found themselves holding unusually high numbers of foreclosed properties in their portfolio, which created several problems that the REIT rules were not designed to handle. Unlike most mortgage businesses, these companies could not sell the newly acquired properties without risking a disqualifying prohibited transaction.[111] In addition, foreclosure may have meant assuming management of the former owner's business until a new property manager or tenant for the property could be found, which could also result in potentially disqualifying income.

To cope with these problems, the foreclosure rules were added to the Code in 1974. If a REIT forecloses on property or reacquires property following a lease default, it may make a foreclosure election. This election permits the REIT to hold the property for sale to customers and treat the gains as qualifying income under the 75 and 95 percent income tests, while excluding them from the 30 percent gross income limitations. Trade or business income from foreclosure properties receive similar treatment for REIT qualification purposes.

Regular rental income or gains from foreclosure properties are treated like other REIT qualifying income and may be offset with a dividends-paid deduction. However, to the extent foreclosure income consists of prohibited transaction gains, it is subject to the highest regular corporate tax rate rather than the 100 percent punitive tax. In addition, nonqualifying rents received under preexisting leases, or trade or business income derived from foreclosure properties, are subject to the highest corporate tax rate.[112] The excess of net foreclosure income over the taxes imposed thereon is included in the calculation of the dividend distribution requirement.

Foreclosure elections are irrevocable and must be made with respect to specific properties in the tax return in the year in which the REIT acquires the property. The election is valid until two years following the date of the property acquisition and may be extended twice, in two-year increments, with the permission of the IRS. A foreclosure election is terminated automatically if the REIT enters into a lease after foreclosure, which by its terms produces nonqualifying income, or if the REIT in fact derives nonqualified income under such lease.

The foreclosure election also may be terminated if the REIT uses the property in a trade or business beginning 90 days after foreclosure, unless the trade or business is conducted by an independent contractor. The trade or business exception applies to the business of property leasing, as well as operating a health care facility or managing a hotel. Thus, if a REIT forecloses on rental property, it must use independent contractors to manage the property, notwithstanding that it is permitted to manage directly any nonforeclosure rental properties. However, unless the REIT intends to sell the property in a prohibited transaction, loss of foreclosure status in this case should not result in any disqualified income.

Finally, foreclosure property status is lost if any construction takes place on the property, other than the completion of a building or other improvement that was at least 10 percent completed before foreclosure became imminent. This rule prevents a REIT from developing land for resale purposes. Unfortunately, it also hampers a REIT's ability to spruce up property for the purpose of reselling it.[113]

3. Prohibited Transactions Tax

A tax equal to 100 percent is imposed on the net income derived from prohibited transactions. A prohibited transaction is a transaction described in Section 1221(1), which includes sales of inventory and property held by the REIT primarily for sale to customers in the ordinary course of its trade or business. Net income from prohibited transactions may be reduced for directly connected expenses, but not by losses from other prohibited transactions.[114] Gross income from prohibited transactions does not affect a REIT's qualification under the 75 percent and 95 percent qualifying income tests, but is taken into account as bad income under the 30 percent gross income restrictions.

The Code provides a safe harbor that a REIT may use to avoid prohibited transaction treatment. The statute specifically provides that the safe harbor terms are not to be considered in determining whether a sale, which fails to satisfy the safe harbor requirements, is a prohibited transaction. Nevertheless, many REITs scrupulously follow its terms rather than risk an adverse factual determination.

In order for a sale of property to qualify for the safe harbor, the REIT generally must have held the property four years, have made capital expenditures on the property during such period equal to 30 percent or less of the selling price, and either (1) not have sold more than seven properties (other than foreclosure properties) during the taxable year or (2) not have sold properties with aggregate tax bases in excess of 10 percent of the REIT's tax bases in all its assets (determined at the beginning of the year). If the REIT relies on the tax bases safe harbor, it must use an independent contractor for substantially all marketing and development expenditures.

Special rules apply with respect to the determination of expenditures made by the REIT and property acquired through foreclosure. Importantly, a sale of multiple properties to a single buyer as part of one transaction is considered a single sale for purposes of the safe harbor.[115]

4. Qualifying Income Shortfalls

If a REIT fails either the 95 percent or 75 percent qualifying gross income tests, it may avoid disqualification under Section 856(c)(7) if the shortfall was due to reasonable cause and not willful neglect. However, if a REIT relies on this provision to maintain its qualified status, it may be subject to a punitive tax. The tax is 100 percent of the net income attributable to the gross income shortfall. If both qualifying income tests are failed, the tax is based on whichever shortfall is greater.[116]

5. Net Operating Losses

REITs are subject to several special rules regarding net operating losses. For example, a REIT's dividends-paid deduction cannot be used to create a NOL.[117] As a result, if its dividends exceed its taxable income, a REIT generally will lose the benefit of the dividends-paid deduction to the extent of the excess. In order to realize a NOL, a REIT's losses or business expenses (other than dividend distributions) must exceed its income (determined without the dividends-paid deduction).

On the other hand, if a REIT has a NOL from a prior year that is carried forward to the current year, the NOL carryover deduction is made after taking the current dividends-paid deduction. This treatment permits the NOL carryover to be preserved for future years when the REIT's income is not otherwise distributed to shareholders as dividends.[118]

Although a REIT is permitted a NOL carryover deduction, it cannot claim any NOL carrybacks, whether or not it was a qualified REIT in the prior years. A related rule prohibits the carryback of any loss from a nonREIT year to a prior REIT year (generally, years in which the entity qualified as a REIT).[119] Finally, certain forms of nonqualifying income that are subject to punitive tax rates (for example, prohibited transaction income under Section 857(b)(6) and qualifying income shortfalls under Section 857(b)(5)) cannot be offset by either NOL carryovers or carrybacks.[120]

6. Alternative Minimum Tax

Prior to 1986, corporations were subject to an add-on minimum tax of 15 percent on certain tax preference items. For REITs, the primary items of tax preference were capital gains and the excess of accelerated depreciation over straight-line depreciation (using a 19-year life). Capital gains were a tax preference item only to the extent they were not distributed to shareholders (in which case they were a shareholder preference item). In the case of REITs with depreciation tax preference items, old Section 58(f)(2) imposed the add-on tax on the REIT rather than passing it through to REIT shareholders. However, most REITs elected 19-year straight-line depreciation, thereby avoiding the minimum tax.

Permissible depreciation methods were changed in 1986 to straight-line depreciation and recovery lives were extended to 31.5 years (later changed to 39 years) for nonresidential and 27.5 years for residential. In lieu of the foregoing, a property owner may elect to recover any real property over a 40-year period under the Alternative Cost Recovery System (ACRS). Today, any difference between actual depreciation taken and ACRS is subject to the alternative minimum tax. However, capital gains that are retained by the REIT are no longer subject to the minimum tax.

The 1986 Act also required that differently treated items (tax preference items) be apportioned between the REIT and its shareholders in accordance with regulations to be prescribed by the IRS.[121] Although the IRS has never issued the apportionment regulations, most REITs currently apportion their tax preference items to their shareholders in proportion to their dividend distributions. Such apportionment should be limited to the tax preference associated with accelerated depreciation. A tax preference associated with a net operating loss should not be apportioned to shareholders, because it is not possible to distribute the benefit of a NOL to shareholders. As discussed above, a NOL deduction is useful to a REIT only for purposes of reducing the amount of its required distribution. To the extent a REIT makes actual distributions, its income will be offset with a dividends-paid deduction. Once the distributions equal the REIT's taxable income, the NOL deduction cannot be utilized and is deferred until the following year. Thus, a REIT benefits from the NOL only to the extent it is applied against income that the REIT does not distribute to shareholders.

For purposes of computing the alternative minimum tax, the Code starts with taxable income and makes adjustments for items of tax preferences in arriving at alternative minimum taxable income. In the case of a REIT, taxable income means REIT taxable income after the dividends-paid deduction.[122] If a REIT's alternative minimum taxable income is greater than its taxable income (and creates a minimum tax exposure), the REIT can simply increase its distributions and take a larger dividends-paid deduction for the difference, provided it has sufficient E&P. The excess dividends-paid deduction will reduce the REIT's E&P but will not generate a net operating loss carryover. Accordingly, if this route is chosen the REIT should be sensitive to whether it will have sufficient E&P to meet future dividend distribution requirements.

B. Dividend Distribution Requirements

The REIT dividend distribution requirement states that a REIT's annual dividends-paid deduction equal at least 95 percent of its REIT taxable income, computed before taking the dividends-paid deduction (and excluding net capital gains and certain forms of excess noncash income), plus at least 95 percent of its net income from foreclosure properties (reduced for taxes paid thereon).[123] Income that is not required to be distributed and which is retained by the REIT is subject to tax at regular corporate rates.

Although the amount of the distribution requirement is computed by reference to REIT taxable income, qualifying distributions must be dividends, which are based on available earnings and profits. Situations can and do arise in which a REIT's available earnings and profits are less than its taxable income and are inadequate to support the required amount of deductible dividends.[124]

1. C Corporation Earnings

A REIT is required to distribute before the close of any taxable year any earnings and profits it may have accumulated in a nonREIT year (that is, any taxable year in which it was not a qualified REIT).[125] In recently issued regulations, the IRS has taken the position that this requirement applies to E&P inherited by a REIT in a merger with a C corporation, as well as E&P earned by the REIT before it made a REIT election. The regulation also provides that the deficiency dividend procedures for regulated investment companies under Section 852(e) will be available to REITs for purposes of satisfying the E&P distribution requirement.[126]

2. Corporate Gain Recapture

The special corporate recapture rules under Section 291 can have a significant effect on a REIT's required distributions. Under Section 291, 20 percent of capital gain (to the extent attributable to prior depreciation deductions) on the sale of real property is recharacterized as ordinary income. This is in addition to depreciation that is recaptured as ordinary income under Section 1250. Gains in excess of all prior depreciation deductions are not subject to Section 291.

To the extent the Section 291 recapture amount is retained by the REIT, and thus recharacterized as ordinary income, it will increase the REIT's required dividend distribution. On the other hand, the Section 291 amount will not be subject to recharacterization in the hands of a REIT to the extent it is distributed as a capital gain dividend. If the Section 291 recapture amounts are distributed to corporate shareholders, they retain their character for purposes of Section 291.

By way of example, assume a REIT realizes $80 gain on the disposition of real property on which it had taken $60 of depreciation, $20 of which is subject to recapture as ordinary income under Section 1250. If the REIT makes no capital gain dividends, then it must treat $28 (20 percent of $40 (the Section 291 amount), plus $20 of Section 1250 recapture) as ordinary income that is subject to the ordinary dividend-distribution requirement. On the other hand, if the REIT declares a capital gain dividend of $30 (half of total capital gain, before the application of Section 291), it must treat $24 of the remaining amount as ordinary income (20 percent times half of $40, plus $20) and $26 as capital gain. In this case, corporate shareholders would treat the $30 capital gain dividend as including $20 that is subject to Section 291. Of this amount, $4, or 20 percent, is treated as ordinary income and the remaining $26 distribution is capital gain.

3. Spillover Dividends

Dividends that are declared for shareholders of record near the end of the year (that is, in October, November, or December) and that are actually distributed to shareholders before the end of January of the following year are treated as having been paid by the REIT and received by the shareholders on the last day of December. This provision is intended to mitigate the timing mismatch that occurs with respect to dividends paid at the end of the year, but not received by shareholders until the following year.[127]

Unlike the rules for late dividend elections, discussed below, neither the statute nor the regulations address the treatment of earnings and profits with respect to spillover dividends. For administrative simplicity, the characterization of a spillover distribution should be determined by the available current E&P as of December 31 of the prior year and any distribution in excess of such E&P should be treated as a return of capital for the prior year. However, the statute provides that spillover treatment is available for dividends only, without any reference to return of capital distributions. Accordingly, a literal reading of the statute mandates that any distribution in excess of the prior year's E&P is not entitled to spillover treatment and is considered to be a distribution in the following year.

4. Late Dividend Elections

It is often difficult for a real estate company to estimate accurately its required dividend distribution in time to declare and pay a dividend before the end of the year. Under these circumstances, the Code permits the REIT to declare and pay a dividend after the end of the year and claim a dividends-paid deduction as if the distribution occurred in the prior year. In order to make a late dividend election, the REIT must declare the dividend before the due date for its return (including extensions) and make the dividend distribution on or before its next regular dividend date (and within the 12-month period following the close of the taxable year to which the election relates).

The election only applies at the REIT level and, unlike the spillover dividend, it does not affect when a shareholder is considered to have received the dividend. Consequently, a timing mismatch occurs from the government's standpoint, since the REIT claims a deduction in one year for an item of income that is not reported by shareholders until the following year. The excise tax, discussed below, addresses this problem.

The late-dividend election is available only to the extent of the current earnings and profits for the taxable year to which it relates. Current E&P is determined after the application of the special E&P rules in Section 857(d) (relating to E&P adjustments in the case of nondeductible items and minimum E&P to avoid excise tax exposure), but before reductions for deficiency dividends and prior year late dividend elections.

The current earnings and profits limitation means that a distribution made pursuant to a late-dividend election will not include any return of capital. For example, if a REIT's current E&P in year one is $100 and it declares and pays a distribution of $150 in February of year two, the REIT can make a late-dividend election only with respect to $100 of the $150 distribution. The remaining $50 is considered to be a distribution in the second year and its character as a dividend depends on available E&P in such year.

5. Deficiency Dividends

If an adverse determination results in an increase of a REIT's taxable income or a decrease in its dividends-paid deduction for a prior taxable year, it may be able to make a deficiency dividend to eliminate any tax increase resulting from the determination. The deficiency dividend qualifies for the dividends-paid deduction for the prior year, notwithstanding that it is made long after the close of such year.[128]

In order to claim a deficiency dividend, a REIT must have a determination, which is any final decision by a court, a closing agreement with the IRS, or a written agreement with the IRS that fixes the amount of the deficiency dividend. The determination must result in an increase in the REIT's taxable income, foreclosure income, or net capital gains (to the extent not offset with a capital gains dividend deduction), or a decrease in its dividends-paid deduction (determined without regard to any capital gain dividends).[129]

A deficiency dividend generally can be made up to the full amount of the adjustment, whether or not it is required to maintain REIT qualification, provided it would have qualified as a dividend if actually made in the taxable year for which it is claimed. If the determination results in an increase in the dividends-paid deduction as well as an increase in taxable income, then a deficiency dividend is allowed only to the extent the increase in taxable income exceeds the adjustment made to the original dividends-paid deduction. A similar principle applies with respect to capital gain adjustments.[130]

Although the deficiency dividend mitigates any tax liability resulting from an adverse determination, interest and any additions to tax must still be paid. Furthermore, these amounts are calculated based on the amount of the deficiency dividend deduction rather than the amount of the mitigated tax liability. However, interest should be deductible in the year in which it is paid or accrued.[131]

A deficiency dividend must be made within 90 days of the determination, and a claim for a deficiency dividend must be filed with the IRS within 120 days of such determination. The deficiency dividend deduction is not available in the case of fraud or willful failure to file a return.[132]

6. Liquidating Distributions

Under Section 562(b)(1)(A), a distribution in complete liquidation is treated as a dividend for purposes of the dividends-paid deduction to the extent of accumulated earnings and profits. Furthermore, if a REIT adopts a plan of liquidation and completely liquidates within two years, then any distributions made pursuant to the plan during that period may qualify for the dividends-paid deduction. For this purpose, E&P is not reduced for capital losses during the period of the plan of liquidation.[133] Care should be taken to ensure that all liquidating distributions are timely and proportional with respect to all shareholders to avoid a preferential dividend problem, discussed below.

The treatment of liquidating distributions as dividends applies only for purposes of the dividends-paid deduction. It does not affect the character of the distributions in the hands of the shareholders. In the hands of a shareholder, such distributions are treated as full payment in exchange for the stock.[134] Further, a liquidating dividends-paid deduction cannot offset gains that are subject to the built-in gains tax.[135]

7. Preferential Dividends

A REIT is not permitted a deduction for preferential dividends. This restriction does not refer to dividends on preferred stock, but rather to dividends that are not proportional with respect to all shareholders of a particular class of stock, or that prefer one class of shares over another (except to the extent required by the terms of the respective classes).[136] The IRS permits reasonable discounts (5 percent) on acquisitions of shares under dividend reinvestment plans, since the preference represents savings in administrative and underwriting costs of the REIT.[137]

A preferential dividend may occur if a REIT delays the payment of a dividend for some shareholders but not others, even if the distributions are proportional in amount.[138] In such case, none of the dividends are deductible. Similarly, a REIT could lose its dividend deduction in a current or liquidating distribution if some shareholders receive property and others receive cash or other property. Although using a liquidating trust may avoid this problem in the context of a liquidation, it is of no help with respect to current distributions.

A preference may also exist between classes of stock. For example, if an entire preferred class of shares forgoes its right to an unpaid and accumulated dividend, a preference may occur when the REIT pays its next dividend on the common shares. In this case, any distributions on the common or preferred are disqualified for purposes of the dividends-paid deduction.[139]

8. Excise Tax

The REIT excise tax in Section 4981 is intended to recapture revenue that may be lost when a REIT receives a deduction for dividends in a taxable year prior to the taxable year when it is recognized by shareholders. This can occur in the case of a calendar-year REIT that makes a late dividend election under Section 858, or a fiscal-year REIT that pays dividends near the end of its taxable year but before the end of the calendar year. The excise tax does not apply in the case of spillover dividends, since no timing mismatch occurs, nor in the case of deficiency dividends.[140]

Since 1976, Section 859 has required all new REITs to report income on a calendar-year basis. Because relatively few REITs today remain on a fiscal-year basis, the excise tax will apply in most cases only to REITs that make late dividend elections.

Generally, the excise tax is 4 percent of the amount by which a REIT's dividend distributions during the calendar year are less than 85 percent of its ordinary income and 95 percent of its capital gains. To the extent a REIT chooses to retain income and pay regular corporate tax (up to 5 percent of ordinary income and all capital gains), such income is deemed timely distributed for purposes of the excise tax. Thus, the tax only applies to the extent the REIT eventually claims a deduction under Section 858 for amounts in excess of 15 percent of its ordinary income or 5 percent of its net capital gains, or in the relatively rare cases of fiscal-year REITs.[141] The tax is not deductible from REIT taxable income.

Amounts that are subject to the excise tax in one year are considered shortfalls and are part of the required distribution in the following year. These amounts plus the requisite percentage of the REIT's current ordinary income and capital gains in the second year must be timely distributed to avoid another excise tax.[142] In most cases, if the REIT has made distributions sufficient to maintain REIT qualification, it will have already distributed a prior year's shortfall and will avoid a second excise tax on the same amounts. If a REIT overdistributes in one year, that is, it distributes amounts in excess of its taxable income and prior year shortfalls, the excess may be credited toward the required distribution in the following year provided the original distribution was made from earnings and profits.[143]

Although retained income that is subject to a regular corporate tax is generally deemed timely distributed for purposes of the excise tax, foreclosure property income is excluded from both the calculation of required distributions and distributed amounts.[144] This treatment effectively exempts foreclosure income from the excise tax, but it also increases the percentage of the REIT's other income that must be distributed. Since the REIT is not permitted to credit its distributed amounts with the already taxed foreclosure income, it must make up the difference with actual distributions.

Similarly, income from prohibited transactions and qualified income shortfalls that are subject to a 100 percent punitive tax are excluded from the calculation of both the required distribution and distributed amounts for purposes of the excise tax.[145]

The excise tax presents unique problems for those few REITs that still use a fiscal year for tax reporting purposes. For purposes of the excise tax, their income is determined on a calendar-year basis. If a fiscal-year REIT realizes a loss after the end of the calendar year, but before the end of its own taxable year, it may not have sufficient earnings and profits to make dividend distributions to meet the required distribution under the excise tax. In this case, Section 857(d)(2) provides that a REIT will be deemed to have sufficient E&P to meet the required distribution for purposes of Section 4981.

VII. TAXATION OF REIT SHAREHOLDERS

Generally, REIT shareholders are taxed the same as other corporations' shareholders for federal income tax purposes. Typically, they are not liable for tax on REIT income, except to the extent it is distributed to them in the form of dividends. However, because of the REIT's special tax status, a number of unique issues arise with respect to REIT shareholders that do not apply to regular C corporation shareholders.

As mentioned previously, REITs may pay capital gain dividends to shareholders and such dividends are treated as long-term capital gains for reporting purposes.[146] As in the case of mutual funds, if a shareholder has held the shares less than six months and receives a capital gain dividend, then any subsequent loss on the sale of the shares is treated as long-term capital loss to the extent of the dividend. This rule prevents taxpayers from converting short-term gains or ordinary income into long-term gains.[147]

Like regular corporate dividends, REIT dividends are treated as portfolio income for purposes of the passive activity loss rules and cannot be offset with passive losses. They also are treated as dividends for tax-exempt shareholders and, thus, generally are not subject to the unrelated business income tax (UBIT).[148] REIT dividends may be subject to UBIT if the REIT is predominantly held by a few tax-exempt entities.[149]

In the hands of corporate shareholders, REIT dividends are not entitled to a dividends-received deduction under Section 243.[150] In addition, some or all of a capital gain dividend may be subject to recapture as ordinary income under Section 291.[151] Although a corporate shareholder may own more than 80 percent of the shares of the REIT without violating the REIT share ownership tests, a REIT cannot be a member of an affiliated group or file a consolidated return.[152]

If a REIT holds a residual interest in a REMIC, the extent to which excess inclusion income that is realized by the REIT exceeds the REIT's taxable income (excluding net capital gains) will be allocated among shareholders in proportion to the dividends they receive.[153] This is perhaps the only situation in which REIT shareholders may be allocated phantom income as a result of holding shares in a REIT.

In the case of foreign shareholders, REITs are generally required to withhold 30 percent on the distribution of ordinary dividends under Section 1441 of the Code, except to the extent the amount is reduced under a treaty. Under the Foreign Investment in Real Property Tax Act (FIRPTA), withholding may also be required on capital gain dividends (35 percent) and by the purchaser of REIT shares from a nonresident alien (10 percent). FIRPTA liability may be avoided if the REIT is domestically controlled or publicly traded, but generally is not reduced under tax treaties.[154] In 1996, the Small Business Job Protection Act extended the 10 percent withholding under Section 1445(e) to apply to distributions in excess of earnings and profits. It is anticipated that withholding exemption certificates will be available to avoid the 10 percent withholding in appropriate cases.

VIII. FAILURE TO QUALIFY AS A REIT

A REIT may lose its qualified status for failing to meet the income or asset tests, share ownership tests or other organizational requirements, the dividend distribution requirement, the recordkeeping requirements, or the non-REIT earnings and profits distribution requirement. A REIT may also affirmatively revoke its election following its first taxable year as a REIT.[155]

Generally, if an election has been revoked or terminated, an entity may not re-elect REIT status until the fifth year following the first year for which the termination or revocation is effective.[156] In the case of a termination (but not revocation), in certain circumstances the IRS may permit an entity to re-elect REIT status before the end of the five-year period.

If a REIT's status is terminated because it failed to meet either the 75 percent or 95 percent income tests, the IRS may waive the violation if the nature and amount of all items of qualifying gross income are set forth in a schedule in the return, the inclusion of any incorrect items is not due to fraud, and the failure was due to reasonable cause and not willful neglect.[157] This exception may be available for the year the violation occurs. However, it is not available for failing to meet the 30 percent gross income restriction or other REIT qualifying tests. As discussed previously, any net income attributable to the gross income tests shortfall is taxed at a 100 percent rate.

If a REIT's status is terminated for reasons other than a qualifying income shortfall, the IRS may still waive the five-year waiting period for re-electing provided the entity did not willfully fail to file a timely return for the year the violation occurred, it did not include any fraudulent information in such return, and the failure was due to reasonable cause and not willful neglect.[158] The statute does not expressly empower the IRS to waive the violation as in the case of a qualified income shortfall, but only the five-year waiting period. Read literally, this provision would not permit the IRS to allow a REIT to maintain its qualification during the year of the violation, regardless of the circumstances.

From a policy standpoint, a REIT that is inadvertently disqualified should have the opportunity to seek a waiver from the IRS for the year of the violation. This would encourage better voluntary compliance and would help such REITs resist the temptation to ignore qualification problems until they are detected on audit.

If a REIT is disqualified, it will be liable for corporate income taxes and any applicable interest or penalties for the disqualified years that are not closed by the statute of limitations. To the extent a REIT pays such amounts, its earnings and profits will be reduced and may require amended Forms 1099. In addition, shareholders may be entitled to claim refunds for years in which dividends were over-reported. A net operating loss incurred while the entity is not a REIT cannot be carried back to any REIT years, but may be carried forward to years after the entity re-elects REIT status.[159]

ENDNOTES

1. The author appreciates the invaluable review and editorial comments of Mr. Tony Edwards, General Counsel for the National Association of Real Estate Investments Trusts, Inc., and Mr. Neil Rosenburg, partner, Coopers & Lybrand L.L.P., New York.
2. Revenue Act of 1909.
3. 220 U.S. 178 (1910).
4. See, e.g., *Crocker v. Malley*, 249 U.S. 223 (1918).
5. 296 U.S. 344 (1935).
6. See *Commissioner v. North American Bond Trust*, 122 F.2d 545 (2d Cir. 1941); cert. denied 314 U.S. 701 (1942).
7. Pub. L. No. 86-779, e 10(a), 74 Stat. 1004. See Lynn & Bloomfield, *Real Estate Investment Trusts*, e 1.02 (Warren, Gorham & Lamont 1994), for a thorough discussion of the judicial and lobbying history of the REIT.
8. 102 Cong. Rec. 15,304–305 (1956).
9. See Kelley, *Real Estate Investment Trusts Handbook*, e 1.02 (ALI-ABA 1990), for a synopsis of the legislative changes.
10. Pub. L. No. 99-514, Section 663(a) (1986).
11. While the old independent-contractor rule was based on the historic distinction between passive and active entities, it also forced an economic misalignment between the interests of investors and the REIT's sponsor, who often retained profitable advisory and management contracts. These

problems have been largely eliminated with the change in the law and virtually all new public REITs today are internally managed.

12. Section 351(a) of the Internal Revenue Code ("Code").

13. Section 351-1(c) of the Income Tax Regulations ("Regulations").

14. Section 1.351-1(c)(5) of the Regulations.

15. Section 337(d) of the Code.

16. Notice 88-19, 1988-1 C.B. 486. See also Notice 90-27, 1990-1 C.B. 336, for the treatment of built-in losses, and Notice 88-96, 1988-35 I.R.B. 25, regarding built-in gains realized during a short period when a regulated investment company is disqualified.

17. Although Notice 88-19 is almost nine years old, the Service has not yet issued proposed or final regulations regarding the built-in gains tax. Consequently, there is no built-in gains tax for REITs at the time of this writing. Because of the obvious threat that final regulations will be made fully retroactive, most REITs with built-in gain assets elect to hold those assets for 10 years. In 1996 and 1997, the Administration recommended repealing the 10-year election to avoid the built-in gains tax.

18. See VII. REIT Taxable Income, Part B.1. C Corporation Earnings, *infra.*

19. Section 1.701-2(d), *Example (4)* of the regulations. The example offers an UPREIT structure in which the partners may convert their units into shares based on relative fair market values at the time of conversion, rather than on a one-for-one basis. In addition, in the example the REIT is free to acquire investment assets separate and apart from its interest in the operating partnership.

20. Section 856(a) of the Code.

21. Section 1.856-2(b) of the Regulations.

22. Section 856(b) of the Code.

23. Section 542(a)(2) of the Code.

24. Section 856(h)(2) of the Code.

25. 1972-1 C.B. 207.

26. See Rev. Rul. 77-23, 1977-1 C.B. 197; Rev. Rul. 76-534, 1976-2 C.B. 215; **V. Operational Requirements**, Part A.1.(b) Definition of Independent Contractor, *infra.*

27. Section 856(h)(2) of the Code.

28. Section 544(a)(1) of the Code.

29. Section 544(a)(3) of the Code. Holders of units in umbrella partnership REITs often are given the right to convert units into either cash or REIT shares at the REIT's or operating partnership's discretion. Because the

REIT is not obliged to issue shares upon exercise, such conversion rights should not be treated as call options to acquire REIT shares, but rather as put options for the underlying partnership units.

30. Rev. Rul. 66-106, 1966-1 C.B. 151.

31. Typical commingled fund vehicles include common trust funds, tax-exempt group trusts, and insurance company segregated accounts.

32. Section 856(h)(3)(C) of the Code.

33. Section 514 of the Code.

34. Section 1.857-8 of the Regulations.

35. Real Estate Investment Trust Tax Simplification Act, or REITSA, H.R. 2121 (July 28, 1995).

36. Five transferees owning 9.8 percent each of outstanding shares would collectively own 49 percent of the REIT. In some cases, insiders may own more than 9.8 percent, which mandates a smaller percentage transfer restriction with respect to the remaining outstanding shares.

37. Section 1.856-1(d) of the Regulations.

38. PLR 8921067 and PLR 9205030.

39. PLR 9430022.

40. Rev. Rul. 71-218, 1971-1 C.B. 209 (holding that the tax-free reorganization of an ordinary corporation into a business trust under Section 368(a)(1)(F) does not end the tax year of the entity and, thus, the entity did not qualify as a REIT during the period it was an ordinary corporation); Rev. Rul. 67-376, 1967-2 C.B. 142 (holding that a business trust REIT qualifies as a corporation for purposes of a Section 368(a)(1)(F) reorganization).

41. See, e.g., PLR 8729076.

42. Rev. Rul. 89-130, 1989-2 C.B. 117. Some states, such as Delaware, permit a foreign corporation to register as a domestic corporation under their state corporation laws. These dual-citizenship entities should be entitled to elect REIT status.

43. Section 856(c)(4) of the Code.

44. Section 1.856-4(a) of the Regulations.

45. Prior to 1976, a REIT could offer customary tenant services through its independent contractor, but could not separately charge the tenant for such services without disqualifying the tenant's rents. 26 C.F.R. 1.856-4(b)(3) (April 1, 1977).

46. The rule for customary services was added to the REIT provisions by the Tax Reform Act of 1976.

47. Section 1.856-4(b)(5)(i) of the Regulations.

48. Section 1.856-4(b)(1) of the Regulations.
49. Section 856(d)(3) of the Code.
50. Section 1.856-4(b)(5) of the Regulations; Rev. Rul. 77-23, 1977-1 C.B. 197; Rev. Rul. 76-534, 1977-2 C.B. 215.
51. Rev. Rul. 74-471, 1974-2 C.B. 198; *modified by* Rev. Rul. 74-626, 1974-2 C.B. 200; Rev. Rul. 75-136, 1975-1 C.B. 195.
52. Section 1.856-4(b)(5) of the regulations; Rev. Rul. 74-520, 1974-2 C.B. 201.
53. Rev. Rul. 66-188, 1966-2 C.B. 276.
54. Section 663(a) of the Tax Reform Act of 1986.
55. Section 1.512(b)-1(c)(5) of the Regulations.
56. This position was acknowledged by IRS representatives at 1993 and 1994 Law and Accounting Conferences, sponsored by the National Association of Real Estate Investment Trusts, Inc.
57. PLR 9436025 and PLR 9340056 (independent contractors serve as aerobics and fitness instructors); PLR 9216007 ("substantial" remodeling services performed by independent contractor); PLR 9233008 (minor remodeling or maintenance performed by REIT employees, but only for purposes of re-letting the premises).
58. PLR 9440026; PLR 9340056; PLR 9248022; PLR 9012032; PLR 8914048.
59. PLR 9313010; PLR 9507007.
60. PLR 9152030; PLR 9635032. These rulings suggests that the parking facilities must at least be associated with or tangential to other REIT rental property and used partly by REIT tenants.
61. PLR 9510030; PLR 9436025.
62. PLR 961309; PLR 9428033; PLR 8830076.
63. Section 1.856-4(b)(5)(ii) of the Regulations.
64. Section 856(d)(2)(B) of the Code.
65. Section 856(d)(1)(C) of the Code.
66. Section 1.856-4(b)(2)(i) of the Regulations.
67. Section 1.856-4(b)(2)(ii) of the Regulations.
68. PLR 961309.
69. Section 856(d)(2(A) of the Code.
70. Section 856(d)(6)(A) of the Code.
71. *Cf., Harlen E. Moore Charitable Trust v. United States*, 93-2 U.S.TC d50,601 (7th Cir., September 29, 1993), *affirming* 812 F. Supp. 130 (DC-Ill); 93-1 U.S.TC d50,090, in which the court found that a percentage sharecropping lease was not based on the "income or profits" of the ten-

ant (interpreting statutory language in Section 512 that is identical to the analogous provisions in Section 856). In this case, the farm lease revenues were found to be qualified rents (i.e., tax-exempt income) to the tax-exempt landlord, even though the landlord shared in the costs of seed, fertilizer, herbicides, electricity, and soil tests, in addition to maintaining the farm buildings. The court noted that other significant expenses, such as labor, farm equipment, and fuel were borne by the farmer.

72. Section 856-5(a) of the Regulations.

73. Section 1.856-5(c) of the Regulations.

74. Section 856(f) of the Code.

75. PLR 8626023.

76. Section 856(c)(3)(G) of the Code; *cf.* Rev. Rul. 74-258, 1974-1 C.B. 168; Rev. Rul. 70-362, 1970-2 C.B. 147.

77. A REIT's higher return may have been based on declining interest rates when the pool was sold, a subordination feature, and/or its obligation to service the mortgages.

78. PLR 843709.

79. PLR 8618065 and seven related PLRs, suspending prior favorable rulings after the enactment of Section 1286 of the Code.

80. PLR 8601032.

81. 1991-2 C.B. 777; See also Rev. Rul. 91-46, 1991-2 C.B. 358.

82. See, e.g., Rev. Rul. 84-10, 1984-1 C.B. 155; Rev. Rul. 74-300, 1974-1 C.B. 169; Rev. Rul. 70-545, 1970-2 C.B. 8; PLR 8601032.

83. Section 856(c)(6)(E) of the Code.

84. 1977-1 C.B. 196.

85. 17 C.F.R. Section 270.2a-7 (1991).

86. Section 856(c)(6)(D) of the Code.

87. Although there are a series of IRS general counsel memoranda (GCM) that consider derivative positions in government securities as producing qualifying gains for regulated investment companies, these memoranda were largely superseded by amendments to Section 851(b)(2) and (b)(3).GCM 38994 (May 27, 1983) and GCM 37233 (August 25, 1977). In addition, two older REIT private-letter rulings found that futures hedges did not constitute prohibited transactions, but declined to rule on whether the gains from the futures were qualifying income. PLR 8118047; PLR 8021110.

88. See Brandon, "REIT Liability Hedges Under the IRS Hedging Regulations," 24 J. Real Est. Tax'n. 167 (Winter 1997).

89. Section 1.856-3(g) of the Regulations.

90. See, e.g., PLR 9508019; PLR 9507007; PLR 9552038; and PLR 9521010.

91. Section 1.856-2(c)(2) of the Regulations.

92. Section 856(c)(8) of the Code. See also, **VI. REIT Taxable Income and Distribution Requirements**, Part B.6. Liquidating Distributions, *infra*, regarding a dividends-paid deduction for gains recognized pursuant to a plan of liquidation.

93. Sections 856(c)(5)(A) and 856(c)(6) of the Code.

94. Section 1.856-3(d) of the Regulations.

95. Rev. Rul. 69-94, 1969-1 C.B. 189; Rev. Rul. 71-220, 1971-1 C.B. 210; Rev. Rul. 71-286, 1971-2 C.B. 263; Rev. Rul. 74-191, 1974-1 C.B. 1970; Rev. Rul. 75-424, 1975-2 C.B. 269; Rev. Rul. 76-197, 1976-1 C.B. 187; Rev. Rul. 77-349, 1977-2 C.B. 239.

96. See, **V. Operational Requirements,** Part A.2.(c) Loans Made to Partnerships, *supra*. The IRS no longer issues these rulings.

97. See Part A.2.(h) Repurchase Agreements, above.

98. Section 1.856-3(a) of the Regulations.

99. Section 1.856-2(d)(3) of the Regulations.

100. *Id.*

101. REITs can hold up to 25 percent of their assets in investments other than real estate or securities, such as gold or foreign currency, but as a practical matter they could not derive significant income or gains from these investments without risking violating the 95 percent income test.

102. GCM 36823 (August 24, 1976).

103. Section 856(i) of the Code.

104. See PLR 9205030.

105. PLR 960924.

106. PLR 9409035.

107. Section 856(c)(5) of the Code; Section 1.856-2(d)(3) of the Regulations.

108. Section 857(b)(2) of the Code.

109. Section 857(b)(3) of the Code.

110. Section 857(b)(3)(D) of the Code.

111. Originally, merely holding property for sale to customers could disqualify a REIT. This rule was replaced with the 100 percent prohibited transactions tax in 1976.

112. Directly connected deductions include real estate taxes, interest, depreciation, and management fees, but do not include general administrative and overhead expenses. Section 1.857-3(b) of the Regulations.

113. Section 856(e)(4) of the Code.

114. Section 857(b)(6) of the Code. However, such losses may be used against other REIT taxable income, thereby reducing the REIT's distribution requirement.

115. Section 857(b)(6)(D) of the Code.

116. Section 857(b)(5) of the Code. For the consequences of other causes of REIT disqualification, see **VIII. Failure to Qualify as a REIT**, *infra*.

117. Section 172(d)(6)(A) of the Code.

118. Section 172(b)(2) and Section 172(d)(6)(B) substitute REIT taxable income (after taking into account the dividends-paid deduction) for taxable income, for purposes of determining the amount of NOL carryovers. See also *Example (1)* of Section 1.172-5(a)(4) of the Regulations.

119. Section 172(b)(1)(B) of the Code.

120. Section 857(B)(5) and (6) of the Code.

121. Section 59(d) of the Code.

122. Section 55(b)(2) of the Code.

123. Section 857(a)(1) of the Code. The separate reference to foreclosure property income is required only because this amount is excluded from the definition of REIT taxable income. Excess noncash income includes amounts recognized under Section 467 (rent leveling) and, in the case of cash-basis REITs, Section 1274 imputed interest and income recognized on failed Section 1031 exchanges. Section 857(e) of the Code.

124. For example, this problem may arise in the case of an installment sale of property. For purposes of the E&P account, all of the gain from an installment sale is taken into account immediately, even though it is deferred for taxable income purposes. Section 312(n)(5). If the REIT makes distributions in excess of taxable income, the excess will be treated as dividends and deplete the E&P account. When the deferred gain is recognized on the installment sale, the REIT may have insufficient E&P to cover the required dividend distribution. A similar problem exists for REITs that use accelerated depreciation when computing REIT taxable income. Since E&P adjustments must be based on straight-line depreciation, the REIT's annual additions to E&P in the early years will usually be larger than its annual taxable income. These larger E&P balances are depleted if the REIT makes distributions in excess of taxable income. In the later years, when accelerated depreciation deductions are less than straight-line, the calculation is reversed. Unless the REIT has retained its excess accumulated E&P, it may find itself without enough current E&P to meet the dividend distribution requirement. In the case of a sale of property for which a REIT had taken accelerated depreciation, Section 562(e) increases the

REIT's E&P by the total amount of gain realized on the sale, rather than the gain that would be realized based on E&P straight-line depreciation. This rule avoids a potential E&P shortfall for purposes of the distribution requirement in the year of sale, but at the cost of including the same income in E&P twice (to the extent accelerated depreciation exceeded straight-line). It does not resolve the E&P problems associated with installment sales or with current distributions before a sale occurs.

125. Section 857(a)(3)(B) of the Code.

126. Section 1.857-11 of the Regulations. The deficiency dividend procedures of Section 860, discussed *infra*, apply only to redeterminations of taxable income or the dividends-paid deduction. They are not an effective remedy for failing to satisfy the E&P distribution requirement.

127. Section 857(b)(8) of the Code.

128. Section 860 of the Code.

129. Section 860(d) and (e) of the Code.

130. Section 860(f)(2) of the Code.

131. Section 860(c) of the Code.

132. Sections 860(f)(1), 860(g), and 860(i) of the Code.

133. Section 562(b)(1) of the Code.

134. Section 331 of the Code.

135. See Notice 88-19, *supra.*

136. Section 562(c) of the Code.

137. Rev. Rul. 83-117, 1983-2 C.B. 98.

138. Example (1) of Section 1.562-2(b) of the Regulations.

139. Example (3) of Section 1.562-2(b) of the Regulations.

140. Section 4981(e)(3) of the Code.

141. Section 4981 of the Code.

142. Section 4981(b)(3) of the Code.

143. Section 4981(c)(2) of the Code.

144. Sections 4981(b)(1) and 4981(c)(1)(A) of the Code. Foreclosure income is excluded from REIT taxable income under Section 857(b)(2)(D) and, therefore, excluded from the definitions of "ordinary income" under Section 4981(e)(1) and "required distribution" under Section 4981(b)(1).

145. Both amounts are excluded from the definition of REIT taxable income and from the 95 percent dividend distribution requirement pursuant to Section 857(b)(2)(E) and (F). Thus, neither amount enters into the calculation of the excise tax. Sections 4981(c)(1)(A) and 4981(e)(1).

146. Section 867(b)(3)(B) of the Code.

147. The conversion technique involved acquiring large blocks of shares after a capital gain dividend was announced, collecting the dividend and then selling the shares at a loss. If the transaction was completed in a short time frame, the loss should be primarily attributable to the distributed capital gain. The realized short-term loss could be used to offset unrelated short term capital gains and a limited amount of ordinary income. As a result, the trader effectively converted the offset short-term gains into long-term gains, as represented by the capital gain dividend.

148. Rev. Rul. 66-106, 1966-1 C.B. 151.

149. See, **V. REIT Qualification: Organizational Requirements,** Part B.3. Pension Fund Ownership of REIT Shares, *supra.*

150. Section 857(c) of the Code.

151. See Part VI.B.2. Corporate Gain Recapture, *supra.*

152. Section 1504(b)(6) of the Code.

153. Section 860E(d)(1)(B) of the Code.

154. Section 1445 and Section 897(h) of the Code.

155. Section 856(g)(2) of the Code.

156. Section 856(g)(3) of the Code.

157. Section 857(c)(7) of the Code.

158. Section 856(g)(4) of the Code. In the case of a REIT that fails to meet the dividend distribution requirements, disqualification may be avoided by making a deficiency dividend, without regard to the conditions required for a waiver from the Service.

159. Section 172(b)(1)(B) of the Code.

CHAPTER

5

OVERVIEW OF THE STATE TAX CONCEPTS AFFECTING REITs[1]

Thayne T. Needles, *Manager, REIT Advisory Services, Coopers & Lybrand L.L.P., and former Associate Counsel, National Association of Real Estate Investment Trusts*

Recent years have shown states to be increasingly aggressive in seeking receipts to meet the demands of their ever-burgeoning budgets. REITs face considerable state franchise and income tax scrutiny as heavily capitalized entities that rely on their ability to produce a growing income stream to attract investors. This chapter provides an overview of the important state tax principles affecting REITs.

For each state and the District of Columbia, the reader is offered insight into the variety of taxes imposed (income, gross receipts, net worth, or capital stock)[2] upon income a REIT generates in a state[3] or for the benefits afforded any REIT choosing to operate a business in that state. In addition, this chapter provides information regarding each jurisdiction's rule concerning such issues as (1) the apportionment or allocation of income, (2) the taxation of REIT shareholders, (3) the treatment of qualified REIT subsidiaries, (4) the taxation of REITs that hold interests in partnerships, and (5) the title issues and taxes associated with REITs' holding and transferring ownership in real estate.

Also, this material summarizes the underlying principles concerning a state's ability to subject nonresident persons to tax and explores certain state tax-planning opportunities that may serve to limit the impact of state taxes.

For most states, the Internal Revenue Code serves as the foundation for their income tax. Accordingly, state officials' interpretation of the extent to which the state tax system abides by the federal Code is a significant factor in determining each state's treatment of the REIT vehicle. The prevalence of these administrative interpretations means that information presented in this chapter should be viewed with some degree of caution, as these administrative positions do not provide the certainty of statutes, case law, or published rulings.

I. IMPACT OF THE INTERNAL REVENUE CODE ON STATE TAXES

Internal Revenue Code Sections 856 through 860 govern REIT taxation for purposes of the federal corporate income tax. These provisions allow the REIT to deduct dividends paid to shareholders and do not impose either a net worth or capital stock tax. As a result, it can be stated as a general proposition that the REIT does not face a federal tax liability.[4]

Unlike the federal government, which has the federal Code, the majority of states have no existing statutory authority directly addressing the tax treatment of REITs.[5] As a result, state taxation is often a product of each state's administrative policy regarding the adaptation of that state's general corporate tax statutes to the REIT vehicle. Nevertheless, it is important to note that almost all states (by statute or regulations) conform their tax rules with those of the federal government. This conformity generally extends to the federal REIT rules, and as a result, a majority of states recognize all items of income and deduction considered at the federal level, including the dividends-paid deduction. Accordingly, a state tax liability based on income usually is found to exist in connection with a federal tax liability.[6]

It also is important to review each state's tax rules for items of income or deduction, at the federal level, that may not be observed for purposes of the state tax. For example, certain states require the add-back of net operating losses. But, a number[7] of states have indicated that they use federal REIT taxable income as the starting point for their income tax computations. If no adjustment is made, those states should not tax income resulting from prohibited transactions or foreclosure property.

Of course, in general, the income tax considerations of the federal rules have no application to a state-imposed franchise tax. Such taxes are likely to be the major concern of most REITs.

II. POWER TO TAX

A state must evidence both jurisdiction and nexus prior to taxing a person's activities. This subsection addresses in general terms when a state may require that a REIT file a tax return with, and pay taxes to, that state on its operations as a whole or selected transaction.

A state's ability to tax a REIT that is neither incorporated in that state nor has its principle place of business located in that state is limited by the federal Constitution and self-imposed policies (that is, a state choosing not to enforce its state's authority to tax). Although self-imposed limits will most narrow the scope of a state's ability to tax, also of importance in the area of jurisdiction and nexus are the mandatory limits provided by the Constitution's due process[8] and commerce clauses.[9]

The due process clause imposes two requirements on a state that seeks to impose jurisdiction over a taxpayer from another state. First, a "minimal connection" must exist between the interstate activity and the state seeking to impose a tax.[10] Second, the income attributed to the state must represent a fair apportionment when compared to the taxpayer's intrastate activity.[11]

Under the commerce clause, a tax involving interstate commerce must satisfy the following four requirements: (1) The tax is applied only to activities with a substantial nexus with the state, (2) the tax is fairly apportioned, (3) the tax does not discriminate against the interstate commerce, and (4) the tax fairly relates to the services provided by the state.[12] (The rules concerning the fair apportionment of a business's income are addressed in the next section.)

It is a long established and indisputable principle that physical presence of a REIT's property or employees in a state establishes nexus for an income, franchise, or gross receipts tax for purposes of the constitutional limitations.[13] However, when a REIT's only contact with a state is limited to the ownership of certain intangible or contingent property rights such as a security interest in real property, the nexus determination becomes less settled.[14] A majority of states rule that either making loans secured by real property located in a state or entering into shared-appreciation mortgages or other participatory loans constitutes a sufficient level of activity to result in nexus.[15] No clean-cut rules can be cited for when such loan-making activity crosses the nexus threshold. Many of the states that find nexus in such activity should be expected to condition that determination on a finding of a regular and continuous loan-making activity. Other limitations imposed by states to a finding of nexus include a requirement that an employee/agent be present in the state or that some repair or maintenance activities related to the property have occurred with respect to the property securing the loan.

With regard to franchise taxes, a state of incorporation or organization may impose such a tax on a REIT even though it has no operations in that state. For example, Delaware imposes a franchise tax (based on the number of authorized shares) of up to $150,000 on a Delaware REIT, even if the REIT owns no Delaware properties.

Additionally, REITs commonly conduct business through a partnership format, for example, using an operating partnership in an umbrella partnership (UPREIT) structure. In short, a partnership's activities generally establish nexus for the partnership's partners for income tax purposes, with a few states providing exceptions for certain limited partners. For purposes of a franchise tax, the state rules providing for the attribution of partnership's nexus to the partners are divergent and less settled.

III. APPORTIONMENT AND ALLOCATION OF INCOME AND CAPITAL

A. Purpose

For REITs with operations in more than one state, an important factor in determining the tax liability in each of those states is the division of a REIT's tax base among those various states. For reasons of fairness and to avoid constitutional challenges to their tax schemes, states employ several methods to determine a reasonable portion of the interstate corporation's tax base that it subjects to tax.

B. Methods

There are three predominant methods used to assign income in the case of an interstate business: (1) formula apportionment; (2) specific allocation; and (3) separate accounting. No state currently requires a REIT to use separate accounting, which seeks to source all elements of revenue and expense (including overhead costs) of an interstate corporation's operations to each state. Thus, this overview focuses on the first two methods.

1. Formula Apportionment

Unlike separate accounting, formula apportionment does not require that income and expense items be assigned to each individual activity of a business. Instead, formula apportionment seeks to assign income based on an estimate of the level of the entity's overall income-producing activity occurring in each individual state in comparison with the activity in all states in which the entity operated during the taxing period. States consider such factors as the payroll expense, property used, or sales concluded in each jurisdiction.

2. Specific Allocation

Specific allocation calls for the allocation of the income items to their geographic source. In general, allocation applies to nonbusiness (nonoperating) income, such as interest, dividends, capital gains incidental to the main business, and rents. However, in the case of a REIT, rental income and capital gains resulting from the sale of real estate most likely is treated as apportionable income because those sources relate to the conduct of a trade or business.

Although some states have developed their own systems (by statute or regulation) for apportioning or allocating income of an interstate business, many states are affected by two statutory developments in this area, the Multistate Tax Compact (MTC) and the Uniform Division of Income for Tax Purposes Act (UDITPA). Every state that imposes a tax on income has adopted UDITPA or a modified version of UDITPA, or has developed a method for dividing income that uses one or more of the factors considered in UDITPA's formulary apportionment calculation.[16] Therefore, the principles of UDITPA and a brief introduction to the MTC are provided below.

C. UDITPA

The concepts of formula apportionment and specific allocation are both elements of UDITPA. UDITPA was adopted by the National Conference of Commissioners on Uniform State Laws and approved by the House of Delegates of the American Bar Association in 1957. It was created to serve as a model for state apportionment and allocation, thereby reducing the diversity of methods employed by the various states to divide income and decrease the chance for double taxation.[17]

Although developed to govern the assignment of net income between the various states, one or more of the UDITPA factors are often relied on for purposes of assigning the franchise tax base. However, as noted above, some states may modify the factors. For example, states may expand the property factor, which under UDITPA applies only to real or tangible property, to include all forms of property (that is, intangibles).

Under UDITPA, a corporation's income is divided into business and nonbusiness components. Business income, which represents income derived from a corporation's regular business activity, is apportioned through formula apportionment using a three-factor formula discussed below. Nonbusiness income is allocated specifically to a geographical location.

1. UDITPA Formula Apportionment

As noted above, under the traditional concept of formula apportionment, all apportionable income (business income) from a multistate operation is divided among the states according to a formula that seeks to provide a general estimate of the business activity taking place in each taxing jurisdiction.

Under UDITPA, formula apportionment is based on an interstate corporation's level of three income-producing factors (sales, property, and payroll). Income attributable to a state is determined by applying a percentage comprised of a fraction contrasting a corporation's total of these three factors in the taxing state with the total in all jurisdictions.

EXAMPLE: REIT has operations in State A and several other states. REIT's total net income is $8,000,000 and in State A it (1) holds property totaling $10,000,000, (2) had a payroll of $100,000, and (3) had rental receipts of $6,000,000. In all states (including State A), the apportionment factors were (1) $20,000,000 in property, (2) $150,000 in payroll, and (3) receipts of $10,000,000. The portion of REIT income apportioned to State A is calculated as follows:

> A percentage of in-state activity is calculated with respect to each factor ($10 million ÷ $20 million = 50%; $100,000 ÷ $150,000 = 67%; and $6 million ÷ $10 million = 60%). Those percentages are then summed and divided by 3 (177% ÷ 3) to achieve an apportionment factor (59%) that is multiplied by the net income of the REIT ($8 million × 59% = $4,720,000).

a. UDITPA Property Factor The property factor, described by UDITPA Section 10, represents the average value of the REIT's real and tangible personal property owned or rented and used during the taxing period. Owned property is valued at original cost plus capitalized improvements or additions.[18] For rented property, the value is set at eight times the net annual rent. However, that figure is offset by any rent received by the REIT from a subtenant.

When a REIT holds an interest in a partnership and is required to combine that partnership's income and apportionment factors with its own,[19] a potential approach for establishing how much of the cost should be assigned to each partner is to use a liquidation scenario similar to the one employed by the I.R.C. Section 752 regulations. Assuming a sale of all assets for their original cost, each partner's share of the sale proceeds plus a share of the nonrecourse debt secured by such property would represent that partner's share of the original cost.[20]

b. UDITPA Payroll Factor UDITPA Sections 13 and 14 detail the payroll factor. A REIT's compensation expense is assigned to the factor's numerator or denominator based on the jurisdiction to which the REIT makes an unemployment compensation contribution with respect to those wages.

Amounts paid to independent contracts or third-party property managers should not be considered for purposes of the payroll factor.

c. UDITPA Sales Factor Under Sections 15 through 17 of UDITPA, the sales factor includes all receipts. Accordingly, a REIT's rental receipts are included in the sales factor. It is important to remember that many states do not apply UDITPA in its totality, and there may be states that do not consider the receipt of rents as "sales" for purposes of their particular apportionment formula. Receipts from the sale of business property are assigned to the state where the property is located.

d. Zero Factor As a general rule, the states that rely on formula apportionment provide that a factor is ignored for purposes of determining apportionment if the denominator (activity in all states) for that factor is zero. For example, a REIT with no payroll in any state eliminates that factor, and the percentage representing the in-state versus out-of-state activity is divided by two instead of three.

e. Challenge to UDITPA. Generally, most states provide under UDITPA Section 18 or equivalent provisions that either the taxpayer or the taxing authority can use another method if the formula is "unreasonable." The courts are divided as to whether the state can do this on an ad hoc, case-by-case basis. Some courts have held that the state may use the authority of this provision only to promulgate a regulation for such special cases (that is, a special formula or factor for the airline industry). Cases under Section 18 include *Donald W. Drake Co. v. Dep't of Revenue*, 773 P. 2d 1290 (Ore. 1989) (cite for burden of proof); *American Airlines v. Porterfield,* 21 Ohio St. 272, 257, N.E.2d 348 (1970); *Twentieth Century Fox Film Corp v. Dep't of Revenue,* 700 P. 2d 1035 (Ore. 1985); *FW Woolworth Co. v. Dir., Div. of Tax'n.* 45 J.J. 466, 213 A.2d 1 (1965); and *RA Macy & Co. v. Lindley,* Ohio BTA (Aug. 7, 1985), Ohio Taxes (DDH) par. 201–637.

2. Specific Allocation

UDITPA uses specific allocation to assign nonbusiness income. In general, examples of nonbusiness income include interest, dividends, and rents. However, because rents received by a REIT represent income generated in connection with a trade or business, many states provide that a REIT's rental income is treated as business income. Nevertheless, Delaware appears to require the allocation of all rental income.

D. Unitary Business and Combined Reporting Principles[21]

Formulary apportionment is used whenever a business has income[22] from business activity that takes place in more than just the taxing state. Conceptually, this can raise issues as to the total scope or base of the total business activity that is to be assigned[23] under the formula. If an entity has an unrelated line of business that takes place solely in another state, it may seek to carve such a business out using principles of separate accounting to that other state, so no part of that income could be assigned to the operations in the taxing state. Conversely, if a corporation has related corporate affiliates engaged in similar or related activities, a state may attempt to argue that those business activities (even of other corporations) are so closely related with those in the taxing state that they should be included in the total income base to be assigned by formula apportionment.

Thus, the test of whether out-of-state activities are included in the income base to be assigned is the concept of a "unitary business." If the operations of the part of the business done within the state is dependent or contributes to the operation of the business outside the state, the operations are unitary. See, for example, *Wisconsin Dep't of Revenue v. Exxon,* 90 Wis.2d 700, 281 N.W.2d (1979). States and courts look to whether the in-state operations, for example, of a qualified REIT subsidiary under I.R.C. Section 856(i) (QRS), are so related to the out-of-state operations of that company or a corporate affiliate, such as the parent REIT or another QRS, that they should be treated as a unitary group.24 Factors considered include the lines of business; common ownership and control; common officers; centralized management; purchasing, accounting, or other support functions; economies of scale; flow of goods or services; and functional integration.[25]

1. Forms of Unitary Combination

As addressed above, a unitary combination[26] exists when several affiliated corporations engaged in a unitary business are included in a combined report.[27] Unitary combinations are a part of the taxing scheme in many states. In each of these states, unitary combinations generally apply only to United States sourced income. Prior to the last few years, worldwide combinations[28] were part of the taxing scheme in several states. The constitutionality of California's past imposition of worldwide reporting was upheld by the Supreme Court in 1994.[29]

E. Treatment of Income from Partnerships

In general, if a unitary relationship exists between a REIT and a partnership in which it is a partner, the REIT must combine its share of the partnership's income and apportionment factors with its own for purposes of determining its state tax liability. This rule also may apply for purposes of a state's gross receipts and franchise tax. However, a few states impose their gross receipts tax directly on the underlying partnership.

In most instances, the rental activities of partnerships are deemed "business income" when received by a REIT. The same result is even more likely with respect to any management fees the REIT might receive from the partnership. Accordingly, the REIT's share of partnership income generated from the renting of real property is subject to apportionment.

UDITPA provides that for purposes of allocating business income, a REIT is required to include in its apportionment factors an amount of each of the partnership's apportionment factors "to the extent of its interest in the partnership." In light of the complex partnership tax rules that often affect the allocation of partnership earnings, this direction may seem inadequate.

The UDITPA language suggests an allocation of apportionment factors in a manner similar to that provided by Income Tax Regulations Section 1.856–3(g), which controls the allocation of income to REIT partners for purposes of federal income taxes and is not in accord with the subchapter K rules. Nevertheless, many practitioners believe that a REIT would appear to comply with the UDITPA requirement if it reported its distributive share of partnership items as set forth under I.R.C. Section 704(b).[30]

F. Qualified REIT Subsidiary (QRS)

For federal income tax purposes, I.R.C. Section 856(i) provides that a QRS is not a recognized entity and has no filing responsibility. Accordingly, all assets, liabilities, income, or losses are deemed to be those of the parent REIT. In essence, the REIT is taxed as if the QRS never existed.

In those states that follow the federal tax rules, it appears that the QRS's apportionment factors are passed through to the REIT parent. The same holds true in those jurisdictions that recognize the QRS as a separate entity for purposes of a filing responsibility (sometimes imposing a minimum tax) but nevertheless require that the income of the QRS be reported on the REIT's return.[31]

With respect to those states imposing a franchise tax, the QRS generally has a franchise return filing responsibility separate from the REIT. Accordingly, apportionment issues are not raised for the REIT. However, a QRS conducting business in more than one state will raise apportionment issues.

IV. INCOME TAX TREATMENT

Section I of this chapter details the basic concepts of state taxation and the impact of the federal rules. This section provides more detailed information with respect to several individual issues affecting state income taxation of REITs.

A. Dividends-Paid Deduction

As a result of conforming with the federal tax treatment of REITs, states generally allow for the dividends-paid deduction. In addition, most states that compute taxable income without strict reliance on the federal rules provide for a dividends-paid deduction as part of their income tax. States where authorities once have or currently do challenge the deduction for dividends paid or provide only a limited deduction include Hawaii, Kentucky, New Hampshire,[32] New Jersey,[33] Pennsylvania,[34] and Texas.[35] Additionally, Michigan does not allow for the deduction for purposes of the single business tax.

B. Income from Foreclosure Property and Prohibited Transactions

As previously mentioned, income from foreclosure property and prohibited transactions are not included in federal REIT taxable income.[36] Therefore, a REIT's income from such sources should not be subject to tax in the few states using REIT taxable income as the starting point for their income tax computation. Nevertheless, officials for those states that do not have state-specific REIT statutes but merely reference the federal Code indicate that the majority of those states would tax such income. This treatment appears to be based on the proposition that the state taxes any income taxable at the federal level unless a specific state modification is made. This rationale for taxing such income appears susceptible to challenge or at least an assertion that such income should be offset at the state level by the dividends-paid deduction.

In states that key their taxes to "federal taxable income," it would seem appropriate for REITs to interpret that term as REIT taxable income (Form 1120-REIT, line 22). Thus, the state starting point for its income tax computation would be read so as not to include the contested forms of income.[37]

As an alternative, an argument could be made in support of the dividends-paid deduction as an offset to all forms of income received by a REIT. This position is born out of a recognition that states do not adequately distinguish between the various forms of income, as is the case with the federal system. I.R.C. Section 857(b)(2) specifically provides for separate taxes on general REIT income, while income from foreclosure property or prohibited transactions are taxed under I.R.C. Sections 857(b)(4) and (b)(6), respectively. While states clearly incorporate the Code for purposes of classifying entities or even categories of income, there is little or no support for the proposition that by referencing the Code the specific taxes it imposes become state taxes. If that were so, each state that references the Code would impose an alternative minimum tax, something few states do. Consequently, it would appear that any taxes must be affirmatively imposed by the state. Due to the failure of states to distinguish between the various forms of REIT income, the federal tax limits on the use of the dividends-paid deduction would not be recognized at the state level.

All of that said, when states eventually address this area, it seems likely they will find that such sources of income should be treated in a manner similar to that afforded by the federal Code. In fact, their willingness to conform with such federal concepts as the dividends-paid deduction and qualified REIT subsidiary through administrative decisions may suggest that REITs would be willing to accept a state's administrative decision to conform with the federal treatment of foreclosure property and prohibited transaction income.

C. Qualified REIT Subsidiary (QRS)

An important tax concept involves the treatment of a QRS in a state that to some extent exempts the REIT parent from taxation. For example, Ohio exempts REITs from the state's franchise tax, which has both an income and net worth tax component. Specifically, the issue is whether a state granting an exemption to REITs extends that exemption to a QRS.

Many of the states that grant specific exemptions to REITs take the informal position that the exemption also applies to a QRS. Those positions appear to be based on the federal tax concept that a REIT and QRS are, in fact, one entity. However, the potential exists for states to take the position that an exemption granted to REITs does not extend to a QRS, based on the QRS being a separate entity and recognizing that it does not meet the definitional tests for REIT status set forth in I.R.C. Section 856. (Some practitioners believe this position states the current rule in Ohio and possibly other states).

In states that reference federal taxable income but not specific REIT sections or concepts, one must determine whether the QRS is viewed as having no taxable income by virtue of the pass-through treatment under I.R.C. Section 856(i). Under this analysis, the QRS tax items flow through to the parent level, as under the federal rules.

Some states appear to treat a QRS as a separate REIT, allowing it to deduct dividends paid to its parent. Although this achieves the correct "bottom line" result, one should monitor the state's position closely to become aware of any change of policy. Hopefully, no state that references federal taxable income will view a QRS as a separate taxable entity for income tax purposes without the benefit of a dividends-paid deduction.

V. FRANCHISE (NET WORTH/CAPITAL STOCK) TAX

Numerous states impose a franchise tax as a compliment to their income tax. Because REITs tend to be heavily capitalized entities, this tax can present a substantial tax liability. With limited exceptions, a state's franchise tax applies to REITs. A REIT's exemption from franchise taxes may be predicated on the fact that its operations are conducted as a business trust or because of a statutory exception.[38]

A. Forms of Franchise Taxes

The franchise tax comes in several forms. The two most common forms of franchise tax are the net worth and capital stock taxes. The capital stock tax is imposed solely on the entity's capital account. The capital account, depending on the state, represents either authorized, issued, or outstanding capital stock at their par value or at some fixed amount when the shares have no par value. The net worth tax is imposed on a broader base that takes into consideration the entity's going-concern value. Accordingly, the base may represent corporate worth as assets over liabilities or the fair market value of the entity's stock.

Delaware's franchise tax is in part based on the number of authorized shares, not on the dollar value of the company or its stock.

In several states,[39] the franchise and income tax serve as components of a single tax. In such instances, a REIT determines the tax on its income and franchise tax base, and then pays the higher of the two liabilities.

B. Apportionment

For REITs operating in more than one state, the constitutional limitations outlined above require that the tax base subjected to the franchise tax represent a fair apportionment of that entity's operations in that state.

C. Qualified REIT Subsidiaries (QRS)

Because franchise taxes are not based on income, the federal tax treatment of either the REIT or QRS has a nominal impact on the imposition of a franchise tax for either form of entity. In addition, most states treat the QRS as a separate entity for purposes of their franchise tax. This is true in the great majority of instances, including many of the states that ignore the existence of the QRS for income tax purposes.

VI. OTHER TAXES

A. Gross Receipts Tax

Gross receipts taxes are imposed by Delaware, Indiana, New Mexico, and Rhode Island. In addition, Michigan imposes a single business tax that is based in part on gross receipts. The tax in these states varies depending on the type of business conducted in the states. New Mexico's tax is imposed on the sale of personal property and receipts generated in providing services to others.

B. Alternative Minimum Tax

Some states impose an alternative minimum tax similar to that of the Internal Revenue Code. Thus, a REIT could have an income tax liability even in states that allow for a dividends-paid deduction. For example, New York levies an alternative minimum tax that adds back not only the preference items provided for under I.R.C. Sections 56 and 57 but net operating losses as well. Alaska, California, Florida, Iowa, Maine, Minnesota, and North Dakota also impose an alternative minimum tax. However, Minnesota exempts REITs from its alternative minimum tax.

C. New Hampshire Business Enterprise Tax

Under the new business enterprise tax (BET), applying to any business with a tax year ending on or after July 31, 1993, a tax is imposed on an enterprise's outlays for labor or capital within New Hampshire. The tax is imposed on a base of three components: (1) compensation, (2) dividends,[40] and (3) interest. Because New Hampshire does not allow for a dividends-paid deduction and the fact that any tax liability resulting from the BET can be used to offset any New Hampshire income tax liability, the impact of the new tax may be minimal in many cases.

D. Personal Property Taxes and Transfer Taxes

The imposition of a state or local transfer tax must be considered when property is transferred between the REIT, a qualified REIT subsidiary, or a partnership in which the REIT holds an interest. These taxes can have a substantial impact on a REIT and must be considered when choosing a locale in which to operate. It is important to ascertain whether such transactions are exempt when no, or a limited, beneficial ownership change occurs.

VII. TAXATION OF THE REIT SHAREHOLDER

A. Taxability of the REIT Dividend

REIT dividends generally are taxable as ordinary divided income. In every state that imposes a tax on income or receipts, dividends from a REIT are considered part of the tax base. The same treatment is applied to a REIT that characterizes a part of its dividend as a capital gain. However, any amounts paid to shareholders that represent a return of the shareholder's capital should not be subject to tax in the hands of the shareholder, consistent with the federal rules.

B. Nexus Issues

Most states adhere to a general rule that dividends are sourced to the recipient's state of domicile for purposes of imposing taxation. Nevertheless, this position is under review, and several states[41] may have decided to impose a tax on any dividend that is a product of operations within their borders.[42] This position is often adopted by states that do not impose an income tax on a REIT itself or that provide a REIT with the dividends-paid deduction. Such states base the decision to tax the dividend on the fact that they will otherwise collect no tax on operations within their state (compare I.R.C. Section 1441). Obviously, this position can present problems for a REIT shareholder when its state of domicile imposes the traditional allocation rule to dividends.

Taxation of a nonresident on the receipt of a dividend representing income earned in that state requires that the state find a taxable nexus merely from the receipt of the dividend. Such taxes would appear susceptible to challenge under the constitutional limitations outlined in the section concerning nexus and jurisdiction.

REIT shareholders subject to a franchise tax (corporate shareholders) are faced with the nebulous issue of whether the receipt of the REIT dividend income creates a separate tax return filing responsibility or constitutes an includable sales apportionment value in the states in which the REIT conducts business. In general, the receipt of a REIT dividend should not produce a filing responsibility or a sales apportionment value in the states where the REIT operates.[43]

VIII. PLANNING STRATEGIES

A. Use of Business Trust Format

A primary tax-planning opportunity offered by the state taxation patterns currently in place is to conduct the REIT's operations in the business trust format. However, the tax advantages that can be gained from using this format must be contrasted with the potential nontax limitations the format may present.

1. Tax Consequences

No fewer than nine states exempt a REIT formed as a business trust from their income tax, franchise tax, or both. The list of states offering such an advantage includes Delaware, Kentucky, Illinois, Massachusetts, Missouri, Nebraska, New York, Pennsylvania, Rhode Island, South Carolina, Texas, and Wisconsin.[44] Each of these states exempt the business trust from its franchise or license tax, and Massachusetts, Pennsylvania, and Texas also provide protection from their income taxes.

2. Nontax Considerations

Probably the most significant advantage of the corporate form of organization over that of the business trust is the well-defined laws that provide legal liability protection for shareholders, officers, and directors. Business trusts are creatures of common law and subsequently do not offer the security of statutory language.[45]

In addition to the possible tax savings, many new REITs have chosen the trust format for such reasons as the flexibility provided by the trust's governing instrument. Unlike corporations that have much of their corporate governance matters prescribed by state statutes that cannot be altered, the declaration of trust instrument provides the luxury of determining which of the common corporate governance matters to include. Significant examples include the opportunity to set a par value in states that impose a tax on capital, standards of conduct for the trustees and officers, the ability to provide additional protection to trustees against breach of fiduciary lawsuits, and whether to allow for appraisal rights.

B. Qualified REIT Subsidiary (QRS)

The use of a QRS can result in reduced income or franchise tax liabilities if the QRS is recognized as a separate entity. Another consideration is the unitary combination rules previously addressed.

1. Franchise Taxes

EXAMPLE: REIT operates in State A and State B. State B has a much higher net worth rate and recognizes the QRS as a separate entity for franchise tax purposes. By creating a thinly capitalized QRS to conduct operations in State B, the REIT protects its capital from tax. The QRS's capital needs can be met primarily through debt held by the REIT. Care must be exercised to be certain that the QRS has sufficient equity capital so that the state does not reclassify the debt as equity for state tax purposes.

EXAMPLE: REIT, which for nontax reasons is formed as a corporation, operates in States C and D. State D imposes a much higher capital stock tax rate, recognizes the QRS as a separate entity, and exempts business trusts from the capital stock tax. By creating a QRS in the form of a business trust to conduct operations in State D, neither the QRS nor REIT owes capital stock taxes to State D.

2. Income Taxes

Generally, by financing operations with debt from the REIT, the QRS can use the interest payments associated with that debt to lower the QRS's income tax liability. This planning technique may be limited by the unitary reporting principles previously discussed.

3. Potential Pitfall

The contribution of appreciated property from the REIT to QRS is a nontaxable event at the federal level since the QRS is not recognized as a separate entity for tax purposes. Uncertain, however, is the potential for tax at the same level if the QRS is recognized in that jurisdiction. However, most states incorporate the full Internal Revenue Code into their own rules, and therefore, those states should treat the transaction in a manner consistent with the tax-free principles of I.R.C. Section 351.

C. Partnerships

1. Franchise Taxes

EXAMPLE: Similar to the examples presented for the QRS, franchise taxes may be avoided by conducting operations in a partnership format in those states that impose high capital stock tax rates.

2. Income Taxes

EXAMPLE: State E imposes a much higher income tax than does State F. REIT directly operates its leasing activities in State F. However, REIT participates in a partnership that operates property in State E and has provided the financing for that partnership's operations. The partnership's repayment of the note to REIT reduces the income generated in State E. However, the application of this planning tool also is subject to reduced effect by the unitary business rule.

EXAMPLE: The potential for using a QRS as a tax-saving device becomes more complex when the REIT uses an UPREIT structure, due largely to all of the property interests being downstreamed to the umbrella partnership (also known as an operating partnership). In particular, the umbrella partnership is unable to form a QRS since 100 percent of the QRS's stock must be held by the REIT (see I.R.C. Section 856[i]).

The creation of a "tandem" structure may allow for advantageous use of the QRS form. An example of such a structure for a Texas situation is discussed below. (The principles also apply to other states).

REIT is a partner in the Operating Partnership which holds assets in Texas as well as other states. Because REIT is a corporation and Texas is a tax-advantaged state for business trusts, REIT would like its share of the income resulting from the Texas properties to pass through a QRS that is organized as a business trust.

This is accomplished either by the QRS forming a partnership with the Operating Partnership to hold the Texas properties, or the QRS can become a partner in the Operating Partnership and through special allocations receive the income from the Texas properties that would otherwise be allocated to the REIT.

In the case of a QRS that joins with the Operating Partnership to hold the Texas properties, the Texas partnership mirrors the umbrella partnership because the QRS's interest in the Texas partnership is identical to the REIT's interest in the umbrella partnership. (In variations of this structure, the REIT still may hold a limited partner interest in the Texas properties through the umbrella partnership since such contact, by itself, does not currently establish nexus with Texas.) The QRS may be organized as a business trust and thus be excluded from the Texas franchise tax.

The REIT holds its interests in the non-Texas properties through the umbrella partnership.

The umbrella partnership contains an allocation provision specifically allocating to the nonREIT partners all items pertaining to the Texas partnership. These allocations should satisfy the requirements of I.R.C. Section 704.

There are potential problems with this structure. The need to maintain equal ownership interests for the REIT and the other Operating Partnership partners may make the structure impractical, particularly for those variations of the structure when the QRS is formed to hold the general partner interest in addition to the REIT's limited partner interest in the Operating Partnership. Another potential problem is that if a nonREIT Operating Partnership partner exercises its put options and converts a portion of its units to REIT shares, the REIT's interest in the umbrella partnership increases. However, there is no mechanism for adjusting the REIT's interest in the Texas partnership. A similar problem occurs if the REIT conducts a secondary offering.

It is important to consider whether the QRS is recognized for tax purposes by the state offering the exemption to business trusts. For purposes of their income tax, many states either do not recognize the QRS or require it to file an informational return and report its income on the REIT's tax return. If the REIT is formed as a corporation, the exemption from tax may be lost.

With respect to the other possible structure, which calls for the REIT's QRS to acquire a limited partnership interest in the Operating Partnership (which would continue to directly own all of the properties) through special allocations, the nonREIT partners of the Operating Partnership have an interest of Y percent in all properties owned by the Operating Partnership. Through special allocations, the REIT has an interest of X percent in all of the non-Texas properties, while the QRS has an interest of X percent in the Texas properties.

For federal income tax purposes, all income, expense, assets, and liabilities owned by the QRS are treated as belonging to the REIT. Therefore, there may not be significant federal issues with respect to the substantiality of the allocations for I.R.C. Section 704(b) purposes. Thus, the threshold issue becomes whether the state recognizes the integrity of the special allocations. Since Texas recognizes the QRS, it appears that the state should likewise recognize the special allocations, assuming such allocations have economic substance.

For Texas purposes, the REIT is presumably not doing business in Texas and thus would escape the Texas franchise tax if the QRS were in a trust format.

As noted in the previous example, a consideration in using this structure is whether the QRS is separately recognized for tax purposes in the state offering the exemption to business trusts.

D. Other Strategies

1. Avoid Property Transfers

Care should be taken when structuring your organization to ensure that property is placed in the proper form of entity at the start. The need to reorganize at a later date may raise issues over the transfer of property and result in substantial transfer tax liabilities. In addition, keeping alive the operating partnership in an UPREIT structure might forestall a state's attempt to classify property as transferred.

IV. SUMMARY

Although most REITs are not likely to have federal income tax liabilities as a result of their operations, the same is not always true with respect to state taxes. As noted, much of the authority governing the taxation of REITs at the state level comes from administrative decisions rather than statutes. In many cases, especially in the case of net worth taxes, state liabilities can be substantial.

These factors, and the ever-increasing aggressiveness of state governments to find fiscal resources, make clear the need to monitor changes in state taxation and to consider the impact of such taxes when structuring transactions.

ENDNOTES

1. This overview is taken from the NAREIT *State and Local Tax Compendium for REITs.* Special thanks to Linda A. Amsbarger of Morrison & Foerster, Washington, DC, and Stephen T. Ryan of Ernst & Young, Chicago, for their contributions to this overview.
2. Throughout this overview, taxes on net worth, capital stock, or authorized shares may be replaced with the generic term *franchise tax.* However, it is

important to be aware that some states may use the term *franchise tax* to represent a tax based on income, or a tax comprised of both income and capital stock or net worth components.

3. Throughout this overview, the term *state* is used to signify the 50 states and the District of Columbia. At other times, the term *jurisdiction* is substituted for the word *state.*
4. A separate method of taxation applies to income from foreclosure property [I.R.C. Section 857(b)(4)] and prohibited transactions [I.R.C. Section 857(b)(6)] and such income is not subject to offset by the dividends-paid deduction. Thus, amounts from those sources create a federal tax liability. The taxability of income from these sources at the state level is discussed later in this overview.
5. The great majority of states either tax REITs under a general principle of incorporating the federal rules or a statute that specifically incorporates I.R.C Sections 856 and 857. States providing specific statutory rules regarding the taxation of REITs include Alabama, California, Ohio, New Hampshire, Pennsylvania, and Utah.
6. As noted above, the typical reasons for a REIT to be subject to tax include the REIT having (1) net taxable income that exceeds the dividends-paid deduction or (2) income arising from foreclosure property or prohibited transactions.
7. States that recognize REIT taxable income are Alabama, Colorado, Florida, Illinois, Maryland, Minnesota, Missouri, Utah, Virginia, and Wisconsin.
8. U.S. CONST. amend. XIV. Section 1.
9. U.S. CONST. art. I, Section 8, cl.3.
10. *Moorman Mfg. Co. v. Bair,* 437 U.S. 267 (1978); *Cf. ASARCO, Inc. v. Idaho State Tax Comm'n,* 458 U.S. 307 (1982); and *FW Woolworth Co. v. Taxation & Revenue Dep't,* 458 U.S. 354 (1982).
11. *Id.*
12. *Complete Auto Transit Inc. v. Brady,* 430 U.S. 274 (1977); *cf. Quill Corp. v. North Dakota,* 112 S.Ct. 1904 (1992).
13. See Hellerstein & Hellerstein, *State Taxation,* Para. 6.06 at pp. 6–12 (2d ed. 1993) ("Hellerstein") *citing to Northwest States Portland Cement Co. v. State of Minnesota,* 358 U.S. 450 (1959) and *International Shoe Co. v. State of Washington,* 326 U.S. 310 (1945) regarding the relationship between taxable nexus with a state and the presence in that state of property or employees, respectively.
14. Ryan, "Real Estate Investment Trusts Face Surprising State Taxation," *Journal of State Taxation* 12, no.14 (Spring 1994).

15. Some of these states draw a distinction between participatory and nonparticipatory loans, deeming the participatory loan to equate with an equity interest in the underlying real property. Accordingly, it is more likely that the participatory loan results in a finding of nexus.
16. In many of these states, the traditional three-factor formula is applied with variations. Generally, these variations involve a different weighing of the traditional factors or the exclusion of one or two of the factors. It is also important to remember that states may use different apportionment formulas for their income and franchise taxes.
17. The Multistate Tax Compact (MTC) Regulations are another important piece of the puzzle that is the assignment of income for an interstate business. The MTC, formulated in 1966 by the National Association of Attorneys General and the National Legislative Council, is a document to which states may subscribe in the interest of uniform taxation of multistate corporate income. Under the MTC, a taxpayer may elect either the established state law on allocation and apportionment or Article IV of the MTC, which substantially incorporates UDITPA. Most jurisdictions subscribing to the MTC also have adopted UDITPA as their governing law, thus eliminating any meaningful election for taxpayers in such states. Currently 18 jurisdictions are members, and 24 other jurisdictions have adopted some of the MTC regulations or have similar provisions.

    Even in states where the MTC regulations have not been formally adopted, they may serve as an important interpretative source to the extent that a state's own laws and regulations are unclear concerning issues of allocation and apportionment.
18. As noted earlier, UDITPA is not applied literally in every state. Consequently, certain states may use such sources as a real property tax assessment as the measurement of a property's value for purposes of the apportionment computation.
19. See subsection III.B., *infra.*
20. A Guide to State Taxation of Real Estate Investment Trusts, p. vi (Deloitte & Touche, 1992).
21. See Hellerstein, *supra* at n. 12, for a detailed examination of the issues raised in this overview.
22. The unitary business concept discussed in this section does not apply for purposes of determining a franchise tax liability.
23. The term *assigned* is used in place of the terms *apportioned* or *allocated* that would apply depending on the nature of the income.
24. The common relationship between a REIT and a qualified REIT subsidiary or the operating partnership in an UPREIT structure generally is one

that would result in the determination that a unitary business relationship exists. Accordingly, the income and apportionment factors of those entities are added to the REIT's for purposes of determining the REIT's income tax liability.

25. See generally *Container Corp. of America v. Franchise Tax Board,* 463 U.S. 159 (1983); *ASARCO supra* at n. 9; *Woolworth supra* at n. 9; and *Mobil Oil Corp. v. Commissioner of Taxes of Vermont*, 445 U.S. 425 (1980).

26. Two distinct, but closely related, concepts are at play in this section. The unitary business principle addresses a single corporation conducting business in several jurisdictions, and whether the nature of those businesses warrant the combination of all income from those businesses for apportionment and allocation between the various states. Alternatively, the concept of a unitary combination is exemplified by several corporations involved in a similar (unitary) business that should report their results on a combined basis.

27. Note that the combined reporting principle could have a significant effect on REITs that use a management subsidiary. A REIT and its sponsors create management subsidiaries to provide management services to third parties that the REIT itself may not provide. Such subsidiaries are structured so that voting control is held by nonREIT participants, while the REIT receives a significant portion of the income produced (either through the ownership of nonvoting stock or interest payments on loans made by the REIT). See, e.g., PLR 9340056.

28. Upheld in *Container supra* at n. 23.

29. See *Barclays Bank v. Franchise Tax Board*, 510 U.S. 1107, 114 Supreme Court 1044 (1994).

30. See, e.g., A Guide to State Taxation of Real Estate Investment Trusts p. vi (Deloitte & Touche, 1992).

31. Connecticut, Georgia, Massachusetts, New Jersey, New Mexico, New York, Pennsylvania, Rhode Island, and Vermont are examples of states that appear to impose a filing requirement on the qualified REIT subsidiary even though its income is reported on the parent REIT's return.

32. In addition to denying the dividends-paid deduction, a recently enacted New Hampshire tax imposes a tax on a REIT on the dividends it pays. However, the effect of this new tax is mitigated because any tax paid may be used to offset any income tax liability.

33. As a result of a court decision, REITs have a right to the dividends-paid deduction. *Corporate Property Investors v. Director, Division of Taxation,*

Superior Court of New Jersey, Appellate Division A-5993-93T3 (May 23, 1995).

34. The Pennsylvania Department of Revenue informally has advised corporate REITs that they may use the dividends-paid deduction for income but not capital stock purposes. A REIT organized as a business trust is not subject to either tax.

35. An April 1997 decision of a Texas Administrative Law Judge upheld a REIT's right to the dividends-paid deduction. The state is appealing that decision.

36. Income generated by foreclosure property or prohibited transactions are taxed at the federal level (see I.R.C. Sections 857[b][4] and [6]). However, the tax imposed on such amounts, which may not be offset by the dividends- paid deduction, is computed apart from the computation of tax imposed on "real estate investment trust taxable income."

37. But see n. 33, *supra.*

38. The states exempting business trusts include Delaware, Illinois, Kentucky, Massachusetts, Missouri, Nebraska, Pennsylvania, Rhode Island, South Carolina, Texas, and Wisconsin. Alabama, Connecticut, New York, Ohio, and Oklahoma appear to exempt all REITs from their franchise tax.

39. Examples include Texas and Rhode Island. Ohio's franchise tax has both an income and net-worth component, but Ohio exempts REITs from that tax.

40. Defined as "any distribution of money or property, other than the distribution of newly issued stock of the same enterprise, to the owners of a business enterprise with respect to their ownership interest in such enterprise from the accumulated revenues and profits of the enterprise." RSA 77–E:1, VI. The statutory language can be interpreted as applying only to dividends paid from profits earned in years prior to the current tax year. However, an official with the state's Department of Revenue indicated that the tax applies to dividends paid from accumulated *and* current-year earnings. Note that the tax base excludes a payment constituting a return of capital (i.e., a payment in excess of earnings and profits).

41. The list of states includes Indiana, Iowa, Missouri, Nebraska, Oklahoma, and Texas (34 TAC Section 3.549). In addition, the recent law change in Delaware that exempted REITs from the state income tax also included a provision providing that any REIT dividend representing income arising from the ownership or disposition of Delaware property is considered Delaware source income for purposes of the taxation of nonresidents. However, no withholding requirement is imposed on the REIT.

42. There is no indication that any of these states impose a withholding requirement on the REIT.

43. Ryan Article at 18, *supra.*

44. Ohio statutorily exempts all REITs, both corporate and trust, from its taxes on income and net worth. In addition, Delaware exempts the two forms of REITs from its income tax.

45. However, the "Maryland REIT Law," the "California REIT Law," and the Delaware Business Trust Act provide statutory protection from trustee liability. The extent to which traditional comity principles apply when a trust organized in these states owns property in another state is not clear.

PART

III

BUSINESS AND FINANCIAL STRATEGIES OF REITs

CHAPTER

6

THE CEO's PERSPECTIVE

Thomas P. D'Arcy, *President and Chief Executive Officer, Bradley Real Estate, Inc.*

INTRODUCTION

This chapter provides an overview of the REIT business from the perspective of a REIT chief executive officer. In my role as the CEO of Bradley Real Estate, I have primary responsibility, in concert with the board of directors, for devising and implementing Bradley's strategic plan. Bradley's strategy is focused on becoming the dominant owner of grocery-anchored, open-air shopping centers in the Midwest. Founded in 1961, Bradley is the nation's oldest REIT and has a current total market capitalization of $650 million. The company is a fully integrated operating company and owns and operates a portfolio of 42 properties totaling 8.5 million square feet located in 12 states. Over the past year, the company has undergone a number of significant changes, including my being named CEO following the sudden death of my predecessor and the acquisition of another REIT, which doubled the size of our company.

In this chapter, I will share my perspective of the role of a REIT CEO by addressing in particular those issues and challenges that are distinctive and unique to REITs as well as the issues that face CEOs in all businesses.

While the stewardship of a modern REIT is a challenging and complex endeavor requiring a wide variety of skills, the relative success of this stewardship is quite simple to measure. I know full well that my job is to deliver superior returns to our share owners and that the market will let me know daily how our company is doing in this regard. This is not to say that I spend the day fixated on the quotron. But I do understand that the public market, together with its assorted players, is a relentless watchdog of management and corporate performance. When I took the reins at Bradley, I did so with the complete understanding that the company under my watch would either fulfill our investors' expectations or that the board would find someone who could make sure it would. I not only find this dynamic rational but healthy, as the measurement of success and failure are clearly defined.

While the measure of performance is easy to understand—that is, total return to our share owners—achieving it can be both complex and challenging. The skills involved in running a modern REIT are numerous and include an in-depth knowledge of all aspects of the real estate business, including management, leasing, acquisition, and development as well as a thorough understanding of the capital markets, micro- and macroeconomic trends, capital costs, and numerous other related factors. The CEO must apply these skills to a business that is capital-intensive yet possesses structural limitations on retained cash, thus creating constant pressure to maintain fairly priced capital sources. Additionally, as a publicly traded company, REITs adhere to formal reporting guidelines, including the quarterly reporting of earnings in a business that in certain circumstances does not easily lend itself to such reporting.

VISION AND STRATEGY

In order to succeed in delivering superior total returns, I believe one of the most important roles of the CEO is to have a clear and attainable vision for the company and a sound and flexible strategic plan. The vision provides the foundation for all of the company's activities and serves as the basis for the development of the company's strategic direction, which is critical to the company's position in the REIT marketplace. My vision for Bradley is based on my years of experience in the real estate and capital markets, industry knowledge, analytical capabilities, and an innate feel for how Bradley can best create value for our owners.

While having a clear vision is critical, the CEO must be able to transform this vision into action through a strategic plan. In my mind, the importance of both the core corporate vision and a well-devised strategic plan cannot be overstated. Without either one, the REIT CEO has little chance of delivering superior share owner returns over the long term. While it is true that for a period of time a solid core group of real estate assets in a growth market may be able to outperform a peer group, it cannot do so on a sustainable basis without a firm vision and a clear, flexible, and well-thought-out strategic plan. While I have heard it argued that since REITs manage hard assets, vision and strategy are less important, I could not disagree more. The management of a modern real estate operating company creates an entirely different dynamic than that of a passively managed group of properties. Vision and strategy are essential to running a successful REIT because without them resources are ultimately expended on activities that do not contribute to core earnings. Over time, this scenario can prove fatal since, for the most part, REITs are relatively lean organizations without a lot of built-in redundancies. In addition, investors will easily perceive this lack of direction and begin to have difficulty assessing the company's progress, which will eventually lead to a reassessment of ownership positions and ultimately to the devaluation of the company's equity.

I believe that having a vision and implementing a strategy is what differentiates today's REITs from the private and public real estate entities of the past. Since a REIT's strategic plan is capable of generating value in excess of carried assets, it is not merely a collection of properties but an enterprise worthy of a valuation in excess of the net asset value of the property portfolio. This premium must be earned in the marketplace through demonstrated earnings growth and a well-conceived strategic plan. Admittedly, there are companies that trade at a discount to asset value for a variety of reasons. For these companies, it is the CEO's task to create this premium or reduce the discount by applying his or her vision to the enterprise.

At Bradley, a significant amount of time and resources are expended on the development and maintenance of the strategic plan. This is an ongoing process, which involves the board of directors, senior management, and certain levels of employees from all departments. The management team analyzes our core business and the economic factors affecting our markets, and conducts a general review of the macro- and microeconomic trends. This analysis involves a critical self-assessment, marshaling all available resources to ensure that decisions are based on the best information available. I believe it critical that this process be conducted in as free-flowing a forum as possible, where "out of the box" thinking is not only encouraged but rewarded. In addition to senior management, we also involve property managers and leasing and acquisition personnel in the formulation and assessment of our strategic direction in order to take advantage of the perspective of "frontline" employees.

During the process, management receives critical input from the board of directors. At Bradley, we have an experienced and talented board that is fully committed to this process. Since six of the seven board members are outside directors (I am the only inside director), the board brings a truly independent and objective mind-set to the process, which creates a healthy atmosphere for working through the planning process.

In addition to the input of company personnel and board members, we also work with external consultants who have both strategic planning and real estate expertise. We find that consultants, as objective observers, facilitate discussion and self-examination. They provide feedback regarding the company's direction and use their perspective of the REIT business and their knowledge of the investment community to test the plan's assumptions and to ensure that it is capable of accomplishing our stated corporate objectives.

Throughout this process, the CEO's involvement is crucial. It is the CEO who must review the gathered data and take into account the internal and external forces affecting the business. No company exists in a vacuum. The CEO must weigh how best to position the company to compete in the current operating environment. I believe it is critical that the CEO be realistic in his or her evaluation of the unique abilities and competitive advantages as well as the weaknesses and disadvantages that he or she believes the company brings to the marketplace. Ultimately, the CEO must determine whether he or she can make the company perform and support the vision and plan or whether the vision, the management team, or both must be reevaluated and reshaped.

As the strategic plan evolves, it is critical that the best information available is used in order to understand the company's competitive position. Often, this information can be difficult or expensive to obtain. For instance, a significant part of our research efforts involve specific demographic factors, job and population growth, and retail capacity studies. In order to most effectively compile this data, we tap into raw economic and socioeconomic data sorted by ZIP code, which is supplied by an independent consultant. This information helps to raise questions regarding numerous factors in target markets, which we then analyze by a more in-depth study of the particular market. The process is clearly one in which hypotheses are conceived and then critically examined, researched, and tested in order to ascertain whether they can stand up to scrutiny and prove viable and flexible over the long term.

Once the plan has been developed, an important element that should be incorporated in the plan is an ongoing process of testing the plan's underlying assumptions. This is necessary in order to continually quantify the plan's impact on the operating numbers, the ultimate arbitrator as to whether a plan is worth the paper it is written on. At Bradley, we have developed sophisticated modeling programs that produce cash flow results broken down by quarter, which take into account all the variables included in the strategic planning process.

Our analysis begins with a financial model of all our properties measured over a long-term holding period, which contains tested assumptions for leasing, capital expenditures, tenant improvements, and so on for the core portfolio. The model then layers in anticipated acquisition, disposition, development, and redevelopment transactions to test the impact these events will have on earnings. Additionally, we model the capital-raising and deployment assumptions we must make in financing our business, including the ratio of debt to equity; the type, maturity, and cost of our debt; and any assumed equity or equity-linked offerings. Ultimately, this information is converted into FFO per share per quarter. We then run sensitivity analyses to review alternative strategies with regard to both the capital structure and our investment decisions. The introduction of stresses into the company's earnings stream or capital structure, and the management team's capabilities must be understood and weighted against potential returns. The final test is whether the plan as conceptualized fulfills the goals that have been articulated to the various constituencies both in the short and long term or whether the plan must be modified to accomplish the level of cash flow growth the CEO believes the equity holder requires.

The ultimate goal of the strategic-planning process and corresponding financial modeling is to convert the vision of the company into a workable plan that can be employed throughout the organization as the blueprint against which all decisions will be based and all progress judged. It is the CEO's role to ensure that the plan and the rationale behind the plan's objectives are understood by all levels of the company. The CEO is ultimately responsible for the successful implementation of the strategy, which involves making some tough, final calls. The CEO along with senior management must also convey to the share owners and to the investment community the company's short- and long-term strategies, including the potential risks and anticipated benefits.

IMPLEMENTATION AND EXECUTION

Following the development of the plan and its conveyance throughout the organization and the investment community, the CEO must implement and execute the plan by converting the vision and operational plan into action. In many ways, it is easy to articulate a grand vision for a company so long as the CEO is familiar with the various forces that affect the business. It can also be easy to construct a strategic plan around this vision by using the numerous templates and modeling tools that are available. What is more difficult, and what separates the superior CEO from the rest of the pack, is translating the plan into reported earnings that exceed the expectations of investors and the market in general.

It is at this point that the REIT CEO's role changes from visionary and strategic planner to organizational leader—one who takes the blueprint of the strategic plan and begins to execute the steps necessary to achieve it. The strategy must always be subjected to constant scrutiny to ensure it is capable of delivering the results the financial model predicts. Part of the responsibility in executing the plan is keeping an eye on when it needs to be flexible and when adjustments need to be made along the way. Certain time frames, benchmarks, and milestones need to be incorporated into the plan to monitor progress effectively and adjust issues as they arise.

As we implement our strategic plan, we first focus on the various departments required to run a successful real estate operating company, which include the following:

- Asset and property management
- Leasing
- Acquisitions
- Finance
- Accounting/legal/MIS
- Construction/engineering
- Research
- Investor Relations

These departments must be carefully structured so that they are able to accomplish the objectives of the strategic plan. This is especially true today since one of the most meaningful aspects of the REIT resurgence in the 1990s is the marketplace's demand that a company possess the disciplines necessary to run its business within its organizational structure. This change, which has transformed the REIT industry into a group of disciplined, focused real estate operating companies, has also created increased pressure on the CEO to strike the proper balance between being mindful of the amount of share owner money expended on corporate General and Administrative (G&A) expenses and the need to sufficiently staff the company with professionals in various disciplines who are capable of carrying out an aggressive growth agenda.

Clearly, it is the CEO's responsibility to put teams into place that can deliver the targeted cash flow growth from the company. The challenge is to get these professionals to operate as one unit, striving for common goals in a highly energized fashion. In my mind, it is here that the CEO earns his or her pay. The CEO must motivate, administer, referee, and compel all employees to work toward the share owners' common good.

At Bradley, we seek to achieve this objective by establishing clear short- and long-term goals for the company and for each department. These goals are directly tied to our corporate objectives. Furthermore, all employees (including the CEO) annually establish their goals and objectives that must reflect how they will contribute to the success of their department and ultimately to the corporation. Our incentive compensation program couples individual progress with the achievement of corporate performance. The criteria used for incentive pay is tied directly to the goals of the strategic plan, including growth in FFO per share and the total return earned by our owners, the mandate being that if our owners are not making money, we should not be receiving incentive-based pay.

While the planning and organizational structure must be devised and implemented, these processes must be managed in concert with day-to-day operational demands. In order to manage all of these facets, the CEO must use and manage his or her time effectively and efficiently. One of the most important facets in which the CEO should be involved is capital allocation, including recurring capital expenditures, tenant improvements, acquisitions, and corporate infrastructure needs. At Bradley, we take a highly programmed approach to these issues, predicated on the understanding that capital is our most precious commodity and that for every dollar we expend, whether on property operating expenses, corporate G&A, tenant capital improvements, or acquisitions, we must earn a return in excess of our cost of capital. We also realize that in the longer term we must exceed this cost by a healthy amount in order to create the superior long-term returns we seek for our share owners.

These capital allocation decisions, while ultimately made by the CEO, must be well understood by all members of the senior management team as well as field personnel. At Bradley, the understanding and clear sense of direction I try to provide is reinforced by a series of systems and procedures we have put in place to clearly quantify the impact these capital allocation decisions have on the value of our equity. For example, in making decisions about a specific lease transaction, we use a lease-approval form that I must sign that clearly shows the impact of each transaction on value. The form reduces the value of the lease's income stream (taking into account all inflows and outflows) and reduces the cash flow into an equivalent level rent, or ELR. The ELR is the flat rate per square foot that if paid in nominal dollars would equal the same present value as the proposed lease's variable cash flows. We factor the ELR concept into all lease decisions so that we have a clear and common tool to use when discussing any lease transaction.

Since the CEO's role is critical to the capital-allocation process, establishing a clear tool of measurement for acceptable returns becomes an important aspect of creating superior value. By using ELR, we focus on what I believe to be the critical aspect of creating value for the share owner: the return earned on incremental capital dollars invested. It is not difficult for a REIT to source suitable product that will produce an acceptable first-year return. True value, however, is created when superior returns are generated on the dollars invested subsequent to purchase. At Bradley, we quantify these returns by comparing the yield generated by using the ELR per square foot of a lease transaction against the gross per square foot value of the property into which the tenant is leasing space. The resulting yield is then compared with our corporate cost of capital (using an FFO discount model and the current market rate for debt) in order to determine whether the transaction is additive or dilutive to the value of the company stock.

While it could be argued that this approach to the lease-approval process does not take the "big picture" into account, it does get the organization to focus on the concept of value in all aspects of the business. At Bradley, we take the added step of tying a portion of the leasing agent's compensation (in addition to that tied directly to corporate performance) to the amount of positive ELR generated in a year (ELR in excess of the corporate cost of capital). We've found that this focuses agents and managers on the economic result of each transaction rather than simply on filling vacant space.

Another aspect of the business that I believe the CEO must constantly strive to improve is financial accounting and reporting and the management information systems (MIS). These departments must be able to produce the financial information required of a public corporation as well as information that the field personnel can use to effectively compete for tenants, manage the tenant billing process, track retail sales, and provide construction and leasing data. While the responsibility for financial systems rests with the CFO and controller, the CEO must always be mindful of the effect this function has on overall company efficiency. This is one area I would contend that recent IPOs have had great difficulty understanding and coordinating. The rigorous reporting requirements of a REIT demand a sophisticated level of MIS.

At Bradley, in addition to the regular quarterly and annual reports, we also provide our investors with detailed property information. This supplemental information provides key financial ratios for both operating performance and the balance sheet. Our disclosure philosophy is that current and prospective investors are entitled to as much information as they need to make an informed decision about our company. The desire to provide this information is tempered only by our commitment to not disclose information we believe could affect the company's competitive position. The enhanced property detail included in this supplement requires an investment in technology and, more importantly, a clear statement from the CEO that technological expertise is an important company goal.

In addition to the benefits that I believe accrue from providing our investors with better information through additional disclosure, our management information systems also provide senior management sound benchmarks and a detailed scorecard from which to gauge performance and indicate areas in which we need improvement. Reporting the type of information we provide on a quarterly basis imparts a great deal of discipline on the company.

Another daily activity of a CEO involves the management of numerous and sometimes complex relationships. These relationships include those between the CEO and the board, the chairman of the board, managers, share owners, the investment community, REIT analysts (both on the buy and sell side of the business), real estate industry professionals, and external advisers, including investment bankers, legal advisers, members of the accounting community, and other professional groups. Each of these relationships has a different dynamic, both from a power perspective and from an expectation perspective. The role of the CEO is to foster a healthy and productive relationship with each of these players.

One of the most important relationships the CEO has is with the board of directors. While the nature of this relationship varies in every company and with the personality of the CEO, a healthy, productive, and mutually trusting relationship is critical to success. At Bradley, the board is experienced, not only in terms of the real estate industry, but also in managing and serving as directors of other public companies. The perspective they bring to the decision-making process is invaluable to me. We seek to keep the board well informed of the company's status and to involve them in all significant investment decisions, in the setting of compensation policy and levels, and in the development of the company's strategic direction.

The CEO must also foster relationships with share owners and with members of the investment community. While long-term investors in the REIT industry remain key players, a new group of investors, including members of the pension community and their advisers, have become significant participants in the business. The challenge for the REIT CEO is to establish a sense of trust and an understanding of the company plan with both the existing share owner base and potential new investors. The fostering of these relationships is also critical to establishing realistic expectations about current earnings, earnings growth, the pace of acquisitions, potential new markets, and other information that provides the investor a clear sense of direction and purpose. If the CEO is successful in this regard, he or she can establish a level of comfort in the investment community that will hold the CEO and the company in good stead in both good times and bad.

CONCLUSION

In summary, the CEO must have a solid understanding of the company's targeted property type and focus. This day-to-day knowledge must be supplemented by a clear understanding of the capital markets for both debt and equity, the workings of the investment banking community, as well as GAAP accounting and the impact it has on the company's strategic plan. It goes without saying that a CEO must have a firm grasp of the critical elements of the business in which the company operates. Since there are so many new companies in the industry, many of which came in during the boom of 1993, it is fair to say that a certain number of these companies adapted better to the public nature of the REIT business than others. This was and continues to be a result of the specialized nature of the REIT vehicle in addition to the obvious differences between running private and public companies. Lack of industry knowledge was clearly one of the reasons that some of these companies were less than successful. While there is no shortage of available research and other industry information, there is no substitute for having dealt with the issues that affect the business and the knowledge that this experience imparts.

Being the CEO of a REIT is both challenging and rewarding. While the pressures of the job can at times be intense, the opportunity to shape the direction of an enterprise where success or failure are easily determined is stimulating. The REIT business is clearly just beginning to find its role in the real estate market, and the CEOs of all REITs must help this to happen. At Bradley, we are hard at work turning our plans into reality. In my role as CEO, I am focused on making the decisions and taking the steps that the pursuit of superior value requires.

CHAPTER

7

REITs AND COMMERCIAL LENDERS

The Evolving Relationship

Kenneth S. Nelson, *Managing Director, First Chicago/NBD*

INTRODUCTION

While REITs have existed for over 30 years, commercial lenders have had a sporadic relationship with them. Most commercial lenders turned away from REITs in the late 1970s, but in the 1990s, commercial lenders have rediscovered REITs. This chapter will examine this second stage of the evolution between commercial lenders and REITs. It begins with a definition of commercial lenders and then distinguishes among these lenders on the basis of whether they make primarily long- or short-term loans. Next, the chapter will consider the capital needs of REITs as businesses, followed by an evaluation of their interaction within the public and private debt markets. The emerging role of commercial lenders is then discussed, followed by a detailed examination of institutional lenders' roles in financing REITs through traditional mortgage loans, commercial mortgage-backed securities, and private and public unsecured debt. This narrative is followed by an extensive discussion of the roles of banks in providing mortgage debt, secured and unsecured revolving credit facilities, as well as such products as interest-rate swaps, interest-rate caps, floors, and collars to REITs. Following a consideration of bank roles as a source of bridge and acquisition financing, the focus will shift to a consideration of how to choose and manage relationships with commercial lenders. The chapter then ends with a number of concluding observations.

It is useful to begin with a definition of a commercial lender. For the purposes of this chapter, a commercial lender is a financial institution that provides loans on either a secured or unsecured basis to business enterprises, usually with the intention of keeping a significant portion of such loans on its own balance sheet. A commercial lender also considers the making and holding of loans to commercial enterprises a principal part of its business and employs professionals dedicated to making and managing such loans. Since this chapter focuses on commercial real estate lending, *commercial lenders* in this context refers to those parts of financial institutions that do commercial real estate lending as the principal focus of their business. This chapter will primarily focus on commercial lenders that are either institutional lenders or banks.

Commercial lenders fall into two broad groups, based principally on the predominant type of loans they make: longer-term or shorter-term. Most commercial lenders can make both types of loans, but the distinction between long-term and short-term is often important.

Long- and Short-Term Lenders

Long-term lenders typically include life insurance companies and pension funds, through their advisers. Referred to as "institutional lenders," these organizations' sources of funds and investment objectives are longer-term. Some debt mutual funds may act like long-term lenders; however, they comprise only a modest component of this commercial lending segment.

Life insurance companies invest for their own account and on behalf of pension funds. Life insurance companies participate in both the public and private side of the capital markets for REITs. In their equity portfolios, they may invest in the public stock of REITs. In their debt portfolios, they may invest in public debt issued by REITs. Additionally, they may be: (1) a source of funds for private equity or debt placed by a REIT, (2) a joint venture partner with a REIT in a real estate project, or (3) a long-term mortgage lender to a REIT. (See Chapter 8 for a more detailed discussion of the role of life insurance companies as a source of investment funds for REITs.)

Short- to intermediate-term lenders, on the other hand, typically include commercial banks, thrifts, and nonbank lenders, who usually finance their own balance sheets with short-term funds. Their sources of funds and investment objectives are shorter-term. Recently, some investment banks have become active in providing bridge loans and revolving-credit facilities to REITs. Thus the term *banks* can be interpreted fairly broadly. Still, most lenders in this category—institutions providing short-term and intermediate loans—are commercial banks, thrifts, and finance companies, as opposed to mutual funds, investment banks, opportunity funds, and other lenders that make such loans more sporadically.

The Capital Needs of REITs as Businesses

The marketplace for capital and financial services encompasses equity capital, debt capital, interest-rate hedging, cash management, shareholder services, corporate financial advisory services (mergers and acquisitions advice), asset sales and acquisitions, and other services. A REIT's management is concerned with all of these activities in addition to managing, developing, and acquiring assets. Acquiring capital and financial services comprises a major activity in managing REITs.

Today, both management and shareholders view REITs as more than passive investment vehicles for holding real estate asset portfolios. Most REITs are actively managed corporations, designed to maximize shareholder value through active management of existing assets and prudent asset growth. While the term *assets* generally refers to the property owned by a REIT, a broader definition would include employees and information as assets. Commercial lenders who understand this are more likely to be value-adding to REIT management than those who do not. Commercial lenders who focus on one deal at a time may tend to look one-dimensionally at a REIT rather than focusing on what financial products the REIT needs.

One critical element in maximizing shareholder value for any company is successfully managing the company's capital structure. This vital and continual process enables REIT management to develop the company and maximize cash flow per share. As any REIT goes through different growth stages and as the debt and equity markets move through their cycles, management must continually adjust both the firm's capital structure and its capital sources, an activity as important as adjusting the firm's property ownership to changes in the marketplace. Through the adjustment process, management can anticipate and proactively deal with changes in the availability, cost, and other characteristics of capital. This process requires long-term plans to change the characteristics of the REIT's capital structure, such as lowering its overall cost of capital or achieving an investment-grade credit rating. Again, commercial lenders who understand this will be more valuable to a REIT through the business and capital market cycles.

Managing the capital structure requires choosing the appropriate providers of debt and equity capital and the appropriate type of capital. Since most REIT managers will employ debt in their capital structure, understanding the debt marketplace will help them define the role commercial lenders can play in REIT management.

REITs AND THE PUBLIC AND PRIVATE DEBT MARKETS

REIT management must also understand what motivates their prospective debt providers and what specific products they offer. These entities act as prospective financial partners in the constantly changing capital markets. These lenders, in many cases, view their prospective dealings with a REIT as a partnership. By understanding these prospective partners, REIT management can much more effectively focus on the right lenders, with the right products, at the right times. When REIT management considers its lenders as stakeholders in the firm, a more productive relationship with those lenders can develop; lenders share a real interest in a REIT's success with the REIT's shareholders.

The Public Debt Market

Debt comes from two broad marketplaces. The first is the public debt market. It is registered with the Securities and Exchange Commission and is generally sold on the open market. Underwriters take the debt issuer through the underwriting process and either commit to take the debt at specific terms or sell the debt on a best-efforts basis. This debt can be raised through bonds, medium-term notes, commercial paper, or commercial mortgage-backed securities. Underwriters can be investment banks or the investment banking subsidiaries of commercial banks.

The Private Debt Market

The second marketplace is the private debt market. This market differs from the public market in several respects:

1. The debt does not need to be registered.
2. The debt is typically placed with only one or a small number of lenders by a placement agent who does not commit to take the debt at specific terms. In some cases, the borrower may be dealing directly with a potential lender with no placement agent involved.
3. This market involves direct negotiation with the ultimate lenders.
4. Private means private. The terms of the debt are not disclosed to the marketplace unless both parties wish them to be.
5. This debt is issued on a one-time-only basis as opposed to medium-term notes and commercial paper, which are "continuously offered."

Commercial banks, mortgage bankers, and investment banks can serve as placement agents. In most cases, life insurance companies, pension funds, commercial banks, thrifts, and finance companies are the ultimate investors in this type of debt. The private debt market also includes secured and unsecured lines of credit from commercial banks, thrifts, finance companies, and investment banks as well as bridge financings, acquisition financings, and term loans.

THE EMERGING ROLE OF COMMERCIAL LENDERS

Today, REITs benefit from renewed interest by commercial lenders in providing debt to this industry. The commercial lenders now have a vibrant, modestly leveraged ownership format characterizing the REITs they do business with. In 1991, banks provided fewer than 20 significant credit facilities to REITs. Institutional lenders provided debt in the form of mortgage debt. The relatively small number of REITs that existed in 1991 had experienced limited asset growth in the 1980s as debt and equity capital flowed to different entities in the private sector due to both tax laws and the continuing neglect of REITs. Only a handful of REITs could access the public debt markets by 1991, and few commercial lenders called on REITs. At this point, many commercial lenders had greatly reduced their real estate lending. Some commercial lender real estate departments virtually disappeared. At the same time, enormous amounts of the existing real estate debt had to be refinanced. Who was going to do it?

In late 1991, Wall Street rediscovered and reinvented REITs. The Resolution Trust Company and Wall Street pioneered the securitization of real estate debt, which in turn led to the securitization of real estate equity. REITs provided the only credible entity that retained some of the traditional tax advantages. However, most real estate owners could not stand the immediate tax hit from selling their assets to the public well above book value. The development and exploitation of the umbrella partnership structure in the ensuing four years allowed more private owners to securitize their equity and deleverage at the same time. The UPREIT "twist" allowed a new beginning for many real estate owners.

As the public debt and equity markets accepted these REITs, the commercial lenders took note. Lending officers, previously contemplating new careers outside of real estate, suddenly could point to public market acceptance of real estate. It gave hope to banks and institutional lenders. In the bargain, these lenders would also get lower leveraged loans. Also, REITs were public companies with greater disclosure requirements, and thus many other pairs of eyes were watching their moves. And finally, these prospective new REIT customers were companies with a greater need for a full range of financial services.

At year-end 1995, over 75 banks were offering credit facilities to REITs. Through direct long-term mortgage financings, purchases of commercial mortgage-backed securities, and purchases of bonds, institutional lenders furnished long-term debt to the capital structure of many REITs. In the process, short-term bank financings were replaced by these longer-term debt sources. Also, as 1994 ended, REIT management increasingly took advantage of institutional lenders' rising appetites for debt and the capital markets' declining appetite for REIT equity. During 1995 and 1996, REITs role in the debt market grew significantly. REITs issued all manner of public and private debt, much of it only imagined a few years earlier.

Commercial lenders had significantly boosted their own equity capital levels in the early 1990s, and after incurring the cost of real estate write-offs, needed to find loans to produce a suitable return on that equity. This need was greater than it otherwise would have been because these same commercial lenders had significantly reduced their real estate loans in the early 1990s. As noted earlier, the REIT world presented opportunities to lend on more conservative loan structures than in the late 1980s. Loan pricing was also much higher than in the 1980s. In short, a major correction in the supply and demand for bank financing in real estate allowed the resurgence in commercial lenders' involvement in REITs and other real estate lending. Also, for those banks that provided a range of banking services beyond loans (for example, cash management, debt placement, interest-rate hedging products, debt underwriting, and shareholder services), REITs looked more and more like customers they could market multiple products and services to.

With institutional lenders, two interesting and very important developments have significant consequences for the capital flows to real estate in the future. First, total equity capitalization of the REIT universe has risen dramatically, as have the number of individual REITs with over $500 million in equity capitalization. Second, rating agencies increasingly assign investment grades to the debt of real estate companies as well as secured packages of real estate assets. These two developments have led to rapid growth in rated debt issues that are outstanding and trading in the marketplace. This deepening market for securitized real estate equity and investment-grade debt addresses the issues of investment liquidity and pricing, issues that caused the exodus of institutional lenders from real estate investment in the early 1990s.

INSTITUTIONAL LENDERS

Since Chapter 8 provides a detailed perspective on the financing roles of institutional lenders, this section will briefly discuss their loan products, expanding investment horizons, and importance to REITs. While the focus here is on the debt side of the equation, it is important to note the growing role for institutional lenders as equity investors in REITs. Increasingly, institutional lenders have both debt and equity perspectives on capital structure decisions.

Most institutional lenders have long-term investment horizons. REIT management must also consider the evolution taking place in institutional lenders' views of real estate debt. The securitization of real estate debt and equity and the development of investment-grade secured and unsecured real estate debt significantly affects how institutional lenders think about real estate investment. The traditional relationship between an institutional lender and a real estate borrower now can develop in different ways for REITs, as a special class of real estate borrower, due to the increased capital-raising options available to REITs. Today, institutional lenders have three primary types of loan structures to offer REITs:

- Traditional mortgages
- Commercial mortgage-backed securities (CMBSs)
- Unsecured term debt

REIT management, based on prior dealings with institutional funds as providers of secured mortgage financing, may think of relationships with institutional funds only in one dimension. And public unsecured debt, by the nature of the public underwriting and sales process, seems to have less of a relationship orientation. When institutions invest in such debt, they may be more passive than when they fund mortgage loans or invest in private unsecured debt. Often the decision to buy or not buy a public debt issue is based on pricing and investment guidelines. However, managers of REITs should develop broad relationships with institutional lenders. It would be a mistake not to consider all the investment capabilities of these sources of funds.

In practice, this may mean that REIT customers will access one area at an institutional lender for CMBSs and will access another area for rated unsecured debt. Ultimately, institutional lenders will hold the majority of long-term, real estate debt dollars in one form or another. Institutional lenders also provide a major source of equity for real estate. Establishing relationships with institutional lenders on the debt side can offer an entry to the equity side and vice versa. Understanding the changing motivations of institutional lenders can enable REIT management to work more effectively and efficiently in matching and timing the debt requirements of their company with the investment requirements of the institutional lenders. Following is a discussion of the three types of loan structures that institutional lenders offer REITs.

Traditional Mortgage Financing

Because of their investment horizons and objectives, institutional lenders typically prefer long-term fixed-rate debt. Historically, most institutional lenders have only invested in mortgage debt with respect to REITs and other real estate owners. They have done this through the real estate side of their organizations, viewing this mortgage debt, for a variety of reasons, as a unique investment type. Until recently, most of this debt was done one property at a time, secured by a mortgage on a single property.

With the development of the commercial mortgage-backed security (discussed below), institutional lenders and other mortgage lenders have had to expand their investments to deal with rated, multitranched notes secured by mortgages on multiple properties. However, traditional mortgage financings still dominate real estate financing, and thus traditional mortgage debt represents a deep and efficient market for REITs to tap when it fits their financial objectives. Following is a discussion of the advantages and disadvantages of a REIT's using traditional mortgage financing.

Depending on a REITs perspective, such financing offers several advantages:

1. It eliminates interest risk since it is typically fixed-rate.
2. It is usually long-term and thus matches the long-term nature of REIT assets.
3. It has loan-to-value ratios that are often higher than those obtainable from banks.
4. It permits REITs to obtain higher overall leverage in their capital structures.
5. It involves debt that is often nonrecourse or limited recourse to the REIT and its subsidiaries and affiliates.
6. It entails few or no financial covenants that can adversely affect the REIT or its subsidiaries and affiliates.

In addition, institutional lenders will finance joint venture assets with such financings, and the product is well-developed with a deep lender pool.

Again, depending on a REIT's perspective, the disadvantages fall principally in two general categories, those affecting the firm's financial flexibility and asset-management flexibility. Such financing has several disadvantages:

1. The mortgage often has some amortization, and this drain on cash flow can create strains on meeting dividend payments for a REIT that is using primarily mortgage debt for leverage. (There may be no easy way to raise replacement debt for this amortization, although the development of bank lines of credit can moderate this disadvantage.)
2. Stiff prepayment penalties exist, reducing refinancing flexibility and the ability to sell secured properties.
3. It encumbers assets, often a negative with rating agencies when they are considering giving a rating for unsecured debt.

4. Secured debt is disliked by unsecured lenders and may inhibit a REIT's access to unsecured loans.
5. Documentation is heavy and can consume much of the REIT's finance staff's time.
6. The lender often has approval rights with respect to leasing, redevelopment, and most other actions that might affect properties serving as collateral.

Commercial Mortgage-Backed Securities

This product is similar to traditional long-term mortgage financing in the sense that such securities are ultimately secured by mortgages on properties. However, a special, bankruptcy-remote legal entity is established to hold the properties. The institutional lender lends to that entity on a stand-alone basis and seldom looks to any other entity for required transaction support. These transactions may be highly structured with full, partial, or no cross-collateralization of the underlying properties. The transactions are often tranched to meet the objectives of both the REIT and institutional lenders. Mutual funds, banks, mortgage REITs, and special purpose funds may all invest with institutional lenders in a given CMBS.

The development of the CMBS market, with respect to the evolution in thinking by the rating agencies, the creativity of Wall Street, and the growth of investors in real estate debt, has created more options for REIT management when considering secured financing. REIT management should note that institutional lenders and banks invest in these securities as well as underwrite and service them. A bank or institutional lender that understands these securities can better advise a REIT positioning itself to issue a CMBS.

Many advantages of a CMBS can become disadvantages depending on whether the security structure was dictated more by the REIT or by a marketplace that is not aligned with the types of debt the REIT desires. CMBS issues may have tranches with varying maturities, with some tranches at fixed interest rates and others floating. How these tranches match up with a REIT's needs can determine the advantages or disadvantages of the structure.

One clear advantage the CMBS offers is that the REIT gains a pricing benefit by offering investors a rated security that typically spreads the benefits of risk diversification across many properties. Pricing based on the weighted all-in spread over U.S. Treasury notes of comparable average term may accomplish more than a series of individual mortgage financings. Also, CMBS issues allow the REIT to put higher leverage on a group of assets than might be obtained with a series of individual mortgage financings. This benefit results from investors who will purchase junior, noninvestment-grade tranches of CMBS issues, drawing comfort from how such junior tranches have performed in the past few years. The CMBS also allows tranches to be structured to meet market demand for particular maturities, ratings, and fixed- or floating-rate debt.

The disadvantages of the CMBS are as follows:

1. Extensive documentation.
2. Limited flexibility in adding and removing assets from the collateral pool.
3. Restrictions on prepayment.
4. Long execution time.
5. Dislike by the rating agencies with respect to rating unsecured debt.
6. Dislike by unsecured lenders.
7. The size of CMBS issues, which tend to be large relative to other individual loans of a REIT, lumping a disproportionate amount of refinancing risk into one product and one time.

Unsecured Term Debt: Private and Public

This type of loan product is typically available to REITs with investment-grade ratings from one or more rating agencies, or a National Association of Insurance Commissioners (NAIC) rating of 2 or better. It can be fixed-rate or floating-rate.

Privately Placed Unsecured Term Debt

The principal investors for this type of debt are institutional lenders. Banks will occasionally enter this market, but banks typically focus on floating-rate debt with maturities of five years or less. Bond mutual fund managers might also invest in the product but will typically prefer publicly issued, investment-grade debt. This debt can be privately placed with or without some type of debt rating, though having the equivalent of a Standard and Poor's rating of BBB– increases both the number of potential institutional lenders that may invest and moves the pricing and covenants much closer to what can be achieved in a public, investment-grade debt issue. In a private placement, the institutional lender will be even more thorough in underwriting the REIT and have covenants unique to particular REIT characteristics. In a private placement, the institutional lender becomes more of a partner. Institutional lenders can act directly in providing this debt through a private placement arranged by a placement agent or directly solicited and negotiated by an institutional lender.

Why would a REIT issue private term debt? In some cases, where a REIT is six months to a year away from obtaining the necessary ratings for issuing public debt, there may be an immediate need for capital. Management, if it plans to become an issuer of investment-grade, unsecured debt, may not wish to pursue secured debt. Since some institutional lenders invest in both secured and unsecured REIT paper, REIT management can sometimes convince an institutional lender already knowledgeable about the REIT that an unsecured, private debt issue with appropriate covenant protections does not pose much more risk than a secured loan. Also, management can argue that the unsecured private debt helps improve the chances of obtaining an investment-grade rating. And when such a rating is obtained, the value of the private debt being held by the institutional lender will likely increase.

Sometimes a REIT will issue private term debt because it obtains an investment-grade rating from only one rating agency or it gets a split rating: One or more agencies gives it investment grade, and one or more rates it below investment grade. The REIT's debt underwriters may not advise a public issue since the downside of an unsuccessful public issue is probably greater than the downside of an unsuccessful private placement.

When a REIT needs less that $100 million in financing and does not have a medium-term note program in place (see below for a discussion of this type of financing), a private placement may make sense. REIT management and the placement agent can focus their time and effort on institutional lenders whom they know have the interest and capacity for debt in the below $100 million range.

Public Unsecured Term Debt

In exchange for maintaining the lower leverage and higher debt service coverage requirements of obtaining an investment-grade rating, a REIT gains considerable advantages with public unsecured debt. The investor base for this debt extends beyond just the traditional institutional lenders. Today, the debt can be issued at virtually any maturity from 2 to 15 years, through either individual bond underwritings or on a virtually continuous basis through a medium-term note program. The debt can be issued as fixed or floating rate. No properties are specifically encumbered, and documentation is minimal.

With few or no properties encumbered, the REIT has much more flexibility in selling assets. Within limits, the REIT can encumber assets should a secured financing become particularly advantageous, such as in a joint venture arrangement. Issuance time is relatively short. The interest spreads over comparable term U.S. Treasury notes are between 50 basis points and 175 basis points for investment-grade rated REITs. On a floating-rate basis, the spreads range from 35 basis points to 125 basis points over LIBOR.

On the negative side, typically three principal covenants come with this type of debt:

1. The REIT must maintain between 1.5 and 1.75 dollars in unencumbered assets for each dollar of unsecured debt.
2. The REIT must maintain a minimum debt service ratio or fixed charge coverage ratio of from 1.5 to 2.0 times.
3. The REIT must maintain some minimum net worth level, typically set somewhere near the REIT's current book net worth.

Some REIT managers may feel that maintaining lower leverage could cause them to forgo growth opportunities that could be financed with higher leverage. Others disagree, in that many of the fastest growing REITs have very low leverage and use equity to finance much of their growth.

BANKS

In a short period of time during this second courtship of commercial lenders and REITs, many banks have undergone a dramatic change in their understanding of the real estate capital markets and the role that banks can and should play for their real estate customers. These banks now realize that REITs, particularly equity REITs, represent the type of customer they seek in their corporate lending departments: a customer that needs many bank services and loan products, a customer whose capital needs are constantly changing, and a customer who values financial flexibility. The material that follows presents the loan products offered by banks and their advantages and disadvantages relative to REITs.

Secured Term Loans: Mortgages

Banks have traditionally offered only two loan products to real estate customers:

1. A mortgage on one or a few properties, for a term of between one and seven or eight years, at a floating interest rate, sometimes fully or partially guaranteed by the customer.
2. A construction loan with a term varying from the time it takes to complete construction to as much as four or five years after construction is finished, requiring a floating rate, with full or partial guarantees, and often, acceptable takeout financing.

Banks still provide these loans, and for some REITs they can make sense. The following are some of the potential advantages of obtaining a secured term loan from a bank:

- Faster execution than from an institutional lender.
- The ability to do both small and large deals.
- Adjustable loan terms.
- No prepayment penalties for most loans since they usually have a floating rate and banks can often underwrite more unusual situations than can a typical institutional lender—such as a property that is undergoing redevelopment. These loans may be nonrecourse to the REIT or operating partnership (in the case of an UPREIT), or they may be partial or full recourse.

One disadvantage of any secured bank loan is that many banks must comply with regulatory guidelines that can add costs (such as appraisals) and time. However, some banks (realizing the broad definition of *bank)* do not have such regulatory considerations. Another disadvantage is that banks do not typically wish to lend longer than five years. Also, most banks are floating-rate lenders, so if the REIT wants fixed-rate debt, it will need to execute an interest-rate swap. This can be problematic for some REIT managers who may not have the credit credentials to obtain an unsecured swap and may not wish to pledge other collateral to obtain the swap.

Depending on REIT management's perspective, another possible disadvantage of these loans is that sometimes they may carry amortization requirements. This can pose difficulty for some REITs and may conflict with, or at least make more difficult, the execution of their strategies for managing debt levels, average debt maturities, and in some cases, dividend policies.

As banks approach more traditional advance rates (loan-to-value ratios) in their secured lending, some REITs may find it advantageous to place more leverage on fewer assets, freeing some assets from secured debt. The trade-off may be somewhat higher loan interest rates against lower transaction costs. Additionally, the REIT has more unencumbered assets available.

Some REITs, as they become unsecured borrowers, can employ this strategy since rating agencies are particularly sensitive to assets being encumbered by mortgages. Rating agencies see a clear difference between two REITs with identical leverage but where the less-favored REIT has more of its assets secured than the other.

The ability to prepay these bank-secured loans with no or little penalty also means that REIT management can "warehouse" debt capital, waiting until one of the following takes place:

1. Enough has been accumulated to refinance in a CMBS.
2. A window in the equity market opens, allowing repayment of the debt.
3. A desired unsecured debt rating comes through, allowing the REIT to refinance the secured debt with unsecured debt.

For most banks, these loans are not long-term, and a REIT that accumulates a large percentage of its debt in such loans may create potential problems as large amounts of debt may mature in relatively constricted time frames. Many banks, while desiring to make these loans, view an overreliance on such loans by a REIT as poor financial management.

With regard to construction loans, the following points can be made. REITs that are active developers often need to finance development projects with construction loans in cases where their revolving-credit facilities either cannot provide the financing or where management does not wish to use the revolving-credit facility for such purposes. Some revolving-credit facilities may even prohibit their being used for development financing, though this limitation is somewhat archaic today. In other cases, a REIT may be developing in the form of a joint venture and either chooses not to or cannot borrow directly for the benefit of the venture. In such cases, a bank may provide the REIT a separate construction loan on a limited recourse basis. In some cases, such loans may be completely nonrecourse.

The underwriting guidelines for construction loans today are more conservative than in the 1980s. However, given the target leverage for most REITs, the advance rates likely requested by most REITs fall well within the range acceptable to most banks. REIT management should keep in mind, however, that many lenders will have a problem funding an advance rate on a development project dramatically higher than the overall leverage of the REIT.

Secured Revolving-Credit Facilities

This loan product is one of the critical developments in REIT lending. It can serve all of the purposes that the traditional bank secured loans serve, with one main difference. These facilities permit the REIT to borrow, repay, and reborrow during the facility's term.

This product has reacquainted banks with REITs in the early 1990s. These facilities, while somewhat complex to underwrite and administer, offer the banks a diversified collateral pool, which is typically cross-collateralized. Additionally, these credit facilities are usually full recourse to the REIT, and there are financial covenants applicable to both the collateral pool and the REIT itself. In exchange for providing a collateral pool, the REIT gains the flexibility, in most cases, of being allowed to add and remove assets from the collateral pool. This is the greatest benefit of the secured revolving facilities. The flexibility of being able to remove assets, sometimes subject to certain constraints, allows REIT management to more effectively take better advantage of capital-raising opportunities, both debt and equity. A REIT's management may desire to reduce the outstanding balance under the revolving credit facility with proceeds from an equity issue or a debt issue unrelated to the assets in the collateral pool. Given such a reduction in borrowings under the revolving-credit facility, management may decide that it no longer wishes to "tie up" as many assets.

In this type of revolving credit, it is important to understand the difference between the commitment amount and what is often referred to as the borrowing base. The commitment amount is the maximum amount that the REIT could borrow if it provided sufficient collateral. The borrowing base is the amount that the REIT can borrow at any given time based on the collateral currently available and the advance rate (the percentage factor to be multiplied times the value of the collateral).

As an example, a REIT could have a $50 million commitment for its revolving-credit facility with an advance rate of 50 percent. Thus, if the REIT had $100 million in collateral, it could borrow the full commitment amount. Assume that the facility is fully borrowed because over a six-month period the REIT used the credit facility, in combination with equity raised from a past stock offering, to acquire properties. Also assume that REIT management had a strategy in place that once it accumulated $75 million in new assets it would seek to place long-term financing on those assets at a loan-to-value of ratio of 66.7 percent. At the time of closing, the REIT takes the $50 million raised from the new long-term financing, repays the revolving credit outstandings, and releases the $75 million in properties to the new lender. When it does so, it still will have a commitment amount of $50 million under its revolving-credit facility; however, its borrowing base—the amount it can borrow—will have been reduced to $12.5 million ($25 million in properties remaining multiplied times the advance rate of 50 percent). Should the REIT now wish to acquire properties relying only on the revolving-credit facility, it could purchase $12.5 million of properties. If it placed these properties in the collateral pool, it would then have $37.5 million in properties, creating a borrowing base of $18.75 million (50 percent multiplied by $37.5 million). With $12.5 million already borrowed, the REIT has $6.25 million available for further purchases. While this bootstrap process could theoretically continue, a REIT might have trouble finding small enough properties for it to effectively continue to use the facility.

Prior to the exploitation of this credit product, REITs often would issue equity and hold cash while frantically searching for assets to acquire. When interest rates or short-term investments were closer to dividend yields, this strategy was feasible. However, in low interest-rate environments, this strategy was undesirable. The secured revolving-credit facility allows REIT management, at an acceptable cost, to avoid parking idle cash on the balance sheet and to avoid excessive pressure to act too rapidly in making property acquisitions.

The price of this "liquidity" is the up-front loan fee in the revolving credit facility and the unused commitment fee. Banks charge these fees because they must earn a return on the capital allocated to their loan commitments. REIT management must determine the value of having this "liquidity" and the certainty of knowing that the commitment exists and is in place. A REIT that assumes it can always get financing when an actual need arises takes a big risk in order to avoid paying the insurance premium for "liquidity." Most major corporations choose to pay for this financial insurance by always having revolving-credit facilities in place. Many REITs began with secured revolving-credit facilities and then developed these facilities into the next product: unsecured revolving-credit facilities.

Unsecured Revolving-Credit Facilities

There are several advantages to a REIT's having an unsecured revolving-credit facility. The REIT never needs to get approval from its lenders to admit or release a property to the borrowing base, never needs to get approval on a new lease, never needs to get a mortgage or pay legal and recording costs associated with secured lending, and seldom needs to provide extensive operating statements property by property to lenders. Until 1994, there were few REITs that had experienced this facility. Today, a growing number of banks are comfortable with such lending. Many of these same banks said they would never do such lending, yet now they are. REIT management must understand this change, which will be briefly discussed before exploring unsecured revolvers.

Many bank real estate departments, particularly the largest banks most active in real estate lending in the 1980s, have undergone a painful education about the capital markets and real estate. These banks have learned the importance of liquidity in an industry that historically had illiquid assets. Instead of betting on future appreciation or future cash flow, they recognize the importance of today's cash flow. They understand the variability of debt and equity capital sources as well as the risks of putting large loan amounts against single properties. They have learned about the risks of insufficient financial disclosure. They clearly differentiate between professional real estate management and speculative development. In short, many banks see that the more a real estate customer operates like a corporation, the more the risks will diminish and the more they can comfortably provide credit products to those real estate customers.

Most REITs are now managed like corporations. For knowledgeable banks, a REIT's tax status works well for a real estate company. Because the public equity market appears to favor it, many real estate companies have chosen to take this tax election in the 1990s. Banks prefer dealing with professional management in a corporate format.

When banks see rating agencies and public debt markets endorse a REIT and its management, the banks become comfortable providing unsecured credit facilities. In fact, many banks also provide such unsecured facilities to REITs that do not yet have investment-grade ratings. In these instances, they see REIT's management as moving the REIT toward receiving an investment-grade rating as the REIT already has met many of the necessary characteristics.

Unsecured revolving credit facilities to REITs have few differences from general corporate revolvers. The fundamental characteristics can be generalized as follows:

1. The term is seldom over five years, with three years being typical.
2. The interest rate is typically quoted as a spread over LIBOR, with various LIBOR maturities available.
3. The spread over LIBOR may vary as the REIT's debt rating or some other credit risk measure changes.
4. An up-front fee is paid at the closing of the facility.
5. An unused commitment fee is typically paid quarterly on the average unused amount of the facility during the quarter.
6. Financial covenants addressing interest coverage by some measure of cash flow, such as earnings before interest, taxes, and depreciation (EBITDA), are standard.
7. Leverage covenants measured using either book value or market value of assets are standard.
8. Minimum book net worth covenants are standard.
9. A minimum level of unencumbered assets relative to total unsecured debt is standard.

10. Other covenants specific to a given REIT, dealing with things such as the level of development assets or specialization in the ownership of certain property types, may exist.

REIT management must remember that, with respect to unsecured revolvers, banks' real estate departments (where lending to REITs is usually conducted) have ready access to the vast corporate lending experiences of other bank executives. Most real estate lenders at such banks are learning about unsecured lending at much the same time that REIT management is obtaining such knowledge. The loan characteristics of unsecured revolvers to REITs are quickly incorporating the characteristics found in general corporate revolvers. Of course, industry-specific considerations exist in such revolvers, and the REIT industry's revolvers carry some of these specifically crafted covenants. A prime example is the unencumbered asset covenant (number 9 above). REIT management must recognize that when a bank provides an unsecured revolving-credit facility, dozens of unsecured facilities exist that the REIT's facility can be compared with within that bank. The unsecured lending market is very efficient, and a mispriced or improperly structured credit facility will stand out clearly when reviewed against the backdrop of dozens of similar facilities. Bank credit approvers have few rationales for giving a REIT better covenants than other unsecured customers, particularly given the recent experience of most lenders with real estate lending.

Other Financial Products

Commercial lenders, particularly banks, offer REIT management a number of other products that help REITs manage their debt. When a commercial lender understands a REIT's strategic objectives, particularly regarding managing its capital needs and its capital structure, it can better anticipate which other financial products might help a REIT's management meet its objectives. Following is a discussion of a number of other financial products.

Interest-Rate Swaps

Commercial lenders, as well as some other institutions, actively provide interest-rate swaps. These swaps enable management to change the characteristics of existing debt or can be put in place as hedges against debt yet to be issued. Generally, most REITs are concerned with converting their floating-rate debt, or a portion of that debt, to fixed-rate debt if certain hurdle rates can be achieved. Many REITs believe that real estate held for the long term should be financed with fixed-rate debt. Also, managing FFO is easier when less of a REIT's debt carries a floating rate. Fixed-rate debt can be converted to floating-rate debt with reverse swaps in those cases where REIT management may wish to have more floating-rate debt on its balance sheet. Commercial lenders, particularly banks, are a logical place for REITs to look for swaps. These swaps might be secured or unsecured, depending on the credit characteristics of the REIT. Many lenders desire this additional business as part of a broader relationship with a REIT.

Interest-Rate Caps, Floors, and Collars

Similar to swaps, these financial instruments provide additional options for a REIT to manage its interest-rate profile. Again, banks in particular actively provide these financial instruments, and in their relationship with a REIT, they expect to bid on this business as part of that relationship.

Bridge and Acquisition Financing

Sometimes REITs require unusual financings: the turnaround time is short and the ultimate source of repayment for financing may be a subsequent debt and/or equity offering. The requirements of bridge and acquisition financings are often outside the lender's normal underwriting guidelines. Commercial lenders, particularly banks, are the primary providers of such facilities. Investment banks also actively provide these facilities. Having a well-established relationship with commercial lenders makes it much easier for these lenders to respond to these often large financing requests where minimal new information may be available and a commitment is needed quickly. REITs enjoying established relationships with commercial lenders may have competitive advantages over REITs that do not.

CHOOSING COMMERCIAL LENDERS

REITs evolve over time, changing in size, capital structure, geographic focus, property type, joint venture activities, and acquisition criteria. The commercial lenders a REIT selects may well change over time if the REIT is to obtain the best products for any given point in its evolution. The decision about choosing the appropriate commercial lenders falls into roughly three stages in the life cycle of most REITs.

During the first stage, the REIT has limited needs. Local or regional commercial lenders, particularly banks, are adequate. The REIT needs lenders that can provide secured financing against single or multiple assets in modest amounts. The REIT is not yet as focused on what its ideal capital structure might be since it is too soon to know its full development potential. Management may have time to deal with several commercial lenders. REIT management may choose commercial lenders according to opportunistic considerations or previous relationships with lenders. Floating-rate debt is often dominant, and shorter-term debt is acceptable because management wants the flexibility to reposition the capital structure as the REIT grows and more financing and equity-raising options become available to the REIT.

REITs don't have many options in the capital markets at this stage; the alternatives are equity, bank debt, or permanent mortgages from institutional lenders. Few commercial lenders will know of the REIT, and because the REIT is likely to be small, the lenders may have limited interest in establishing a relationship. So, in stage one, REIT management often must be more opportunistic than calculating in choosing commercial lenders.

The next stage in a REIT's life—when it has between $250 million and $500 million in total market capitalization—is critical. The selection of commercial lenders involves many more considerations at this stage. Lending capacity; speed of execution; flexibility; unsecured lending capacity; interest-rate hedging capabilities; the ability to provide financial advice; the ability to underwrite large dollar amounts for revolvers, acquisitions, or to bridge facilities; and the ability to syndicate loans with an appropriate group of lenders are all important considerations in commercial lender selection. In stage one, banks tend to dominate. In stage two, while banks may dominate, institutional lenders can participate in a more significant way because a REIT may now begin to implement a more long-term capital structure plan that incorporates longer-term debt, either secured or unsecured. The choice of commercial lenders begins to reflect the REIT's characteristics. Just as a REIT may expand from dealing with regional investment banks to large investment banks as their need for capacity and sophisticated financial advice grows, larger and/or more sophisticated commercial lenders will enable them to expand their banking relationships.

In the third stage, REITs have many choices available. For debt capital, REITs increasingly rely on the institutional lenders, directly or indirectly, through pooled mortgage financings, CMBS issues, and public and private unsecured debt. Banks become the principal providers of working capital/acquisition facilities and bridge loans. As a REIT deals with larger commercial lenders, the lines become more blurred with respect to accessing the broader debt markets through financial institutions such as banks, institutional lenders, and investment banks. Some institutional lenders own investment banks. Many banks do investment banking. Increasingly, many investment banks provide revolvers, acquisition, and bridge loan facilities to REITs. REIT management must often choose from a bewildering array of financial service providers.

Consequently, REIT management should consider the following list of desirable qualities when selecting commercial lenders as financial service providers:

1. Commitment to and understanding of the REIT industry.
2. Financial capacity—based both on their own assets and the ability to facilitate access to the assets of other commercial lenders.
3. Financial sophistication—understanding the capital markets and ability to advise management on developments in the capital markets.
4. Flexibility and speed of execution.
5. Quality of the frontline people that REIT management must deal with on a regular basis.
6. Depth and width of financial services and products that the commercial lender can deliver to the REIT.
7. Reputation of the commercial lender in the broad marketplace.
8. Vulnerability of the commercial lender to abrupt changes in policy due to events such as acquisition by another commercial lender, pending changes in business lines, or financial difficulties.
9. Ability to create and deliver new financial products and services as the evolution of the REIT industry continues.

As the REIT industry reaches maturation, perhaps sometime in the next few years, additional considerations may become important in selecting commercial lenders. However, the most qualified commercial lenders and their REIT customers will understand that successfully evolving to meet the changing competitive marketplace will distinguish those who thrive from those who simply survive.

MANAGING RELATIONSHIPS WITH COMMERCIAL LENDERS

The following are seven simple considerations that should help REITs enjoy a fruitful relationship with any commercial lender:

1. Remember that the commercial lender is in business for its shareholders, just as the REIT is. It is motivated by profit potential with a REIT.
2. Understand the strengths and weakness of the commercial lender. Be honest with the lender about where there are good fits and opportunities for business. Don't push a lender to do something that is too far outside its capabilities or policies.
3. Help educate your commercial lender about your business and your strategies.
4. Communicate frequently with your commercial lender.
5. Meet senior management of the commercial lender if possible. Deepen your contacts at the lender beyond the relationship banker.
6. Make your commercial lender feel like a partner in your business, not a passive investor.
7. Don't burn bridges. The commercial lending industry is a consolidating industry. The commercial lender that a REIT management treats harshly today may acquire a commercial lender tomorrow that the REIT wants to have a good relationship with.

CONCLUDING OBSERVATIONS

The REIT industry has enjoyed a renaissance in the last decade. However, more than once in the past 20 years, commercial lenders and the real estate industry, including REITs, have managed to produce a boom-and-bust cycle almost unrivaled by any other industry. If, together, REITs and their commercial lenders are to expand beyond this current renaissance, they must incorporate the lessons learned so painfully in the past.

Perhaps the next few years will tell if the relationship between REITs and commercial lenders has evolved to a new level of mutual understanding that will lead to a long and profitable relationship.

CHAPTER

8

LIFE INSURANCE COMPANIES' INVESTMENTS IN REITs

Eugene R. Skaggs, *Vice President, The Northwestern Mutual Life Insurance Company*
Robert M. Ruess, *Vice President, The Northwestern Mutual Life Insurance Company*
Richard T. Garrigan, *Professor of Finance, Kellstadt Graduate School of Business, DePaul University*

This chapter provides broad perspectives on life insurance companies' investments in REITs. The material has been organized into six sections. An introductory section provides an overview of recent life insurance company (LIC) real estate investment patterns. This material is followed by a discussion of the impact of both rating agencies and regulators on real estate investment by LICs. Next, the concept of four-quadrant investing is briefly considered prior to a detailed discussion of the role of LICs in providing debt capital to REITs. A companion section then considers both the objectives and forms of REIT equity investments by LICs.

INSURANCE COMPANY INVESTMENT PATTERNS

Real estate in the form of both mortgage loans and real estate equities has been a major type of investment for LICs throughout the entire 20th century. For example, mortgage loan investments accounted for about one-third of LIC assets in 1920, with real estate equities accounting for an additional 2 percent. Since then, the proportion of real estate in the typical life insurance company portfolio has gradually declined to its current level of approximately 14 percent, with mortgage loans at 11 percent and equities at 3 percent. These figures do not include real estate investments made either through partnerships or stock ownership. Such investments are considered miscellaneous assets under LIC statutory reporting criteria.

Historically, the sources of most LIC investment funds were their internal, or general, accounts. LICs acted as principals, and thus their real estate and other investments were held as long-term assets for the benefit of policy owners. However, in the 1970s, several major life insurance companies formed REITs to attract third-party capital through the public markets. Their motive was typically to access additional sources of capital to level out the impact of the credit cycle on their investible funds and to add to their profitability by serving as investment managers. Most of the REITs sponsored by LICs during this period were mortgage loan investment oriented. The equity component of their investments typically was fairly minor. Due to the inflation and higher interest rates that characterized the late 1970s and early 1980s, these fixed-income-oriented REITs typically did not fare well from a stock price standpoint. Most were subsequently bought back by their sponsors or liquidated.

During the latter half of the 1970s, several large LICs established commingled real estate separate accounts. These actions were motivated by the desire to attract third-party capital in order to generate income in the form of investment management fees. The trend of LICs acting as investment managers accelerated throughout the 1980s and into the 1990s to the point where the majority of funds for real estate investments at many of the large LICs came from third-party sources, namely public and private pension funds, rather than being generated internally through these firms' general accounts.

As noted above, LICs were very active as both lenders and equity investors in real estate in the 1980s. Capital sources grew significantly during this period, not only from their traditional product lines, but also through the sale of GICs (guaranteed investment contracts). Much of this capital was directed toward mortgage lending activities because they provided the level of financial returns required on the product lines being marketed. This substantial flow of capital led many companies to invest heavily in mortgage loans. With commercial banks aggressively pursuing mortgage lending during the same time frame, the market became extremely competitive, which resulted in the overleveraging of many real estate projects. Many life insurance companies increased their real estate investment portfolios (mortgage loans and equities) to levels in excess of 30 percent, with some exceeding 40 percent. The economic downturn that began in 1990, coupled with the excessive overbuilding that occurred in the 1980s, led to a major downward adjustment in real estate values.

It is important to distinguish the source of LIC capital for purposes of addressing LICs' investments in REITs. To the extent that such companies are acting merely as investment managers, their characteristics do not differ notably from those of other investment managers, such as pension fund investment advisers or mutual funds. In the material that follows, the primary focus will be on LICs' investments as principals, using their general account funds as the source of capital for investing in REITs.

IMPACT OF RATING AGENCIES AND REGULATORS

Rising delinquencies, foreclosures, and restructured loans were the natural result of the real estate recession of the early 1990s. Such real estate problems became the focus of the rating agencies, with the result that many life insurance companies experienced downgrades of their credit ratings. Consequently, several of these firms were forced to cease their real estate and mortgage lending activities, and a number of LICs securitized their mortgage portfolios in order to reduce the level of capital required. At the same time, the National Association of Insurance Commissioners (NAIC) instituted new regulatory measures regarding real estate investments in light of the real estate problems that were occurring in many insurance company portfolios. These new regulatory measures included both required asset valuation reserves for mortgage loans and real estate equities, and the institution of risk-based capital (RBC) factors. Asset valuation reserves had previously existed for common stock and bond investments. Such reserves were designed to cushion the valuation fluctuations that occur with publicly traded securities. Under the new regulatory measures, this concept was extended to other assets in the portfolio, including mortgage loans and equity real estate.

The more significant new regulation by the NAIC was the development of RBC factors for the various forms of investment. Through RBCs, NAIC has established capital requirements for each asset type and risk level. These factors, which are presented in Table 8–1, are designed to measure the relationship of an insurance company's surplus relative to the perceived risk in its investment portfolio. These new RBC measures have greatly influenced the allocation of funds to real estate at several firms because the

TABLE 8–1

NAIC Investment Limitation Comparison

Bonds	Rating	Risk-Based Factor
Class one	A or better	0.3%
two	Baa	1.0%
three	Ba	4.0%
four	B	9.0%
five	C	20.0%
six	default	30.0%
Mortgage loans[1]		2.25%
Equity real estate		10.0%
Common stock		
Unaffiliated public		30.0%
Private		30.0%
Other equities[2]		Based on asset nature

[1] The applicable percentage will be adjusted for problem loan experience. A minimum of 1.125 percent can be used if a LIC's delinquency experience is much better than the industry average, while a maximum of 7.875 percent can be required if a LIC has a very adverse delinquency experience.

[2] The RBC factors for rated preferred stock are determined by adding 2 percent to the RBC factors for comparably rated bonds.

RBC factors assigned to real estate related assets were higher relative to other asset categories. Consequently, LICs that had allocated higher proportions of their investment portfolios to mortgage loans and real estate equities were affected most by the new RBC requirements. Many of these firms have subsequently reduced their allocations to real estate, especially in their real estate equity accounts.

As is evident from Table 8–1, REIT common stock investments, which have a 30 percent RBC factor, represent a particularly expensive way to own real estate as compared to outright real estate equity ownership, which has an RBC factor of only 10 percent. This differential in RBC factors in and by itself would likely diminish the appetite of LICs for investing in real estate through the REIT common stock. Additionally, however, LICs do not maintain large common stock portfolios. The typical firm normally holds only 2 to 4 percent of its investments in the form of common stock. A real limit therefore exists on the amount of REIT common stock that can be held in most LIC portfolios because real estate, as a specific industry sector, would likely make up only 5 to 10 percent of all stock held. This point will be considered further when alternative REIT equity investments are evaluated.

FOUR-QUADRANT INVESTING

In this section, major consideration will be given to various means for LICs to invest in REITs. Before considering REIT investments specifically, it is useful to first consider the growing trend for institutional investors to categorize their debt or equity investments within four distinct quadrants. Two of these quadrants consist of either traditional mortgage or real estate equity investments, including joint ventures in the case of the latter. The remaining two quadrants pertain to securitized forms of both debt and equity. REITs can and do use traditional mortgages as a means of raising debt capital. Increasingly, however, REITs provide investment alternatives through the issuance of various kinds of securitized debt. In the case of equity, increasingly REIT shares offer an alternative form of investing to that of direct real estate ownership. Such shares provide investors the opportunity to balance their real estate equity portfolios as to both geographic diversity and property sector. For example, in the retail property sector, regional malls are now owned extensively by publicly traded REITs. Therefore, institutional investors now have the opportunity to broaden their equity portfolios by indirectly acquiring these assets through the selective acquisition of REIT shares.

PROVIDING DEBT CAPITAL TO REITs

In this section, several types of REIT debt will be discussed. First, conventional mortgage debt will be considered, followed by a consideration of various kinds of securitized loans. Next, attention will be given to arrangements whereby secured loans can be changed to unsecured debt. Finally, various types of unsecured debt will be examined.

Traditional Mortgage Loans

The most basic form of REIT debt is the traditional or one-off loan, for which the REIT provides a single property as collateral. Portfolio mortgage loans, on the other hand, arise from the LIC simultaneously funding mortgage debt on a number of properties. In the case of portfolio loans, cross-collateralization exists, whereby each property collateralizes not only its own mortgage debt but also serves as collateral for the mortgage debt on each of the other properties making up the portfolio. Under such an arrangement, REITs seek the right to substitute other properties in the future to permit them to sell individual properties on an unencumbered basis or to refinance them through use of unsecured debt, a bank line, or a commercial mortgage-backed security (CMBS). A typical arrangement might permit the substitution for, say, up to 4 properties out of a portfolio of 10 properties in return for a fee being paid to the LIC. Also, there may be a limit as to how many substitutions may occur in any one year.

Individual or one-off loans are more likely to be made on office buildings and regional mall-type properties because of their larger average size. Multiple or portfolio loans are typically made on numerous apartment or warehouse properties, as these properties tend to be smaller and more commodity-like in their individual characteristics. If a REIT's debt is not rated as investment grade, traditional mortgage debt will generally be the least costly source of financing available, especially in the case of a portfolio. Advantages of traditional mortgage debt include:

1. Cost efficiencies resulting from the terms and related documentation being negotiated for many mortgage loans simultaneously by parties having great familiarity with these transactions.
2. The possibility of greater financial leverage being attained by the REIT due to the advantages of using cross-collateralization.
3. More flexibility as to prepayment or substitution, especially in comparison to using mortgage debt to collateralize a CMBS.
4. Earlier interest rate locks than for a CMBS, say, a 60- to 90-day period between the lock date and the funding date.

On the other hand, there are notable costs involved with such portfolio lending. The environmental report expenses, attorneys fees, and title insurance costs associated with these deals add measurably to the total cost of such funding. Consequently, when the REIT is financing an individual property, it may be advantageous to use unsecured debt, as these costs would not be elements of the financing.

Commercial Mortgage-Backed Securities

Commercial mortgage-backed securities are a growing and important part of the mortgage finance business. These securities come in many forms.

They are both public and private. In the case of a REIT, a bankruptcy-proof subsidiary would be formed to own the real estate to be used as the CMBS collateral. Investment-grade rated securities are rated either Aaa, Aa, A, or Baa. Noninvestment-grade securities carry lower ratings. The CMBS may be secured by a mortgage on a single property or by many mortgages on multiple properties. In the case of a conduit transaction, mortgages issued to a number of unrelated borrowers are combined as collateral for a CMBS. Numerous major commercial bank and investment banking firms are aggressively seeking to originate this product in competition with the traditional mortgage loans. As yet, not much securitization of REIT loans has occurred, and thus REITs are a small part of this market.

The opportunity also exists for a REIT to first obtain traditional mortgage debt from a LIC with the intent to later securitize all or a portion of it, possibly through substitutions. A disadvantage of this arrangement is that the terms and documentation for both types of debt have to be in place at the time the mortgage loans are made.

A variation of this arrangement pertains to converting traditional mortgage financing into unsecured debt where the overall financing requirements of the REIT makes this desirable. Under this process, a LIC would permit a portion of a REIT's traditional mortgage debt to be converted into unsecured debt in order for the REIT to qualify for an investment-grade rating of its debt. For example, if a LIC were financing $125 million of a REIT's traditional mortgage debt, the LIC might permit $50 million to be converted. Upon conversion, the LIC would continue to finance a total of $125 million, but only $75 million would be secured.

Unsecured Debt

Unsecured debt issued by REITs can be either private or public. Private unsecured debt incorporates a negative pledge whereby the REIT borrower typically agrees to own unencumbered real estate in an amount equal to at least one and one-half times its unsecured debt. This arrangement facilitates the debt being funded by a qualified institutional lender, such as a LIC or pension fund. Private unsecured debt takes one of two forms: private negotiated or private 144A, that is, subject to the requirement of Section 144A of the Securities Act of 1933. A major distinction between private and public unsecured debt is that the private unsecured debt has reduced secondary market liquidity. Often a smaller to mid-size REIT creates debt that initially is private but that it intends, upon maturity, to roll over into public debt. Or the REIT might have no rated public debt outstanding, but it wants to create rated debt through issuing private debt for which a rating is obtained. In such cases, the unsecured debt would be a bridge between private and public financing.

The LICs and other institutional lenders typically trade off the lesser liquidity of private unsecured debt for better restrictive covenants and/or a higher interest rate at the time the loan is made. Covenants are of a financial and nonfinancial nature. Financial covenants will generally specify minimum net worth requirements, limitations on secured debt as a percentage of assets, a total debt-to-capitalization ratio, a minimum debt-service coverage requirement, and a minimum unencumbered-assets test. Nonfinancial covenants will generally restrict the level of turnover in a REIT's board of directors, limit changes in control, and deal with key management retention issues.

EQUITY INVESTMENTS IN REITs

As noted above, a RBC factor of 30 percent for common stock together with limitations on the proportion of a LIC's investments that are placed in common stock limit the amount of LIC investment in REIT common stock. The material in this section deals with several different kinds of REIT equity investments, including the operating units of an UPREIT, private or public common stock, and convertible preferred stock. Before considering these forms, however, it is useful to first consider REIT equity-investment objectives.

REIT Equity-Investment Objectives

Four primary objectives to be served through LIC equity investment in REITs include:

1. Attaining liquidity.
2. Facilitating private property exit strategies.
3. Arbitraging against private market property values.
4. Coinvesting with REIT management.

Attaining Liquidity

While the REIT public market remains relatively small by overall market standards, there has been meaningful growth in its market capitalization in recent years. Market values have grown from $8 billion in 1990 to about $100 billion in 1997. REITs, especially those with market capitalizations of $1 billion or more, can provide liquidity not present through direct real estate ownership. There are now 25 REITs with market capitalizations in excess of $1 billion. With the growing size of this market, a real estate investor can now begin to achieve the benefits of liquidity attendant to the public stock market in comparison to the relative lack of liquidity inherent in the private market. This greater liquidity is attractive to institutional investors, including LICs, as it permits them to invest in real estate-based assets that have real-time pricing and permits them to acquire and dispose of such assets on a more timely basis as compared to the ownership of real estate assets in the private market. This objective can be especially important when it is deemed desirable for a LIC to reduce its level of investment in a particular property sector. As the public REIT market continues to grow in size and efficiency, so will the importance of the liquidity factor in asset-allocation decisions.

Facilitating Private Property Exit Strategies

Institutional investors, including LICs, are increasingly concerned about exit strategies when contemplating new real estate investments. With the growth of the REIT public market, REITs have become a major acquirer of privately held real estate assets. Their ability to raise capital on a cost-effective basis through the public markets has made them very competitive.

LICs, along with other institutional investors, now view REITs as being among their most likely targets for providing exit strategies for their privately held real estate assets. In selling a specific property, the highest amount of consideration might be obtained through the LIC's exchanging the property for shares of a REIT whose stock is viewed as an attractive real estate investment. Alternatively, the consideration might be in the form of partnership assets, using a subsidiary partnership of the REIT and the LIC. Or the structure might include some cash in addition to stock in an outright sale. The LIC also might be willing to place some debt on the property in return for fewer shares of stock.

Arbitraging against Private Property Market Values

Pricing of real estate assets in the REIT public market has tended to be a lead indicator of real estate pricing and performance in the private market. This pricing variation has created periodic opportunities to invest in the public market at attractive prices for real estate assets not available in the private market. For example, a regional mall sold as real property might require a capitalization rate of 6 or 7 percent, while the stock of a REIT investing in regional malls might be able to be purchased at an effective capitalization rate of 9 percent. As the REIT market grows and more institutional investors become active in both the public and private real estate markets, the opportunities for such arbitrage will diminish. Likewise, the public market has tended to lead the private market in repricing assets by about 12 to 18 months. As the efficiency of the market improves, the degree to which the public market is a lead indicator to the private market will also diminish.

Coinvesting with REIT Management

One of the reported benefits of investing in REITs is that it provides the institutional investors with an opportunity to, in essence, coinvest with REIT management. Many REIT managers have a substantial portion of their net worth tied up in the stock (or UPREIT units) of their respective companies. Their future fortunes are thus tied to the performance of their REIT's stock. This provides for an alignment of interests between the investor and the REIT that has not always been present in the private market.

ALTERNATIVE FORMS OF REIT EQUITY INVESTMENT

At this point, it is useful to give more detailed attention to alternative forms that REIT equity investment might take. This section will consider various aspects of the following four forms of ownership:

1. Operating units of an UPREIT
2. Stock of a private REIT
3. Stock of a public REIT
4. Perpetual preferred stock or convertible preferred stock

Contributing Properties for Operating Units in an UPREIT

The UPREIT structure provides owners of privately held real estate the opportunity to exchange their investment interests, in essence, for stock in the REIT on a tax-effective basis. So long as investors continue to hold their units in the UPREIT, recognition of any gain on the transfer of the assets can be deferred. While this is generally a far more important tax-planning feature for individuals, it can also be important to taxable institutional investors such as LICs. The exchange of property interests for UPREIT units is attractive, of course, only if the investor desires to make an investment based on the anticipated future performance of the REIT. The only reason for an LIC to sell properties to a REIT in exchange for UPREIT units is for tax-deferral purposes.

Acquiring Stock in a Private REIT

The principal motivation for investing in a private REIT is to obtain better pricing than is available for like assets in the public market, based on the REIT's property holdings and property sector focus. Selected opportunities have been available for institutional investors to make strategic investments in private REITs. These investments have provided the capital required to recapitalize these firms, facilitating their growth and/or the restructuring of their balance sheets. The primary objective for such an investment has been to obtain meaningful positions in the private entity at favorable pricing. The ultimate goal of such an investment is usually for the REIT to go public and thereby achieve more attractive public market pricing.

Acquiring Stock in Public REITs

The public REIT market offers LICs an opportunity to invest not only in real estate assets but also in real estate operating companies. This form of investing provides enhanced liquidity for this asset category plus the opportunity for coinvestment with the REIT's management. Another major advantage of such investment is that it permits the LIC to achieve its diversification objectives, both in terms of property types and geographic diversity. As indicated previously, it may also offer asset pricing arbitrage as against the private real estate market.

LICs and other institutional investors obviously can acquire their interest in REITs through participation in initial public offerings (IPOs), public secondary offerings, private secondary offerings, or open market purchases. In the recent past, the IPOs of many REITs have proven attractive investments. In many cases, the property-owning firms became REITs of necessity because there was a major need to raise equity capital in the aftermath of the overexpansion of the 1980s, when many balloon and bullet loans were maturing and many lenders were not willing to roll over the debt at previously funded levels. This pressure to take on REIT status does not exist today, as most of the firms so affected have already converted to REIT status. Consequently, while REIT IPOs are still coming to market, LICs have substantial opportunities to invest through either open market acquisitions of the shares of existing REITs or secondary offerings of these companies. Alternatively, LICs can invest in the private placements of these public REITs.

As noted previously, the recently established RBC factors make REIT stock a relatively expensive way for LICs to own real estate, in that the RBC factor for stock is 30 percent versus 10 percent for directly owned real estate. The relative importance of this constraint will be determined by the level of an LIC's asset allocation to real estate and the level of its surplus.

Acquiring Perpetual Preferred Stock and Convertible Preferred Stock

The institutional market has not traditionally been a major acquirer of perpetual preferred stock; it has largely been a retail product. Many REITs find this stock to be an attractive form of raising cheap equity to finance their growth or to restructure their balance sheets. A few LICs have shown interest in this form of investment. Since the performance of such stock is determined by its fixed-income characteristics, the motivation for investing in perpetual preferred is a function of its pricing relative to that of other fixed-income investment alternatives. It is not expected that many LICs will find perpetual preferred stock attractive on an ongoing basis.

A more attractive form of preferred stock for many LICs is convertible preferred. The principal attractiveness of this form of security is that it is slightly more defensive while providing much, if not all, of the upside potential of the common stock. A growing number of REITs are issuing such convertible preferred. Some issues have been public, while others have been issued on a private basis. The public issues have generally been rated prior to issuance, while most private placements have been without ratings. One very attractive feature of convertible preferred to LICs is their treatment from a risk-based capital perspective. The exact RBC factor depends on the rating of the preferred issue but varies from a level of 3 percent for an investment-grade preferred stock rated Baa to 11 percent for a noninvestment-grade preferred stock rated B. Compared to an RBC factor of 30 percent for common stock, there is a decided advantage in investing in convertible preferred stock.

CONCLUSIONS

In concluding this chapter, a number of observation can be made about LIC investments in REITs:

- REITs offer LICs good lending opportunities through a variety of forms, including secured, combination secured and unsecured, and unsecured loans. The opportunities for making secured loans are greatest for pre-IPO REITs and public REITs that do not have investment-grade ratings for their debt.
- REITs offer LICs an opportunity to meet some of their equity investment objectives through a form of real estate investment that is both more liquid and that has real-time market pricing. They offer an LIC the opportunity to achieve diversification objectives (geographic and property type) that might not be achievable in the private market. They also provide a chance to coinvest with management where the investors' objectives are more aligned with that of management.
- The REIT market provides an opportunity for smaller LICs that may not have the organization to participate effectively in the private real estate equity market to achieve exposure to this asset class.
- Many large LICs cannot satisfy their appetite for real estate equities through the public market because of overall internal limitations on the level of common stock investment by the LIC and the higher RBC factors associated with stock investments as compared to the direct ownership of real estate. However, convertible preferred stock investments can be used to ameliorate this disadvantage.

In summary, REITs provide LICs with many very interesting alternative forms of investment in real estate that can supplement and compliment an LIC's direct investment in real estate.

CHAPTER

9

REIT MERGERS AND ACQUISITIONS

Dale Reiss, *Managing Partner, Chicago Real Estate Group, E & Y Kenneth Leventhal*
Elizabeth Plzak, *Partner, Chicago Real Estate Group, E & Y Kenneth Leventhal*

REIT mergers are becoming an increasingly important aspect of the REIT industry as the securitization of income-producing properties has become a proven trend. With real estate continuing to enter the corporate sphere, the normal cycles of growth and consolidation are becoming increasingly apparent within the REIT industry. The phenomenal growth of the REIT market between 1992 and 1996 has created an industry ripe for consolidation. This chapter will explore some of the capital market, real estate industry, and economic factors leading to an environment conducive to REIT merger activity as well as some of the key transactional, accounting, valuation, and tax issues that are a consequence of merger transactions.

MARKET, ECONOMY, FOUNDERS' STYLES AND PERFORMANCE CAN LEAD TO MERGERS

The increase in both the number and the market capitalization of REITs since 1992 has been significant. Figure 9–1 details the dramatic increase in the cumulative dollars raised in the public markets since 1992. During the years 1993–1994, 95 new REITs were formed, which raised $16.4 billion

FIGURE 9–1

REIT Investment Has Increased Dramatically Since 1992

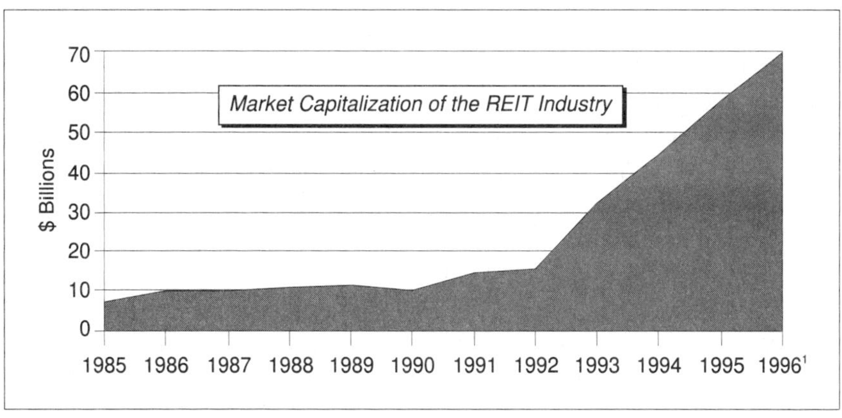

[1] As of September 1996.

from the public markets; and 102 secondary offerings occurred, which raised $7.8 million. During 1995, only eight new REITs were formed, but 93 existing REITs raised $7.3 billion from the public markets. As of September 1996, there were approximately 300 public REITs with a market capitalization of $70 billion. The average size of a REIT was just over $150 million, and only 10 REITs existed with a public market capitalization in excess of $1 billion. With so many small to mid-size REITs, the resulting industry was very fragmented, and most REITs were focused by property type or geographic area.

This separation between the large and the small to mid-size REITs, as well as other market and economic factors and stylistic issues of the founders, caused a shift from many new REITs being formed to a limited number of existing REITs being able to raise additional equity beginning in 1995. In part, the number of IPOs decreased in response to rising interest rates (as from an investment perspective, REITs are particularly interest-rate sensitive, given their relatively high yields). This, combined with a perceived saturation in the marketplace from the high volume of REIT IPO activity during 1992–1994, decreased the number of private real estate companies choosing to go public.

As a result, the ability of existing REITs to access the public capital markets became even more limited. Between 1992 and 1995, the sophistication of the investors and their ability to analyze REITs improved, and they could better distinguish between well-run, strong-performing REITs and lower-quality REITs. In addition, some founders of REITs realized they did not like being in the limelight of a public company or being held to the increased level of scrutiny from public markets as compared to private markets. Not only are there significant compliance and reporting requirements of the IRS and the SEC, but the REITs, often run by individuals used to managing privately held companies, found themselves being questioned by and answering to shareholders and market analysts.

Additional economic issues led to an environment ripe for mergers. The REITs that "overpromised but underdelivered" on performance, both in terms of increased growth and dividends, generally suffered stock price declines, in some cases significant, as the marketplace reacted to the disappointing news. As of December 31, 1995, approximately 30 REITs that had been formed during 1992–1994 were trading below their IPO price. In addition, many other REITs ran out of growth opportunities, both internally and externally, as certain property types and geographic areas faced limited opportunities. Internally, many REITs found that their opportunity to develop additional property or to increase occupancies and rents at their existing properties became more limited, and externally they found they were having more difficulty completing acquisitions as a result of increased competition and prices for acquisition properties. Finally, the cost of operating a public company was not only higher than the cost of operating a private company but often turned out to be higher than the costs anticipated at the time the REITs went public. Costs for items such as annual reports, SEC filings, financial reporting, and investor relations, including the personnel to support these functions, all resulted in expanding overhead structures, which became difficult to justify and absorb in small and midsize REITs.

At the same time, as the marketplace began to differentiate between well-run and poorly managed REITs, the range of yields being paid on REIT stocks began to widen as the market penalized the lower-performing REITs with higher yields and rewarded the well-run REITs with premiums to net asset value. This significantly increased the cost of equity for some REITs, in some cases to levels that made "traditional" bank debt financing more appealing. As a result, some REITs with limited growth opportunities and capital market access began to consider the option of merging with other, stronger-performing REITs. The following are some of the additional performance-related reasons for some REITs to consider mergers:

- **Rebalance debt/equity ratios.** Many private real estate companies had used the opportunity to go public to raise capital in order to pay off existing debt on the properties and had relatively low (30 to 40 percent) debt-to-market capitalization ratios at the time of their IPO. However, after going public, the need to finance growth and, in some cases, existing operations resulted in REITs taking on increased levels of debt.
- **Expand operational capabilities and enhance growth.** The capabilities required to operate a self-managed REIT and the continuing need to generate growth resulted in significant capital requirements.
- **Increase market dominance or obtain geographic diversity.** Many REITs found it difficult to create market dominance or achieve geographic diversity at a rapid pace and at the level of the shareholders' expectations due to lack of access to capital, lack of opportunity, increased competition, and lack of managerial depth and ability.
- **Improve overall management talent.** The management requirements for a public company are typically broader than the requirements for operating a private company. Many real estate companies, once they went public, found that they lacked the depth and breadth of management talent that the marketplace demanded.
- **Reduce corporate overhead relative to asset size.** In order to effectively operate a public company, a certain base level of overhead structure for investor relations and financial reporting is necessary regardless of the size of the company. As a result of economies of scale, in many cases, small to mid-size REITs cannot as readily absorb this cost as larger REITs, which have a larger asset base over which to justify the necessary base amount of overhead.
- **Improve funds from operations (FFO) or cash flow.** Due to the disproportionately high dividend that REITs pay relative to other types of publicly traded companies, REITs face a strong demand from the market to generate FFO and cash flow growth. If REITs find it difficult to improve FFO or cash flow because of size, lack of access to capital, or lack of growth opportunities, they may begin to stagnate and look to merge with other, stronger REITs in order to generate such growth for their shareholders.

- **Create synergies.** Weaknesses in REITs can be offset by strengths in other REITs. For example, a REIT that lacks in-house development capabilities but that has strong asset-management capabilities may find it advantageous to merge with a REIT with strong development abilities.
- **Provide opportunities for private portfolios to team with existing public REITs.** The cost of going public is high, and the premium the market provides the larger REITs makes it expensive and difficult for owners of small to midsize portfolios to complete an IPO. A merger offers an opportunity for a private owner to team with an existing public REIT, potentially on a tax-free basis if operating partnership units are used in the transaction.
- **Provide an exit strategy for those who may not want to or be able to continue operating a public company.** As previously mentioned, the increased requirements of reporting to the shareholders, the SEC, and the IRS is a responsibility that not all real estate operators want or are suited for. For those developer/owners used to working within a privately structured company who do not want to or cannot adapt to the public environment, a merger provides a possible exit strategy, again on a tax-free basis if operating partnership units are used in the transaction.
- **Provide better liquidity opportunities for investors.** Although public REITs generally provide more liquidity to investors than partnerships, owning a share in a midsize REIT does not provide the same level of liquidity as many other publicly traded companies. Most REIT stocks are very thinly traded and have a relatively small population of investors. Therefore, the larger the REIT, the more liquidity opportunities for the existing shareholders.

Although a number of compelling market, economic, and performance reasons explain why REIT mergers make sense, only three REIT mergers had been completed as of December 31, 1995. Effecting a merger transaction is an involved, expensive, and difficult process. In particular, because one of the existing REITs in the merger generally will survive as the controlling entity and both entities would generally be backed by founders with significant wealth tied up in their respective REITs, issues related to who will control the merged entity arise. This issue can become

TABLE 9–1

Recent Public REIT Transactions as of December 31, 1996

Effective Date	Purchaser	Acquiree
December 1994	Wellsford	Holly
June 1995	Mid America	America First
July 1995	Horizon	McArthur/Glen
March 1996	BRE	REIT of California
March 1996	Bradley	Tucker
April 1996	Security Capital	Carr
August 1996	Simon	DeBartolo
September 1996	Highwoods	CRO
December 1996	United Dominion	Southwest

very difficult to satisfactorily resolve and in some cases may result in proposed mergers that for many reasons should not occur. The difficulty of one party giving up control can be partially negated by providing board of directors seats or employment positions to the nonsurviving REIT investor. In addition, the difficulty that a REIT may have with relinquishing control can result in a REIT that needs to merge for economic or performance reasons to search for other alternatives, such as merging with private portfolios or portfolios that may have previously tried to go public but were unsuccessful in their efforts. As of December 31, 1996, however, as the market, economic, and performance factors for consolidation continued to be present and the marketplace had witnessed the occurrence of several REIT mergers, six additional REIT mergers were completed, and a number of additional mergers were either pending or being contemplated. Table 9–1 highlights recent public REIT merger transactions.

ANTITAKEOVER PROVISIONS MINIMIZE OPPORTUNITIES FOR HOSTILE TAKEOVERS

REIT mergers can be either hostile or friendly. Hostile takeovers are very difficult, if not impossible, to complete because many REITs have adopted antitakeover provisions. Antitakeover provisions can consist of excess share provisions, which restrict the number of shares any shareholder can own, purportedly in order to protect the REIT from violating the "five-or-fewer" rule imposed by the IRS, under which five or fewer individuals are not permitted to own in excess of 50 percent of a REIT's stock during the last half of the taxable year. As a result, a typical excess-share provision restricts the maximum number of shares that any shareholder can acquire to generally in the range of less than 10 percent. Excess-share provisions strip any shares acquired by a shareholder in excess of the 10 percent (or other) restriction of any voting rights or rights to secure dividends until the "excess" shares are transferred to a holder who can own them without violating the ownership restriction. However, a REIT's board of directors (BOD) usually also has the discretion to waive the limitation with respect to certain parties if the BOD is comfortable that the five-or-fewer rule will not be violated.

Alternatively, antitakeover provisions include "poison pills," or rights plans, which carry a more significant economic threat to potential acquirers than excess-share plans, as they can be dilutive to the acquirer. Under a rights plan, an abnormally high level of dilution affects the acquirer when a group of shareholders exceeds an established threshold, generally 10 to 20 percent of the target's stock, and the other shareholders have the right to acquire either the target or the acquirer's stock at a substantial discount. As a result, a potential acquirer would normally negotiate directly with the BOD, which usually has the authority to redeem the rights, instead of on an unsolicited basis.

In addition to these antitakeover measures, hostile takeovers are difficult to complete because REITs are generally thinly traded, meaning that a relatively small number of investors actively trade in a REIT's stock, and the principals/founders usually own significant blocks of stock and/or units. However, "friendly" mergers, those that have the approval of the BOD, are easier to complete and more fairly represent mergers that have occurred to date.

In order for a proposed merger to be acceptable to the existing shareholders of the surviving REIT, the transaction must generally be "accretive" to the existing shareholders. In other words, there must be a belief that the merger will result in increased growth, FFO, cash flow, dividends, and share price. In addition, if the performance, growth, or other problems that the nonsurvivor REIT historically has experienced are well understood by the nonsurvivor REIT investors, a merger is more likely to be regarded as the most viable alternative for the company, and the existing shareholders will be more likely to approve the merger. Finally, existing shareholders are skeptical of and typically will not accept a "special deal," such as an extra payment of cash or shares to the founders or other key executives of the nonsurviving REIT.

TRANSACTION AND IMPLEMENTATION COSTS ARE SIGNIFICANT

Mergers are expensive. The amount of time executives and certain employees spend on a proposed merger is extensive and detracts from the amount of time available for other issues and ongoing business. Out-of-pocket transaction costs are also significant, and any REIT entering into a proposed merger should be able to financially bear the impact, both from an earnings and from a cash flow perspective, of the consequences if the deal is not consummated. Generally, "dead-deal" costs should be expensed to earnings as soon as it is evident that the merger will not be completed. During 1995, in the case of several proposed mergers that were not successfully completed, REITs had to report extraordinary losses, sometimes millions of dollars, related to dead-deal costs.

Not only are the transaction costs high, but once completed, as evidenced by shareholder vote, the implementation process can be costly, difficult, and time-consuming. Assuming that one of the reasons for merging is to take advantage of economies of scale and synergies that exist between the two merging REITs, there will likely be some overlap of functions between them. Generally, only one corporate, finance, accounting, development, leasing, and acquisition department will remain with the merged entity. For control reasons, the acquirer is usually the survivor for these areas of operations and management. Although the increased size of the company may dictate a need for the acquirer to expand beyond its premerger size, generally that need is not enough to absorb all duplicate employees.

The cost of terminating employees is not only significant but can result in a difficult human resource issue. Many of the employees may have a long history of working for the founder, making it difficult for the founder to terminate them. In addition, many employees may feel threatened by lack of job security once it is known that the merger may be occurring and therefore begin to look for other employment. This creates a particularly difficult situation for the acquiree, as on a long-term basis the REIT may need to terminate certain employees but on a short-term basis may need to retain employees until the integration of the two companies has occurred in an orderly manner. Thus, in addition to termination benefits, mergers may result in additional payments to those employees who need to be retained on a short-term basis, in an amount sufficient to deter them from undertaking a job search and accepting a new position until their services are no longer needed.

In connection with merging the two entities, it may be necessary to relocate certain employees to the vicinity of the newly merged company's offices. Again, employee relocation costs can be high, and relocation can be difficult to complete, as employees may not want to uproot and relocate their families, thus requiring the REIT to begin a search for new employees.

There is a high probability that the two merging REITs operate from different financial reporting, accounting, property management, leasing, and development systems. In addition, neither of the systems the REITs use prior to the merger may be sufficient to accommodate the size of the merged entity as well as its anticipated future growth. As a result, at a minimum, the merger will require one of the REITs to convert to the surviving system, or alternatively, both will need to convert to a third system. The financial and time costs of selecting a surviving or a new system and the resulting implementation of the conversion can be significant to the surviving REIT.

Finally, implementation costs can include certain costs to exit an activity of the acquired REIT. For example, assume REIT A (the surviving REIT) merges with REIT B and that, before the merger, REIT B handled certain operating activities in-house. However, subsequent to the merger, it is determined that such activities will be handled by REIT A's existing third-party service providers. As a result, additional implementation costs would be incurred to exit those operating activities of REIT B. (See page 217 for a discussion of the accounting treatment of implementation costs.)

Integrating two REITs is not only costly, it takes time to complete. Savings and synergies predicted to occur as a result of the merger may not all be realized immediately, which may affect the surviving REIT's ability to deliver the increase in FFO and/or dividends that shareholders anticipate. For example, either REIT may have in place noncancelable contracts that prohibit certain synergies from occurring immediately. Integration efforts also require significant internal resources to effect, and therefore the remaining employees may be overloaded for a period of time while performing their regular duties as well as their integration responsibilities. This can significantly increase the workload for the surviving REIT in the short term immediately following the merger. Finally, even after employees and systems are integrated for the surviving REIT, it will take time for management to become familiar with the specifics of new properties and employees, which can result in additional delays before anticipated savings and synergies are realized.

Accounting Issues

A merger is accounted for either as a purchase or as a pooling of interests. Historically, IPOs have almost always been accounted for as a pooling of interests, which means that the historical cost basis of the assets prior to the formation of the REIT is "carried over" and becomes the basis of the surviving REIT's assets. This contrasts with the purchase method of accounting, which "steps up" the basis of the assets to reflect the purchase price. However, mergers can be accounted for by either method, depending on the facts and circumstances of the merger.

A complex set of rules has been established by the Financial Accounting Standards Board (FASB), the American Institute of Certified Public Accountants (AICPA), and the SEC, which govern the purchase and pooling methods of accounting. The most comprehensive published guidance is Accounting Principles Board (APB) Opinion No. 16, which was published in 1970. APB 16 established specific criteria, all of which must be met in order for a transaction to be accounted for as a pooling. Within the context of REIT mergers, the criteria are such that they are very easy to fail, and therefore purchase accounting often prevails. In 1995, the Emerging Issues Task Force (EITF), which discusses the recognition of liabilities in connection with a purchase business combination. In general, exit, employee-termination, and relocation costs expected to be incurred should result in a liability being recorded in connection with the transaction. However, any costs regarded as integration costs or costs incurred to integrate the two companies should be expensed at the time incurred.

The accounting for a merger can look quite different, depending on the accounting method used to record the transaction. As a result, it is important to understand the implications of both methods, as in many cases, it is possible to structure a merger to achieve the desired method of accounting. The following points highlight some of the key differences between the purchase and pooling methods of accounting:

- **Basis of assets.** Purchase accounting results in a "step-up" of the basis of the assets to reflect the purchase price. In other words, if Company A purchases Company B's assets (which were recorded on Company B's books at $.7 million) for $1 million, Company A will record the basis of those assets at $1 million. However, under pooling, Company A would record Company B's assets at $.7 million. As a result, the equity in the assets of Company B would also be "stepped up" to $1 million under purchase accounting. The increase in net assets and equity that results from use of purchase accounting is generally considered the more favorable treatment. As the REIT market continues to mature, an increasing number of REITs are seeking unsecured debt, which generally requires that the REIT be rated. Two of the biggest problems that REITs face in getting a rating are size and product type. In the case of a merger, a step-up under purchase accounting would be the favored financial statement treatment. Table 9–2 highlights the effect of purchase versus pooling accounting.
- **Shareholders' equity.** For financial statement purposes, shareholders' equity is increased by the value of the new shares issued under purchase accounting and is presented on a combined basis at historical cost for pooling.
- **Premerger income.** Profit and loss prior to the date of the acquisition is not included in the income statement of the surviving REIT under purchase accounting. However, under pooling, the in-

TABLE 9–2

Effect of Purchase versus Pooling Accounting

	Historical Basis of Net Assets
Company A	$2.0 million
Company B	$0.7 million
	Company A Basis of Net Assets (Post-Merger)
Pooling	$2.7 million
Purchase[1]	$3.0 million

1 Assumes Company A acquired Company B for $1 million.

come statement of the merged entity would reflect the combined earnings of both REITs as of the first day of the reporting period. As a result, it is important to ensure that a proper cutoff on operations is obtained when using purchase accounting and that all appropriate levels of reserve have been reflected in the premerger income statement of the acquiree.

- **Disclosures.** The SEC requirements for disclosures of prior period income statements vary, generally from one to three years, depending on the size of the acquisition under purchase accounting, as prescribed in the SEC Regulation S-X. If pooling is used, the SEC requires income statement disclosure going back for as much as three years, two years of historical and balance-sheet disclosure on a combined basis, assuming the merger had occurred at the beginning of that period.
- **Transaction costs.** Transaction costs are generally capitalized as part of the purchase price under purchase accounting, with the exception of the costs to register and issue equity securities, which are reflected as a reduction of equity. Transaction costs are generally expensed under the pooling method of accounting.

To summarize, the purchase method of accounting has often been used to account for the acquisition of one REIT by another. The acquiring entity (under purchase accounting, only one REIT could be designated as the acquirer) records as its cost an amount equal to the amount tendered for the net assets or equity of the acquired REIT, plus transaction costs, and including the fair market value of the liabilities assumed as part of the transaction. Note that if the cost of the acquisition exceeds the fair market value of the assets acquired less the liabilities assumed, the difference would generally be recorded as goodwill. Within the context of a real estate company, it may be difficult for the shareholders and the marketplace to rationalize the existence of any goodwill resulting from a merger transaction. Finally, the income statement of the acquirer would include the operations of the acquired REIT on a going-forward basis from the date of the merger.

The pooling method of accounting would generally be used to account for a merger as the combination or uniting of two or more companies by exchange of equity securities. Therefore, the recorded assets and liabilities of each REIT would be carried forward at historical cost, and the income of the combined REIT would include income of both entities in the merger for all periods required to be presented, on a restated, combined, basis.

Twelve conditions for pooling must *all* be present for pooling to be used in a merger:

1. The stockholder groups must neither withdraw nor invest assets, and the transaction must be effected by exchange of voting common stock. Withdrawals of up to 10 percent of the assets would not be considered a violation of this condition.

The next two requirements describe certain attributes of the combining REITs that must be present.

2. Each of the two REITs entering into the merger must have been autonomous for a two-year period immediately preceding the date of the merger.
3. Each of the combining entities must be independent of each other.

The remaining conditions describe certain attributes of the combined interests resulting from the merger that must be present.

4. The combination must be effected in a single transaction or plan completed within one year.
5. There must be an absence of planned transactions.
6. There must be an exchange of common stock for common stock.
7. Neither of the combining companies can change the equity interests of the voting common stock within two years of the merger.
8. Distributions from either company are not allowable except in the normal course of business.
9. Reacquisitions of voting common stock may only occur for nonbusiness combination purposes.
10. The ratio of interests of individual shareholders must remain unchanged after the effect of the merger.
11. Stockholder voting rights may not be restricted.
12. Any existing provisions of the combination regarding issuance of securities or consideration must be settled as of the date the plan is consummated.

Disclosure requirements for public mergers and acquisitions are governed by the SEC. In addition to the required historical disclosures, the SEC requires disclosure of pro forma financial statements pursuant to Article 11 of Regulations S-X. The purpose of pro forma financial statements are to show, on a pro forma basis, what the acquirer would have looked like, assuming the merger or acquisition had occurred on the first day of the period presented. For public companies, the SEC requires a pro forma balance sheet for the most recent balance sheet date required to have been filed by the registrant. (The registrant is generally the acquirer, although in the case of a merger between two public companies, it may be necessary for both REITs to file statements regarding the exchange of shares.) In addition, a pro forma income statement is required to be filed that covers (1) the most recent fiscal year that is required to have been filed with the SEC and (2) the most recent interim period that is required to have been filed with the SEC.

Pro forma financial statements are not audited and are generally presented in a columnar format in enough detail to be readily understood by the reader. A pro forma balance sheet generally reflects the historical cost balance sheet of the acquirer and the target followed by a column of adjustments to reflect the specifics of the merger or acquisition. The adjustments typically will include such items as the form of payment for the transaction, including any exchange of shares or units that may occur, any additional debt that is assumed, any adjustments for certain assets or liabilities that may not be assumed as part of the transaction, and any necessary adjustments to reflect the fair value of the assets and liabilities being assumed. (See Table 9–3 for an example of a pro forma balance sheet.)

The required pro forma income statement disclosures generally reflect the historical cost income statements for the acquirer and the acquiree

TABLE 9–3

Pro Forma REIT Merger Balance Sheet Highlights

	Historical Cost		*Pro Forma*	
	Company A	Company B	Adjustments	Balance Sheet
Real Estate	$2.0	$1.0	$1.3[1]	$4.3
Other Assets	$0.5	$0.5	($0.3)[1]	$0.7
Debt	$1.0	$1.0	($0.2)[2]	$1.8
Equity	$1.5	$0.5	$1.2	$3.2

in millions

[1] Assumes total purchase price of $2.5 million, prior to any fair value adjustment to the liabilities assumed, allocated based on fair value of assets and liabilities assumed in accordance with APB Opinion No. 16.

[2] Assumes fair value of debt assumed is $.8 million.

followed by a column of adjustments to reflect the specifics of the merger or acquisition. The adjustments will typically include such items as an adjustment to depreciation to reflect the purchase price; an adjustment to interest to reflect any additional financing or other financing activity that may have occurred in connection with the transaction; an adjustment to reflect any fees or expenses of the merger or acquisition that should be expensed (which would include any costs incurred by the target as well as any internal costs, such as payroll or other overhead costs, incurred by the acquirer of the target); if either the acquirer or the target is an UPREIT, an adjustment to reflect the revised minority interests ownership of the unit holders in the operating partnership; and finally, an adjustment to reflect any overhead or other anticipated cost savings to occur as a result of the merger or acquisition. Note that some synergies and savings may result in reduced capitalized overhead, while others may result in reduced general and administrative costs, depending on the accounting policy of the acquirer for such costs. In addition, other synergies and savings may result in reduced operating expenses as a result of conforming the way two companies do business.

ASSET-VALUATION ISSUES

A number of asset valuation issues must be considered for any merger or acquisition. Usually, preliminary merger discussions focus primarily on purchase-price determination and valuations of the real property and debt, as discussed in the following paragraphs, and if applicable other soft assets such as deferred costs, contracts, and potential goodwill.

- **Purchase price determination.** Generally, an exchange ratio based primarily on the relative trading prices of each REIT's stock is negotiated. In some cases, a premium may be negotiated into the exchange ratio as a result of a belief that the market price of the acquiree's stock does not reflect the underlying value of the real estate assets. In other situations, the exchange ratio may be negotiated at a fixed rate based on the relative stock prices at the time the merger is negotiated and publicly announced; however, the market prices of the stocks may subsequently change relative to each other so that, upon closing, a premium or discount is a part of the exchange ratio. In addition to analyzing the relative trading prices of each REIT's stock, each REIT will most likely hire an outside party to issue a fairness opinion on the exchange ratio and the resulting implied purchase price. Such fairness opinions normally are based on an analysis of the historical trading prices of each company, the exchange ratios in other completed REIT mergers, the purchase price in other known private acquisitions, and an analysis of the underlying real estate properties.

- **Value of underlying real estate.** In connection with the fairness opinions generally issued for each REIT in a merger and in connection with the due diligence performed by each REIT on the other, a detailed analysis of the underlying real estate would normally be performed. Such analysis would generally be based on a model of the executed leases for each property, the anticipated future market conditions (including rental rates, occupancy, and tenant rollover), as well as the operating expenses and capital improvements for each property. Typically a 10-year cash flow model for each property would then be developed, with the aggregate cash flow analysis being used to estimate value for the REIT. This approach to valuation is generally given significant consideration in determining the final exchange ratio/purchase price for a merger.
- **Value of existing debt.** In addition to valuing the underlying real estate, a valuation of the existing debt is normally made. If a REIT has previously entered into debt arrangements that at the time of the merger are either favorable or unfavorable relative to market terms, such incremental or detrimental value will be considered in establishing the overall exchange ratio and purchase price. Other factors, such as the ratio of debt to real estate value, the amount of unused borrowing capacity of a potential REIT acquiree, and the existence of favorable or unfavorable caps, swaps, or other hedges on existing debt agreements are also considered in establishing purchase price.

Ultimately, the analysis of the relative market prices of each REIT's stock and the valuations of the underlying real estate assets, debt, and any other valuation issues are reconciled in determining the final exchange ratio and purchase price. This analysis is important to determine if the amount being paid for a REIT could result in any goodwill to the acquiring REIT.

Goodwill is defined as the amount of the purchase price in excess of the value of the net assets acquired. Because in real estate transactions the amount paid for real estate assets would normally not exceed the value of the underlying properties, it would be unusual if goodwill were associated with a REIT merger and most likely would be interpreted by the market as a sign that the acquiring REIT had overpaid for the acquisition.

TAX ISSUES

Business combinations involving REITs can be structured in a variety of ways. The particular structure used depends on the facts and circumstances of the transaction as well as the parties' desire to minimize the tax implications.

A transaction can be structured to receive fully taxable treatment for the target company or its shareholders. For example, the acquirer can purchase all, or substantially all, of the assets of the target in return for securities, cash, or some other form of consideration. The acquirer can also obtain control of a target by purchasing the stock directly from the target's shareholders.

Although these forms can satisfy the parties' business desires, the tax consequences can be significant. As an alternative, a business combination can be structured as an acquisitive reorganization under Section 368 of the Internal Revenue Code and receive tax-free treatment. When it is desired to combine two or more corporations on a tax-free basis, often the most flexible means is a statutory merger or consolidation under Section 368(a)(1)(A), or an "A" reorganization. The IRS has ruled that a statutory merger of two REITs qualifies as a tax-free A reorganization.

A reorganization under Section 368(a)(1)(C), or a "C" reorganization, requires that a corporation issue its voting stock in exchange for substantially all of the properties of another corporation. The IRS has also approved this form of tax-free reorganization, whereby the REIT exchanges its voting stock for substantially all of the assets of another REIT. The acquiring company in a reorganization can drop the acquired assets to a subsidiary without causing the transaction to become taxable. A REIT, which is now permitted to have a qualified REIT subsidiary, may desire to drop down the assets acquired from the target REIT for a variety of nontax reasons.

A "B" reorganization, provided for in Section 368(a)(1)(B), requires a corporation to issue voting stock in exchange for stock representing control of another corporation. This type of reorganization is generally not available to REITs because a REIT cannot own more than 10 percent of the voting securities of another corporation, and under the rules of Section 368, control requires 80 percent ownership of the stock of the corporation to be acquired. The exception to the rule, a wholly owned REIT subsidiary, does not provide relief because the REIT must hold 100 percent of the stock of the subsidiary for the entire existence of the corporation.

A straight REIT-to-REIT merger is often the most simple, whereby the target corporation merges into the acquirer pursuant to state law. This A-type merger offers maximum flexibility from a tax perspective, but this form is sometimes avoided because of the need in some cases for approval by the acquirer's shareholders.

The reorganization of a REIT and a non-REIT entity can involve many additional obstacles that may need to be considered. Under current law, if a corporation converts to REIT status or is acquired in a tax-free reorganization by a REIT, either the C corporation recognizes and pays tax on net built-in gain on assets at the time of conversion or acquisition, or the REIT may elect to be taxed on such net built-in gain inherent in the C corporation's assets if and when such gain is recognized within 10 years of the conversion or acquisition. These rules are similar to those governing election by existing C corporations when electing S corporation status. The merger of a REIT and non-REIT entity can also involve issues regarding the REITs continuing qualification as a REIT.

The popular UPREIT structure has provided valuable tax advantages to merger transactions. Unlike REITs, UPREITs have the ability to issue operating partnership units to the target or its equity holders, which may provide them with the ability to defer income taxes that would otherwise be payable in connection with the transaction. Generally, when an existing UPREIT is involved in a merger, the surviving entity will maintain its status as or become an UPREIT since it is likely that the existing UPREIT will want to keep its operating partnership in existence.

In a typical merger using the UPREIT structure, the target REIT or nonREIT entity contributes substantially all of its assets to an operating partnership in exchange for operating partnership units. (See Figure 9–2 for a diagram of a typical UPREIT-to-UPREIT merger.) The surviving REIT is the general partner in the operating partnership, and the unit holders may elect to convert their operating partnership units into REIT shares, as mutually agreed. Although the UPREIT structure can offer advantages, material and complex tax consequences can result to the acquired entity or its owners in connection with the receipt of operating partnership units.

FIGURE 9-2

Typical UPREIT-to-UPREIT Merger

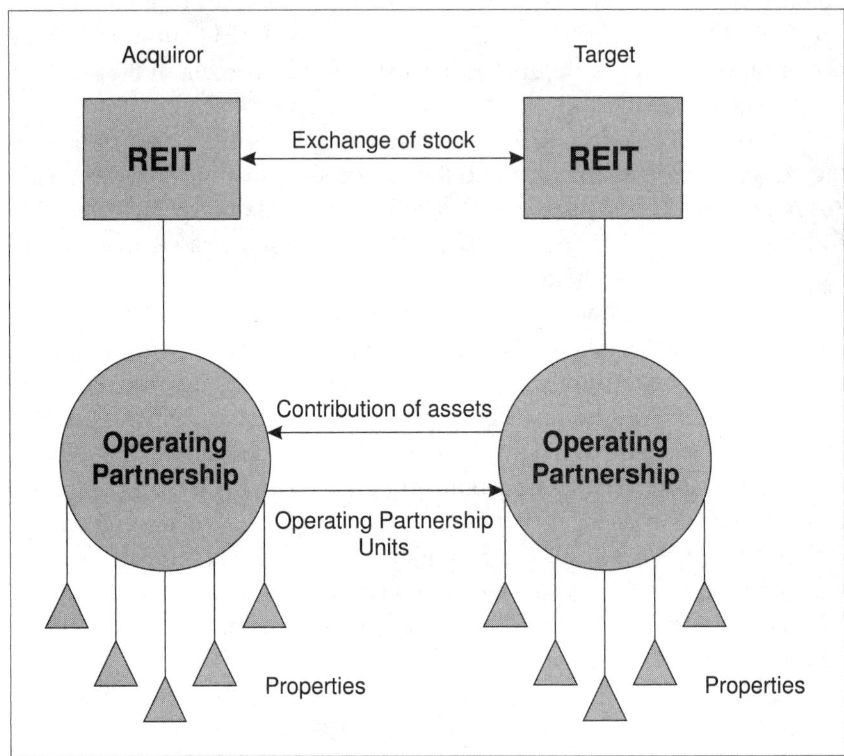

Under the tax rules, a "deemed cash distribution" may result if there is either a repayment of debt on contributed property or a reduction of a unit holder's "share" of debt for tax purposes. In addition, the "built-in gain" that exists upon contribution of property must be specially allocated back to the contributing partner upon a subsequent sale by the operating partnership. Therefore, in order to preserve the tax deferral, the UPREIT typically agrees not to sell or pay down indebtedness on the properties for some period of time except in connection with a sale or refinancing of all or substantially all of the UPREIT's assets.

The UPREIT structure offers other benefits, such as the ability of the UPREIT to issue different classes of units that have rights that are different from other units, for example, rights to preferred distributions. This flexibility is not offered through pure stock ownership structures. In planning for a merger involving an UPREIT structure, the tax consequences to the voting partners of the existing operating partnership must be considered. The parties should consider, for example, the tax consequences from a dilution of the existing interests in the partnership as a result of the issuance of new units as well as the resulting reduction in the unit holder's "share" of partnership liabilities.

The availability of any type of reorganization is dependent on a state law permitting such a merger or consolidation. Historically, many REITs have been organized as business trusts that are not corporations, although they are treated as associations taxable as corporations for tax purposes. A REIT formed as a business trust may have to be reformed as a corporation under state law in order to effect a merger with a corporation. The IRS has ruled that the reincorporation of a REIT formed as a business trust will qualify as an independent tax-free reorganization. Other state considerations involve potential transfer tax liabilities. The use of the UPREIT structure can help to greatly minimize any state transfer tax liabilities.

The organization and structure of a REIT must meet strict requirements under Section 856 of the Code. It is extremely important that the parties involved a REIT merger incur the time and expense on tax-related due diligence to ensure the REIT status will not be jeopardized. In addition, the ownership of the newly merged REIT must be monitored carefully to ensure the REIT is not closely held at any time. A prospective look at the post-merger income and assets test requirements of a REIT is an important step in the due diligence process.

In addition, many REITs own substantially all of the economic interest but 10 percent or less of the voting stock of a corporation set up to conduct businesses that the REIT could not conduct directly. Any acquisition of a REIT that owns an interest in such a third-party service corporation must take into account the voting stock of that corporation. Premerger due diligence can alert the parties to any potential problems that may arise from the ownership of these and other REIT assets following the merger.

OTHER TYPES OF MERGER AND ACQUISITION ACTIVITY

In addition to REIT-to-REIT mergers, which have been the primary type of merger activity discussed in this chapter, other types of merger and acquisition activities occur in the marketplace. As a result of the changes in interest rates and the marketplace during 1995 (which were previously discussed in this chapter), many companies that wanted to go public as REITs found that the appropriate market conditions were not present. Accordingly, some existing public REITs have acquired or would like to acquire large portfolios, where such portfolios are unable to go public on a stand-alone basis.

In addition, investors have looked at acquiring existing public REITs with the intent of taking the REIT private. This alternative exists because certain investors believe that the market value of some REITs, based on the stock price, is less than the underlying value of the real estate. Depending on the size of the investment in the REIT, the ultimate strategy may be to take the public REIT private. Economically, this is more feasible for smaller REITs and results in the elimination of the time-consuming and costly requirements of maintaining a public REIT. As a private company, the REIT distribution requirements can be avoided, and needed capital can be retained within the portfolios for growth. Finally, investors are looking at buying smaller REITs to use as a vehicle to make additional acquisitions. Particularly, if the stock price of a REIT is trading below its underlying real estate value, it may be cheaper, quicker, and easier to acquire an existing REIT than to establish a new REIT.

CONCLUSION

Although REIT mergers are complex transactions, involving many issues including capital market, economic, accounting, and tax, the underlying economic fundamentals will likely continue to result in industry consolidation. Any REIT traded in the capital markets at a discount to its underlying net asset value could be considered a potential merger candidate, and as the marketplace increases its knowledge and understanding of REITs, mergers will increasingly be viewed as a good opportunity for some REITs to achieve growth, economies of scale, and critical mass. The trend toward the corporatization of real estate, and particularly the economies of scale that are inherently present in larger organizations, will motivate certain REITs to seek out merger targets that can be acquired at an accretive price.

CHAPTER

10

REIT GOVERNANCE FOR DIRECTORS AND TRUSTEES

Paul D. Lapides, *Director, Corporate Governance Center, Kennesaw State University*
Michael A. Torres, *Principal, ERE Rosen Real Estate Securities, L.L.C.*

The success of a REIT depends on management's ability to function effectively as a public company. One of the key indicators of this ability is the effectiveness of the board of directors (or trustees in the case of a REIT organized as a trust rather than a corporation). Therefore, successful market performance demands that directors and trustees address the challenges of effective corporate governance.[1] Among these challenges is the need for directors to recognize the impact of two factors: the public marketplace and institutional investors.

As a public company, a REIT can easily be compared with other investments (for example, other REITs, direct investments, commingled funds, common stocks, and fixed-income securities). Additionally, a large percentage of REITs have attracted institutional investors. The investment goals of these institutions include managing investment risk, enhancing shareholder value, and attaining short-term returns. Accordingly, blocks of REIT shares may be acquired or sold on the basis of financial performance, expectations about future performance, or an institution's portfolio management strategy.

The combination of the public marketplace and institutional investors has resulted in powerful "activist" shareholders.[2] In the past, unhappy investors were likely to sell their shares and take their losses. Today, institutional investors who are unhappy with a company's performance often decide to acquire more shares at what they perceive to be an attractive discount. In addition, these shareholders are likely to continue the 1993 trend where shareholders and boards "showed the boss who was boss."[3] Such activism may range from holding informal and formal discussions with management to engaging in a proxy fight for control of the enterprise. Effective corporate governance can help REIT management benefit from the public marketplace and institutional investors.

This chapter will help directors and trustees address the challenges of effective corporate governance.

BOARD RESPONSIBILITIES

The board of directors is elected by shareholders, whose interests it is legally required to protect. Directors are responsible for overseeing the conduct of the REIT's business and directing the affairs of the corporation but not for actively managing the business. The chief executive officer (CEO) and other members of management do that. The board is charged with the responsibility to do the following:

- Supervise operations to ensure that adequate controls exist to safeguard assets, prudently provide stable returns, and comply with laws and regulations.
- Establish, with management, and approve a business strategy, objectives, and policies.
- Deliberate and counsel management on the enterprise's mission, strategy, policies, decisions, and operations.
- Hire, retain, and when necessary, fire the chief executive officer and other principal operating officers.
- Ensure that information is disclosed honestly, objectively, routinely, and efficiently to those entitled to receive it.

These responsibilities are consistent with the North American Securities Administrators Association policy (NASAA policy) regarding REITs, which states that the board should do the following:[4]

- Establish written policies on investments and borrowing.
- Monitor the administrative procedures, investment operations, and performance of the REIT.
- Assure that such policies are carried out.

The National Association of Corporate Directors (NACD) suggests the role of board members should be to ensure that long-term strategic objectives and plans are established, and that the proper management and management structure are in place to achieve those objectives, while at the same time making sure that the structure functions to maintain the corporation's integrity, reputation, and accountability to its relevant constituencies.[5]

Recognition of these primary objectives by REIT CEOs and directors is indicated in their ranking of selected issues in response to the "1996 Board Practices Survey of Public Real Estate Organizations."[6] In terms of their importance for the board, the issues that ranked highest were corporate performance, oversight of corporate strategy, deal approval, corporate governance, and portfolio management. Performance and strategy were also ranked as the top two issues in the National Association of Corporate Directors' 1995 corporate governance survey.[7]

We are not suggesting that good corporate governance is required for good market performance. Many real estate entrepreneurs have demonstrated that success does not require a strong board of directors. Nevertheless, our experience with underperforming companies is consistent with that expressed by noted corporate lawyer, Martin Lipton, and Harvard Business School professor, Jay Lorsch: "We are convinced that if a company is underperforming due to poor management or persisting with a failed strategy, good corporate governance is the safety valve that can provide the means to deal with the problem and improve performance."[8]

DIRECTORS' DUTIES AND RESPONSIBILITIES

The following guidelines are intended to help directors meet their duties and responsibilities in this changing and challenging environment. These guidelines can serve as a foundation for REIT boards. Our goal is to begin to establish a shared understanding of the board's purpose. This will enable directors to engage in intelligent and meaningful discussions and reach decisions about matters that come before the board.

Recognizing that director responsibilities are governed by a complex framework of federal and state laws and regulations, these guidelines make no attempt to modify the legal framework in any way, nor do they cover every situation that may confront a REIT director. Rather, they are intended only to offer general assistance to directors in meeting their responsibilities. Underlying these guidelines is the assumption that directors are making an honest effort to deal fairly with their enterprise, comply with all applicable laws and regulations, and follow sound practices.

Maintain Independence

The first step both the board and individual directors should take is to establish and maintain the board's independence. Effective corporate governance requires a high level of cooperation between an enterprise's board and its management. Nevertheless, a director's duty to oversee the conduct of the enterprise's business necessitates that each director exercise independent judgment in evaluating management's actions and competence. Critical evaluation of issues before the board is essential. Directors who routinely approve management decisions without exercising their own informed judgment are not serving the enterprise or the stockholders adequately.

Keep Informed

Directors must keep themselves informed of the activities and condition of their enterprise and of the environment in which it operates. They should attend board and assigned committee meetings and should be careful to review closely all meeting materials and auditor's findings and recommendations.

Directors should stay abreast of general industry trends and any developments pertinent to their enterprise (for example, reading industry publications, specific property-type publications, and general business press, and attending related educational programs and conferences). Directors should work with management to develop a program to keep members informed. The pace of change in real estate finance and valuation today makes it particularly important that directors commit the amount of time (8 to 24 days per year) required to be informed participants in the affairs of the enterprise. This is critical when assessing the merits of single-asset or portfolio acquisitions, dispositions, or financings.

Periodic meetings or briefings with shareholders should be considered, especially when accessing the capital markets. Routine briefings by management, counsel, auditors, or other consultants are often helpful. Formal director education programs should also be considered.

Ensure Qualified Management

The board of directors is responsible for ensuring that day-to-day operations of the enterprise are in the hands of qualified management. If the board becomes dissatisfied with the performance of the chief executive officer or other principal officers, it should address the matter directly. If hiring a new chief executive officer is necessary, the board should act quickly to find a qualified replacement. Ability, integrity, and experience are the most important qualifications for a chief executive officer.

Supervise Management

Supervision is the broadest of the board's duties and the most difficult to describe, as its scope varies according to the circumstances of each enterprise. Nevertheless, the following general suggestions should provide a framework for each board to develop its own supervision.

Establish Policies and Risk Controls

The board of directors should ensure that all significant activities are covered by clearly communicated written policies that employees can readily understand. All policies should be monitored to ensure that they conform with changes in laws and regulations, economic conditions, and the enterprise's circumstances. Specific policies should cover the following:

- Code of ethics or conduct.
- Conflicts of interest.
- Capital structure strategy and plan.
- Internal controls, audit programs, and compliance activities.
- Operations strategy, plan, and budget.
- Cash and short-term investment management plan.
- Acquisition strategy and due diligence protocol and procedures.
- Investment and divestment authorization protocol and process.
- Disclosure strategy, protocol, and plan.
- Investor relations strategy, protocol, and plan.

These policies should be formulated to further the enterprise's business strategy. They should be supported by procedures, including a system of internal controls, designed to foster sound business practices, to comply with laws and regulations, and to protect the enterprise against external crimes and internal fraud and abuse.

Monitor Implementation

The board's policies should establish mechanisms for providing the board with information needed to monitor the enterprise's operations. Perhaps the most important of these will be management reports to the board. These reports should be carefully framed to present information in an objective form that is meaningful to the board. The appropriate level of detail and frequency of individual reports will vary with the circumstances of each enterprise. Reports should include information on:

- Capital outlays and adequacy.
- Income, expenses, and cash flow of the enterprise.
- Investment pipeline, setting forth properties under consideration, negotiation, and letter of intent.
- Investment watch list setting forth properties or investments that are not performing in line with expectations, their present status, and remedial plans.
- Portfolio diversification and concentrations.
- Compliance with financial covenants and terms.
- Management of interest-rate risk.
- Performance in all of the above areas compared to past performance and to peer group performance.
- All insider transactions that benefit, directly or indirectly, controlling shareholders, directors, officers, employees, or their related parties.
- Activities undertaken to ensure compliance with applicable laws (including IRS regulations pertaining to REIT status) and any significant compliance problems.
- Any extraordinary development likely to affect the integrity, safety, or profitability of the enterprise.

Reports should be provided to board members far enough in advance of board meetings (one to two weeks) to allow meaningful review. Management should be asked to respond to any questions raised by the reports.

Provide for Independent Reviews

The board has direct responsibility for hiring, firing, and evaluating the enterprise's independent auditors and should have access to the enterprise's regular corporate counsel and staff. The board should review the auditor's findings with management and should monitor management's efforts to resolve any identified problems. The board should also establish additional mechanisms for independent review and testing of compliance with board policies and procedures, applicable laws and regulations, and for accuracy of information provided by management. It is recommended that an independent review and quality assessment of the REIT's assets be performed periodically (every one to three years).

In some instances, outside directors may wish to consider employing independent counsel, accountants, or other experts, at the enterprise's expense, to advise them on special problems arising in the exercise of their oversight function. Such situations might include the need to develop appropriate responses to problems in important areas of the enterprise's performance or operations.

Plan Board Activities

To fulfill their numerous duties and responsibilities, the directors should set an annual agenda for board activities.[9] This will enable the board chair, CEO, and other directors to agree in advance when various topics will be reviewed and deliberated. An annual agenda will enable directors and committees to prepare for and give in-depth attention to specific topics at each meeting, in addition to addressing the inevitable urgent matters and routine compliance tasks. The annual agenda should include meetings that address the following:

- **Strategic planning.** To review, formulate, and approve corporate and business mission statement and strategy, including investor-relations goals.
- **Portfolio planning.** To review and approve portfolio quality characteristics, investment and divestment goals, and other capital allocations.
- **Operations planning.** To review and approve operational strategies and plans and to compare results to plans, competitors, and performance measures or benchmarks.

- **Financial planning.** To review and approve financial standards, policies, and controls.
- **Human resource planning.** To select senior management, review management succession plan, and provide for management development and training.
- **Performance appraisal.** To evaluate top management and board effectiveness and, if necessary, take steps to improve.

These guidelines should help directors approach their responsibilities with clarity, assurance, and effectiveness, thereby ensuring shareholder democracy with effective corporate governance. If directors succeed in meeting these goals, the larger goal of maintaining confidence in the public real estate market will be achieved.

BOARD COMPOSITION

The New York Stock Exchange (NYSE), American Stock Exchange (AMEX), NASDAQ National Market System (NASDAQ/NMS), and other securities exchanges (hereafter referred to as the exchanges) require that all domestic listed companies have at least two independent directors.[10] NASAA policy requires that the majority of the directors shall be independent directors.[11] In additional to these requirements, the Code of Ethics of The National Association of Real Estate Investment Trusts (NAREIT) requires that each member have a majority of independent directors. We recommend that the board include a majority of independent directors.

NASAA policy states that a REIT must have a minimum of three directors. In most cases, three directors will not be enough to provide effective corporate governance for a REIT. We believe the board needs seven to nine directors to enable it to fulfill its duties and responsibilities. This size board should allow directors to get to know each other well, thereby ensuring more effective discussions and decision making at board and committee meetings, with the CEO and other members of management, and among the board members.

Director Independence

The role of independent directors (also known as outside directors) has received a lot of attention from institutional investors and the business press.

This attention prompted Congress to convene a hearing in 1993 to consider legislative action on the subject.[12] Investors, management, and directors must recognize the importance of independent judgment and thought when the company's affairs are debated. Independent directors are one of the least expensive and often one of the most effective means for companies to gain perspective.

REIT shareholders, like shareholders of all public companies, need independent directors to represent them by overseeing the business and management. After all, management cannot oversee itself and, if entrenched, can dangerously affect the well-being of the enterprise. Additionally, conflicts of interest may interfere with the judgment of management and others with a vested interest in the outcome of their decisions.

Regulatory requirements regarding independent directors are fairly clear. However, institutional investors, the investing public, and the courts are demanding a much higher standard regarding corporate governance and the role of independent directors. We believe that REIT boards are taking appropriate steps to improve their boards, thereby satisfying the governance demands of their various constituencies and avoiding the need for legislative action.

NASAA policy presents standards for independent directors that are not only more specific but are higher than those of the exchanges. REITs listed on the exchanges are generally exempt from compliance with NASAA policy. Regardless of this exemption, NASAA policy provides important guidelines that make considerable progress in meeting the demands of a REIT's various constituencies.

Definition of Independent Director

The exchanges all define *independent director* in similarly broad terms. For example, AMEX defines independent directors as "directors who are not officers nor represent concentrated or family holdings of its shares; and who, in the view of the company's board of directors, are free of any relationship that would interfere with the exercise of independent judgment."[13] The NYSE also explicitly excludes "directors who are affiliates of the company or officers or employees of the company or its subsidiaries."[14]

NASAA policy defines independent directors as the directors of a REIT who are "not associated and have not been associated within the last two years, directly or indirectly, with the REIT's sponsor or adviser of the REIT."[15]

The Council of Institutional Investors, a Washington, DC-based group representing major pension funds, defines an independent director as "someone whose only nontrivial connection to the corporation is that person's directorship."[16]

Tests of Independence

The exchanges clearly indicate that the board of directors' opinion regarding a director's "independence" should be based on an assessment of the ability of each individual to exercise independent judgment in carrying out his or her responsibilities as director. Unfortunately, reasonable people have differed and will continue to differ on what circumstances interfere with an individual's ability to exercise independent judgment.

NASAA policy provides a list of relationships that disqualify an individual, such that an individual cannot be considered an independent director "if he or she does any of the following:

- Owns an interest in the sponsor, adviser, or any of his or her affiliates.
- Is employed by the sponsor, adviser, or any of his or her affiliates.
- Is an officer or director of the sponsor, adviser, or any of his or her affiliates.
- Performs services, other than as a director, for the REIT.
- Is a director for more than three REITs organized by the sponsor or advised by the adviser.
- Has any material business or professional relationship with the sponsor, adviser, or any of his or her affiliates."[17]

To determine whether a business or professional relationship is material, NASAA policy suggests determining the materiality of the income a prospective independent director derives from the sponsor, adviser, and affiliates. If such income exceeds 5 percent of his or her gross income, a material relationship exists.[18]

NASAA policy also disqualifies individuals whose relatives are or have been associated with the REIT.

Similar to NASAA policy, the Council of Institutional Investors includes as part of its definition of independent director a list of relationships that members believe pose the greatest threat to a director's independence. The existence of any one of these relationships removes a director from the independent category. The Council's list says, "a director will not generally be considered independent if he or she

- has been employed by the corporation or an affiliate in an executive capacity;
- is an employee or owner of a firm that is one of the corporation's or its affiliate's paid advisers or consultants;
- is employed by a significant customer or supplier;
- has a personal services contract with the corporation or one of its affiliates;
- is employed by a foundation or university that receives significant grants or endowments from the corporation or one of its affiliates;
- is a relative of an executive of the corporation or one of its affiliates; or
- is part of an interlocking directorate in which the CEO or other executive officer of the corporation serves on the board of another corporation that employs the director."[19]

Recommendations Regarding Independence

We believe that determination of independence should not be limited to the board's assessment of an individual's ability to exercise independent judgment, a test of materiality, or other similar tests. The board should also consider how investors or other interested stakeholders may view the director candidate and his or her relationship with the CEO and the REIT. For example, could a friend of the CEO, while not an officer or employee of the REIT, be an independent director? There are many situations in which an individual qualifies as an outside director but may have difficulty acting as an independent director.

Additionally, REIT legal counsel, investment bankers, and other service providers can provide considerable insight about opportunities and threats facing the company and in the marketplace, but they may have problems being totally objective—because of real and perceived conflicts of interest. The valuable opinions of these individuals should be available to the board, but these individuals should not be members of the board.

Avoiding conflicts of interests and the appearance of such conflicts is likely to reduce investor and media speculation about such conflicts and, in conjunction with that, reduce the likelihood of shareholder litigation and governmental intervention.[20] Considering shareholder perceptions in the selection process sets even higher standards than those criteria set forth above.

NOMINATING DIRECTORS

Although REIT board members are elected by the shareholders, for all practical purposes the initial members of the board of directors are selected by the individuals forming the REIT. With the exception of satisfying the demands of large shareholders or major lenders, the independent directors are generally selected by the CEO.

NASAA policy requires that independent directors nominate replacements for vacancies among the independent director positions. To comply with this requirement, the board can form a nominating committee to identify, recommend, and recruit candidates for membership on the board. Executive search firms should be considered to provide expertise and assistance with this work.

All of the recommendations regarding nominating committees suggest that the nominating committee be composed of a majority of independent directors. Many suggest it be composed entirely of independent directors. The selection of these independent directors should consider each candidate's experience, ability, diversity, and time constraints.

Experience Requirements

It is easy to agree that an independent director should have good judgment, business sense, and integrity. Unfortunately, there are no easy tests to determine these qualities.

The exchanges do not address experience requirements for directors. NASAA policy requires that directors "shall have had at least three years of relevant experience demonstrating the knowledge and experience required to successfully acquire and manage the type of assets being acquired by the REIT."[21] In addition, NASAA policy requires at least one of the independent directors to have three years of relevant real estate experience.

The relevant experience requirement is generally defined broadly such that the assets being acquired by the REIT include not only real property, but financial, human, and technological resources. Accordingly, board candidates can satisfy this requirement with three years of prior management or board of director experience. Experience as a director or officer of another public company is particularly desirable, as it should help management make the transition from an entrepreneurial organization with little public disclosure responsibilities to one capable of communicating with its diverse group of shareholders, industry analysts, regulators, and other constituencies. An ideal candidate may be the CEO or a board member of another REIT—one operating in a different segment of the real estate market. Not all director candidates need to have public company experience.

In order for a candidate to comply with the relevant real estate experience requirement, he or she should have experience in the specific property type of the REIT (for example, apartments, office buildings, shopping centers, manufactured housing communities, industrial properties). If such a candidate is not available, one with significant experience in another type of investment real estate is acceptable.

Diversity

Although there are no requirements regarding experience other than those noted above, companies will benefit by seeking board members who have a diverse set of backgrounds, experiences, and skills. This diversity will provide for stronger management—one more likely to meet the challenges of today's marketplace as well as those to come. A list of desirable board members should include CEOs of REITs or other public companies; retired CEOs; CEOs of private companies; corporate lawyers; CPAs; commercial bankers; investment bankers; real estate developers, operators, and brokers; large shareholders; economists; community leaders; and academicians.

Consideration should be given to each individual's particular area(s) of expertise (finance, international business, strategy, marketing, operations, human resources, ethics, technology) and how that expertise will complement current management. Also, the board should make efforts to be representative of the REIT's various constituencies, particularly in terms of gender and race.

Time Commitment

Candidates should be willing and able to devote a substantial amount of time to performing board duties. While board meetings may be held 4 to 12 times annually, preparation for and attendance at committee meetings (audit, compensation, nominating) and special meetings, visiting REIT properties, and similar duties demand that independent directors devote many more days to their board duties. To be effective, a director is likely to spend a minimum of 8 to 12 days (a maximum of 18 to 24) annually performing board duties.

With more attention being given to the role of independent directors, this time commitment is likely to increase. States are legislating and companies are adopting bylaws requiring that the audit, compensation, and nominating committees be composed of only independent directors. In some companies, the chair of the board of directors is an independent director, thereby separating the management of the board from the management of the company. In others, the board has adopted the lead director concept, whereby the independent directors select one independent director who agrees to accept a call to leadership, should the need arise. Still others are scheduling additional regular meetings exclusively for the independent directors. All of these are examples of the expanding scope of independent directors' work.

This commitment of time is the primary reason it is difficult to attract independent directors, particularly CEOs of other public companies. In the search for qualified people who can make such a time commitment, retired CEOs can be an excellent source for director candidates.

The demands on a director's time highlight the need to consider limiting the number of boards on which an individual serves. Although there are no legislative or regulatory guidelines, many directors and corporate governance experts believe that two or three boards are the most one can effectively serve on.[22]

While some real estate entrepreneurs have demonstrated that success does not require a strong board of directors, the long-term success of many REITs (and investor confidence in the REIT industry) may depend on the composition of the board and contribution of the independent directors.

Among REITs participating in the FPL survey, the most common number of board members is seven (for 43 percent of those responding). On average, two directors—the CEO and president/COO—represent management (insiders), with the other five being outside directors. Twenty-five percent of respondents had one or more female board members, while 12 percent had one or more minority directors.

Director qualities considered most important by survey respondents included intelligence, integrity, and personality, followed by time and commitment, profit and loss experience, and a real estate background.

NINE PRINCIPLES FOR MORE EFFECTIVE BOARDS

EVALUATING THE CEO AND THE BOARD

The board of directors is responsible for hiring, retaining, motivating, and when necessary, removing the company's CEO and other principal operating officers. In addition, the board is responsible for reviewing and approving management succession plans and management development programs. Proactive human resource planning will increase an enterprise's productivity and performance, provide early warning of potential challenges and opportunities, and minimize the impact of crises that may confront the enterprise. Accordingly, the CEO and other officers and employees should have their performance appraised. Unfortunately, directors are often reluctant to evaluate the performance of the CEO and do so only in times of crisis—often too late to be of any constructive use.

CEO Evaluation Issues

The task of evaluating the CEO is a difficult one that is often ignored. One of the reasons is that the CEO probably recommended most of the directors to the board. For the new real estate enterprises, primarily REITs, the task is even more challenging given the "insider" ownership of most senior managements. Additionally, for the majority of real estate enterprises, the CEO also chairs the board of directors. To address this conflict, some companies have separated the CEO position from that of the board chair. After all, how can the CEO/chair evaluate his or her own performance? With support from institutional investors and other groups, this separation of the chair's leadership and management of the board of directors from the CEO's leadership and management of the company is likely to become more common.

With the termination of CEOs at many Fortune 500 companies in the last few years, evaluating the CEO has received increased attention.[23] A landmark report, "Performance Evaluation of Chief Executive Officers, Boards, and Directors," was issued by the National Association of Corporate Directors (NACD) in 1994.[24] The NACD report addresses such issues as how the board of directors should evaluate the CEO, the criteria and standards to be used in assessing CEO performance, how the board should evaluate its own performance, and how the board should evaluate the performance of individual board members.

Whether or not a formal evaluation process exists, CEO and company performance and problems should always be a part of board discussions. After all, the board of directors is responsible for ensuring that the enterprise is in the hands of qualified management. Including a formal CEO performance evaluation as part of the annual board agenda will help to assure that the important issues relevant to the leadership and management of the company are addressed.

According to the FPL survey, only 20 percent of the REITs that responded have a formal written process to evaluate the CEO's performance. Twenty-seven percent do not evaluate the CEO, and 53 percent evaluate the CEO informally.

Benefits of CEO Evaluation

CEO evaluations make sense for all CEOs. They are not just for inexperienced CEOs, CEOs of recently formed REITs, companies with CEO problems, or CEOs whose companies are having difficulties. Properly conducted, CEO performance evaluations can do the following:[25]

- Facilitate board-CEO communication regarding company and CEO performance expectations.
- Improve communication between the board and the CEO regarding the evaluation of actual performance.
- Help the CEO identify personal strengths and weaknesses, and ways to capitalize on or correct them.
- Provide warning signs of potential problems to the CEO and the board.
- Provide clear guidelines for CEO compensation decisions.
- Help foster a sense of teamwork between the board and the CEO.
- Provide a clear signal to shareholders and regulators that the board is monitoring and evaluating the actions of the CEO and senior management.

Harvard Business School professor Walter Salmon, writing about CEO performance reviews, said, "Evaluating the CEO also helps to preserve his or her humility, a trait that's hard to come by if you're the unchallenged leader of a sizable corporate entity. In addition, annual evaluations may encourage CEOs to appraise their own subordinates more thoroughly."[26]

Evaluating the Board

In addition to evaluating the CEO, boards should evaluate their own performance and the performance of individual board members. A 1993 survey by the Heidrick Partners shows clearly that CEOs want their corporate directors to know how their performance as board members measures up against the needs of their companies.[27] CEOs surveyed said that nearly 40 percent of the members of their boards were only "somewhat effective" or worse. CEOs said it would benefit their companies if board members knew how they were doing in key areas.

Similar to directors' reluctance to evaluate the CEO, most of the CEOs surveyed said they had never spoken with an ineffective or marginally effective director about shortcomings in board performance. The CEOs also said they rarely ask ineffective directors to resign.

CEO and Director Position Descriptions

Successful performance evaluations require a clear and shared understanding of expectations. With this in mind, many companies have developed position descriptions for the CEO, directors, and board chair. For example, a position description for the CEO might include the following:[28]

- Develops and recommends to the board a long-term strategy and vision for the company that leads to the creation of shareholder value.
- Develops and recommends to the board annual business plans and budgets that support the company's long-term strategy.
- Ensures that the day-to-day business affairs of the company are appropriately managed.
- Ensures continuous improvement in the quality and value of the products and services provided by the company.
- Ensures that the company has an effective management team below the level of the CEO and has an active plan for its development and succession.
- Ensures, in cooperation with the board, that there is an effective succession plan in place for the CEO position.

A position description for the board of directors prepared by J. Keith Louden, former president and chairman of the American Management Association's Presidents Association, includes sections on (1) duties and

NINE PRINCIPLES FOR MORE EFFECTIVE BOARDS

1. **The board must understand and support management's vision and strategy.**
2. **Boards should have a majority of independent—not just outside—directors.**
3. **Boards should develop board leadership skills among the independent directors.**
4. **The independent directors should actively participate in establishing board procedures, agendas, and policies.**
5. **The independent directors should schedule regular meetings without insiders.**
6. **The audit committee, compensation committee, governance committee, and nominating committee should be composed solely of independent directors.**
7. **The board should conduct annual performance reviews of the CEO and other key members of management, board members, and the board itself.**
8. **The board should develop an annual agenda of board activities to assure that it fulfills all of its duties and responsibilities properly.**
9. **Directors should have a substantial personal stake in the company, their pay should be only in stock and cash, and directors' compensation should be fully disclosed in the proxy statement.**

Source: Corporate Governance Center, Kennesaw State University.

responsibilities regarding shareholder relations and financial structure and actions; (2) policies, objectives, and plans; (3) management; (4) controls; (5) employee relations; (6) government and the public; and (7) working relationships.[29] The section on management includes the following:

- Elect the CEO and such other corporate officers of the company and delegate management responsibility and authority to them; approve position descriptions.

- Appraise the performance of the chief executive officer.
- Approve overall programs for management development and see to it that such programs exist.

A position description for the board chair (and lead director), in addition to the directors' duties and responsibilities listed above, should provide that the chair (1) provide leadership to the board, (2) establish meeting agenda and schedules, (3) chair (lead) meetings of the board, and (4) manage directors' performance reviews.[30]

CEO Performance Evaluation

The NACD report suggests that directors evaluate the performance of the CEO in each of the following areas:[31]

- **Leadership.** Leads the company and sets a philosophy that is well understood, widely supported, consistently applied, and effectively implemented.
- **Strategic Planning.** Ensures the development of a long-term strategy; establishes objectives and plans that meet the needs of shareholders, customers, employees, and all corporate stakeholders; ensures consistent and timely progress toward strategic objectives; obtains and allocates resources consistent with strategic objectives.
- **Financial Results.** Establishes appropriate annual and longer-term financial objectives and manages to consistently achieve these goals; ensures that appropriate systems are maintained to protect assets and maintain effective control of operations.
- **Succession Planning.** Develops, attracts, retains, motivates, and supervises an effective top management team capable of achieving objectives; provides for management succession.
- **Human Resources/EEO.** Ensures the development of effective recruitment, training, retention, and personnel communications plans and programs to provide and motivate the necessary human resources to achieve objectives; establishes and monitors programs to provide equal employment opportunity for minority employees.
- **Communications.** Serves as chief spokesperson, communicating effectively with shareholders and all stakeholders.

22 QUESTIONS FOR DIAGNOSING YOUR BOARD

If you answer yes to all 22 questions, you have an exemplary board.

1. **Are there three or more outside directors for every insider?**
2. **Are the insiders limited to the CEO, the COO, and the CFO?**
3. **Do your directors routinely speak to senior managers who are not represented on the board?**
4. **Is your board the right size (8 to 15 members)?**
5. **Does your audit committee, not management, have the authority to approve the partner in charge of auditing the company?**
6. **Does your audit committee routinely review "high-exposure" areas?**
7. **Do compensation consultants report to your compensation committee other than to the company's human resource officers?**
8. **Has your compensation committee shown the courage to establish formulas for CEO compensation based on long-term results—even if the formulas differ from industry norms?**
9. **Are the activities of your executive committee sufficiently contained to prevent the emergence of a "two-tier" board?**
10. **Do outside directors annually review succession plans for senior management?**
11. **Do outside directors formally evaluate your CEO's strengths, weaknesses, objectives, personal plans, and performance every year?**

- **External Relations.** Ensures that the company and its operating units contribute appropriately to the well-being of their communities and industries. Represents the company in the community and industry affairs.
- **Board Relations.** Works closely with the board of directors to keep them fully informed on all important aspects of the status

12. Does your nominating committee rather than the CEO direct the search for new board members and invite candidates to stand for election?

13. Is there a way for outside directors to alter the meeting agenda set by your CEO?

14. Does the company help directors prepare for meetings by sending relevant routine information, as well as analyses of key agenda items, ahead of time?

15. Is there sufficient meeting time for thoughtful discussion in addition to management monologue?

16. Do the outside directors meet without management on a regular basis?

17. Is your board actively involved in formulating long-range business strategy from the start of the planning cycle?

18. Does your board, rather than the incumbent CEO, select the new chief executive—in fact as well as in theory?

19. Is at least some of the directors' pay linked to corporate performance?

20. Is the performance of each of your directors periodically reviewed?

21. Are directors who are no longer pulling their weight discouraged from standing for reelection?

22. Do you take the right measures to build trust among directors?

Source: Walter J. Salmon, "Crisis Prevention: How to Gear Up Your Board," *Harvard Business Review,* Jan.–Feb. 1993, p. 73.

and development of the company. Facilitates the board's governance, composition, and committee structure. Implements board policies and recommends policies for board consideration.

This evaluation should provide a basis for discussion of the CEO's strengths and weaknesses, ways for the CEO and the company to capitalize on the strengths, and how to overcome or minimize the weaknesses identified. In many cases, the board can help the CEO by sharing experience and expertise. In some situations, shifting duties, responsibilities, and roles among members of the management team may be warranted.

Unfortunately, there may be times when the board will need to remove the CEO. Removal may be warranted for any number of causes, including decline in competency, lack of vision, or even personality differences. CEOs of recently organized REITs are faced with the challenge of managing a public company with numerous constituencies in a marketplace that evaluates the company daily. Some will meet the challenge. Some will not.[32]

Successful human resource planning requires developing a shared understanding of performance expectations. It also requires addressing the sometimes difficult task of evaluating the CEO, other officers and employees, the board of directors, and individual directors. An essential element of human resource planning is performance appraisal, with each employee receiving feedback on his or her performance relative to objectives and standards. Most appraisal programs also identify areas for employee development, specifying and assisting with training and development programs for continued personal development.

Effective performance appraisals help the CEO and other employees grow, increasing creativity, productivity, and job satisfaction. This will result in a stronger, more profitable enterprise.

ENDNOTES

1. Martin Lipton and Jay W. Lorsch, "A Modest Proposal for Improved Corporate Governance," *The Business Lawyer,* vol. 48, no. 1 (November 1992), pp. 59–63.
2. Robert C. Prozen, "Institutional Investors: The Reluctant Activists," *Harvard Business Review,* Jan.-Feb. 1994, pp. 140–149.
3. Dana Wechsler Linden and Nancy Rotenier, "Good-bye to Berle & Means," *Forbes,* January 3, 1994, p. 100.
4. "Statement of Policy Regarding Real Estate Investments Trusts," (NASAA Policy) as revised and adopted by the North American Securities Administrators Association membership on September 29, 1993.
5. Definition of effective corporate governance included in each issue of *DIRECTOR'S Monthly,* published by the National Association of Corporate Directors, Washington, DC.

6. "1996 Board Practices Survey of Public Real Estate Organizations" (FPL survey) surveyed approximately 300 public real estate entities, of which 70 responded. The FPL survey was conducted by FPL Associates, the Corporate Governance Center at Kennesaw State University, and the Newman Real Estate Institute at Baruch College.
7. "The 1995 Corporate Governance Survey" (NACD Survey) (Washington, DC: National Association of Corporate Directors, 1995). A survey of 7,000 CEOs, with a response rate of 8 percent.
8. Lipton, p. 64.
9. Jay W. Lorsch, *Pawns or Potentates: The Reality of America's Corporate Boards,* (Harvard Business School Press, 1989), pp. 179–180.
10. See New York Stock Exchange Listed Company Manual (NYSE), New York, June 1986, p. 3-1; American Stock Exchange Requirements for Original Listing (AMEX), New York, April 1993, p. 11; and NASD By-laws, The NASDAQ Stock Market, as amended Oct. 5, 1990, Washington DC, Part III, Sec. 5(c). Requirements for other exchanges are not specifically addressed.
11. NASAA Policy.
12. "Corporate Governance: The Role of the Independent Directors on Corporate Boards," Hearing before the Subcommittee on Telecommunications and Finance of the Committee on Energy and Commerce, House of Representatives, April 21, 1993, Serial No. 103-56.
13. AMEX, p. 11.
14. NYSE, p. 3-1.
15. NASAA Policy, Section I(B)(14).
16. Definition of Independent Director, as adopted by the Council of Institutional Investors (CII Definition) on April 5, 1991, Washington, DC.
17. NASAA Policy, Section I(B)(14)(a).
18. *Ibid,* Section I(B)(14)(b).
19. CII definition.
20. See "Boardrooms: The Ties That Blind?" *Business Week*, May 2, 1994, pp. 112–114; and "Corporate Governance: The Role of the Independent Directors on Corporate Boards."
21. NASAA Policy, Section II(D).
22. "Report of the NACD Blue Ribbon Commission on Director Professionalism," Washington, DC: National Association of Corporate Directors, 1996.
23. See Michael A. Verespej, "CEOs Under the Magnifying Glass," *Industry Week,* April 19, 1993, pp. 60–64; Richard M. Ferry, "CEOs and Boards:

Reform or Gridlock?" *Directors & Boards,* Summer 1993, pp. 59–60; Walter J. Salmon, "Crisis Prevention: How to Gear Up Your Board," *Harvard Business Review*, Jan.–Feb. 1993, pp. 68–75.

24. "Performance Evaluation of Chief Executive Officers, Boards, and Directors" (NACD Report), Washington DC: National Association of Corporate Directors, 1994.

25. *Ibid,* pp. 1–2.

26. Salmon, p. 71.

27. "Board Quality and Performance Evaluations: A Survey of Fortune 1000 Chief Executives" (Chicago: The Heidrick Partners Inc., Fall 1993).

28. NACD Report, p. 25.

29. J. Keith Louden, "A Position Description for the Board," *Directors & Boards,* Spring 1993, pp. 25–27.

30. Donald H. Thain and David S. R. Leighton, "Improving Board Effectiveness: The Problem and the Solution Begin with the Chairman," *Business Quarterly,* Summer 1992, pp. 19–33.

31. NACD Report, pp. 25–26.

32. See Gary B. Roberts and Laura L. Matherly, "Removal, Resignation, and Retirement of the CEO," *Handbook for Corporate Directors* (New York: McGraw-Hill, 1985), Chapter 37; and James F. Calvert, "When It Becomes Necessary for the Board to Remove the CEO," *DIRECTOR'S Monthly,* Washington, DC: NACD, October 1992, pp. 1–4.

CHAPTER

11

INVESTOR RELATIONS

Stephanie M. Mishra, *Partner, The Financial Relations Board*
Frederick J. Nachman, *Senior Vice President/Director of Investor Relations, Golin/Harris Communications*

In a publicly traded real estate investment trust (REIT), ownership of the company changes from top management and its small circle of investors to a disparate group of shareholders: officers and directors; institutions, including global investment banks, securities and mutual fund firms, insurance companies, bank trust departments, pension funds, and independent money managers; and individual investors. The practice of investor relations (IR) involves communicating the quantitative and qualitative information needed for investors to plan their investment strategies and make informed decisions about the company's securities. Although the investor relations function can be fulfilled simply by providing the public with required documents—annual and quarterly reports, and news releases on company earnings and significant corporate events—the successful IR practice is in fact a sophisticated marketing activity involving a unified communications message, audience targeting and research, and frequent telephone and personal contact with investors. The ultimate goal is to lower the cost of capital, raise the price of the stock to a realistic value, and keep an orderly liquid market for the stock.

The investor relations function is handled in a number of ways. Many companies set up a separate IR department managed by a director or manager of investor relations. Where a separate department is not established, investor relations is most typically the responsibility of the chief financial officer and the finance department. To a lesser extent, the corporate communications or public relations department handles the functions. In all cases, either the president or chief executive officer must be actively involved to ensure the success of any program since investors' perceptions of top management are a critical factor in whether they purchase stock.

In recent years, consultants have played an increasing role in investor relations. Since only the largest REITs have the need and resources for a full-time IR person, who commands benefits and deferred compensation as well as a salary, the use of consultants is growing. These consultants include specialized investor relations firms, the investor relations divisions of large public relations agencies, and individual consultants. They perform a wide range of services for the company and charge on an hourly, fixed fee, or per-project basis.

COMPONENTS

All investor relations programs—for either a newly public REIT or a veteran of the securities markets—must begin with an agreed-upon program that includes objectives, costs, and responsibilities. As you will see, a comprehensive IR program contains a large amount of printed materials and requires management to spend a good portion of its time talking directly with investors.

Investor relations is simply another form of communication: Your company's credibility is at stake with almost every public pronouncement, and goodwill that has been developed over a period of time can be dissipated almost immediately by poorly communicated information. It is therefore imperative that the investment message be consistent from day one and that it be reviewed continually when putting together or revising major IR materials and presentations.

DISCLOSURE

There is no definition of *material disclosure,* and in the absence of a court ruling, the IR veteran usually views disclosure as "I know it when I see it, or at least I think I do." The spate of class-action suits has further clouded the issue, in that it inhibits many companies from making disclosures, particularly of a forward-looking nature, for fear they will be sued down the road when said pronouncement turns out to be less than true. Unfortunately, the very caution that prevents companies from making disclosures—often at the advice of counsel—will cause unhappiness from shareholders when lower-than-expected earnings, a cost overrun on a new development, or a lost management contract is finally announced.

The following is a general definition of material information: *Material information is information that when known would cause an investor to buy or sell the stock.* Generally, an event requiring an 8-K filing should be broadly disclosed.

The gray area is how to respond to investor or media inquiries during the time a possible material event is developing: a pending acquisition or merger, restructuring, earnings decline, and so on. The prudent action is not to comment at all but to simply say, "No comment." If a company does choose to comment, it must be absolutely accurate and consistent in its response and follow up regularly as the event unfolds.

The disclosure and any necessary follow-up are done either via news releases distributed to approved disclosure wires (see "News Releases" below) or via an exclusive interview with one of these media sources (see "Media Relations" below). Under no circumstances should material information be disclosed to investors prior to release to the public, for this information can send a stock plummeting and prompt an inquiry from the SEC.

RESEARCH

In making the case for your REIT as a good investment, comparisons with peer companies are important. Analysts and portfolio managers will look at certain quantitative information when making their assessments of the many companies on the market, which are then factored into their perceptions of the quality of management, the growth strategy, and prospects for success.

For REITs, peer groups are mainly constructed using two main factors: the REIT type and the size. Investors tend to compare commercial/industrial REITs with other commercial/industrial REITs, retail mall REITs with other retail mall REITs, and so on. Some classifications, such as manufactured housing, are small enough that the peer group covers all of the REITs in the industry. For other classifications, number of properties, revenue, and square footage of the properties owned are used to determine a peer group. REIT indexes are also used for comparisons of total return.

Publications and news services such as Media General's *Industriscope,* Standard & Poor's Stock Reports, and Bloomberg Business News have constructed peer groups. It is best to check these periodically because they are not always accurate. We have found the services to be very amenable to making changes when given sufficient supporting information.

The following areas are most often used by investors for peer company comparisons: annualized yield, payout ratio, long-term debt as a percent of capitalization, implied cap rate, estimated annual funds from operations (FFO) growth, FFO multiple, and return on equity. This comparative information is very important. You should use it in news releases, conference call overviews, and presentation materials to make the case for your REIT as a good investment.

NEWS RELEASES

The typical REIT issues several types of news releases on a variety of subjects, including quarterly earnings, dividend declarations, acquisitions/divestitures, and management changes.

The quarterly earnings release is more than simply a forum to report financial results that can be picked up in the 10-Q. This release gives management the opportunity not only to discuss what happened during the last quarter and why but also to talk about the outlook for the future. In fact, the most successful news releases are those that comment beyond the quarter, especially if quarterly results are as expected, and provide investors with insights into corporate strategies for enhancing earnings growth, strategies for coping with a difficult market or interest-rate environment, and information as to whether there is an expected change in earnings expectations. Changes in earnings expectations should be announced in this venue since a news release constitutes full disclosure.

To measure what we call the information content of the news release, eliminate all of the information that can be found in the financial tables. If you are left with just a few paragraphs, the news release is not doing its job. We often hear, "But very little of the release makes it onto the wires or into the newspapers. Why should the release be so long?"

There are several reasons for a lengthy release: (1) The release is "of record" for the quarter and must take care of all disclosure situations, (2) technology enables the full text of news release to get into the hands of millions of people shortly after distribution, and (3) the release is sent to investors and the media, either on the day of distribution or days/weeks later, who know little or nothing about your REIT.

Because of their unique structure, REITs report quarterly earnings in a different way than a manufacturing company, bank, or insurance company. For any type of REIT, the following must be reported: rental revenue, property expenses, depreciation and amortization, net income, earnings per share, funds from operations (FFO), FFO per share, and number of common shares outstanding. UPREITs should also report total shares and operating partnership units. Some REITs also report funds available for distribution (FAD) and FAD per share. Balance sheet items that should be included on the asset side are: properties, cash and short-term investments; investments in unconsolidated partnerships; interest, rents, and other receivables; and deferred expenses. On the liabilities side, you should include mortgage notes payable and accounts payable, and investments in unconsolidated partnerships. If applicable, include minority interests as well.

Following the large number of public offerings in 1993 and 1994, the wire services have become more sophisticated about reporting REITs' quarterly financial results after they are released. Dow Jones, Reuters, and Bloomberg still report net income and earnings per share numbers because of their GAAP status, but they now generally report FFO and FAD numbers without prompting from company officials. The financial tables, where wire service reporters will look first when preparing to report financial results, should be set up so that the important FFO and/or FAD data are easily discernible.

News releases are distributed basically in two ways: by fax or by a for-fee distribution service. Occasionally, news releases are hand-delivered but only after they have been distributed by the other means because of the need for simultaneous disclosure. None of the services like to receive a release after it has been sent to its competitors, and wire service reporters will not hesitate to call a company if they feel slighted by seeing news on another wire before receiving their copy of the release. Distributing releases by fax requires that the company keep an up-to-date roster of the disclosure points' fax numbers and be dedicated to faxing to all the points as soon as possible. These disclosure points are Dow Jones News Service, Reuters, Bloomberg Business News, Standard & Poor's, Moody's, Fitch, and Associated Press.

The two major services—PR Newswire (800/832-5522) and Business Wire (800/227-0845)—are not only far more efficient than faxing yourself, the media prefer their means of distribution. Your release is sent simultaneously to the aforementioned disclosure points, where the text and tables can be downloaded directly into the reporter's computer. The full text of the release is also distributed to the myriad on-line services used by professional and individual investors, including Bridge, First Call, CompuServe, America Online, and Prodigy; leading media outlets in either a targeted area or nationwide; and investor networks set up by the companies. To ensure error-free transmission, the services accept computer-to-computer transmission, which also facilitates getting news on the wire as soon as possible after management approves the release.

For releases on dividend declarations, acquisitions/divestitures, and management changes, include the following:

- **Dividends.** Amount of quarterly payment, period for which it is being paid, payment date, record date, number of shares and/or OP units, and annualized yield based on most recent closing price.
- **Acquisitions/divestitures.** Property/portfolio being acquired or sold, buyer/seller, price and terms, cap rate, and expected date of completion (for letter of agreement).
- **Management changes.** Name of executive, age (Dow Jones prefers this information), new title, former title and/or company, and responsibilities (if not evident from title).

The distribution of news releases does not stop with their delivery to the wire services and media outlets. The company should maintain a fax list for sending the news release to investors as soon as possible after the news crosses one of the disclosure wires. By using a broadcast fax system (several companies offer this service), hundreds of copies of a news release can be distributed simultaneously to fax machines across the nation and around the world simply by sending one copy to a central distribution point. Professional investors have come to rely on this type of distribution, as it gets the full text and financial tables of a news release into their hands by the fastest possible means.

MEDIA RELATIONS

Media relations can play a significant role in a REIT's investor relations program. The so-called "third-party endorsement" of a newspaper, wire service, or magazine feature helps develop interest in a REIT and provides backing for the investment message being disseminated to the public.

For our purposes here, we will limit the discussion to media policy and procedures that pertain to the REIT as a public company. Publicity for mall openings, employee honors, and the like are often handled separately from the functions of the investor relations media program.

An excellent time- and cost-effective method of widely disseminating information about your REIT is through the wire service interview, most notably with Dow Jones News Service, Reuters, or Bloomberg Business News. These interviews are typically given shortly before earnings are announced because this allows management to give investors an indication of how the quarter went—in both quantitative and qualitative terms—while fulfilling full disclosure requirements. These interviews are typically referred to as earnings preview interviews or, in the case of Dow Jones, "Dow Jonsers."

Typically, two to four days before quarterly results are announced, the interview is arranged by calling the appropriate reporter at one of the news services and explaining that the company wishes to discuss earnings in advance of the actual distribution of the news release on an exclusive basis. Most often, the reporter is the service's REIT expert either in New York or in the local bureau nearest to the REIT's location. The interview consists of the CEO providing the expected range for FFO per share in the quarter (within a range of about 5 percent) and approximate revenues. As part of the interview, the reasons for successes are given, as well as areas that may have fallen short of expectations, and some indication of how the future is shaping up. Earnings projections are not required; however, this is the ideal forum for giving the Street an early indication that future results look certain to be better or worse than expected.

The reporter usually gets the text on the wire within hours. He or she occasionally will check back with management to make sure the numbers are correct and clear up any uncertainties about the interview. The coverage is almost always impressive; rather than the financial tables and a one- or two-line comment that runs on the wire following the distribution of the earnings release, the preview interview runs several paragraphs and contains much valuable information for investors. Parts of the interview can also run in newspapers that subscribe to these services, including *The Wall Street Journal, Investor's Business Daily,* and the *New York Times.*

Additional opportunities exist for spreading your investment message through the new video networks for professional investors. Bloomberg Forum interviews are conducted in New York, and NBC/First Call tapes industry conference presentations, significant news conferences, and executive interviews.

Crisis communications is another component of the total media relations program as it pertains to the investment community and material events. Management should have a contingency plan for considering whether certain information needs to be disclosed that includes appropriate directors, members of management, and outside legal, audit, and investor relations counsel. These persons should serve as sounding boards to give early warning on whether or when an action should be made public.

PRINTED MATERIALS

REITs wishing to expand their investor universe should use a variety of printed materials. The sooner a newly public REIT can produce a document to replace its offering prospectus, the better. Communications efforts must continually stress the positives of the investment thesis, and the offering prospectus—loaded with legalese and risk factors, and constrained from stating much more than a general growth strategy—cannot do this. One should still send prospectuses to interested persons, but a prospectus should not be the foundation of an investor relations effort.

Annual Report

The most important document produced during the year is the annual report. While the SEC only requires that a form 10-K be filed within 90 days of the close of the year, every REIT should publish a separate annual report that goes beyond reporting mandated numbers. The two can be combined into a "10-K wrap," in which a letter to shareholders and, often, an operations review are bound with the 10-K. REITs with long and complicated financial statements and notes often use the 10-K wrap format to save printing and production expenses.

The annual report has many audiences, but a good annual report is written primarily with the *potential* investor in mind, not the current shareholder. The primary objective should be to answer this two-part question: Why should I invest in this REIT, and why should I do it now? If this question is answered well, the annual report will serve all the audiences: shareholders, employees, banks, residents/tenants, suppliers, and acquisition targets.

An annual report usually contains eight main parts: company description, letter to shareholders, operations review or narrative, five-year financial summary, management's discussion and analysis (MD&A), financial statements, notes to financial statements, and corporate information. All sections except the company description, shareholders' letter, and operations review have fairly clear SEC requirements, down to the type size of the financial statements and notes. We will confine our discussion to the letter and operations review.

The tone of the shareholders' letter is almost as important as the content, since the previous year's results are not only available in the "back" of the report but for many investors are actually old news. While it's fine to be "pleased and proud" about last year's results, investors typically want a candid, no-holds-barred discussion of how well the REIT accomplished its goals, what management is doing about those that were not met, and a realistic assessment of the next year and beyond. Goals should be reiterated or revised, as the case may be, so that investors know exactly what management expects of itself, and investors in turn can decide whether this meets their requirements and goals.

A good operations review section can be used to expand on ideas discussed in the shareholders' letter as well as to explore other areas. When the annual report has a theme, this section is used to develop the theme; for example, if the theme is diversification of the portfolio, either by geography, tenant type, or other means, the operations review can give complete commentary on these efforts and include tables and graphs to illustrate points.

Quarterly Report

Like the annual report, a quarterly report is not required. Filing of a form 10-Q within 45 days after the close of the quarter is all that is needed.

Much has been written lately about the demise of the quarterly report. Surveys have shown an increasing number of companies eliminating them, scaling back the cost and production time, or simply sending a copy of the quarterly earnings release. The accessibility to earnings information, especially by individual investors, has put a premium on getting the information out to shareholders more quickly than in the past.

The quarterly report provides yet another opportunity to put your investment message in front of the public. The following will allow you to make maximum use of space while making the report more cost-effective:

- **Use the front panel to grab attention.** Add bullet points, such as "FFO Increase 11%"; "Construction of Mill Valley Mall Begins"; and "$63 Million REMIC Completed" to the usual "Meyer Properties, Inc., Third Quarter 1996 Report."
- **Pare down repetitive information in the letter.** Don't give a long reiteration of numbers that can be found in the tables: "FFO in the third quarter of 1996 was $16.8 million versus $15.7 million in the third quarter of 1995, an increase of 7.0%." Instead, talk in terms of percentage changes and the factors that caused the results.
- **Concentrate on the future.** Even the most timely report gets into the hands of investors well after results are announced. To justify the additional cost of the report, talk about your REIT's growth strategy in terms of how well it has been accomplished, what (if anything) needs to be altered in terms of goals and strategy, and a likely time frame for these accomplishments.

There are several ways to keep down costs. Instead of a fancy four-color report, use one or two colors. Desktop publishing is also an option. Design the report as a self-mailer with a permit number, saving the cost of envelopes and first-class postage. Finally, ADP has a computer-driven program called StreetLink that allows you to input the information on personal computer and send it to ADP for production. The completed report is mailed within 48 hours. For information, call ADP at (516) 254-7450.

Fact Books/Corporate Summary

An annual report, especially an expensively produced one, is not your best investor prospecting piece. For several dollars less per copy, a fact book or corporate summary provides professional investors with complete but concise information on your REIT.

A good fact book should contain:

- A description of the REIT.
- An investment thesis for the REIT.
- The market outlook.
- Your growth strategy.

- A financial review and profitability outlook.
- A 5- to 10-year financial summary containing selected income and cash flow statement and balance sheet data. The exact entries will vary with the REIT type.

Broker Sell Sheets

With their above-market divided returns, REITs are attractive investments for individuals. A relatively inexpensive way to get information to brokers is with a sell sheet. These are one-page, desktop-published sheets that contain the investment thesis for the REIT, which a broker can use virtually verbatim in pitching a client, and summary financial data. In addition to being mailed to thousands of brokers, these sell sheets can also be distributed, for a fee, directly to investment clubs and individuals by the two major individual investor organizations: the National Association of Investors Corp. (NAIC) and the National Association of Individual Investors (NAII).

PROFESSIONAL INVESTORS

Having reviewed the written materials needed for a top-quality investor relations program, we will now turn to the next major component of an IR program: investor contact.

Before determining the appropriate investment audience for a REIT, keep in mind that the investment community is comprised of buy- and sell-side analysts, institutional investors, independent money managers, pension fund advisers, retail brokers, and individual investors. Successful investor prospecting and presentation arrangements require that management first understands the role each of these investors plays in the financial community.

Buy- and Sell-Side Analysts

Buy-side analysts are responsible for carrying our research on a public company or industry sector for the exclusive use of their firm's portfolio managers. In contrast, sell-side analysts publish and market stock recommendations—known as research reports—through a broker network that often "sells" their research to portfolio managers, institutional investors, and pension fund advisers. Sell-side analysts are the most difficult to convince of a REIT's investment merits because they choose stocks based on both the story's appeal and the transaction opportunities the stock represents. Often, sell-side analysts require a corporate finance relationship before they will consider formal coverage.

A buy-side analyst is typically compensated by a salary-plus-bonus arrangement. Again, the base is typically a reflection of the individual's experience and track record. The bonus depends on how handsomely the analyst's recommendations have paid off in the investment firm's portfolios.

A sell-side analyst is usually compensated with a combination of a base salary plus commission. The base salary, as one would imagine, is also related to experience and track record. The commissions are determined by the analyst's ability to generate trading commissions for his or her firm from its (usually buy-side) clients.

The analyst's ability to evaluate a REIT's growth prospects accurately and continually, on one hand, and the ability to provide service to the buy-side client, on the other hand, determines income levels. While specific percentages are impossible to pinpoint, the amount of a successful analyst's commission often exceeds 50 percent of base salary.

When it comes to the research side and the corporate finance side of the investment company, the Chinese wall (supposedly as impenetrable as the Great Wall of China) separates the two in theory. Typically, the sell-sider will receive a handshake and an expression of appreciation when a company that he or she is following brings a deal to the firm. At the other end of the spectrum, the sell-sider could receive a commission of 10 percent to 20 percent of the profit from the deal. However, it's rare for an analyst to successfully make a case that his or her relationship with a client, rather than the corporate finance executive's relationship, actually brought investment banking business to the firm. As you can imagine, this is a highly sensitive area involving ethical issues, inside information, and other contentious matters.

Institutional Investors and Independent Money Managers

Institutional investors who manage at least $100 million in equity assets are required by the SEC to file a quarterly report of their equity holdings within 45 days after the end of each calendar quarter. This document is a most important source for identifying major owners of the stock. Because these are public documents, any individual can access the institutional holdings of any publicly owned company or the stock ownership of any institution through companies including CDA/Spectrum and Technimetrics.

Depending on the size of the institution, it may conduct its own in-house research or it may rely on outside sources. The larger institutional investment firms can have a significant impact on a company's stock price, depending on the level of their trading activity and percentage ownership in a company.

In contrast, independent money managers are those investment professionals who manage less than $100 million in assets. Some of these money managers may file 13-F holdings, although they are not required to by the SEC. Within this sector are boutique firms that conduct, publish, and sell research to a select audience and have no stock-transaction service. The research boutique generally sells its research for an annual fee, subscription, or one-shot price ("hard dollars") to clients. The boutique stakes its reputation and ultimately its revenues on its product.

Pension Plan Sponsors

There are four basic types of pension funds: public pension funds—namely the large public employee and teacher retirement systems—corporate plans of Fortune 500 companies, foundations, and endowments. These large investors may invest in REITs directly through their real estate or equity investment staff or more commonly through a fiduciary that provides real estate investment services. Pension plans are a particularly important investor audience because of their ability to also consider large private placements and joint venture transactions with a REIT.

Retail Brokers

Retail investors are valuable because they buy in smaller volumes than institutions, thereby reducing the price volatility that large orders can create. They also demonstrate a potential demand for shares, which is the "holy grail" for analysts who produce written research reports. Although there is no supporting documentation, most believe that retail investors typically hold their investments longer than other types of investment professionals.

INSTITUTIONAL OWNERSHIP

Although growth, value, and income are popular self-descriptors that asset managers use to describe their own investment styles, these self-descriptors hide more than they reveal about an institution's investment preferences. Value investors may or may not actually hold inexpensive stocks. Growth investors may or may not invest in smaller capitalization stocks with rapid top-line growth. Income investors may or may not hold stocks with high yields. For this reason, we classify active managers into five main styles:

- **Cash and value investors** seek to buy stocks that are undervalued relative to their intrinsic net worth due to temporary market inefficiencies. Discounting cash flow is the most dominant value strategy. Investors using this strategy attempt to compute the net present value of a business on the basis of its recurring cash flow. Other value investors use EVA/MVA or cash flow return on investment as tools to decide if companies are undervalued relative to their ability to generate wealth. Asset-based models estimate a firm's value by aggregating the value of the firm's assets and liabilities. These investors invest in firms whose market value is less than the sum of its parts.
- **Earnings investors** seek companies with growing earnings streams. These investors believe that stock price is largely a function of net income. The analyst's task is to estimate the rate of earnings growth. Some prefer companies with modest increases in earnings and dividends—"growth and income" investors—while others seek growth exclusively. The latter can be classified into discrete sets: those seeking earnings growth rates between 5 and 15 percent, those seeking growth rates between 15 and 25 percent, and those willing to pay PE multiples for growth in excess of 25 percent. A popular variant is earnings momentum investors. These investors require a company to have successively larger rates of earnings growth.
- **Dividend/reinvestment investors** focus on reinvestment rates, dividend growth rates, dividend yields, and discounted future dividend streams. Reinvestment, or plowback, rates are particularly important to these investors since reinvestment contributes to the company's growth rate. Some dividend investors invest in

companies that do not pay a dividend if they believe management can reinvest capital better than the investor can. Dividend discount investors focus on the stream of cash disbursements being paid to shareholders. The net present value of the expected stream of cash disbursements to shareholders provides these investors with a means to value firms. Yield investors constitute a small minority of dividend/reinvestment investors.

- **Economy investors** employ top-down selection criteria as the first stage of their analysis. They seek companies that will benefit from forecast events over which a firm has no control. Economic, demographic, political, and other exogenous factors that can benefit certain kinds of stock while injuring others are the focus of the analysis. Fads, fashions, and technological developments are as important as interest rates, the balance of trade, and industry cycles to these investors. Once the classes of stocks that will benefit from the forecast conditions are identified, economy investors typically employ bottom-up, fundamental analysis to select portfolio candidates.
- **Theme investors** concentrate on selecting corporate attributes or management behaviors that management controls. These investors believe such attributes as incentive compensation for line employees, excellent customer service, growing investments abroad, and high insider ownership will provide companies a commanding edge over rivals that do not possess similar investment appeals. Socially responsible investors practice a form of theme investing. These investors limit their investment universe to firms they believe promote socially desirable practices.

INVESTOR TARGETING

It is important to keep in mind that there are over 250 public REITs vying for the attention of these various investment managers. As a result, it is important to have a well-defined strategy in targeting and communicating with these investors. Earlier in the chapter, we discussed how to create effective written materials. Now we will review how to target the appropriate institutional holders through one of two different targeting methods: industry peer comparison and investment peer comparison.

Industry Peer Comparison

A common targeting practice is to analyze the 13-F filings of REITs in a similar property sector. By using any one of the many databases available to investors today, it is relatively easy to compile a list of institutional investors who own 13-F peer holdings.

Before proceeding with your targeting efforts, it is important to keep in mind the investment styles of each institution. As we explained above, there are five dominant investment styles: earnings growth, value, economic, dividend, and theme. As an example, you should avoid contacting an earnings growth investor if your FFO is stagnant or declining. In addition, you should avoid contacting "IR immune" investors or institutions that are essentially unaffected by management's attempts to fully communicate with the Street. This group includes index, quantitative, and short-term investors.

Investment Peer Comparison

By statistically examining the holding of institutional investors, we can determine which companies are comparable to XYZ REIT on the basis of their investment appeals. We call the comparable companies "investment peers." The investment peers are discovered by correlating the dollar-weighted holdings of XYZ REIT's institutional shareholders with those of all other companies having comparable or larger institutional share ownership bases. High degrees of correlation result when XYZ REIT and its investment peers have many institutional investors in common.

Highly correlated stocks are often found in the same portfolios. Although these stocks are diversified across industries, they share other characteristics, attributes, and investment risks. These common attributes are the factors portfolio managers believe will help their portfolios beat the market. Consequently, portfolios are overweighted in these factors. By identifying a portfolio manager's revealed preferences through quantitative means, we are able to present those facets of XYZ REIT that will be most interesting to the targeted portfolio manager who overweights his portfolios with other companies possessing attributes like those of XYZ REIT. Portfolio managers who hold the investment peers but who hold little or none of XYZ REIT generally will buy your stock if it is shown to possess the factors or investment appeals that are key value drivers for the portfolio manager.

Targeting retail brokers and independent money managers through a systematic approach is more difficult because these investors are not required to file 13-F holdings. Since many of the national wirehouses have extensive retail networks, it is important to establish relationships with these analysts and encourage their formal research coverage. In addition, broker sell sheets (as described earlier) should be produced and mailed to members through a variety of services.

CONFERENCE CALLS

Recent articles on investment analyst teleconferences have appeared in *The Wall Street Journal* and other media, raising the visibility of this communications approach. We have long maintained that conference calls are an essential part of a successful investor relations program and have strongly advocated this technique for many years as one of the most efficient, cost-efficient, democratic, and credibility-building steps a company can take to maintain an orderly flow of news and uniform understanding of the facts.

Teleconference calls provide access to management for institutional followers, strengthening relationships with current holders and attracting the attention of interested prospects. By offering analysts and institutional investors a common meeting place and an opportunity to converse with management, companies can meet the informational needs of institutional investors on an individualized basis yet maintain the consistency of the investment message. At the same time, conference calls are a highly efficient use of executive time, reducing the number of phone calls that must be handled individually.

However, there are limits to the conference call format. The conference call is *not* a forum for new ideas. Conference calls enable management to *amplify* concepts already introduced in an earnings release to provide a greater understanding of specific aspects of the business. Analysts and institutional investors will generally ask more penetrating questions than individual investors; they are also more capable of understanding and using the more involved detail provided by management's answers. Therefore, on conference calls, management should provide a more complex level of detail for more knowledgeable investors, not new sets of material information.

Conference calls also have pitfalls, mainly the "minefield" of selective disclosure. During a conference call, if companies disclose information that can be material to investment buy or sell decisions, management has created a selective disclosure problem by disclosing material information to a select group of individuals without disseminating that information to the entire investment community. In this case, a news release should be written and issued as soon as possible.

While selective disclosure can occur any time management speaks to an investor, the benefits of conference calls far outweigh the risks. Independent studies continually show that companies that speak openly with investors have greater followings of analysts and more accurate consensus earnings estimates. These risks of selective disclosure underscore our recommendations for comprehensive earnings releases, complete with a detailed discussion of financial results and business conditions and how these results and conditions may affect future performance.

Well-managed conference calls, in conjunction with comprehensive earnings releases and a complete investor relations program, will help the investment community gain a greater understanding of a company. This will enable investors to price that company's stock more efficiently, more fully reflecting the company's investment potential. Longer term, this should reduce the company's cost of capital and provide it with access to the low-cost funds it needs to achieve its growth objectives.

Conference calls typically consist of opening remarks by management that are then followed by a question-and-answer session. In preparing for a quarterly conference call, one should consider the following:

- **Recommended frequency.** Conference calls should be a matter of course for all significant developments. Many companies with large or very active Street followings hold quarterly conference calls to discuss earnings. Conference calls can also be conducted following announcements of major acquisitions, unanticipated earnings declines, and top management changes.
- **Timing.** Conference calls should be conducted as soon as possible after the news crosses the Dow Jones, Reuters, or Bloomberg wires. There must, however, be enough time to reach investors by phone and to fax the release to all interested parties via the broadcast fax system described earlier. In addition, investors need time to review the news release. If a release is sent out before the market opens in the morning, it is best to have the conference call either later in the morning or in the afternoon. Waiting more than 24 hours creates the risk of losing large numbers of participants.

Note: Once a company has established a pattern of regular quarterly conference calls tied to earnings announcements, the call can be set up in advance. Unprecedented conference calls or conference calls tied to special announcements must not be set up until the news crosses the tape because there is some informational content in the disclosure that a call is taking place.

- **Content.** Management should begin with a brief overview, using the publicly disseminated earnings release as an outline. Because the investors should have a copy of the news release, it is not necessary to do a number-by-number recitation of financial results. As you are aware, there is frequently no disclosure difficulty in providing analysts with supporting background. You should be careful, however, to answer questions on not-yet-public subjects with "We cannot comment on that." A group conference call does not qualify as disclosure.
- **Management preparation.** Several days prior to the conference call, management should prepare a list of talking points to cover in the formal comments: introductory remarks, a list of questions likely to be asked (and the answers), approaches to avoiding repetitive questions, and strategies for limiting the length of the call if necessary.

INSTITUTIONAL CONFERENCES

Each year, there are numerous opportunities for corporate REITs and investors to participate in institutional and industry conferences. Many of the large investment banking firms sponsor REIT conferences that are attended by the firms' institutional and corporate banking clients. The National Association of Real Estate Investment Trusts (NAREIT) also sponsors an Institutional Investor forum each year, in which participating REIT members have the opportunity to listen to REIT panels, designated by investment strategy and moderated by an industry analyst. The moderator of each panel leads a discussion with management on issues, including current business conditions, capital structure, growth strategies, development, redevelopment, acquisition opportunities, management vision, managing growth, mergers and acquisitions, market conditions, opportunities, risks, overall portfolio strategy, market depth, and size.

The International Corporate Forum sponsors three- and four-day conferences during which 65 to 85 public corporations meet with the U.S.

and international institutional investment communities. Each forum includes three related industry groups, and is complemented by participating *Institutional Investor* magazine's "All-America Research Analysts" representing 12 leading brokerage firms. Four institutional investment conferences are held annually.

ADDITIONAL CONFERENCES

In addition to these institutional conferences, investors can attend company presentations sponsored by various investor relations agencies: the Financial Analysts Society, the National Association of Stockbrokers, the American Stock Exchange Security Analysts Forum, and the National Association of Investors Corporation (NAIC).

Investor relations agencies arrange formal presentations on behalf of their corporate clients throughout the year. These agencies should personally identify and invite via telephone the appropriate analysts, institutional portfolio managers, independent money managers, and retail brokers. Further, as a third party, they should follow up with participants to elicit comments about the company's presentation and determine the next steps in obtaining either sell-side coverage or new investors.

The Financial Analyst Society has 76 chapters worldwide with approximately 24,000 members, most of whom are analysts, portfolio managers, and bankers, and a very small number of whom are retail brokers who have a CFA. Its mission is to provide a forum for the exchange of information among investment professionals, corporate management, and other interested members of the public to maintain an active program of continuing education, to encourage the pursuit of high standards of ethics and professional conduct, and to promote integrity and professionalism. Each chapter sponsors monthly luncheons at which a public company presents to interested members who saw the Society's announcement of its presentation.

The National Stockbrokers Society has chapters in over 48 cities, including Los Angeles, San Francisco, Seattle, Portland, Denver, Chicago, Cleveland, New York, Hartford, Philadelphia, Boston, St. Louis, Dallas, Houston, Austin, Atlanta, Tampa, Palm Beach, and Ft. Lauderdale. Luncheons are held in all chapters; receptions and dinners are held in some cities. Each meeting features one company, with a presentation by a senior member of management, followed by a Q&A session. The audience is comprised of a select group of top-producing retail brokers from regional and national firms, plus portfolio managers and bank trust officers. Attendance varies by company and city.

The American Stock Exchange Security Analysts Forum holds several meetings per month for AMEX-listed companies in each of eight cities, including Chicago, Hartford, San Francisco, Minneapolis, Toronto, Montreal, and New York. The audience is typically a small group of securities analysts and portfolio managers from major brokerage firms and key institutions, usually averaging 10 to 15 attendees.

The NAIC was founded in 1951 to increase the number of individual investors in common stocks and to provide a program of investment education and information for new as well as experienced investors. NAIC has three classes of membership: Individuals, which has 50,000 members; Investment Club, which has over 13,000 clubs with 260,000 members; and Corporate, which has over 230 members.

The NAIC sponsors investors fairs for individual investors, held in key cities throughout the country. Four corporations and an analyst speak to groups ranging from 100 in smaller cities to more than 600 in larger cities.

Generally, given management's need to prioritize demands on time, we do not recommend presentation forums where the audience cannot be both quantified and qualified prior to the meeting. Many of these clubs and forums claim strong attendance; however, there is no guarantee of their interest. It's a shotgun approach, which in our experience doesn't work.

GROUP ONE-ON-ONE MEETINGS

An integral part of any investor relations program is formal analysts' presentations and one-on-one appointments. Face-to-face meetings between investment professionals and management are critical to closing the sale. The overwhelming majority of investors and research analysts want the opportunity to develop a personal assessment of management prior to committing their time and money. After all, they are banking on management's ability to implement strategies that will allow the company to grow and prosper.

When preparing for a group presentation, it is important that your formal remarks are geared toward the appropriate investment audience. If you are targeting institutional investors and sell-side analysts, your formal presentation must reflect a comprehensive analysis of your industry, strategies, markets, competitive position, and financial performance. On the other hand, if you want to enhance your retail ownership by addressing retail brokers, your presentation should not have too much detail and instead should emphasize three or four key investment appeals. Keep in mind that retail brokers have a limited amount of time to convince their clients of a company's investment prospects and its risks. In an effort to reinforce a message, we strongly recommend broker sell sheets.

During the formal presentation, management's prepared remarks should last no longer than 25 to 30 minutes so that the audience has sufficient time for the Q&A sessions. Slides are still the preferred medium. Companies often augment slides with video presentations, which can be run before and after the presentation. We recommend that the presentation get right to the REIT's investment appeals and growth strategy; presentations that take up valuable time up front with lengthy descriptions of the company and its portfolio run the risk of putting the audience to sleep. Presenting the "sizzle" first not only will pique the audience's interest but will also require that the script make a point-by-point case for investing in the REIT.

The small luncheon format is informal, at least when compared to a large group meeting. We presume a greater level of preparation by the audience, so we expect a more sophisticated list of questions from a small group. However, we cannot take it for granted that the audience will walk in with our preferred assessment of the company.

FACILITIES VISITS

One of the most effective ways to encourage buy- and sell-side interest is to conduct a property tour or headquarters visit. Not only does this allow investors to "kick the tires," it gives them the opportunity to meet additional members of management who do not typically participate in group meetings or conference calls.

Often, these meetings begin with a group dinner or breakfast, followed by a formal presentation in the morning, a property tour, and a luncheon presentation and Q&A session. Investors tend to like this format because it encourages a healthy dialogue between management and the investment community and allows for interplay between participants. Many REITs conduct their property tour in conjunction with one of the institutional conferences sponsored by NAREIT or an investment banking house.

PART IV

INVESTMENT ANALYSIS OF REITs

CHAPTER

12

THE HISTORICAL BEHAVIOR OF REIT RETURNS

A Capital Markets Perspective

Anthony B. Sanders, *Professor of Finance, Max M. Fisher College of Business, Ohio State University*

INTRODUCTION

Real estate investment trusts offer an alternative to direct-asset investment for institutional investors. REITs allow institutional investors to create a diversified portfolio of public real estate equities more rapidly and at a lesser cost than creating a diversified portfolio by acquiring properties directly. In addition to being more liquid than direct investment in real estate, investment performance can be better monitored with REITs than with appraisal-based indexes such as the NCREIF index.

This chapter will examine the historical behavior of REITs in order to gain a better understanding of how REITs perform. In particular, it is important to examine the historical evidence in order to determine if the behavior of REITs is changing over time. Given the increased trading volume in REITs that has occurred since 1993, it would not be surprising if REITs were priced differently than before 1993, owing to the increased attention by a number of analysts. In fact, one of the conclusions of this chapter is that REITs have been less correlated with other investment vehicles since 1991 than before 1991.

The NAREIT (without health care) and Wilshire equity REIT indexes behave comparably with virtually every broad-based equity index (that is, each portfolio has a beta coefficient of around 0.56). Both indexes seem to behave comparably, in terms of risk, to the Wilshire Small Value index. When a simple mimicking portfolio is created, the Wilshire Small Value index and the high-yield corporate bond index are the investment alternatives that have the most similar risk characteristics to REITs. In the 1990s, corporate bonds became a critical variable in explaining REIT returns, while the Wilshire Small Value index fell in relative importance.

THE DATA

Rather than rely on a newly constructed REIT index (see Chan, Hendershott, and Sanders [1990]), the NAREIT and Wilshire REIT indexes are employed in this study. The NAREIT indexes, constructed by the National Association of Real Estate Investment Trusts, are distributed widely among portfolio managers. Four different NAREIT indexes are examined. First, there is the NAREIT equity index, which includes the health care REITs (hereafter termed NAREIT). Second, there is the NAREIT index excluding health care REITs (NAREIT:EH). Third, there is a hybrid REIT index (NAREIT:H). Finally, there is the NAREIT mortgage REIT index (NAREIT:M). The Wilshire REIT index is composed of equity REITs (WILSHIRE). These indexes can be obtained from the direct sources (NAREIT and Wilshire) as well as from Ibbotson Associates in their portfolio management database.

Table 12–1 contains a description of the data as well as the source. Table 12–2 contains the means and standard deviations for the REIT indexes (less the one-month Treasury bill return) as well as the Wilshire size portfolios (Wilshire Top 750, Wilshire Next 1750, Wilshire 5000), the Wilshire style portfolios (value versus growth adjusted for size), and several bond market portfolios (long-term government bonds, long-term corporate bonds, and high-yield corporate bonds). Tables 12-2a, 12-2b, and 12-2c contain the means and standard deviations of the excess returns over selected subperiods.

As we would expect, the mean monthly excess return on both the Wilshire and NAREIT:EH indexes is below that of the Wilshire size and style portfolios. In terms of average excess returns, equity REITs are closest to the Wilshire Top 750 index, the largest capitalization index among the Wilshire indexes. The NAREIT:EH earned an average excess return that is

TABLE 12–1

Description of Portfolio Returns

Monthly common stock and bond returns are obtained from the Center for Research in Security Prices (CRSP) at the University of Chicago and the U.S. Investments Benchmarks module of the Ibbotson & Associates database.

Portfolio	Definition	Source
	Monthly Portfolio Returns w/Dividends	
NAREIT	National Association of Real Estate Equity Investment Trusts-NYSE, Amex, and NMS tax-qualified equity trusts only	NAREIT
NAREIT:EH	Same as NAREIT but without health care REITs	NAREIT
NAREIT:H	NAREIT hybrid trusts	NAREIT
NAREIT:M	NAREIT mortgage trusts	NAREIT
WILREIT	Wilshire Real Estate Securities Index of equity and hybrid REITs and real estate operating companies	Wilshire Associates
Wilshire Top 750, Wilshire Next 1750, Wilshire 5000	Three value-weighted portfolios of NYSE, Amex, and Nasdaq stocks from market value at previous year's end	Wilshire Associates
LTG	Long-term government bonds	CRSP bond files
LTC	Long-term corporate bonds	Ibbotson & Associates
HIC	High-yield corporate bonds (Baa or below quality rating)	First Boston & Co.
SP500	S&P 500	Ibbotson & Associates
WLG, WLV, WMG, WMV, WSG, WSV	Wilshire growth and value portfolios in terms of large, mid, and small capitalization	Wilshire Associates

TABLE 12–2

Summary Statistics for the Excess Returns on Portfolios

All returns are in percent per month for 1978:1 to 1996:6 (222 observations).

Portfolio	Mean	Standard Deviation
	Asset Excess Returns	
REIT Benchmarks		
WILREIT	0.5763%	4.8215%
NAREIT	0.6223%	3.7048%
NAREIT: EH	0.5501%	3.8165%
NAREIT:H	0.3807%	4.4848%
NAREIT:M	0.0941%	4.3673%
Standard Benchmark		
S&P 500	0.7034%	4.2468%
Size Benchmarks		
Wilshire Top 750	0.6929%	4.2799%
Wilshire Next 1750	0.8757%	5.2949%
Wilshire 5000	0.7122%	4.3783%
Style Benchmarks		
WLG	0.7568%	4.8288%
WLV	0.7436%	3.8295%
WMG	0.9073%	5.6757%
WMV	0.8968%	3.9549%
WSG	0.9198%	6.4294%
WSV	0.9850%	3.8001%
Bond Benchmarks		
LTG	0.2547%	3.4198%
LTC	0.2452%	2.9853%
HIC	0.3831%	2.4572%

less than the average excess return on the S&P 500 index. However, it is important to understand that the NAREIT:EH index earned a higher excess return than the S&P 500 index during the first subperiod (January 1978 through December 1986) and earned close to the same excess return during the last subperiod (November 1990 though June 1996). It is only the middle

TABLE 12–2a

Summary Statistics for the Excess Returns on Benchmarks
All returns are in percent per month for 1978:1 to 1986:12 (108 observations).

Portfolio	Mean	Standard Deviation
	Asset Excess Returns	
REIT Benchmarks		
WILREIT	1.2167%	5.4781%
NAREIT	0.8786%	3.9160%
NAREIT: EH	0.8571%	3.9246%
NAREIT:H	0.8322%	5.0550%
NAREIT:M	0.2881%	4.7253%
Standard Benchmark		
S&P 500	0.6007%	4.3651%
Size Benchmarks		
Wilshire Top 750	0.5890%	4.4747%
Wilshire Next 1750	1.0339%	5.5970%
Wilshire 5000	0.6512%	4.5972%
Style Benchmarks		
WLG	0.5942%	4.9793%
WLV	0.7666%	3.9519%
WMG	0.9732%	5.8693%
WMV	1.1161%	4.2359%
WSG	1.0311%	6.7449%
WSV	1.3160%	4.0788%
Bond Benchmarks		
LTG	0.1857%	4.1892%
LTC	0.1685%	3.7607%
HIC	0.3169%	2.8178%

subperiod (January 1987 through October 1990) following the Tax Act of 1986 that the NAREIT:EH index earned substantially lower excess returns than the S&P 500 index.

In terms of equity REITs and bonds, REITs have earned a slightly higher average excess return than long-term government, long-term corpo-

TABLE 12–2b

Summary Statistics for the Excess Returns on Benchmarks

All returns are in percent per month for 1987:1 to 1990:10 (46 observations).

Portfolio	Mean	Standard Deviation
	Asset Excess Returns	
REIT Benchmarks		
WILREIT	–1.0533%	4.6040%
NAREIT	–0.6263%	3.5646%
NAREIT: EH	–0.8418%	3.9845%
NAREIT:H	–1.7443%	4.3769%
NAREIT:M	–1.6891%	3.5089%
Standard Benchmark		
S&P 500	0.3780%	5.5949%
Size Benchmarks		
Wilshire Top 750	0.3195%	5.5136%
Wilshire Next 1750	–0.3364%	6.4729%
Wilshire 5000	0.2152%	5.6253%
Style Benchmarks		
WLG	0.4297%	6.1634%
WLV	0.1954%	4.8159%
WMG	–0.3551%	6.8786%
WMV	–0.3477%	4.6433%
WSG	–0.5366%	7.6258%
WSV	–0.3977%	4.5292%
Bond Benchmarks		
LTG	–0.0196%	2.7010%
LTC	0.0506%	2.2618%
HIC	–0.3514%	2.4262%

rate, and high-yield corporate bonds. However, the total risk (or standard deviation) of the REIT returns is higher as well. These results support the contention that REITs behave like both stocks and bonds or, put differently, behave like a portfolio of stock and bonds.

TABLE 12–2c

Summary Statistics for the Excess Returns on Benchmarks

All returns are in percent per month for 1990:11 to 1996:6 (68 observations).

Portfolio	Mean	Standard Deviation
	Asset Excess Returns	
REIT Benchmarks		
WILREIT	0.6618%	3.4677%
NAREIT	1.0598%	3.2982%
NAREIT: EH	1.0041%	3.3304%
NAREIT:H	1.1010%	2.9517%
NAREIT:M	0.9923%	3.9904%
Standard Benchmark		
S&P 500	1.0866%	2.7921%
Size Benchmarks		
Wilshire Top 750	1.1105%	2.7814%
Wilshire Next 1750	1.4444%	3.5959%
Wilshire 5000	1.1453%	2.8032%
Style Benchmarks		
WLG	1.2364%	3.3844%
WLV	1.0781%	2.7446%
WMG	1.6565%	4.2181%
WMV	1.3903%	2.6588%
WSG	1.7283%	4.7433%
WSV	1.3946%	2.3719%
Bond Benchmarks		
LTG	0.5498%	2.3455%
LTC	0.4987%	1.8092%
HIC	0.9850%	1.5928%

REITs AND SYSTEMATIC RISK

Rather than focus solely on average return and total risk, it is important to focus on the relative risk of REITs to other investment alternatives. Previous studies (see Chan, Hendershott, and Sanders [1990]) have found that equity

REITs have a beta coefficient (generated by the market model) of approximately 0.55 over the 1980–1987 sample period. Furthermore, previous studies have found that the R-square is sensitive to the specification of the independent variable (as might be expected, CHS found that the equally weighted NYSE index had an R-square that was roughly twice as large as the R-square found using the NYSE value-weighted index). This result indicated that equity REITs behaved in a similar fashion to smaller capitalization stocks rather than larger capitalization stocks.

The market model (or single-factor model) is defined as

$$r_{i,t} - r_{f,t} = a_i + b\,[\,r_{p,t} - r_{f,t}\,] + e_{i,t} \qquad (1)$$

where the left-hand side is the excess return of the REIT index over the return on one-month Treasury bills, and the right-hand side is the excess return of the selected benchmark over the return on the one-month Treasury bills.

Results for the Entire Sample

The results of Equation (1) are presented in Table 12–3 for the NAREIT equity index (excluding health care). Like CHS, the beta coefficient for the NAREIT:EH index is approximately 0.57 for each of the Wilshire size portfolios and the S&P 500 index. The beta coefficients for the Wilshire style portfolios are similar, although the point estimates vary from 0.40 (Wilshire Small Growth) to 0.74 (Wilshire Small Value). The R-square varies depending on the index. The R-square is lowest for the long-term government bond (0.0540) and highest for the Wilshire Small Value index (0.5365).

Over the entire sample, the NAREIT:EH index earned positive risk-adjusted excess returns against long-term government and long-term corporate bonds. These results are signified by the significant intercept (a) term at the 0.10 level. The NAREIT:EH index did not earn risk-adjusted excess returns (either positive or negative) against any of the other benchmarks.

Results for the January 1978 through December 1986 Subperiod

The first subperiod corresponds to the beginning of the Wilshire REIT index (January 1978) and the implementation of the Tax Reform Act of 1986 (December 1986). This delineation will allow the comparison of the coef-

TABLE 12-3

Regression of the Excess Returns on NAREIT Equity (without Health Care) Return Index against Competing Benchmarks

1978:1 to 1996:6 (222 observations). Standard errors are in parentheses.

Portfolio	a	b	R^2
Standard Benchmark			
S&P 500	0.0016	0.5605**	0.3891
	(0.0020)	(0.0474)	
Size Benchmarks			
Wilshire Top 750	0.0016	0.5661**	0.4030
	(0.0020)	(0.0465)	
Wilshire Next 1750	0.0010	0.5175**	0.5154
	(0.0018)	(0.0338)	
Wilshire 5000	0.0014	0.5788**	0.4409
	(0.0019)	(0.0439)	
Style Benchmarks			
WLG	0.0019	0.4764**	0.3633
	(0.0021)	(0.0425)	
WLV	0.0008	0.6363**	0.4076
	(0.0020)	(0.0517)	
WMG	0.0014	0.4486**	0.4452
	(0.0019)	(0.0338)	
WMV	–0.0007	0.6864**	0.5059
	(0.0018)	(0.0457)	
WSG	0.0018	0.3997**	0.4534
	(0.0019)	(0.0296)	
WSV	–0.0017	0.7356**	0.5365
	(0.0018)	(0.0461)	
Bond Benchmarks			
LTG	0.0048*	0.2594**	0.0540
	(0.0025)	(0.0732)	
LTC	0.0047*	0.3176**	0.0617
	(0.0025)	(0.0835)	
HIC	0.0026	0.7608**	0.2399
	(0.0023)	(0.0913)	

Note: ** denotes significance at the 0.05 level, and * denotes significance at the 0.10 level.

ficients with those from the post-Tax Act period (January 1987 through October 1990). Table 12–3a presents the same information for the subperiod of January 1978 through December 1986. The results are quite similar to that of the entire sample. The exception is that the NAREIT:EH index earned risk-adjusted excess returns against the majority of the benchmarks. In particular, the results are most prominent for the corporate bond indexes and less prominent for the Wilshire growth indexes.

Results for the January 1987 through October 1990 subperiod

Table 12–3b covers the January 1987 through October 1990 period. Again, the beta coefficients are similar to those for the entire period and the first subperiod (0.57). However, the NAREIT:EH index earned significant negative risk-adjusted excess returns in this period against the Wilshire size indexes and the S&P 500 index. In addition, significantly negative risk-adjusted excess returns were earned against the Wilshire Growth indexes. The results for the Wilshire Value indexes were less significant. Of particular interest in this subperiod is that the R^2s are particularly large relative to the other periods. The Wilshire Next 1750 index ($R^2 = 0.8024$) and the Wilshire Small Value index ($R^2 = 0.7618$) had particularly large coefficients of determination. Among the bond indexes, the high-yield corporate bond index had an R^2 of 0.5213.

It is clear that REIT returns were poor in comparison to other asset returns in the period following the Tax Act of 1986. The evidence from Tables 12-2b and 12-3b indicates that although the Wilshire Midcap and Small stock indexes suffered over this period, REITs suffered far worse. Like an oil glut that can drive down the prices of oil company stocks, another real estate glut can occur again if an environment is created in which construction becomes excessive relative to the demand for real estate. However, another glut should not come as a surprise to investors given the long cycles of real estate.

Results for the November 1990 through June 1996 Subperiod

Table 12–3c examines the period from November 1990 through June 1996. The beta coefficients are slightly lower for the majority of the equity

TABLE 12–3a

Regression of the Excess Returns on NAREIT Equity (without Health Care) Return Index against Competing Benchmarks

1978:1 to 1986:12 (108 observations). Standard errors are in parentheses.

Portfolio	a	b	R^2
Standard Benchmark			
S&P 500	0.0051*	0.5744**	0.4082
	(0.0029)	(0.0672)	
Size Benchmarks			
Wilshire Top 750	0.0052*	0.5687**	0.4205
	(0.0029)	(0.0648)	
Wilshire Next 1750	0.0034*	0.4955**	0.4994
	(0.0027)	(0.0482)	
Wilshire 5000	0.0048*	0.5756**	0.4545
	(0.0028)	(0.0612)	
Style Benchmarks			
WLG	0.0057*	0.4894**	0.3856
	(0.0030)	(0.0600)	
WLV	0.0036*	0.6443**	0.4209
	(0.0029)	(0.0734)	
WMG	0.0043*	0.4418**	0.4366
	(0.0029)	(0.0486)	
WMV	0.0013	0.6491**	0.4908
	(0.0028)	(0.0642)	
WSG	0.0046*	0.3811**	0.4291
	(0.0029)	(0.0427)	
WSV	–0.0006	0.6944**	0.5208
	(0.0028)	(0.0647)	
Bond Benchmarks			
LTG	0.0008	0.2463**	0.0691
	(0.0037)	(0.0878)	
LTC	0.0081**	0.2830**	0.0735
	(0.0037)	(0.0976)	
HIC	0.0067**	0.5935**	0.1816
	(0.0034)	(0.1224)	

Note: ** denotes significance at the 0.05 level and * denotes significance at the 0.10 level.

TABLE 12–3b

Regression of the Excess Returns on NAREIT Equity (without Health Care) Return Index against Competing Benchmarks

1987:1 to 1990:10 (46 observations). Standard errors are in parentheses.

Portfolio	a	b	R^2
Standard Benchmark			
S&P 500	–0.0106**	0.5709**	0.6427
	(0.0036)	(0.0642)	
Size Benchmarks			
Wilshire Top 750	–0.0100**	0.5859**	0.6572
	(0.0035)	(0.0638)	
Wilshire Next 1750	–0.0066**	0.5514**	0.8024
	(0.0026)	(0.0413)	
Wilshire 5000	–0.0097**	0.5916**	0.6976
	(0.0033)	(0.0587)	
Style Benchmarks			
WLG	–0.0106**	0.5154**	0.6356
	(0.0036)	(0.0588)	
WLV	0.0036*	0.6475**	0.6126
	(0.0029)	(0.0776)	
WMG	–0.0067**	0.4926**	0.7232
	(0.0031)	(0.0459)	
WMV	–0.0058*	0.7391**	0.7419
	(0.0030)	(0.0657)	
WSG	–0.0060**	0.4511**	0.7454
	(0.0030)	(0.0397)	
WSV	–0.0054*	0.7679**	0.7618
	(0.0029)	(0.0647)	
Bond Benchmarks			
LTG	–0.0084*	0.1244	0.0071
	(0.0059)	(0.2216)	
LTC	–0.0085*	0.2098	0.0141
	(0.0059)	(0.2637)	
HIC	–0.0043	1.1858**	0.5213
	(0.0042)	(0.1713)	

Note: ** denotes significance at the 0.05 level and * denotes significance at the 0.10 level.

TABLE 12–3c

Regression of the Excess Returns on NAREIT Equity (without Health Care) Return Index against Competing Benchmarks

1990:11 to 1996:6 (68 observations). Standard errors are in parentheses.

Portfolio	a	b	R^2
Standard Benchmark			
S&P 500	0.0053*	0.4396**	0.1358
	(0.0041)	(0.1365)	
Size Benchmarks			
Wilshire Top 750	0.0049	0.4601**	0.1477
	(0.0040)	(0.1361)	
Wilshire Next 1750	0.0033	0.4676**	0.2549
	(0.0038)	(0.0984)	
Wilshire 5000	0.0043	0.5029**	0.1792
	(0.0040)	(0.1325)	
Style Benchmarks			
WLG	0.0061*	0.3195**	0.1054
	(0.0041)	(0.1146)	
WLV	0.0044	0.5221**	0.1851
	(0.0040)	(0.1348)	
WMG	0.0043	0.3444**	0.1903
	(0.0039)	(0.0875)	
WMV	0.0010	0.6487**	0.2682
	(0.0039)	(0.1319)	
WSG	0.0044	0.3275**	0.2176
	(0.0038)	(0.0765)	
WSV	–0.0007	0.7712**	0.3016
	(0.0040)	(0.1444)	
Bond Benchmarks			
LTG	0.0079*	0.3873**	0.0744
	(0.0040)	(0.1682)	
LTC	0.0071*	0.5986**	0.1058
	(0.0040)	(0.2143)	
HIC	0.0023	0.7847**	0.1408
	(0.0044)	(0.2386)	

Note: ** denotes significance at the 0.05 level and * denotes significance at the 0.10 level.

benchmarks (0.46 versus 0.57). Furthermore, the R^2s are dramatically lower than in the previous subperiod. Like the first subperiod, the NAREIT:EH neither earned significantly positive or negative risk-adjusted excess returns against most of the benchmarks. The interesting exception is the S&P 500 index, for which the NAREIT:EH index earned significantly positive risk-adjusted excess returns.

The results for both NAREIT:EH indexes lead to the following conclusion: REITs behave in a similar fashion to small capitalization stocks, particularly those that are value stocks. Are REITs just another small-cap, value stock? The answer is no. While the R-square is quite high, there is still variation in the REIT returns that has not been explained by the Wilshire Small Value index. However, it is clear that a large percentage of a REIT's risk is redundant with other assets.

Equity REITs and Competing Debt Investments

A number of papers have compared REIT returns with interest rates. For example, Chan, Hendershott, and Sanders (1990) used the returns on the long-term U.S. Treasury bond and the high-yield corporate bond to explain returns on equity REITs. They find that these bond indexes are important macroeconomic variables in explaining the returns of equity REITs. The relationship between REIT returns and interest rates is a logical one since REITs are often compared with bonds rather than stocks (see previous tables).

Recent research by Hemel, Sakwa, and Bhattacharjee (1995) showed that REITs have a lower correlation with interest rates than the S&P 500 index has with interest rates. This is an important finding in that it casts doubts on the argument that REITs behave more closely with bonds than with stocks. However, there are different types of bonds in the economy. While their results are correct for long-term U.S. Treasury bonds, they are inaccurate for risky bonds, such as corporate bonds.

In this section, the excess returns on the various benchmarks are regressed against two variables. The first variable is the excess return on long-term government bonds. The second variable is the spread between the returns on high-yield corporate bonds and long-term government bonds. The first term is intended to capture the effect documented by Hemel, Sakwa, and Bhattacharjee (1995). The second term is intended to capture the sensitivity of REIT returns in comparison to the spread between high-yield corporate and U.S. Treasury bonds. The regression model is as follows:

$$r_{i,t} - r_{f,t} = a_i + b_1 [r_{LTGov,t} - r_{f,t}] + b_2 [r_{HiYld,t} - r_{LTGov,t}] + e_{i,t} \quad (2)$$

Results for the Entire Sample

The results of the regression model, Equation (2), are presented in Table 12–4. Interestingly, the coefficients for the long-term government bond (b_1) and the high-yield corporate bond premia (b_2) are virtually the same for the NAREIT:EH index and the S&P 500 index. The coefficient for default-free interest rates is slightly higher for the S&P 500 index, while the coefficient for risky interest rates is slightly higher for the NAREIT:EH index. The coefficients are not significantly different from each other, indicating that the Hemel, Sakwa, and Bhattacharjee (1995) conclusion is overstated.

The intuition of this result is clear. Although the NAREIT:EH index has a lower correlation of returns with the long-term government bond index, the returns on both the NAREIT:EH index and the S&P 500 index are greatly influenced by the market risk premia, which is reflected in the high-yield corporate bond index. Failing to analyze the long-term government bond index in conjunction with the high-yield corporate bond index causes measurement error since there is an omitted variable problem. Therefore, focusing solely on long-term Treasury bonds as an explanatory variable for REIT returns results in the erroneous conclusion that the S&P 500 index is more sensitive to interest-rate changes than REITs.

Results for the January 1978 through December 1986 Subperiod

Before any conclusions can be drawn about the relationship between bonds and REITs, it is necessary to check to see if the relationship is constant over time. Table 12–4a presents the results for the first subperiod. Once again, the coefficients for the default-free interest rates are higher for the S&P 500 index, while the coefficients for risky interest rates are higher for the NAREIT:EH index. Given the magnitude of the standard errors, the difference between the coefficients is not statistically significant.

Results for the January 1987 through October 1990 Subperiod

The results for the second subperiod (see Table 12–4b) indicate that REITs, whether the NAREIT:EH index or the Wilshire Index, had substantially

TABLE 12–4

Regression of the Excess Returns on Benchmarks against Spreads on Long-Term Government Bonds (b_1) and Corporate Bonds (b_2)

1978:1 to 1996:6 (222 observations). Standard errors are in parentheses.

Portfolio	a	b_1	b_2	R^2
REIT Benchmarks				
WILREIT	0.0018	1.0257**	1.0410**	0.2750
	(0.0028)	(0.1148)	(0.1373)	
NAREIT	0.0039*	0.7258**	0.7653**	0.2379
	(0.0022)	(0.0904)	(0.1081)	
NAREIT: EH	0.0025	0.7449**	0.8209**	0.2431
	(0.0023)	(0.0928)	(0.1111)	
NAREIT:H	0.0000	1.0025**	0.9746**	0.2985
	(0.0026)	(0.1050)	(0.1256)	
NAREIT:M	–0.0033*	1.1511**	1.0180**	0.4068
	(0.0023)	(0.0940)	(0.1125)	
Standard Benchmark				
S&P 500	0.0039*	0.8827**	0.7057**	0.2533
	(0.0025)	(0.1026)	(0.1227)	
Size Benchmarks				
Wilshire Top 750	0.0037*	0.9018**	0.7208**	0.2603
	(0.0025)	(0.1029)	(0.1231)	
Wilshire Next 1750	0.0045*	1.1000**	1.1569**	0.2672
	(0.0031)	(0.1267)	(0.1515)	
Wilshire 5000	0.0037*	0.9266**	0.7973**	0.2618
	(0.0026)	(0.1051)	(0.1258)	
Style Benchmarks				
WLG	0.0042*	0.9264**	0.7593**	0.2153
	(0.0029)	(0.1196)	(0.1430)	
WLV	0.0044**	0.8670**	0.6122**	0.3078
	(0.0022)	(0.0891)	(0.1065)	
WMG	0.0048*	1.1028**	1.0807**	0.2262
	(0.0034)	(0.1396)	(0.1669)	
WMV	0.0054**	1.0067**	0.8125**	0.3795
	(0.0021)	(0.0871)	(0.1042)	
WSG	0.0046	1.1699**	1.2274**	0.2047
	(0.0039)	(0.1603)	(0.1917)	
WSV	0.0062**	0.9926**	0.8826**	0.3998
	(0.0020)	(0.0822)	(0.0984)	

Note: ** denotes significance at the 0.05 level and * denotes significance at the 0.10 level.

TABLE 12–4a

Regression of the Excess Returns on Benchmarks against Spreads on Long-Term Government Bonds (b_1)and Corporate Bonds (b_2)

1978:1 to 1986:12 (108 observations). Standard errors are in parentheses.

Portfolio	a	b_1	b_2	R^2
REIT Benchmarks				
WILREIT	0.0091*	0.9567**	0.9477**	0.2425
	(0.0047)	(0.1654)	(0.2351)	
NAREIT	0.0068*	0.5997**	0.6782**	0.1869
	(0.0035)	(0.1225)	(0.1741)	
NAREIT: EH	0.0066*	0.5980**	0.6746**	0.1849
	(0.0035)	(0.1229)	(0.1747)	
NAREIT:H	0.0053*	0.9748**	0.9341**	0.2972
	(0.0041)	(0.1470)	(0.2089)	
NAREIT:M	–0.0007	1.1421**	1.1003**	0.4665
	(0.0034)	(0.1197)	(0.1702)	
Standard Benchmark				
S&P 500	0.0038	0.7729**	0.5749**	0.2742
	(0.0036)	(0.1290)	(0.1834)	
Size Benchmarks				
Wilshire Top 750	0.0036	0.7976**	0.5916**	0.2783
	(0.0037)	(0.1319)	(0.1874)	
Wilshire Next 1750	0.0074*	0.9505**	0.8750**	0.2327
	(0.0048)	(0.1701)	(0.2417)	
Wilshire 5000	0.0042	0.8136**	0.6468**	0.2659
	(0.0039)	(0.1366)	(0.1942)	
Style Benchmarks				
WLG	0.0038	0.7748**	0.5594**	0.2147
	(0.0043)	(0.1531)	(0.2176)	
WLV	0.0055*	0.7664**	0.5724**	0.3283
	(0.0032)	(0.1123)	(0.1597)	
WMG	0.0070*	0.9165**	0.7748**	0.2022
	(0.0051)	(0.1818)	(0.2548)	
WMV	0.0085**	0.9170**	0.7232**	0.3995
	(0.0032)	(0.1139)	(0.1619)	
WSG	0.0074	0.9563**	0.8531**	0.1636
	(0.0060)	(0.2140)	(0.3041)	
WSV	0.0104**	0.9158**	0.7871**	0.4154
	(0.0031)	(0.1082)	(0.1538)	

Note: ** denotes significance at the 0.05 level and * denotes significance at the 0.10 level.

TABLE 12–4b

Regression of the Excess Returns on Benchmarks against Spreads on Long-Term Government Bonds (b_1)and Corporate Bonds (b_2)

1987:1 to 1990:10 (46 observations). Standard errors are in parentheses.

Portfolio	a	b_1	b_2	R^2
REIT Benchmarks				
WILREIT	–0.0054	1.2633**	1.4666**	0.5597
	(0.0047)	(0.2283)	(0.2000)	
NAREIT	–0.0023	1.0175**	1.1195**	0.5535
	(0.0036)	(0.1780)	(0.1560)	
NAREIT: EH	–0.0041	1.0553**	1.2451**	0.5366
	(0.0041)	(0.2027)	(0.1776)	
NAREIT:H	–0.0137**	0.7765**	1.0688**	0.3235
	(0.0055)	(0.2690)	(0.2358)	
NAREIT:M	–0.0139**	0.9074**	0.8416**	0.3577
	(0.0043)	(0.2102)	(0.1842)	
Standard Benchmark				
S&P 500	0.0084	1.3087**	1.3148**	0.3241
	(0.0070)	(0.3437)	(0.3012)	
Size Benchmarks				
Wilshire Top 750	0.0078	1.3053**	1.3067**	0.3304
	(0.0069)	(0.3372)	(0.2954)	
Wilshire Next 1750	0.0029	1.4578**	1.7938**	0.4188
	(0.0075)	(0.3688)	(0.3232)	
Wilshire 5000	0.0070	1.3373**	1.3934**	0.3528
	(0.0069)	(0.3382)	(0.2964)	
Style Benchmarks				
WLG	0.0095	1.5421**	1.4758**	0.3478
	(0.0076)	(0.3720)	(0.3260)	
WLV	0.0060	1.3419**	1.1306**	0.3764
	(0.0058)	(0.2842)	(0.2491)	
WMG	0.0027	1.6443**	1.7925**	0.3825
	(0.0082)	(0.4040)	(0.3540)	
WMV	0.0007	1.2646**	1.1793**	0.3994
	(0.0055)	(0.2689)	(0.2357)	
WSG	0.0017	1.7281**	2.0286**	0.3893
	(0.0091)	(0.4454)	(0.3903)	
WSV	0.0003	1.1799**	1.2199**	0.4186
	(0.0053)	(0.2580)	(0.2261)	

Note: ** denotes significance at the 0.05 level and * denotes significance at the 0.10 level.

higher coefficients of determination than the S&P 500 index (or other equity indexes). The WILREIT index has virtually identical regression coefficients with the S&P 500 index during this subperiod, while the EREIT:EH index has lower coefficient values for both interest-rate variables (though not statistically significant).

It should be noted that both the NAREIT hybrid and mortgage indexes earned significantly negative risk-adjusted excess returns over this subperiod. The other REITs had negative intercepts, but the results were not significantly different from zero.

Results for the November 1990 through June 1996 Subperiod

The final subperiod indicates that the explanatory power of interest rates (see Table 12–4c) is roughly comparable to the first subperiod from 1978 through 1986. Interestingly, the regression coefficients for both the default-free interest rates and the risky interest rates are greater for the NAREIT:EH index than for the S&P 500 index, although the difference is not statistically significant for the default-free interest rates (b_1). The difference is statistically significant for risky interest rates (b_2).

THE MIMICKING PORTFOLIO APPROACH FOR ANALYZING THE RISKINESS OF REITs

Is it possible to create a portfolio of investment alternatives that mimics the returns on equity REITs? Using the Wilshire-style portfolios and the bond returns, it is possible to weight the various portfolios in such a way as to minimize the sum of squared errors relative to the REIT index. That is, the portfolio that minimizes the sum of squared errors is the portfolio that best explains the variation of REIT returns. The results were obtained by using restricted least squares (all coefficient values were constrained to be zero or positive, and the coefficients had to sum to one) and restricting the intercept to zero.

Table 12–5 presents the results for the NAREIT:EH index. Over the entire sample period, four portfolios have weightings: Wilshire Small Value, Wilshire Small Growth, the high-yield corporate bond index, and the Wilshire Large Value. The Wilshire Small Value has the largest weight, with 46.97 percent, while the high-yield corporate bond index has the second largest weighting, at 35.00 percent. The first subperiod had results

TABLE 12–4c

Regression of the Excess Returns on Benchmarks against Spreads on Long-Term Government Bonds (b_1)and Corporate Bonds (b_2)

1990:11 to 1996:6 (68 observations). Standard errors are in parentheses.

Portfolio	a	b_1	b_2	R^2
REIT Benchmarks				
WILREIT	–0.0017	0.9407**	0.7211**	0.1524
	(0.0047)	(0.2758)	(0.2543)	
NAREIT	0.0024	0.9909**	0.6426**	0.1899
	(0.0043)	(0.2564)	(0.2364)	
NAREIT: EH	0.0016	0.9840**	0.6958**	0.1802
	(0.0040)	(0.2605)	(0.2401)	
NAREIT:H	0.0020	1.0574**	0.7435**	0.2651
	(0.0037)	(0.2186)	(0.2015)	
NAREIT:M	–0.0029	1.5031**	1.0529**	0.2933
	(0.0049)	(0.2898)	(0.2672)	
Standard Benchmark				
S&P 500	0.0047*	0.8412**	0.3650*	0.2383
	(0.0035)	(0.2105)	(0.1941)	
Size Benchmarks				
Wilshire Top 750	0.0048	0.8386**	0.3805*	0.2320
	(0.0036)	(0.2106)	(0.1941)	
Wilshire Next 1750	0.0048	1.0196**	0.9254**	0.1823
	(0.0047)	(0.2809)	(0.2589)	
Wilshire 5000	0.0046	0.8702**	0.4779**	0.2189
	(0.0036)	(0.2104)	(0.1973)	
Style Benchmarks				
WLG	0.0060*	0.8171**	0.4227*	0.1370
	(0.0046)	(0.2716)	(0.2504)	
WLV	0.0048*	0.8932**	0.2502*	0.3565
	(0.0032)	(0.1902)	(0.1753)	
WMG	0.0077*	0.9677**	0.7954**	0.1114
	(0.0058)	(0.3435)	(0.3167)	
WMV	0.0058*	1.0211**	0.5695**	0.3321
	(0.0032)	(0.1877)	(0.1731)	
WSG	0.0075	1.0381**	0.9453**	0.1090
	(0.0065)	(0.3868)	(0.3566)	
WSV	0.0057**	0.9851**	0.6546**	0.3603
	(0.0028)	(0.1639)	(0.1511)	

Note: ** denotes significance at the 0.05 level, and * denotes significance at the 0.10 level.

TABLE 12–5

Mimicking Portfolio Weightings for NAREIT Equity (without Health Care) REIT Index

Portfolio:	78:1/96:6 n=222	78:1/86:12 n=108	87:1/90:10 n=46	90:11/96:6 n=68
WLG	0.000000	0.086416	0.000000	0.000000
WLV	0.081746	0.129214	0.000000	0.000000
WMG	0.000000	0.000000	0.000000	0.000000
WMV	0.000000	0.000000	0.053785	0.000000
WSG	0.098568	0.000000	0.172830	0.151337
WSV	0.469657	0.542179	0.296486	0.370275
LTG	0.000000	0.000000	0.000000	0.000000
LTC	0.000000	0.000000	0.000000	0.226904
HIC	0.350029	0.242191	0.476899	0.251484
SSE	*0.152903*	*0.086945*	*0.011473*	*0.049273*

that were similar, with the Wilshire Small Value index having a weighting of 54.22 percent and the high-yield corporate bond index having a weighting of 24.21 percent. The second subperiod found the high-yield corporate bond index having the greatest weighting with 47.69 percent, and the Wilshire Small Value having the second largest weighting at 29.65 percent. The most recent subperiod found the Wilshire Small Value index with the greatest weighting at 37.03 percent, with the high-yield corporate and long-term corporate bond indexes achieving weights of 25.15 percent and 22.69 percent, respectively. One conclusion that can be drawn from this experiment is that, while the Wilshire Small Value index and the high-yield corporate bond index have had the greatest influence on NAREIT:EH returns, the most recent subperiod has found a more complex pricing of REITs with an emphasis for the first time on highly rated corporate bonds.

The changing nature of REIT pricing can be supported by examining the Wilshire REIT index as well (see Table 12–5a). For the entire sample, the Wilshire Small Value (63.06 percent) and the Wilshire Small Growth (24.65 percent) had the greatest weightings. In the first subperiod (1978-1986), the only portfolios that received weightings were the Wilshire Small Value (69.44 percent) and the Wilshire Small Growth (30.56 percent) indexes. Like the NAREIT:EH index, the weightings in the second subperiod

TABLE 12–5a

Mimicking Portfolio Weightings for Wilshire Equity REIT Index

Portfolio:	78:1/96:6 n=222	78:1/86:12 n=108	87:1/90:10 n=46	90:11/96:6 n=68
WLG	0.000000	0.000000	0.000000	0.000000
WLV	0.000000	0.000000	0.000000	0.000000
WMG	0.000000	0.000000	0.000000	0.000000
WMV	0.000000	0.000000	0.000000	0.000000
WSG	0.246459	0.305641	0.206920	0.218073
WSV	0.630571	0.694359	0.410185	0.408849
LTG	0.000000	0.000000	0.000000	0.000000
LTC	0.000000	0.000000	0.000000	0.188504
HIC	0.122969	0.000000	0.382895	0.184574
SSE	*0.152473*	*0.074095*	*0.018054*	*0.049631*

TABLE 12–5b

Mimicking Portfolio Weightings for NAREIT Mortgage REIT Index

Portfolio:	78:1/96:6 n=222	78:1/86:12 n=108	87:1/90:10 n=46	90:11/96:6 n=68
WLG	0.000000	0.000000	0.000000	0.000000
WLV	0.000000	0.000000	0.000000	0.219339
WMG	0.000000	0.000000	0.000000	0.000000
WMV	0.328551	0.136548	0.000000	0.353282
WSG	0.000000	0.061299	0.000000	0.000000
WSV	0.180169	0.383563	0.292453	0.000000
LTG	0.000000	0.000000	0.085932	0.000000
LTC	0.090510	0.066971	0.005919	0.050351
HIC	0.400771	0.351619	0.615695	0.377029
SSE	*0.198273*	*0.083073*	*0.039668*	*0.068223*

included a large weighting of the high-yield corporate bond index (38.29 percent) in addition to the Wilshire Small Value and Growth indexes. The results for the final subperiod are very similar to those found for the NAREIT:EH index. The portfolio weightings are relatively evenly split among the Wilshire Small Value (40.88 percent), Wilshire Small Growth (21.81 percent), long-term corporate bonds (18.86 percent) and high-yield corporate bonds (18.46 percent). Table 12–5b presents the results for the NAREIT mortgage index. The results are very similar to the previous tables except that the variable HIC is more important and the variable Wilshire Small Value is not important.

In summary, REIT returns are closely related to the returns on the Wilshire Small Value and high-yield corporate bond indexes. In recent years, the relationship has become more complex, as indicated by the presence of the long-term corporate bond index for the first time. One explanation is that before the explosion of REIT trading volume in 1993, a number of REITs were priced off of high-yield corporate bonds and small capitalization stocks that were value-oriented. With the increased attention by analysts due to the increase in volume of trading, REIT pricing became more complex.

Using a simple mimicking portfolio model, it is possible to explain 70 percent of the variation in REIT return. More complicated models (Chan, Hendershott, and Sanders [1990] and Karolyi and Sanders [1996]) have achieved similar results. However, 30 percent of the variation in REIT returns is still unexplained by the mimicking portfolio. This indicates there is a unique contribution of REITs to a portfolio's risk that cannot be achieved by simply forming portfolios of other assets. In other words, REITs are unique.

REITs AND THE FAMA-FRENCH MODEL OF SECURITY RETURNS

In a recent paper, Hsieh and Peterson (1996) employ the Fama-French model of security returns to REITs. The Fama-French model is a variant of the same model used by Chan, Hendershott, and Sanders (1990), with the exception of a variable that reflects the book-to-market ratio for all stocks. The Fama-French model begins with Equation (2):

$$r_{i,t} - r_{f,t} = a_i + b_1 [r_{LTGov,t} - r_{f,t}] + b_2 [r_{HiYld,t} - r_{LTGov,t}] + e_{i,t} \qquad (2)$$

Fama and French add a variable to measure the impact of the market for all U.S. publicly traded equities. This variable is called MTB, which stands for market less Treasury bills:

$$r_{i,t} - r_{f,t} = a_i + b_1 [r_{LTGov,t} - r_{f,t}] + b_2 [r_{HiYld,t} - r_{LTGov,t}] + b_3 [r_{Mkt,t} - r_{f,t}] + e_{i,t} \qquad (3)$$

Equation (3) can be written in terms of risk premiums:

$$r_{REIT,t} = a_i + b_1 r_{Term,t} + b_2 r_{Risk,t} + b_3 r_{MTB,t} + e_{i,t} \qquad (3')$$

Fama and French add two variables that they found add to the explanatory power of Equation (3′). The first variable is the spread between the return on small stocks and the return on large stocks; this spread is termed SMB. The second variable is the spread between the returns on stocks with high book-to-market ratios and the returns on stocks with low book-to-market ratios; this spread is termed HML.

$$r_{REIT,t} = a_i + b_1 r_{Term,t} + b_2 r_{Risk,t} + b_3 r_{MTB,t} + b_4 r_{SMB,t} + b_5 r_{HML,t} + e_{i,t} \qquad (4)$$

The first three variables have been examined previously by Chan, Hendershott, and Sanders (1990). The variable SMB (for small minus big) should be significant for REITs since it has been argued earlier in this chapter that REITs behave similarly to small firms. The variable HML (for high minus low) should be significant if it measures the possibility for mean reversion in stock prices (that is, high book-to-market stocks will behave like value stocks, while low book-to-market stocks will behave like growth stocks).

The results for Equation (4) are found in Table 12–6. As Hsieh and Peterson (1996) have found, the inclusion of the book-to-market variable (HML) increased the R^2 for the regressions relative to those found in Table 12–3. For example, the Fama-French model generates an R^2 of 0.5822 for the NAREIT Equity (without health care) index, while the standard capital asset-pricing model generates an R^2 of 0.3891. In fact, the Fama-French model dominates the simple regression of the excess returns on the NAREIT Equity (without health care) index against the excess returns on the Wilshire Small Value index in terms of adjusted R^2 (0.5822 versus 0.5365). Thus, the Fama-French model does a superior job in explaining REIT returns relative to the capital asset-pricing model.

CAN DIVIDEND YIELDS HELP EXPLAIN REIT RETURNS?

Conventional wisdom among practitioners and academics is that REITs should be priced comparably to other high-dividend-yielding stocks (for example, see Pagliari, Webb, and Lieblich [1996] for a discussion of the importance of dividends in explaining REIT returns). While dividend yields have some explanatory power for REITs when REITs are examined in

TABLE 12–6

Regression of the Excess Returns on Benchmarks against Spreads on Long-Term Government Bonds (b_1), Corporate Bonds (b_2), MTB (b_3), SMB (b_4), and HML (b_5). 1978:1 to 1995:12 (216 observations). Standard errors are in parentheses.

Portfolio	a	Term	Risk	MTB	SML	HML	R^2
REIT Benchmarks:							
WILREIT	–0.0029*	0.1752*	0.0606	0.7701**	0.8023**	0.4144**	0.7227
	(0.0018)	(0.0889)	(0.0569)	(0.0569)	(0.0792)	(0.0852)	
NAREIT	–0.0028*	0.3411**	0.2359**	0.5213**	0.4933**	0.3936**	0.6607
	(0.0016)	(0.0754)	(0.0869)	(0.0483)	(0.0679)	(0.0827)	
NAREIT: EH	0.0010	0.1279*	0.1261*	0.5794**	0.5102**	0.3936**	0.5822
	(0.0018)	(0.0833)	(0.0993)	(0.0551)	(0.0768)	(0.0827)	
NAREIT:H	–0.0039*	0.3671**	0.2507**	0.5815**	0.5604**	0.4906**	0.5479
	(0.0022)	(0.1053)	(0.1214)	(0.0631)	(0.0939)	(0.0959)	
NAREIT:M	–0.0070**	0.6798**	0.4914**	0.4414**	0.3832**	0.3973**	0.5595
	(0.0021)	(0.0998)	(0.1152)	(0.0639)	(0.0892)	(0.0959)	
Style Benchmarks:							
WLG	0.0012**	0.0063	0.0354	1.0126**	–0.1202**	–0.3181**	0.9764
	(0.0005)	(0.0257)	(0.0279)	(0.0166)	(0.0231)	(0.0249)	
WLV	–0.0004	0.0123	–0.0665*	0.9603**	–0.1659**	0.4659**	0.9341
	(0.0007)	(0.0359)	(0.0396)	(0.0219)	(0.0306)	(0.0329)	
WMG	0.0012*	–0.0077**	–0.0459	1.0822**	0.5998**	–0.2387**	0.9693
	(0.0007)	(0.0345)	(0.0399)	(0.0221)	(0.0309)	(0.0332)	
WMV	0.0009	0.1822**	–0.0000	0.8285**	0.3502**	0.4182**	0.9052
	(0.0009)	(0.0425)	(0.0000)	(0.0272)	(0.0379)	(0.0408)	
WSG	0.0005	–0.0673*	–0.1068**	1.1630**	0.9134**	–0.2778**	0.9693
	(0.0008)	(0.0391)	(0.0451)	(0.0250)	(0.0349)	(0.0376)	
WSV	0.0020**	0.2223**	0.0833*	0.7500**	0.4523**	0.4254**	0.9055
	(0.0008)	(0.0408)	(0.0471)	(0.0261)	(0.364)	(0.0392)	

Note: ** denotes significance at the 0.05 level and * denotes significance at the 0.10 level.

isolation, dividend yields have little explanatory power for REITs when viewed in a capital markets context.

Consider the following pricing models for REITs. The first model assumes that only the term and risk structure of interest rates are important in explaining excess REIT returns:

$$r_{REIT,t} = a_i + b_1 r_{Term,t} + b_2 r_{Risk,t} + e_{i,t} \quad (5)$$

Table 12–7 presents the results for Equation (5). As has been found before in this chapter, both the term and risk structure of interest rates are

TABLE 12–7

Regression of the Excess Returns on NAREIT Equity (without Health Care) Return Index against Spreads on Long-Term Government Bonds (b_1) and Corporate Bonds (b_2), Dividends (b_3), and MTB (b_4)

1978:1 to 1995:12 (216 observations). Standard errors are in parentheses.

Portfolio	a	Risk	Term	Div	MTB	R^2
NAREIT: EH	0.0026	0.7434**	0.8204**			0.2354
	(0.0023)	(0.0941)	(0.1129)			
NAREIT: EH	0.0036	0.6983**	0.7350**	−0.3927**		0.3241
	(0.0022)	(0.0889)	(0.1074)	(0.0730)		
NAREIT: EH	0.0009	0.2915**	0.4433**	−0.0245	0.4844**	0.4662
	(0.0020)	(0.0955)	(0.1029)	(0.0810)	(0.0639)	

Note: ** denotes significance at the 0.05 level and * denotes significance at the 0.10 level.

important in explaining REIT returns (R^2 = 0.2354). At this point, the dividend variable is included in the pricing model. The dividend variable is defined as the spread between the return on low dividend-yielding stocks and the return on high dividend-yielding stocks. If dividend yields are important for explaining REIT returns, the coefficient on the dividend variable should be negative and significant.

$$r_{REIT,t} = a_i + b_1 r_{Term,t} + b_2 r_{Risk,t} + b_3 r_{Div,t} + e_{i,t} \tag{5a}$$

The results for Equation (5a) are also presented in Table 12–7. The coefficient on the dividend variable is negative and highly significant, indicating that dividend yields contribute to explaining REIT returns.

Caution should be exercised in overinterpreting the results for Equation (5a). Since that particular model is missing the market as an explanatory variable, the risk associated with REITs is misspecified. In other words, it is unknown whether the results for Equation 5a are meaningful or not. To correct this problem, the Fama and French (1993) MTB variable is included in the pricing model:

$$r_{REIT,t} = a_i + b_1 r_{Term,t} + b_2 r_{Risk,t} + b_3 r_{Div,t} + b_3 r_{MTB,t} + e_{i,t} \tag{5b}$$

The inclusion of the market-risk premium causes the coefficient on the dividend variable to become insignificant. Alternative specifications of dividends lead to exactly the same conclusion. Dividend yields are not an important explanatory variable for REIT returns once a more well-defined asset pricing model is employed, at least for the NAREIT Equity index without health care.

IS THERE A JANUARY EFFECT IN REIT RETURNS?

Thus far, the evidence points to the fact the REITs are highly correlated with small capitalization indexes such as the Wilshire Small Value index and the high-yield corporate bond index. Given the existence of the small-firm effect, in which small firms earn abnormal returns during the month of January, it seems logical to examine REIT returns in order to determine if there is a January effect in public real estate securities.

The returns on several NAREIT indexes as well as the Wilshire Small Value and high-yield corporate bond indexes are presented in Table 12–8. The returns in January for the REITs are clearly larger than the other months, indicating that there is a January effect in REIT returns. Curiously, the average return in January is higher than average for the Wilshire Small Value index; however, the month of August has a comparable return to

TABLE 12–8

Monthly Returns on Various REIT Indexes, the Wilshire Small Value Index, and the High-Yield Corporate Bond Index
January 1978–June 1996

	NAREIT:EH	NAREIT:H	NAREIT:M	WSV	HIC
January	0.034381	0.023595	0.040004	0.025989	0.019642
February	0.014948	0.018027	–0.002727	0.018700	0.010005
March	0.016395	0.018360	0.000657	0.016426	0.010284
April	0.009318	0.016566	0.012227	0.018600	0.015521
May	0.004627	0.006433	0.012201	0.018000	0.006979
June	0.016768	0.007204	0.011166	0.017374	0.010795
July	0.013439	0.016251	0.008976	0.017394	0.008683
August	0.009116	0.009131	0.010686	0.028233	0.011128
September	–0.002504	–0.001403	–0.008216	0.000344	0.000922
October	–0.008483	–0.015273	–0.005372	–0.011550	0.001456
November	0.007702	0.011365	0.007095	0.019356	0.016350
December	0.020921	0.005831	–0.005031	0.020367	0.005561

January. In addition, there seems to be a January effect for the high-yield corporate bonds. This indicates that the January effect may be caused by the same risk premium that is imbedded in the high-yield corporate bond rate. If this is true, there is no January effect, in the sense that the higher returns are simply rewards for greater risk bearing.

SUMMARY

Equity REITs such as the NAREIT equity index without health care (or NAREIT:EH) have earned slightly lower returns than the S&P 500 index since 1978. However, the lower average return is not unexpected, given that equity REIT betas tend to be in the range of 0.57. Unlike what has been found by Hemel, Sakwa, and Bhattacharjee (1995), equity REITs have comparable sensitivity to interest-rate changes with that of the S&P 500 index.

Perhaps the most important conclusion of this chapter is that the Wilshire Small Value index and the high-yield corporate bond index have had the greatest power in explaining equity REIT returns. While the explanatory power has been impressive, there is still a considerable amount of unexplained variation in REIT returns that cannot be diversified away with major stock and bond indexes, particularly since 1991.

REFERENCES

Chan, K. C., P. Hendershott, and A. Sanders. 1990. "Risk and Return on Real Estate: Evidence from Equity REITs." *AREUEA Journal* 18, no. 4., pp. 431–432.

Chen, K. C. and D. T. Tzang. 1988. "Interest-Rate Sensitivity of Real Estate Investment Trusts." *Journal of Real Estate Research* 3, no. 3, pp. 13–21.

Dowd, M. 1993. "How in the World Can REIT Stocks Sell at a Five Percent Yield?" *Real Estate Finance* 10, no. 3, pp. 13–32.

Fama, E. and K. French. 1993. "Common Risk Factors in the Returns on Stocks and Bonds." *Journal of Financial Economics* 33, pp. 3–56.

Hemel, E., S. Sakwa, and R. Bhattacharjee. 1995. "Interest Rate Sensitivity of REITs: Myth and Reality." Morgan Stanley: U.S. Investment Research Paper, 1585 Broadway, New York, New York 10036-8293.

Hsieh, C. and J. Peterson. "Do Common Factors in the Returns on Stocks and Bonds Explain Returns on REITs?" *Journal of Real Estate Economics*, forthcoming.

Karolyi, A. and A. Sanders. 1996. "The Time Variation of REIT Risk Premiums." The Dice Center Working Paper Series of The Ohio State University.

Lieblich, F., J. Pagliari, and J. Webb. 1997. "The Historical Behavior of REIT Returns: A Real Estate Perspective." In *Real Estate Investment Trusts.* R. Garrigan and J. Parsons, eds. Burr Ridge, IL: McGraw-Hill.

Nelling, E., J. Mahoney, T. Hildebrand, and M. Goldstein. 1995. "Real Estate Investment Trusts, Small Stocks, and Bid-Ask Spreads." *Real Estate Economics* 23, no. 1, pp. 45–63.

Sanders, A., 1996, "A Note on the Relationship Between Corporate Bonds and Equity REITs." *Real Estate Finance* 13, no. 1, pp. 61–63.

CHAPTER

13

THE HISTORICAL BEHAVIOR OF REIT RETURNS

A Real Estate Perspective*

Frederich Lieblich, *Director of Real Estate Research, SSR Realty Advisors*
Joseph L. Pagliari, Jr., *President, Citadel Realty, Inc.*
James R. Webb, *Professor of Finance, James J. Nance College of Business, Cleveland State University*

INTRODUCTION

The preceding chapter, "The Historical Behavior of REIT Returns: A Capital Market Perspective," compares historical REIT returns to various capital market indexes. By contrast, this chapter compares historical public REIT returns (proxied by the NAREIT Index) to the private, institutional real estate returns (proxied by the NCREIF Index). The basic motivation of this chapter involves the assertion that the long-run behavior of REITs should generally follow the behavior of the underlying assets. That is, notwithstanding the fact that the NAREIT Index represents leveraged and securitized real estate, the long-run performance of REITs is ultimately determined by the performance of the underlying property markets, which can be proxied by the unleveraged and unsecuritized NCREIF Index.

* This chapter represents an updated and revised discussion of the issues presented in: J. Pagliari and J. Webb, "A Fundamental Examination of Securitized and Unsecuritized Real Estate Returns," *The Journal of Real Estate Research,* Volume 10 Number 4, 1995, pp. 381–426.

Consequently, the balance of this chapter is devoted to comparing these two real estate equity indexes. In order to facilitate this comparison, each of the indexes is examined with respect to their underlying components of return: dividends, investment values, and dividend yields. While dividends and dividend yields have been explicitly part of the REIT pricing calculus for some time, relatively few studies have focused on the "dividends" paid by NCREIF properties. In addition, this chapter emphasizes the long-term behavior of these fundamental components as a crucial initial step in understanding the relationship between securitized and unsecuritized real estate equities. Unfortunately, the relationship between these fundamental components is generally weak from a statistical standpoint, even when quarterly lags of up to two years are examined. Of the three fundamental components, the path of prices for securitized and unsecuritized real estate exhibited the strongest long-term relationship. This might suggest that the weak relationships for explaining total returns may be more attributable to the volatility of dividends and/or changes in dividend yields. Interestingly, the volatility of the (unleveraged) NCREIF dividend series is approximately 150 percent of the NAREIT volatility, whereas the volatility of the NCREIF asset values is roughly only 25 percent of the NAREIT volatility. These results are contradictory: In a simplified setting, the greater dividend volatility should be accompanied by greater asset/price volatility, not less, as observed. However, such comparisons suffer due to the incompatibility of the data sources. As a result, this chapter also suggests ways in which the comparability of securitized and unsecuritized real estate investments might be enhanced.

LITERATURE REVIEW

Like the preceding chapter, much of the earlier REIT literature has focused on the relationship(s) between publicly traded equity REITs and the larger stock market forces for publicly traded equities. For example, Chan, et al. (1990), using a multifactor arbitrage pricing model over the 1973–1987 time period, found that four factors (unexpected inflation, changes in the risk and term structure of interest rates, and the percentage change in the discount on closed-end stock funds) consistently drive equity REIT returns. The impact of these variables is approximately 60 percent of that for common stocks. Equity REITs offered neither a superior risk-adjusted return nor a hedge against unexpected inflation. Earlier, Titman and Warga

(1986) had also applied CAPM and APT models to equity and mortgage REITs over the 1973–1983 time period. Because REIT returns were so volatile, they found that large amounts of abnormal performance were not statistically different from zero.

Other studies have analyzed interest-rate sensitivity, capital structure and other stock market-like effects. For example, Chen and Tzang (1988) examined the interest-rate sensitivity of REITs, finding different results over two subperiods and different sensitivities between mortgage and equity REITs. The issue of capital structure is an interesting one. Because REITs are exempt from corporate taxation (subject to compliance with the U.S. Tax Code), they begin to approximate the frictionless capital markets used by Modigliani and Miller (1958), who assert that there is no advantage to debt financing. Howe and Shilling (1988) examined the market's reaction to announcements between 1970 and 1985 of new security offerings by REITs. They found a positive stock price reaction to debt offerings by REITs and a negative reaction to equity offerings. These findings support "signaling" as an explanation for this behavior. Maris and Elayan (1990) examined capital structure for debt and equity REITs, finding that despite the lack of tax incentives many REITs are highly leveraged. Two nontax factors might encourage the use of indebtedness: agency theory (that is, an optimum capital structure that is the same for otherwise similar firms) and clientele effects (that is, investors in high tax brackets prefer unleveraged firms while those in low [or zero] tax brackets prefer leveraged firms). Colwell and Park (1990) found that the "January effect" also exists for REITs (as it does for common stocks) and that the effect declines with increasing market capitalization.

Liu, et al. (1990), using the NCREIF data, found that the commercial real estate market is segmented from the stock market. Indirect barriers such as the cost, quality, and amount of information seem to be the major sources of this segmentation since they found that equity REITs and the stock market are integrated (that is, not segmented). However, these conclusions were unclear when another proxy, American Council of Life Insurance Companies' data, for unsecuritized real estate was used. Liu and Mei (1992) examined the predictability of equity REIT returns and their comovement with other assets. They found, using a multifactor model with time-varying risk premiums, that expected excess returns are more predictable for equity REITs than for bonds and small-cap and value-weighted stocks. They also found that equity REIT returns move more closely with small-cap stocks than with large-cap stocks.

Myer and Webb (1993) examined the return properties of equity REITs, common stocks, and commercial real estate. They found that, in a distributional and time series sense, equity REITs appear to be more like common stocks. Intertemporally, REIT returns are, however, much more strongly related to unsecuritized real estate. It is this latter finding (that is, the long-run relationship between securitized and unsecuritized real estate) that this chapter explores in a more fundamental way. Interestingly, Corgel, et al. (1995), in their near encyclopedic review of the REIT literature, do not cite any paper expressly dealing with the detailed analysis of REIT fundamentals.

Given that returns from equity REITs seemingly represent some part general stock market effect and some part unsecuritized real estate, some researchers have suggested hedging a REIT index with either the S&P 500 (see Giliberto [1993]) or a small-cap index (see Kerson [1994]) as a means of capturing the "pure" real estate play within a publicly traded framework. Obviously, the success of such a strategy rests in part on the fundamental relationship between securitized and unsecuritized real estate.

THE DATA

This study uses the NAREIT Equity Index (without the health care sector) as a proxy for securitized real estate. In theory, these equity REITs are directly comparable to unsecuritized real estate. However, as noted subsequently, there are many practical limitations in this comparison. This chapter uses the combined NCREIF Property Index as a proxy for unsecuritized real estate. The combined index represents the sum of the (widely quoted) unleveraged NCREIF Property Index and the (less widely quoted) index of leveraged properties reported to NCREIF stripped of their mortgage indebtedness.

The 1993 volume of new equity REIT issues (both initial and secondary) exceeded the volume of the previous 10 years combined. The 1994 volume equaled approximately 75 percent of 1993's volume (see Frank [1994]). The increased volume of REIT activity has benefited the more recent research activities due to wider market coverage, a greater array of REIT operating philosophies, more stringent financial reporting, narrowing of bid/ask spreads, and so on. However, it should also be noted that it will take several years before the impact of this increased volume will significantly manifest itself in the return series. Accordingly, researchers, analysts, and investors would be well served to cautiously view empirical studies, including this one, using this evolving database.

At the end of 1995, the NAREIT equity index had a market valuation of $57.5 billion while the NCREIF index stood at $47.8 billion. Figure 13–1 shows the changing market mix of these indexes over the 1978–1995 time period. As can be seen, the NCREIF index had consistently comprised a greater share of the real estate investment market, averaging more than three times the size of the NAREIT index. However, this dominance has dramatically narrowed since 1992 and reversed itself in 1995.

The two indexes also vary in other important ways. First, the mix of property types comprising the indexes is different. Figures 13–2 and 13–3

FIGURE 13–1

NAREIT Equity Index versus NCREIF Index Values Relative Market Mix and Combined Asset Values for the Years 1978 through 1995

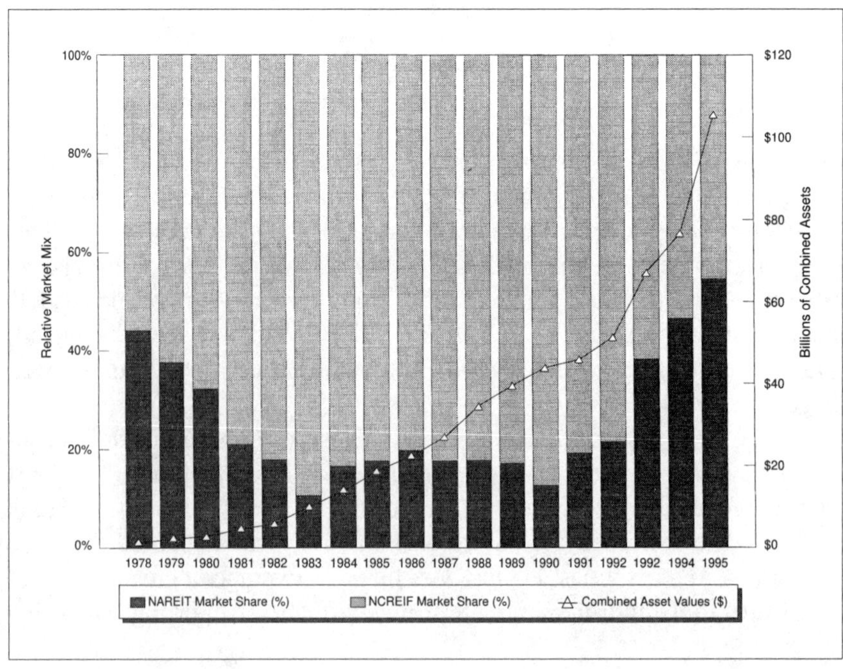

FIGURE 13–2

Mix of Property Types for NAREIT Equity Index as of December 31, 1995

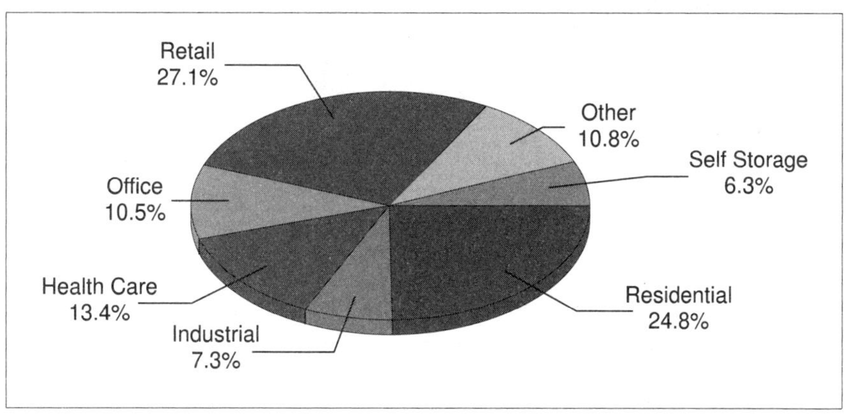

FIGURE 13–3

Mix of Property Types for NCREIF Equity Index as of December 31, 1995

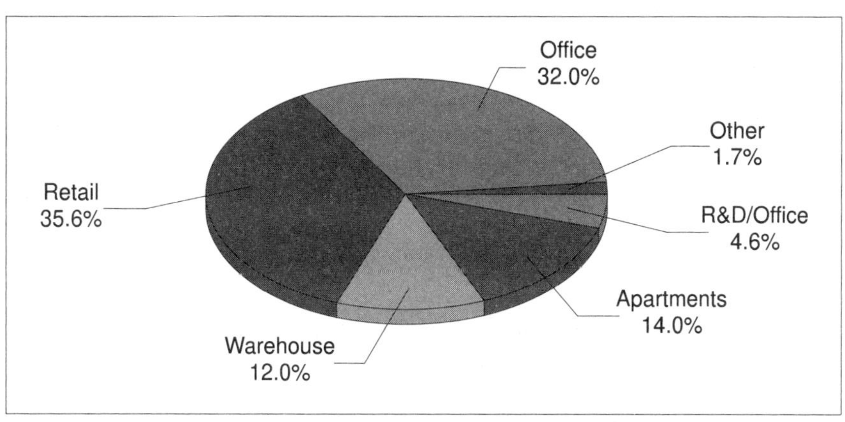

compare the mix of property types by index as of the fourth quarter of 1995. The NAREIT index is overweighted, relative to the NCREIF index, in health care and apartment properties and underweighted in office properties. (Note that NAREIT includes the R&D/office sector in the office sector while NCREIF reports it separately.) Due to recent stock issuances, the

FIGURE 13-4

Comparison of Cumulative Wealth for $1 Investment
Equity REITs (with Health Care) versus Equity REITs without Health Care

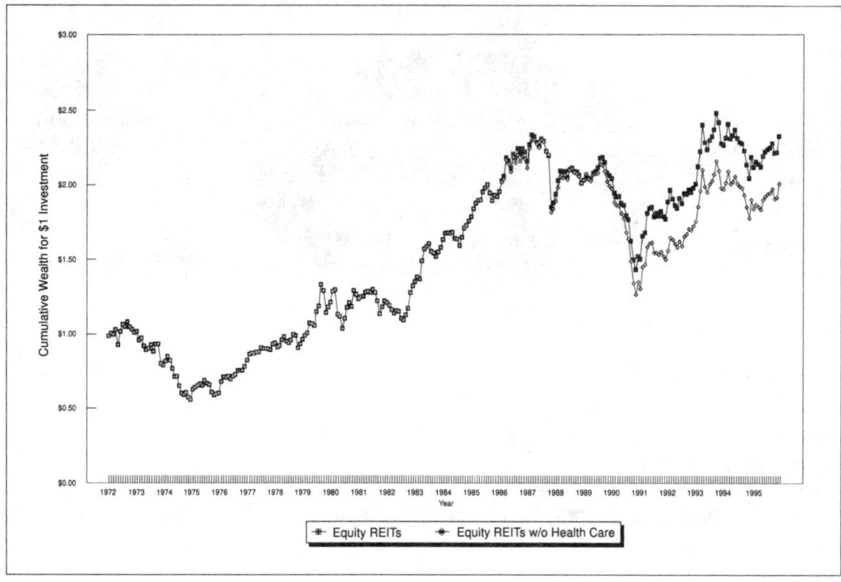

NAREIT index has recently added considerably more apartment and retail properties. Because the health care sector is not present in the NCREIF index, this study uses the NAREIT equity index without health care as a more representative comparison to unsecuritized real estate—as proxied by the NCREIF index. Interestingly, the health care sector has, since its introduction in 1986, on average, outperformed the total NAREIT equity index by 0.67 percent per annum, the result of which can be observed in Figure 13-4.

Second, the indexes also vary considerably by their geographic weightings. In a comparison of the 25 largest equity REITs to an estimate of the national stock of real estate investments, Holden and Redding (1993) found that REITs were substantially overweighted in the smaller markets (for example, Richmond, El Paso, Charleston) and substantially underweighted in the larger markets (for example, New York, Los Angeles, Chicago). Third, the NAREIT series is reported after advisory/reporting fees and costs while the NCREIF series is reported before such fees. Fourth, the equity interests of the properties in the NAREIT series are leveraged while those in the NCREIF series are unleveraged.

Any rigorous comparison between securitized and unsecuritized real estate must make adjustments for the differences in the NAREIT and NCREIF indexes. Several investment banks have begun to report equity REIT performance by property type and geographic weightings, thereby mitigating or eliminating (depending on how far back in time the data series is available and the interests of the analyst) the first two problems noted above. Should the historical data be available, the second problem (different geographic weightings) in conjunction with the first (different property weightings) might be resolved by sorting the NAREIT database according to a geographic and property-type scheme identical to that used to sort the NCREIF database.[1] This still leaves the third and fourth problems unresolved.

The third problem involves investment and asset management fees. In the private arena, the fees charged by real estate advising firms typically represent payment for a blend of investment and asset management services. While in the public arena, these services are typically unbundled: The REIT itself or through an advisory relationship with a third party performs the asset management service; meanwhile, the investment management service can be performed in three basic ways: (1) The investor can internally perform such services, (2) they can be performed via a passive/index fund, or (3) they can be performed via an actively managed fund. (Generally, the second option entails the least incremental direct costs and the third option the most.) The NAREIT series is reported before investment management fees but after the asset management fees while the NCREIF series is reported before both investment and asset management fees. If the investment advisory fees/reporting and costs related to the NAREIT series were constant over time, the third problem (simplistically referred to as fees versus no fees) could be easily rectified: Simply add back a constant percentage and/or amount to the NAREIT series in order to make it directly comparable to the NCREIF series. However, these fees and costs (as measured by amounts and/or percentages) change over time and are complicated as the industry moves from externally advised REITs to those that are internally advised. Additionally, the existence of so-called "UPREITs" (see Frank [1993]) and the multiplicity of agency problems/conflicts of interest (see Sagalyn [1994]) might also contribute to the intractability of identifying fees and costs.

The fourth problem (leveraged versus unleveraged returns) may prove to be the most problematic. Initial adjustments must not only consider the degree of leverage but must also distinguish between fixed- and floating-rate debt. These two types of indebtedness will exhibit opposite behavior on returns, which can be summarized as follows.

A Changing Interest Rate Environment and Its Impact on Equity REIT's Return Components

Type of Interest Rate	Income	Appreciation
Fixed	Neutral	Volatile
Floating	Volatile	Neutral

In a changing interest rate environment, the value of fixed-rate indebtedness should move inversely with the direction of the interest rate change. Consequently, the value of the leveraged equity position (that is, the appreciation return) should reflect the volatility of the interest rate market, *ceteris paribus*.[2] Conversely, the income component of return should be unaffected by the changing interest rate environment as the debt service remains constant (over the life of the loan[s]). The effects of floating-rate debt are opposite those of fixed-rate debt. In a changing interest rate environment, the market value of the indebtedness should remain unchanged. Consequently, the value of the leveraged equity position should be unaffected by the volatility of the interest rate market. Conversely, the income component of the return should be affected by the changing interest rate environment, as the interest expense periodically rolls over to the new floating rate. Moreover, some evidence suggests that the marketplace values REITs using floating-rate debt at a discount from otherwise similar REITs. See Litt, et al. (1994) and Vinocur (1992).

In addition to the distinction between floating- and fixed-rate debt, other characteristics of the indebtedness should be captured. For example, as the term to maturity shortens for the fixed-rate debt, the pricing characteristics begin to roughly emulate the characteristics of the floating-rate debt. Conversely, as the time between "rollover" periods lengthens for the floating-rate debt, its pricing characteristics begin to roughly emulate the characteristics of the fixed-rate debt. Other examples include adjustment for "collars" on floating-rate debt and contingent (or participating) interest. Since all of these terms, rates, and other considerations are changing over time, it is unlikely that a complete "deleveraging" of the NAREIT equity series is amenable to some simple adjustment—as in Fisher, et al. (1994).

TABLE 13–1

Debt-to-Total-Market Capitalization Ratio for 66 Large Equity REITs as of December 1995

Property Type	Average		Standard Deviation
	Simple	Market Weighted	
Apartments	38.7%	34.4%	12.6%
Diversified	20.4%	21.9%	12.4%
Health care	21.8%	21.9%	8.1%
Hotel	14.7%	14.9%	4.2%
Industrial	28.5%	28.9%	9.2%
Mall	53.8%	52.4%	11.1%
Manufactured homes	36.0%	39.2%	13.0%
Office	29.0%	28.4%	5.5%
Retail	37.0%	26.9%	20.1%
Storage	13.9%	14.0%	3.6%
Total	34.7%	32.9%	16.8%

Source: Alex Brown, "Bi-Weekly REIT Valuation Model," December 22, 1995, and authors' calculations.

Furthermore, while the overall leverage ratio is approximately one-third, the ratio varies considerably by property type (see Table 13–1).

To the extent that different property types display different risk/return characteristics, this heterogeneous leverage ratio further obscures the relationship between securitized and unsecuritized returns.

If all these problems were resolved, then securitized and unsecuritized real estate equity could be compared directly. Some of these comparisons are auction- versus appraisal-based valuations, the impact of fractional versus controlling interests, market efficiency, the "correct" pricing of leveraged investments, and the "management" premium. However, the primary role of this study is to examine the long-term convergence/divergence of securitized and unsecuritized real estate equities with regard to dividends, investment values, and dividend yields.

METHODOLOGY

In order to make the securitized/unsecuritized comparison, it is assumed that $100 is invested in each data series at the beginning of 1978. In addition to examining quarterly returns, quarterly dividends and investment values as of the end of each quarter through the end of 1995 are reconstructed.

This reconstruction is fairly simple for the NAREIT series, as dividends, investment values (or prices), and dividend yields have been separately reported in the *REIT Sourcebook* since the beginning of 1972 on a monthly and quarterly basis.

For the NCREIF series, the procedure is a bit more complex. The generally reported NCREIF Property Index discloses income and appreciation returns. The income return, however, is based on net operating income and therefore is not a measure of dividends. As a special data request, NCREIF provides a more detailed report that lists net operating income, capital improvements, partial sales, and beginning and ending asset values. From this information, a "dividend" series can be approximated by subtracting capital improvements from net operating income.[3]

The following two issues illustrate the importance of examining the fundamental return components individually. First, the nature of the traditionally reported income and appreciation (quarterly) returns can lull the unwitting analyst into a false sense of stability with regard to that series' income stream. Consider the following hypothetical (and purposefully extreme) example: Assume that a $50 million building is valued at the end of each quarter by capitalizing next quarter's (annualized) net operating income at 8 percent, that net operating income declines at the rate of 5 percent per annum or 1.25 percent per quarter, and that (for purposes of simplicity) partial sales and capital improvements are zero. The NCREIF methodology[4] would generate the returns shown in Table 13–2.

Notice that the NCREIF reported quarterly income return is approximately 2.0 percent every quarter, even though net income is declining at the rate of 1.25 percent per quarter! This is because the NCREIF methodology constantly revises the denominator to reflect drifting asset values. Because of the constant capitalization rate used in this example, the fundamental approach asserted in this chapter would view (on an annualized basis) this as simply a restatement of the dividend discount model (see Gordon and Shapiro, 1956):

$$k = \frac{Div_1}{MV_0} + g \tag{1}$$

$$3.0\% = 8.0\% - 5.0\% \tag{2}$$

TABLE 13–2

Illustration of Potential Disparity between Net Income Growth and Reported Income and Appreciation Returns Using NCREIF Methodology*

	Underlying Data		NCREIF Returns		
Quarter	Ending Value	Operating Income	Appreciation	Income	Total
0	$50,000				
1	49,375	$1,000.00	−1.24%	1.99%	0.75%
2	48,758	987.50	−1.24%	1.99%	0.75%
3	48,148	975.16	−1.24%	1.99%	0.75%
4	47,546	962.97	−1.24%	1.99%	0.75%
5	46,952	950.93	−1.24%	1.99%	0.75%
6	46,365	939.04	−1.24%	1.99%	0.75%
7	45,786	927.31	−1.24%	1.99%	0.75%
8	45,213	915.71	−1.24%	1.99%	0.75%
9	44,648	904.27	−1.24%	1.99%	0.75%
10	44,090	892.96	−1.24%	1.99%	0.75%
11	43,539	881.80	−1.24%	1.99%	0.75%
12	42,995	870.78	−1.24%	1.99%	0.75%
13	42,457	859.89	−1.24%	1.99%	0.75%
14	41,927	849.15	−1.24%	1.99%	0.75%
15	41,403	838.53	−1.24%	1.99%	0.75%
16	40,885	828.05	−1.24%	1.99%	0.75%
17	40,374	817.70	−1.24%	1.99%	0.75%
18	39,869	807.48	−1.24%	1.99%	0.75%
19	39,371	797.38	−1.24%	1.99%	0.75%
20	38,879	787.42	−1.24%	1.99%	0.75%
21	38,393	777.57	−1.24%	1.99%	0.75%
22	37,913	767.85	−1.24%	1.99%	0.75%
23	37,439	758.26	−1.24%	1.99%	0.75%
24	36,971	748.78	−1.24%	1.99%	0.75%

*Assumes capital improvements and partial sales equal to zero.

Notice that both approaches result in annual returns of 3.0 percent (or a quarterly return of 0.75 percent). It is simply that the fundamental approach leads to a much clearer view of the individual return components.

Second, the effect of fluctuating capitalization rates (or, alternatively, dividend yields) is substantial when the holding period is relatively short. However, in the long run all returns converge toward their fundamental components. Additionally, while shifts in dividend yields can be substantial in the short run, in the long run the percentage change in dividend yields for both securitized and unsecuritized real estate is mean-reverting, as evidenced by their near-zero means—as discussed subsequently.

Consequently, any analysis of short-run returns that ignores the path of the underlying fundamental components encounters substantial "noise" due to short-run deviations from fundamental returns (as dividend yields can shift dramatically) and ignores the fact that this noise is eliminated in the long run by the mean-reverting nature of the shifts in dividend yields.

THE RESULTS

The relationship of securitized to unsecuritized real estate is examined from four vantage points: (1) total returns, (2) dividend amounts, (3) investment values, and (4) dividend yields. Additionally, the discussion of dividend amounts also involves an extension to NCREIF's net operating income series.

Total Returns

Figure 13–5 presents a comparison of total quarterly returns for the respective databases. The greater volatility of the NAREIT series is readily apparent. Moreover, the NAREIT series has historically exhibited higher returns.

In addition to the graphing of concurrent returns, we could also show a fitted linear regression line along with confidence intervals bounded at 95 percent. However, from visual inspection, the relationship between the two data series appears weak. This appearance is supported by a statistical review of the statistics involving the following univariate regression equation used to fit such a regression line for Figure 13–5:

$$y_t = a + b\,x_t + \varepsilon \qquad (3)$$

FIGURE 13–5

Total Quarterly Returns for the Period from 1978:1 through 1995:4
NAREIT Equity Index (without Health Care) versus NCREIF Property Index

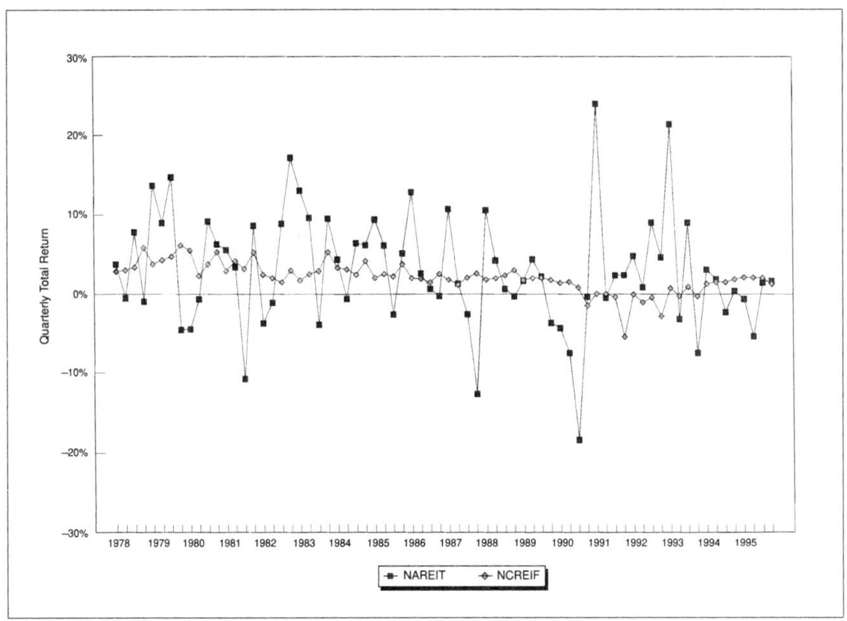

where: y_t = quarterly return on NCREIF index in quarter t,
a = constant (intercept) value,
b = parameter modifying x_t,
x_t = quarterly return on NAREIT index in quarter t, and
ε = error term

The important statistical parameters of this equation are summarized in Table 13–3. This weak statistical relationship between concurrent returns essentially reaffirms the research discussed in the *Literature Review*. Notice that the beta parameter (b) is statistically indistinguishable from zero —suggesting the lack of any linear, concurrent relationship between the two indexes. That the same group (more or less) of underlying assets (that is, real property) should have such widely dissimilar return patterns begs the question: Does "packaging" (that is, same group of assets, one in a securitized format and the other in an unsecuritized format) make such a

TABLE 13–3

Statistical Summary of Univariate Linear Regression Using Concurrent NAREIT and NCREIF Quarterly Total Returns for the Period 1978 through 1995

	Value	t-Statistic
R^2	.002	
F-Statistic	1.146	
a (Intercept)	.0223	8.99*
b (Beta Coefficient)	–.0331	–1.07

*Significant at the 99 percent confidence level.

substantive difference that the two return series are, statistically speaking, independent (or nearly so) of one another?

With regard to the question of the normality of total return, measures of skewness and kurtosis indicate that both distributions are not normal. Moreover, given the leveraged nature of the NAREIT series, it would be expected that this return series is nonnormal (see Pagliari and Sanders [1995]). While these results are also consistent with earlier research (see Myer and Webb [1993] and Young and Graff [1995]), they seem an insufficient explanation as to the statistically weak relationship between the returns of securitized and unsecuritized real estate. This insufficiency leads to the second examination: a lagged relationship between returns.

The lagged relationship between securitized and unsecuritized returns has been previously examined by Gyourko and Keim (1992, 1993). Generally, their 1993 study found a mildly significant relationship between the residual of the unsecuritized real estate returns (after having removed the autocorrelation found in the data series). Geltner (1989, 1993) and Ross and Zisler (1991) have noted previously that there is substantial autocorrelation in the NCREIF series and the lagged one-year returns of a real estate stock index. Not only was their time period (1978–1991) slightly different from that used here, their definition of securitized real estate was also broader (for example, it included non-REIT stocks such as owner/operators, subdividers, developers, and general contractors, which comprised approximately 45 percent of their real estate stock index) and therefore runs counter to our argument of aligning the databases for homogeneity of product type. Consequently, it is important to examine this lag/lead relationship using the databases as discussed herein.

TABLE 13–4

Statistical Summary of Stepwise Multivariate Linear Regression Using Current NCREIF Quarterly Total Returns versus Lagged NAREIT Returns for the Period 1978 through 1995

	Value	t-Statistic
Adjusted R^2	.072	
F-Statistic	2.223*	
a (Intercept)	.0224	8.09***
$b_{NAREIT\ t-8}$	–.0612	–2.12**
$b_{NAREIT\ t-6}$	–.0415	–1.44
$b_{NAREIT\ t-5}$	–.0419	–1.45
$b_{NAREIT\ t-3}$	–.0308	–1.06

* Significant at the 90 percent confidence level.
** Significant at the 95 percent confidence level.
*** Significant at the 99 percent confidence level.

The relationship between current NCREIF (t) quarterly returns and current/lagged NAREIT returns (t–n) can be further examined by using stepwise regression (where missing data are pairwise deleted). For the time period studied, the results of such an approach are shown in Table 13–4.

The ordering of the independent variables noted above also represents their incremental contribution (from highest to lowest) to the equation's explanatory power. NAREIT returns lagged two years (that is, NAREIT t–8) is the most significant independent variable—both with regard to the size of its coefficient and t-statistic—in explaining the variability of current NCREIF returns. While the intercept is positive, all of the independent variables have negative beta coefficients, which suggests an inverse relationship and further points to the confounding, short-term relationship between securitized and unsecuritized returns. Over the 1978–1990 time period, Gyourko and Keim (1992) found a significant relationship between current NCREIF returns and lagged one-year (that is, the preceding annual) NAREIT returns with a dummy variable adjustment for fourth-quarter "seasonality" (see Panel 2 of their Exhibit 2 on p. 464). This preceding annual NAREIT return would correspond to the following periods in this study: NAREIT t–1, NAREIT t–2, NAREIT t–3 , and NAREIT t–4. Notably, only one of these periods (NAREIT t–3) is found to be significant in the stepwise regression approach.

These results are troubling to those who generally believe in market efficiency. How can the two real estate return series exhibit such substantially different risk/return measures (see Figure 13–5) with the covariance statistically indistinguishable from zero (see Table 13–3)? Even lagged NAREIT returns (see Table 13–4) explain less than 15 percent of the variation in NCREIF returns. This pattern has led Giliberto (1990) to examine the residuals from regressions of both data series on financial assets (that is, stocks and bonds). He found these residuals are significantly correlated ($\rho = .44$, significant at the 99 percent confidence level). The alternative approach, used in various forms by Geltner (1989, 1993), Gyrouko and Keim (1992, 1993), and Ross and Zisler (1991), is to remove the autocorrelation in the NCREIF series. Using the "reconstituted" return series, the NCREIF series is more volatile and considered a better estimate of real estate's "true" systematic risk. This study proposes a third alternative: examining the fundamental components of returns (dividends, investment values, and dividend yields).

Quarterly Dividends

An investment of $100 at the beginning of 1978 in each of the real estate series would result in the dividend patterns (without reinvestment) shown in Figure 13–6. Some of the volatility in the NAREIT dividend series may be attributable to imperfect adjustments for capital gains, return of capital, and special dividends (see Culley and Shilling [1990]).

While both series are nonnormal, the NCREIF series has a higher average percentage change in quarterly dividends (4.24 percent for NCREIF versus 3.21 percent for NAREIT) and a wider standard deviation (34.2 percent for NCREIF versus 21.3 percent for NAREIT) and range. All of which is curious, given the unleveraged nature of the NCREIF series. Perhaps quarterly dividend figures are too volatile and preclude drawing any meaningful conclusions. Certainly most investors forecast more than one quarter's worth of dividends when making an investment decision. Accordingly, the following section examines four-quarter rolling dividends in an attempt to dampen the volatile quarterly growth in dividends.

Rolling Four-Quarter Dividends

The rolling four-quarter dividends represent the simple summation of quarterly dividend payments over a given one-year interval. Quite naturally,

FIGURE 13–6

Quarterly Dividends for the Period from 1978:1 through 1995:4
NAREIT Equity Index (without Health Care) versus NCREIF Property Index

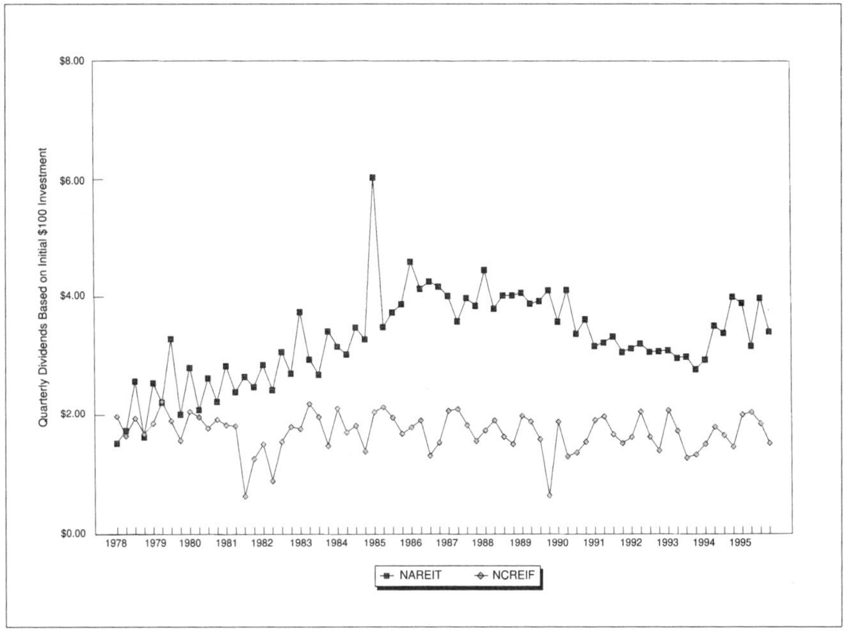

the four-quarter summation of dividends has a smoothing effect, as shown in Figure 13–7.

Summary statistics of the percentage change in rolling four-quarter dividends indicate that the leveraged NAREIT series experienced a higher average growth rate than did the NCREIF series (1.08 percent for NAREIT versus 0.28 percent for NCREIF)—the opposite result from the case of quarterly dividends. (However, the substantially higher volatility and non-normality of the quarterly NCREIF returns makes the mean of its distribution misleading.) Notwithstanding the fact that this time period had large influxes of new construction and large declines in rental rates and property values, it is discouraging that the mean growth (or percentage change) in annual NCREIF dividends is nearly zero. This is all the more troubling given that these dividend series are expressed in nominal (versus real) terms.

Like before, a stepwise regression analysis using the current percentage change in annual NCREIF dividends as the dependent variable and the

FIGURE 13–7

Rolling Four-Quarter Dividends for the Period from 1978:1 through 1995:4
NAREIT Equity Index (without Health Care) versus NCREIF Property Index

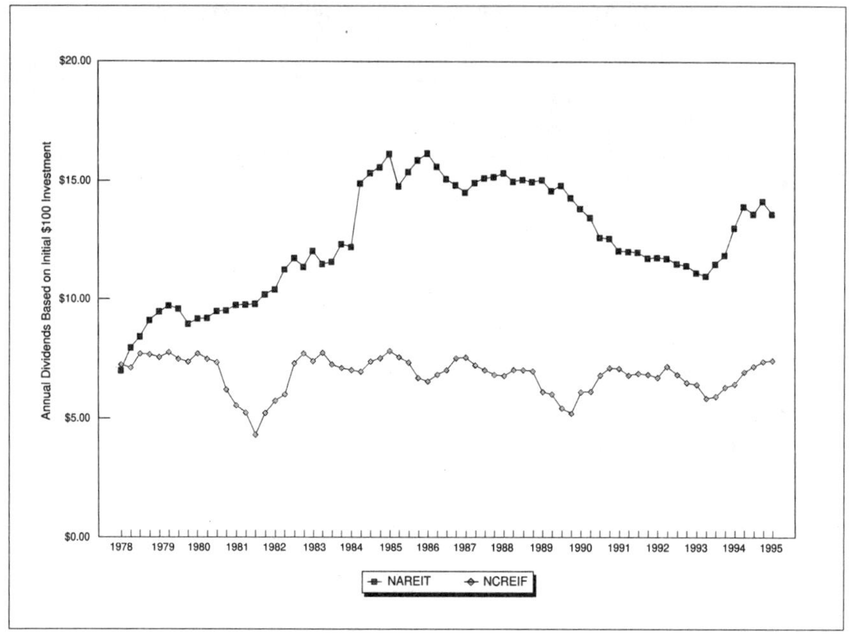

concurrent and leading NAREIT series (that is, NAREIT t through NAREIT t–8) as potentially includable independent variables was generated. The results are shown in Table 13–5.

With the exception of the percentage change in annual NAREIT dividends lagged two and eight quarters (that is, NAREIT t–2 and NAREIT t–8), none of the other quarterly lags were significant at the 90 percent confidence level. The ability of NAREIT dividends to explain future variability in NCREIF returns appears statistically insignificant.

Alternatively, performing the analysis with the percentage change in annual NAREIT dividends and the lagged NCREIF series as the independent variables[5] only marginally changes the statistical significance (as measured, for example, by the adjusted R^2 value). Pragmatically, the variability of neither series explains much of the current and/or future variability of the other series.

TABLE 13-5

Statistical Summary of the Stepwise Multivariate Linear Regression Using the Current Percentage Change in Rolling Four-Quarter Dividends with the NCREIF Index as the Dependent Variable and the Lagged NAREIT Index as the Independent Variables for the Period 1978 through 1995

Adjusted R^2	.1003	
F-Statistic	1.9392**	
	Value	**t-Statistic**
a (Intercept)	.0437	22.98**
$b_{NAREIT\ t-7}$	.0361	.72*
$b_{NAREIT\ t-2}$	–.0840	–1.86*
$b_{NAREIT\ t-8}$	.0904	2.02**
$b_{NAREIT\ t-3}$	–.0718	–1.45
$b_{NAREIT\ t-4}$	.0817	1.58
$b_{NAREIT\ t-1}$	–.0515	–1.19
$b_{NAREIT\ t}$	.0517	–1.07

* Significant at the 90 percent confidence level.
** Significant at the 95 percent confidence level.
*** Significant at the 99 percent confidence level.

NAREIT Dividends versus NCREIF Income

In addition, the relationship of the rolling four-quarter NAREIT dividend series to the rolling four-quarter NCREIF net income series was also examined (see Figure 13–8).

The two data series exhibit a generally tight fit over the 1978–1984 and 1987–1990 time periods. As noted previously, the use of a four-quarter rolling total smoothes each series. However, it does not explain the remarkable similarity—at least in comparison to the dissimilarity of dividends—in the path of NAREIT dividends and NCREIF net operating income. In some sense, senior REIT executives "manage" dividends. That is, they declare dividends based on a variety of factors, which includes compliance with U.S. Tax Code provisions, acquisitions/dispositions, capital improvements, debt restructuring, and "signaling" effects to investors, lenders, and so on. The NAREIT Index reports dividends but not net income (earnings or funds from operations). If dividends are the primary focus of investors and analysts, senior REIT executives might smooth dividends in an effort to

FIGURE 13–8

Rolling Four-Quarter Dividends for the Period from 1978:1 through 1995:4

NAREIT Equity Index (without Health Care) versus Income for the NCREIF Property Index

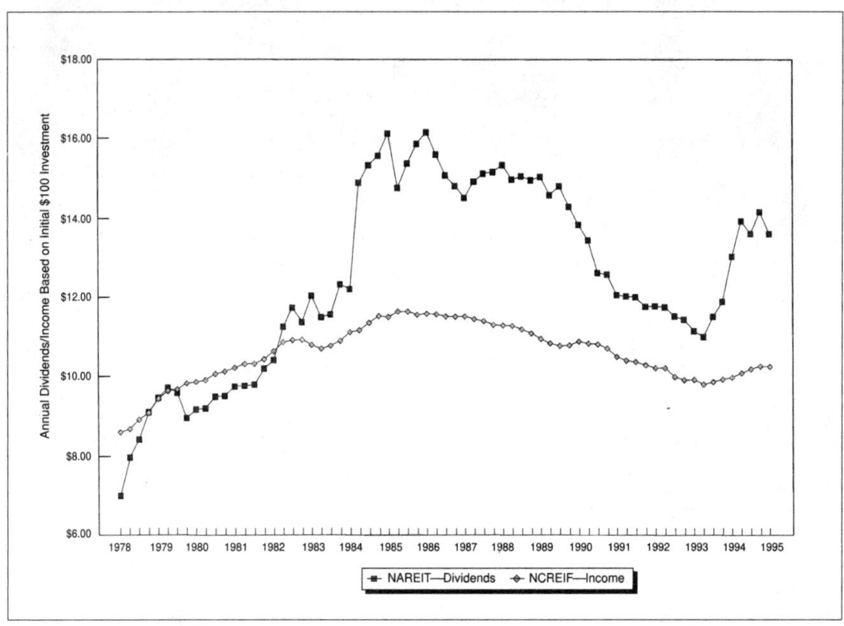

stabilize the pricing of REIT shares. However, the commotion about a NAREIT-proposed change in the way FFO (funds from operations) is to be reported (see Litt and Harris [1994], Martin [1995]) suggests that reported earnings are also a substantial concern to senior management.

Conversely, NCREIF reports income and not dividends. Moreover, the NCREIF dividend series created in this study is relatively unmanaged in the sense that advisory-firm executives make decisions about the timing of capital improvements and (generally) not about Tax Code compliance, new acquisitions, debt restructuring, and so on. Consequently, if the dividend series is unmanaged, a volatile dividend payout ratio might be observed for the NCREIF series. Figure 13–9 tracks the dividend payout ratio (that is, the ratio of dividends to net operating income) on the right vertical axis and net operating income and dividend amounts on the left vertical axis.

FIGURE 13-9

NCREIF Property Index for the Period from 1978:1 through 1995:4

Annual Net Operating Income, Dividend Amounts, and Payout Ratios Based on Initial $100 Investment

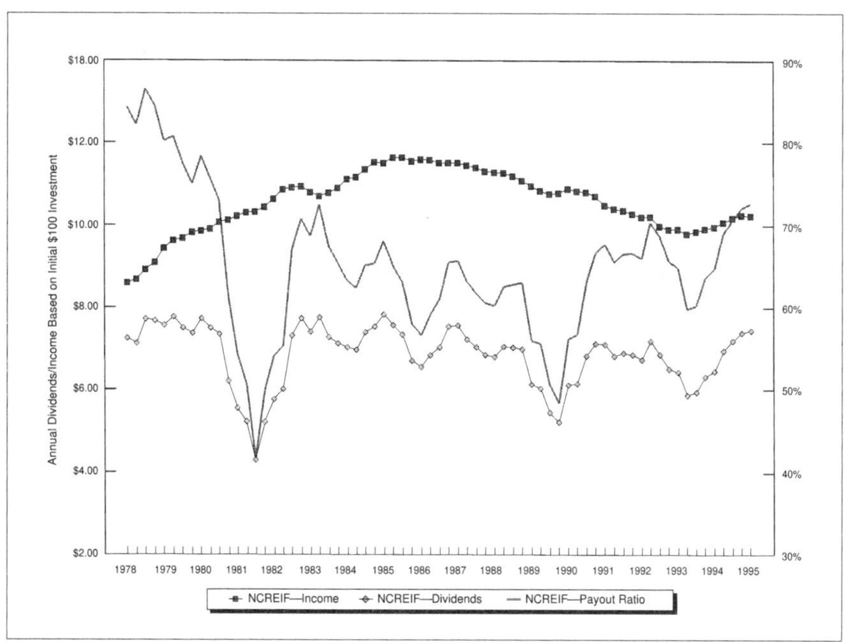

As Figure 13–9 illustrates, the NCREIF series shows substantially more volatility (and less growth) in its dividend series than does its income series. In turn, this suggests the possibility that NCREIF advisers are less concerned about "managing" their dividend series. However, we do not observe the actual cash distributed by advisers to their clients. It is often the case that advisers fund capital improvement escrows in order to smooth their cash distributions to clients.

Investment Values

An investment of $100 at the beginning of 1978 in each real estate series would result in the pattern of investment values (without reinvestment) shown in Figure 13–10.

FIGURE 13–10

Quarterly Investment Values for the Period from 1978:1 through 1995:4
NAREIT Equity Index (without Health Care) versus NCREIF Property Index

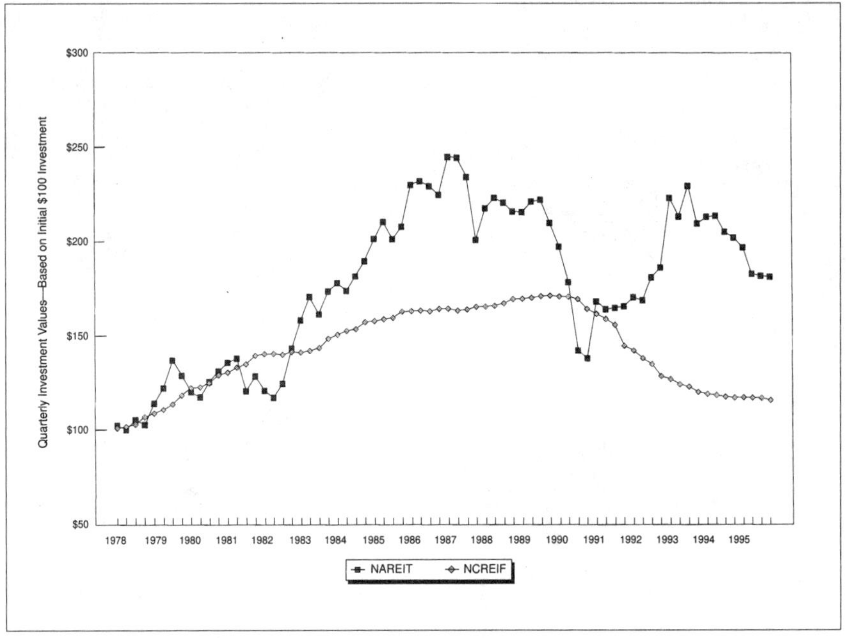

For the NAREIT series, investment values represent the path of aggregate equity REIT stock prices (that is, real estate asset values less mortgage indebtedness and plus/minus any "management premium") as traded on an exchange. For the NCREIF series, investment values represent the path of appraised asset values. The former represents a fractional/minority interest in a securitized portfolio of leveraged real estate, while the latter represents a controlling interest in an unsecuritized, unleveraged fixed asset. Consequently, it is entirely possible that there is considerable short-run divergence between the two series. However, long-run convergence between the two would be expected. Figure 13–10 seems to support this view. Nevertheless, conventional statistical analysis indicates a weak relationship between concurrent investment values.

As compared to dividends where the NCREIF series was considerably more volatile than the NAREIT series, the situation is reversed when

TABLE 13–6

Statistical Summary of the Stepwise Multivariate Linear Regression Using the Percentage Change in Quarterly Investment Values with the NCREIF Index as the Dependent Variable and the Lagged NAREIT Index as the Independent Variables for the Period 1978 through 1995

Adjusted R^2	.147	
F-Statistic	2.778**	
	Value	**t-Statistic**
a (Intercept)	–.0043	–1.920*
$b_{NAREIT\ t-8}$	.0609	2.170**
$b_{NAREIT\ t-5}$	.0623	2.187**
$b_{NAREIT\ t-2}$	.0386	1.391
$b_{NAREIT\ t-4}$	.0473	1.660*
$b_{NAREIT\ t-6}$	.0350	1.221
$b_{NAREIT\ t-7}$	.0330	1.176

* Significant at the 90 percent confidence level.
** Significant at the 95 percent confidence level.

investment values are considered. With regard to the percentage change in investment values, the NAREIT series is approximately four times as volatile as the NCREIF series when standard deviations and ranges are compared.

Lagged relationships are investigated via stepwise regression analysis, with NCREIF t as the dependent variable and NAREIT t through NAREIT t–8 as potentially includable independent variables; the results are as shown in Table 13–6. While all of the beta (slope) coefficients are positive and the first two are statistically significant (at the 95 percent confidence level), the low adjusted R^2 suggests substantial uncertainty in the estimates of the current percentage change in NCREIF asset values as forecasted by earlier changes in NAREIT investment values.

Dividend Yields

As noted earlier, short-run returns are very sensitive to changes in the dividend yield.[6] It is not changing prices per se that distort fundamental returns. In fact, constant dividend yields (or capitalization rates) imply that prices change at the same rate as dividends (or net operating income). When the growth rates for prices and dividends (or net operating income) differ is when dividend yields (or capitalization rates) change. In the aggregate,[7] changing dividend yields represent the manifestation of changing investor sentiment with regard to risk premiums, expected inflation, lease rates, and so on. It is these short-run changes in investor sentiment (more commonly referred to as time-varying risk premiums and cash flow expectations) that can lead to substantial volatility in the quarterly total returns. Consequently, it is extremely important to assess the relationship of changing dividend yields between securitized and unsecuritized real estate.

In an attempt to gauge the correlation between NAREIT and NCREIF dividend yields, this study examines rolling four-quarter dividend yields—computed on a trailing-dividends basis.[8] In this chapter's earlier analysis of quarterly dividends, they were found to be quite volatile and only loosely correlated. The use of the longer period (that is, four quarters) here is also an attempt to dampen this volatility. Not only is there substantial quarter-to-quarter volatility in the underlying dividend streams, most investors are undoubtedly using periods longer than one quarter to value the asset's future dividend stream. Consequently, Figure 13–11 illustrates the rolling four-quarter dividend yields for both indexes.

As noted before, the use of rolling four quarters dampens the volatility of the observation. Nevertheless, the divergence and convergence between the two series —except for the last three years—is obvious and remarkable. It is apparent that the relationship of dividend yields between securitized and unsecuritized real estate is weak. Again, the securitized/unsecuritized relationship is counterintuitive. Notwithstanding the significant number of caveats mentioned earlier, why should dividend yields for the same group of real estate assets (coarsely defined) move inversely with one another?

The disparity in average dividend yields (roughly 265 basis points) is remarkable—given that the standard deviations of the respective distributions are nearly identical and that asset appreciation, over the long run, has been quite consistent for the respective indexes. Also interesting is the mean-reverting nature of dividend yields, which is suggested by the near-zero mean for each distribution accompanied by a substantial deviation and range. For the NAREIT series, the mean percentage change in annual dividend yields was 0.42 percent with a standard deviation of 7.54 percent; for the NCREIF series, the mean percentage change was 0.19 percent with

FIGURE 13–11

Annual Dividend Yields for the Period from 1978:1 through 1995:4
NAREIT Equity Index (without Health Care) versus NCREIF Property Index

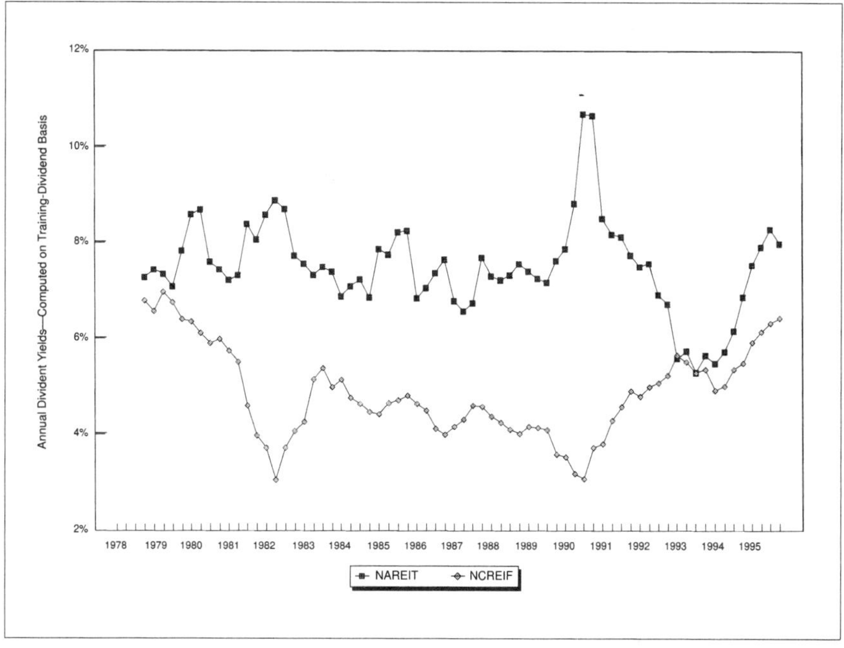

a standard deviation of 7.39 percent. Their mean-reverting nature reinforces the importance of examining the fundamental sources of returns when examining/projecting long-run returns.

As before, a stepwise regression with the current NCREIF dividend yields as the dependent variable and the range of current lagged NAREIT dividend yields as includable independent variables is presented in Table 13–7. Concurrent changes in NAREIT dividends as well as those of two years prior (that is, NAREIT t and NAREIT t–8) are negatively related to current changes in NCREIF dividend yields. They represent the only statistically significant lagged relationships. However, the overall explanatory power of the equation is relatively low—as measured by the adjusted R^2 value. Additionally, similar results are obtained if the percentage change in dividend yields is analyzed.

TABLE 13–7

Statistical Summary of the Stepwise Multivariate Linear Regression Using the Rolling Four-Quarter Dividend Yield with the NCREIF Index as the Dependent Variable and the Lagged NAREIT Index as the Independent Variables for the Period 1978 through 1995

	Value	t-Statistic
Adjusted R^2	.263	
F-Statistic	11.707**	
a (Intercept)	.0922	8.81**
$b_{NAREIT\ t}$	–.4045	–4.65**
$b_{NAREIT\ t\text{-}8}$	–.2043	–2.20*

* Significant at the 95 percent confidence level.
** Significant at the 99 percent confidence level.

CONCLUSIONS AND RECOMMENDATIONS

As with previous research, a weak statistical relationship between total returns for securitized and unsecuritized real estate has been found. In an attempt to resolve this enigma, total returns have been unbundled into their fundamental components: dividends, investment values, and changes in dividend yields. The short-run relationships between these fundamental components as they relate to securitized and unsecuritized returns are generally weak from a statistical standpoint even when lags of up to two years are examined. Of the three fundamental components, the long-run path of prices for securitized and unsecuritized real estate exhibited the strongest relationship (see Figure 13–10). In turn, this suggests that the weak relationships for explaining total returns may be more attributable to the volatility of dividends (see Figure 13–6) and/or changes in dividend yields (see Figure 13–11). Table 13–8 highlights the relative volatility of dividends and prices for the securitized and unsecuritized series.

The third and sixth rows of Table 13–8 compute the ratio of the NCREIF statistic to that of the NAREIT statistic. In comparing the standard deviation of the percentage change in quarterly investment values, NCREIF volatility is roughly one-fourth of the NAREIT volatility. Yet, in comparing

TABLE 13-8

Summary of the Percentage Change in Annual Dividends and Quarterly Investment Values Using the NAREIT and NCREIF Data Series

	Mean	Median	Standard Deviation
Rolling Four-Quarter Dividends			
NAREIT	1.08%	.32%	4.68%
NCREIF	.28%	−.59%	6.96%
Ratio of NCREIF to NAREIT	.257	−1.833	1.488
Quarterly Investment Values			
NAREIT	1.06%	.33%	7.13%
NCREIF	.22%	.24%	1.86%
Ratio of NCREIF to NAREIT	.203	.726	.262

the standard deviation of the percentage change in annual dividends, NCREIF volatility is roughly 150 percent of the NAREIT volatility.[9] This disparity is remarkable. In a simplified setting, greater dividend volatility should be accompanied by greater price volatility, not less, as observed here. These results might suggest some adaptation of the appraisal-smoothing issues raised by Geltner (1989, 1993), Gyourko and Keim (1992, 1993), Ross and Zisler (1991), and others.

While the unbundling of securitized and unsecuritized real estate into their fundamental return components has substantially improved the ability to understand the differences between these two series, at least three areas warrant future investigation.

Alignment of Real Estate Issues

As pointed out in the third section ("The Data"), the considerable differences (that is, property type, geography, fees, and leverage) in the data sets must be resolved before a definitive comparison of the two data series can be made. Myer and Webb (1994) and Liang, et al. (1995) have made initial attempts at doing so, but much work still needs to be done. Additionally, issues related to managed versus unmanaged dividend series demand further research.

Stock Market Inefficiencies

The last several years have witnessed a substantive assault on the market efficiency hypothesis regarding the underlying path of stock prices. These assaults include (1) the excess volatility of stock prices when using a constant risk premium (see Shiller [1981]); (2) the tendency for past losers to become future winners—and past winners to become future losers, though with less magnitude (see De Bondt and Thaler [1985]); (3) the tendency for long-term returns to exhibit a mean-reverting behavior (see Poterba and Summers [1988]); (4) stocks with good fundamentals (for example, low price-to-book ratios, high dividend yields) tend to outperform those with bad fundamentals (see Fama and French [1992], Haugen [1995], and Lakonishok, et al. [1994]); (5) the "January effect," where most of the stocks excess return is generated in the month of January—particularly true for small-cap stocks (see Haugen and Lakonishok [1988]); and (6) questions of separating ownership and operating control (see Fama and Jensen [1983]).

Some of the stock market inefficiencies have already been applied to REITs. See Colwell and Park (1990) with regard to the January/small-firm effect, Gyourko and Keim (1992) with regard to the small-cap effect, and McIntosh, et al. (1994) with regard to control/pricing questions. If, by extension, some or all of these stock market "anomalies" apply to the REIT market as well (but not to the unsecuritized real estate market), further adjustments must yet be made before securitized and unsecuritized real estate can be directly compared.

Type I versus Type II Errors

Poterba and Summers (1988) point out that when too much emphasis is placed on avoiding Type I errors (that is, rejecting the null hypothesis[10] when it is true), the risk of accepting Type II errors (that is, accepting the null hypothesis when it is false) is increased. Thus, traditional tests of random-walk prices/returns may obscure long-run, mean-reverting behavior in prices/returns. They suggest that transitory price components (that is, time-varying risk premiums and/or investor "fads") may account for a substantial part of the variance in common stock returns. Perhaps this is true here as well. Consider the path of asset prices shown in Figure 13–10. The conventional statistical tests reveal little significant correlation. Yet there appears to be a significant long-term relationship.

As this chapter demonstrates, the comparison between securitized and unsecuritized real estate is far from over. We hope this study will stimulate additional research in this evolving and important topic. Finally, the integration of the real estate issues raised in this chapter and the capital market issues of the previous chapter should provide fertile opportunities for an improved understanding of REIT performance.

ENDNOTES

1. We are not advocating that the NCREIF scheme for geographic and property-type disclosure be used necessarily; rather, we suggest that analysts use the most illuminating geographic and property-type scheme common to both databases.
2. While it is possible for properties encumbered with short-term leases (for example, apartments and hotels) to have asset values unaffected by changes in the level of interest rates, this is unlikely for properties encumbered with long-term leases. Consequently, the *ceteris paribus* condition is more likely to apply to properties leased on a short-term basis and/or to portfolios of properties leased on a long-term basis where the lease rollover is equal each year.
3. This is an imperfect solution, as NCREIF uses an accrual-based approach to reporting net operating income. At times, there may be significant timing differences between accrual- and cash-based net operating income (see NCREIF [1988]). Moreover, real estate investment advisers may smooth capital expenditures by accumulating reserves in prior periods to fund current (or future) period capital improvements. The earnings of the NAREIT series were not available to us.
4. Similar illustrations can be created for other indexes (for example, NAREIT, S&P 500, and so on).
5. These analyses and others not shown by summary statistics and/or exhibit are available from the authors upon request.
6. This also applies to capitalization rates or price-earnings ratios where the dividend payout ratio is constant.
7. For an individual building, changing dividend yields or capitalization rates may solely reflect existing fixed-rate leases (that are above or below market) rolling toward their expiration dates. On a portfolio basis where lease maturities are evenly staggered, dividend yields or capitalization rates will, however, remain constant, *ceterus paribus*.

8. On an *ex ante* basis, only trailing dividends are observable. Accordingly, all dividend yields are computed on a "trailings" (versus leading) basis. Additionally, where appropriate, these measures have been annualized to facilitate comparability.

9. The authors thank Anthony B. Sanders (Ohio State University) for suggesting this perspective following Shiller (1981).

10. In this chapter, the null and alternative hypotheses regarding the beta coefficients can be summarized as follows: $H_0 : b_i = 0$v. H_a: $b_i \neq 0$. In other words, we are testing the acceptance/rejection of the null hypothesis of a beta coefficient that is statistically indistinguishable from zero.

REFERENCES

Chan, K. C., P. H. Hendershot, and A. B. Sanders. "Risk and Return on Real Estate: Evidence from Equity REITs." *AREUEA Journal,* Winter 1990, pp. 431–452.

Chen, K. C. and D. D. Tzang. "Interest-Rate Sensitivity of Real Estate Investment Trusts." *Journal of Real Estate Research,* Fall 1988, pp. 13–22.

Colwell, P. F. and H. Y. Park, "Seasonality and Size Effects, The Case of Real Estate-Related Investments." *Journal of Real Estate Finance and Economics,* September, 1990, pp. 251–259.

Corgel, J. B., W. McIntosh, and S. H. Ott. "Real Estate Investment Trusts: A Review of the Financial Economics Literature." *Journal of Real Estate Literature,* January 1995, pp. 13–43.

Culley, S. A. and J. D. Shilling. "REIT Dividend Rates and Their Implications for Valuing Income-Producing Real Estate." *The Appraisal Journal,* July 1990, pp. 386–394.

De Bondt, W. F. M. and R. H. Thaler. "Does The Stock Market Overreact?" *Journal of Finance,* July 1985, pp. 793–808.

Fama, E. F. and K. R. French. "The Cross Section of Expected Stock Returns." *Journal of Finance,* June 1992, pp. 427–465.

Fama, E. F. and M. C. Jensen. "Separation of Ownership and Control." *Journal of Law and Economics,* June 1983, pp. 301–325.

Fisher, J. D., D. M. Geltner, and R. B. Webb. "Value Indexes of Commercial Real Estate: A Comparison of Index Construction Methods." *Journal of Real Estate Finance and Economics,* September 1994, pp. 137–164.

Frank, R. A. "Active First Half Brings 1994 Underwriting to New-Record Level." Alex. Brown & Sons Incorporated, December 9, 1994.

———. "The UPREIT: Keys to the Real Estate Kingdom?" Alex. Brown & Sons Incorporated, March 31, 1993.

Gatzlaff, D. H. and D. Tirtiroglu. "Real Estate Market Efficiency: Issues and Evidence." *The Journal of Real Estate Literature,* July 1995, pp. 157–189.

Geltner, D. "Estimating Market Values from Appraised Values Without Assuming an Efficient Market." *The Journal of Real Estate Research,* Summer 1993, 325–345.

———. "Estimating Real Estate's Systematic Risk from Aggregate Level Appraisal-Based Returns." *Journal of American Real Estate and Urban Economics Association,* Winter 1989, pp. 463–481.

Giliberto, S. M. "Equity Real Estate Investment Trusts and Real Estate Returns." *The Journal of Real Estate Research,* Summer 1990, pp. 259–263.

———. "Measuring Real Estate Returns: The Hedged REIT Index." *The Journal of Portfolio Management,* Spring 1993, pp. 94–99.

Gordon, M. J. and E. Shapiro. "Capital Equipment Analysis: The Required Rate of Profit." *Management Science,* October 1956, pp. 102–110.

Gyourko, J. E. and D. B. Keim. "What Does the Stock Market Tell Us About Real Estate Returns?" *Journal of the American Real Estate and Urban Economics Association,* Fall 1992, pp. 457–485.

———. "Risk and Return in Real Estate: Evidence from a Real Estate Stock Index." *Financial Analysts Journal,* September-October 1993, pp. 39–46.

Haugen, R. A. *The New Finance: The Case Against Efficient Markets.* Englewood Cliffs, New Jersey: Prentice Hall, 1995.

Haugen, R. A. and J. Lakonishok. *The Incredible January Effect.* Homewood, Ill.: Dow-Jones-Irwin, 1988.

Holden, M. P. and K. G. Redding. "The Geographic Distribution of Properties Owned by Real Estate Investment Trusts." The RREEF Funds—Research, September 1993.

Howe, J. S. and J. D. Shilling. "Capital Structure Theory and REIT Security Offerings." *Journal of Finance,* September 1988, pp. 983–993.

Kerson, J. S. "Trading in Fundamental Real Estate Risk with Market-Hedged Equity Indexes." *Bankers Trust Research—Derivatives Focus,* September 1, 1994.

Khoo, T., D. Hartzell, and M. Hoesli. "An Investigation of the Change in Real Estate Investment Trust Betas." *Journal of the American Real Estate and Urban Economics Association,* Summer 1993, pp. 107–130.

Lakonishok, J., A. Shleifer, and R. W. Vishny. "Contrarian Investment, Extrapolation and Risk." *Journal of Finance,* December 1994, pp. 541–578.

Liang, Y., A. Chatrath, and W. McIntosh. "Apartment REITs and Apartment Real Estate." Working paper, January 1995.

Litt, J., D. J. Kostin, and B. T. Hatfield. "Equity is King and Variable Rate Debt is a REIT's Achilles' Heel." Salomon Brothers, July 7, 1994.

Litt, J. D., J. Kostin, B. T. Hatfield, and T. S. Harris. "Understanding REIT Accounting and Disclosure Will Affect Relative Valuations." Salomon Brothers, December 1, 1994.

Liu, C. H., D. J. Hartzell, T. W. Greig, and T. V. Grissom. "The Integration of the Real Estate Market and the Stock Market, Some Preliminary Evidence." *Journal of Real Estate Finance and Economics,* September 1990, pp. 261–282.

Liu, C. H., D. J. Hartzell, T. W. Greig, T. V. Grissom, and J. Mei. "The Predictability of Returns on Equity REITs and Their Co-Movement with Other Assets." *Journal of Real Estate Finance and Economics,* September 1992, pp. 401–418.

McIntosh, W., W. R. Rogers, C. F. Sirmans, and Youguo Liang. "Stock Prices and Management Changes: The Case of REITs." *Journal of the American Real Estate and Urban Economics Association,* Fall 1994, pp. 515–526.

Maris, B. A. and F. A. Elayan. "Capital Structure and the Cost of Capital for Untaxed Firms: The Case of REITs." *American Real Estate and Urban Economics Association Journal,* Spring 1990, pp. 22–39.

Martin, E. J. "Truth or Consequences." *Institutional Investor,* February 1995, pp. 113–116.

Martin, J. D. and D. O. Cook. "A Comparison of the Recent Performance of Publicly Traded Real Estate Portfolios and Common Stock." *AREUEA Journal,* Summer 1991, pp. 184–297.

Modigliani, F. and M. H. Miller. "The Cost of Capital, Corporation Finance, and the Theory of Investment." *American Economic Review,* June 1958, pp. 261–297.

Myer, F. C. and J. R. Webb. "Retail Stocks, Retail REITs and Retail Real Estate." *The Journal of Real Estate Research,* Winter 1994, pp. 65–84.

———."Return Properties on Equity REITs, Common Stocks and Commercial Real Estate: A Comparison." *The Journal of Real Estate Research,* Winter 1993, pp. 87–106.

The National Council of Real Estate Investment Fiduciaries. "Current Value Reporting by Real Estate Fiduciary Managers." *Real Estate Accounting and Taxation,* Fall 1988.

Pagliari, J. L., Jr., and A. B. Sanders. "Option Pricing Models Applied to Asset, Mortgage and Equity Investments: A Real Estate Practitioner's Overview." Working paper, 1995.

Pagliari, J. L., Jr., and J. R. Webb. "A Fundamental Examination of Securitized and Unsecuritized Real Estate." *The Journal of Real Estate Research,* Winter 1995, pp. 381–425.

Poterba, J. M. and L. H. Summers. "Mean Reversion in Stock Prices: Evidence and Implications." *Journal of Financial Economics,* October 1988, pp. 27–59.

Ross, S. A. and R. C. Zisler. "Risk and Return in Real Estate." *Journal of Real Estate Finance and Economics,* June 1991, pp. 175–190.

Sagaluyn, L. B. "Agency Problems in the Structure of REITs." Working paper, September 1994.

Shiller, R. J. "Do Stock Prices Move Too Much to Be Justified by Subsequent Changes in Dividends?" *American Economic Review,* June 1981, pp. 421–436.

———."The Use of Volatility Measure in Assessing Market Efficiency." *Journal of Finance,* May 1981, pp. 291–304.

Titman, S. and A. Warga. "Risk and the Performance of Real Estate Investment Trusts: A Multiple Index Approach." *American Real Estate and Urban Economics Association Journal,* Fall 1986, pp. 414–431.

Vincocur, B. "Floating-Rate Debt May Make High-Yield REITs Investor Traps." *Barrons,* November 9, 1992, p. 51.

Wang, K., J. Erickson, and G. W. Gau. "Dividend Policies and Dividend Announcement Effects for Real Estate Investment Trusts." *Journal of the American Real Estate and Urban Economics Association,* Summer 1993, pp. 185–201.

Young, M. S. and R. Graff. "Real Estate Is Not Normal: A Fresh Look at Real Estate Return Distributions." *The Journal of Real Estate Finance and Economics,* May 1995, pp. 225–259.

Young, M. S., R. Graff, D. M. Geltner, W. McIntosh, and D. M. Poutasse. "Defining Commercial Property Income and Appreciation Returns for Comparability to Stock Market-Based Measures." *Real Estate Finance,* Summer 1995, pp. 19–30.

———. "Understanding Equity Real Estate Performance: Insights from the NCREIF Property Index." *Real Estate Review,* Winter 1996, pp. 4–16.

CHAPTER

14

FINANCIAL ANALYSIS OF REIT SECURITIES

Louis W. Taylor, *Senior Real Estate Analyst, Prudential Securities*

INTRODUCTION

Real estate investment trusts have evolved into fully integrated, dynamic, real estate operating companies that are organized as investment trusts simply to avoid taxation at the corporate level. Their valuation should be approached in a manner consistent with comparable investments, whether publicly traded widget companies or Class A office buildings. That is, a company's value is the present value of its cash flows discounted to compensate the holder for an appropriate level of risk.

Investors in both equity securities and real estate have historically struggled with whether real estate investment trusts are either securities or real estate. At this point, they are becoming less like real property and more like other securities. The reason is the evolution of the REITs into fully integrated, self-funded entities. As they make this transition from a series of assets to an actively managed portfolio, traditional real estate analysis, while still an element of valuation, will be given less weight. Instead, the valuation of companies in other industries with similar market capitalizations and growth rates will become a more important benchmark.

The valuation of real estate investment trusts has three fundamental components:

1. **Determining the nature of the underlying cash flow.** The first component in any valuation is, of course, the underlying cash flow. This involves an analysis of all the elements of revenue and expense to assess the income stream's net cash flow and volatility. This runs the gamut from lease structures to operating expense pass-throughs to upcoming debt maturities, to expected capital expenditures. This is the most important part of the analysis and provides the foundation for the valuation.
2. **Assessing the expected growth in cash flow.** The second component is determining the expected level of growth in the company's cash flows for the determined holding period. This builds off the characteristics of the underlying portfolio to include the following:

   - Supply and demand characteristics for the company's properties.
   - Debt levels that may allow companies to borrow to make further investments.
   - Retained cash flow that can be reinvested to enhance growth and dividend stability.
   - Management's ability to sell assets and redeploy the capital at higher rates of return.

   These and other factors all contribute to a company's growth rate, which can be well in excess of the cash flow growth from the individual properties.
3. **Calculating an appropriate discount rate.** Given the underlying earnings and expected growth rates, investors discount the cash flows at an appropriate rate to compensate them for the real and perceived risks. For securities, a three- or five-year holding period is the most common, with a terminal value based on earnings multiples of similar companies with similar growth rates and liquidity for the shares. Unlike cap rates for properties, the discount rate for securities is much more fluid and dynamic. It is based on constantly changing interest rates and returns on alternative investments. And, of course,

different investors will apply different discount rates, resulting in an implied market rate. Unlike real properties, management's actions can have a profound impact on this discount rate, both positively and negatively. This can result in opportunities to either buy or sell the security based on the changing sentiment. This makes the valuation of real estate investment trusts more volatile than real estate values, but compared to the balance of the equity markets, the volatility would be considered low.

These three considerations set the framework for each company's valuation. As we will discuss below, a wide range of factors affect valuation. Some factors apply to all companies, while some only apply to individual companies based on predominant property type.

After discussing these factors, we will illustrate the methodology with a hypothetical valuation of five companies.

DETERMINING THE NATURE OF THE UNDERLYING CASH FLOW

The determination of the portfolio's underlying cash flow combines the fundamental elements of revenues minus costs. For real estate companies, this combination consists of five major segments:

- Revenue
- Operating expenses
- Administrative costs
- Financial costs (including preferred dividends)
- Capital expenditures

In measuring operating earnings and cash flow, real estate investments use two terms: *funds from operations* and *funds available for distribution.* These terms are unique to real estate investment trusts and are the fundamental measures of earnings and cash flow. Funds available for distribution is generally the operating cash flow available to pay the dividend to common shareholders.

Funds from operations (FFO) is currently the most widely used earnings benchmark for real estate investment trusts. It is defined as net income, as determined by generally accepted accounting principles (GAAP), excluding any gains or losses or deductions for real property depreciation. The formula below illustrates the calculation:

Net Income	
Add Back:	Real property depreciation
Add Back:	Losses from property sales
Deduct:	Gains from property sales
Equals:	**Funds from Operations (FFO)**

The concept behind funds from operations is fairly straightforward. Net income for real estate companies can be very volatile due to property sales and leverage that can inflate the depreciation deduction. Since many real estate assets hold their value and frequently appreciate, especially during periods of higher inflation, the depreciation charge often distorts the true earnings power of a company. Funds from operations, because it excludes volatile property sales and ignores property depreciation, can give investors a better picture of a company's operating performance.

From a real estate perspective, *funds from operations* equals net operating income less all administrative costs (including depreciation of non-real estate assets) and financing costs (including the amortization of financing costs).

Funds available for distribution (FAD) is simply funds from operations less any adjustment for straight line rents, principal amortization on debt, and capital expenditures. The capital expenditures consist primarily of leasing costs and major capital costs, such as roofs and parking lot repair. Funds for distribution attempts to capture leasing and other capital costs required to maintain the revenue stream. Since there is no real estate depreciation charge in FFO, but there are real capital expenditures to maintain the properties and occupancy rates, it is important to recognize these costs. It gives a more accurate picture of the amount of capital available for distribution, and it makes comparisons between companies owning different properties easier. For example, an apartment company and an office company may have similar FFO per share, but the apartment company may have lower capital costs and, consequently, more funds available for distribution to shareholders. As a result, the apartment company may warrant a higher valuation or multiple of FFO.

Items pertaining to substantial renovation are generally excluded from this definition, with the costs being reflected in the total initial cost for a new investment or acquisition. This is a controversial area that represents a weakness in the current definition of funds from operations. For example, several companies have converted existing single-purpose facilities into multitenant facilities at a substantial cost. Under the definition of funds from operations, there is no recognition of these costs, although the companies can recognize the higher revenue stream that frequently results. Ideally, these costs should be amortized over the costs of the improvements, but the companies are not required to do so, even though the amortization would be relatively modest. Instead, investors have to rely on the disclosure of these costs to make their own adjustments.

Funds available for distribution is a fairly good approximation of operating cash flow, although it is not net cash flow. Real estate companies do not have inventory to speak of or large fluctuations in either accounts payable or receivables. This allows funds for distribution to give a fairly reliable picture of operations. However, because of timing differences, it is not net cash flow.

We include this discussion of funds available for distribution because many investors use it in their analytical work. For our purposes, dividend and earnings growth, defined as funds from operations, will be the earnings benchmark because of its wide familiarity. Funds available for distribution will impact the calculation of cash available for the dividend or reinvestment into the company.

Revenue

To determine funds from operations, the first element is revenue. Although most companies do not typically break out revenue into its various components, revenue consists of several items:

- **Base rents.** This is the base rent as defined in a tenant's lease. In many instances, periodic base rent increases are based on the increases in an inflation index, usually the consumer price index, or negotiated increases at specific points during the lease. Rent is typically recognized on a GAAP basis with any difference between cash rent and GAAP rent reflected in the calculation of funds available for distribution.
- **Expense recoveries.** This is the portion of a property's operating costs paid by the tenant. It is typically the tenant's pro rata share of operating costs or pro rata share of operating costs above a negotiated amount.
- **Percentage rent.** Generally pertaining only to retail properties, this component provides for the property owner to receive a percentage of a tenant's sales above a certain negotiated level, known

as a breakpoint. For example, the tenant will pay the higher of a fixed base rent of, say, $10 per square foot or 5 percent of sales above $200 per square foot. When sales are below $200 per square foot, the tenant pays $10 per square foot. Above $200, the tenant pays 5 percent of sales. This rewards the property owner for identifying tenants that can attract customers to the center, thereby increasing the sales potential of all the tenants.

- **Management and leasing income.** Many companies manage and lease properties for other owners and receive a fee. Typically, these contracts are short-term in nature (one year or less) with a 30-day cancellation notice. While it generates incremental revenue and covers overhead costs, management and leasing income can be volatile.
- **Other income.** Other income is usually minor. It consists of interest on cash balances, which are usually kept at a minimum; vending income; parking income; storage income; and other miscellaneous fees.

The sources of revenue vary by property type. For example, only retail tenants receive percentage rent clauses, while apartment owners typically do not receive reimbursements for expenses. As Table 14–1 indicates, every property type begins with a base rent, with the remaining components varying due to different operational characteristics. For example, operating expenses for industrial properties can vary substantially due to the different operating requirements of a manufacturer and a distributor; therefore, industrial tenants historically have paid for their own operating costs. The industrial property owner passes property taxes and insurance costs on to the tenants. However, the operating costs for office building tenants are fairly similar, with the owner expected to maintain the lobby and common areas. Office leases have generally evolved so that office tenants typically only pay expenses above a base year.

Since the nuances of different revenue sources can take up chapters of real estate texts, we will refer the reader to such texts for more detail. Instead, we will focus on operating expenses.

Operating Expenses

Operating costs are the normal, recurring costs to provide for a safe, clean, comfortable, and attractive working environment for a buildings' tenants. As Table 14–2 illustrates, the operating costs vary considerably as a percentage of revenue based on the expense categories for different property types.

TABLE 14–1

Revenue Sources Vary by Property Type

	Apartments	Neighbor-hood Retail	Regional Malls	Office	Industrial	Hotels
Base rent	90.0%	80.0%	70.0%	85.0%	95.0%	
Expense recoveries		15.0%	20.0%	10.0%	2.0%	
Percentage rent		2.0%	5.0%			
Management and leasing	3.0%	1.0%	3.0%	3.0%	1.0%	5.0%
Room revenue						80.0%
Food & beverage						10.0%
Other	7.0%	2.0%	2.0%	2.0%	2.0%	5.0%

Source: Prudential Securities

TABLE 14–2

Operating Expenses Vary by Property Type

	Apartments	Neighbor-hood Retail	Regional Mall	Suburban Office	Industrial
Repairs and maintenance	8.3%	7.4%	20.7%	31.6%	13.9%
Utilities	27.7%	4.9%	13.3%	23.9%	8.5%
Administration and personnel	34.4%	23.0%	17.9%	13.3%	12.7%
Property taxes	18.6%	41.1%	25.5%	28.6%	57.2%
Insurance	2.5%	5.3%	3.2%	1.7%	3.2%
Marketing	5.6%	4.3%	13.7%	0.5%	2.0%
Other	3.0%	3.6%	6.0%	0.5%	2.9%
Total	100%	100%	100%	100%	100%

Source: Prudential Securities

Despite the varying levels of importance, there are six major property expenses:

1. **Property taxes.** Every property has associated property taxes that are a substantial part of operating expenses. This can be a very unpredictable figure due to the whims of local tax authorities. Assessed valuations can increase dramatically as the

result of a comparable property's sale in the immediate area or as a result of the property's sale.

2. **Utilities.** Utilities are a large expense in climate-controlled environments or in areas that have a lot of common-area lighting. As Table 14–2 illustrates, utility costs are high at regional malls and office buildings while relatively small at neighborhood shopping centers and industrial properties. Utility costs can be very volatile due to changing weather conditions. Apartment and hotel owners have the most exposure to variations in utility costs because they are typically not passed through to tenants. However, apartment residents pay for utility costs inside their units. Companies attempt to protect themselves from higher costs by passing the increases on to tenants.
3. **Maintenance.** Maintenance expenses run the gamut from pest control to landscaping to elevator maintenance. No one item contributes a large portion consistently; rather, there are wide variations in maintenance costs by property type. Properties with low site coverage, such as industrial properties or regional malls, have high landscaping and parking lot costs. High-rise office buildings with high site coverage have higher elevator maintenance and cleaning contracts. Generally, repairs and maintenance items are fairly predictable, with most major capital items being capitalized.
4. **On-site management and administration.** This is the on-site staff and the associated administrative costs of leasing and managing the property. Frequently, commercial leasing personnel are on commission, and their costs are capitalized and amortized over the length of the lease. However, the property manager, accounting personnel, and support staff make up the balance of these costs. With the exception of industrial properties, on-site management costs are a major expense although they are fairly predictable.
5. **Insurance.** Insurance covers natural disasters such as fire and earthquakes, liability if someone is hurt on the property, and most often rent insurance in the event tenants cannot use the building for a sustained period. It is usually not a major cost,

except earthquake coverage, and is generally at a consistent level throughout the property types.

6. **Marketing costs.** Marketing costs are an important element of retail and multifamily properties. These costs cover advertising and promotion of the property. Marketing costs can fluctuate widely and be 10 percent of total expenses if a company is trying to fill substantial vacancies. If the property is fully leased and demand for space is strong, the cost can be cut to minimal amounts.

As we alluded to earlier, it is important to know the lease structure to determine who pays for increases. In the long term, higher expenses ultimately affect the total rent a tenant can pay, but in the short term, higher costs are typically passed on to tenants in the form of expense escalations. However, as we noted, apartment leases require the owner to pay these costs, and hotel operators have full exposure for these costs.

The second critical element is that most costs are fixed. Regardless of the occupancy rate, parking areas need to be lit, the heat needs to be on in the common areas, and property taxes and insurance must be paid. As we will discuss below, some capital items can be deferred, but the bulk of the operating costs cannot be. This operating leverage generates some bottom-line volatility since revenue changes go directly to the bottom line. And the effects can be substantial. Because of expense recoveries, operating margins for retail, office, and industrial companies generally approach and can exceed 70 percent. Because so many costs are fixed, virtually every dollar of incremental revenue from the existing portfolio goes right to the bottom line.

Administrative Costs

Administrative costs pertain to the costs to run the company; they represent overhead. The compensation of CEO and CFO are in this category as well as the costs of acquisition and development staffs. These costs also include the corporate communications function, which includes quarterly and annual reports and other shareholder communications. The category includes the compensation for corporate administrative staff along with the office rent, equipment costs, and corporate liability insurance costs.

As we illustrate later in the valuation example, the administrative costs vary by company. Some of this valuation is due to the different operations or property type, but it also has a lot to do with accounting treatment. A number of companies capitalize acquisition and development personnel expenses into the cost of a project. They reflect the cost of uncompleted investments through a quarterly reserve. This of course creates questions about whether the reserve is adequate or not. Conversely, companies that may appear to have higher administrative costs may be expensing all the associated development personnel and writing off canceled projects as incurred.

Like operating expenses, overhead costs are generally fixed. The savings when business slows would come from the investment personnel, whose numbers would be reduced.

Financial Costs

As most readers know by now, real estate is a capital-intensive business. Understandably, the cost of that capital is a major component of operating performance. Companies generally use four main capital sources:

1. Short-term, floating-rate debt in the form of a credit line for acquisitions and development.
2. Long-term, fixed-rate debt that is either secured or unsecured, which is typically used to repay the short-term debt once it reaches certain levels.
3. Mezzanine capital, either in the form of subordinated convertible debentures or preferred stock, which is usually used to repay other forms of debt.
4. Common stock, depending on the equity markets, point in the real estate cycle, and overall debt levels.

From a cash flow standpoint, the most critical element in the short term is the amount of floating-rate debt. Here investors need to make the distinction between interest that is being capitalized as part of a development and interest that is being expensed. Clearly, the more floating-rate debt that is being expensed, the more potential for earnings volatility.

Fortunately, most companies hedge their floating-rate debt through the purchase of an interest-rate cap or a swap. There are times when floating-rate debt is not an issue, but with the volatile interest-rate environment, most investors feel uncomfortable with any modest floating-rate debt exposure for a sustained period.

The second concern is the maturity of the existing debt over the next three to five years and how the interest rates compare to current market conditions. Whether it is short-term debt being repaid with long-term capital sources or the repayment of maturing long-term debt, investors generally feel there is enough risk in the real estate industry that to be burdened with either interest-rate or maturity risk makes a company even less appealing. As a result, companies with long-term, fixed-rate debt are generally viewed more positively.

Capital Expenditures

Capital expenditures are frequently a source of great debate. Investors and analysts spend considerable time determining which capital items are really operating costs that are being capitalized due to liberal accounting stances and which items are true long-term costs that occur infrequently. There is also considerable debate over accounting for such items as tenant improvements and leasing commissions. These costs are clearly long term in nature but are really a cost of maintaining the revenue stream and therefore should be incorporated into the calculation of operating earnings. Currently, the definition of *funds from operations* excludes a depreciation charge for these items.

Regardless of the outcome of the debate, capital expenditures typically follow guidelines established by generally accepted accounting principles. That is, items above a certain dollar amount with a useful life longer than one year are capitalized. These generally include major roof repairs, parking lot repairs, major renovations, and major equipment replacements, such as boilers or heaters. They also include tenant improvement and leasing costs, which are amortized over the term of the leases. The normal threshold for capitalization is $1,000 per item with a useful life beyond one year. For some companies, the threshold is $15,000.

But some companies stretch the definition to include carpeting or apartment appliances when these are normal and recurring replacement items. For example, one apartment company expenses all carpets but capitalizes all invoices over $1,000. Since it buys in bulk, all carpet invoices exceed $1,000, so the company effectively capitalizes its carpet replacements. Some companies capitalize the cost of certain administrative personnel, such as a portion of the CEO's salary, into the cost of a new development. So, clearly, investors not only have to understand the expected costs for the next several years, they need to understand the accounting treatment being used in order to provide a useful estimate of the cost to run the business during the holding period.

Beyond the accounting debate, the most volatile capital expenditures are re-leasing costs. These are a function of the lease expirations occurring each year of the holding period, the negotiating strengths of the landlord and the tenant, and the local market conditions. Disclosures of lease expirations is standard in 10Ks, and most companies have reported historical costs per square foot for both leasing and tenant improvement costs. Investors can at least get some historical guidance to estimate future costs.

Other capital items such as replacing boilers and roofs can be expensive, but because they are fairly infrequent, the yearly fluctuations are often not significant. The exception are portfolios of older properties, which are likely to have an increased level of capital expenditures over time simply due to age. After 10 years, roofs and parking lots begin to wear out. The exterior gets worn and renovation becomes necessary. An aging analysis of the portfolio is always a useful exercise to determine whether these costs are reflected in the operating cash flows. Fortunately, companies can mitigate this risk by selling assets before they need significant capital improvements.

Because capital expenditures can be delayed or scaled down, companies frequently postpone these costs when market conditions are weak, especially if they are struggling to meet debt-service payments. For real estate investment trusts, this is less of an issue because debt levels are low. But several companies have had fairly high capital expenditures after going public because they had deferred capital costs during the weak markets of the early 1990s. If companies do not effectively manage their dividend payout ratios by keeping them too high when markets enter a recession, companies are likely to defer capital costs in order to maintain the dividend.

DETERMINING THE APPROPRIATE GROWTH RATE

Having analyzed a company's operations, investors can then focus on a company's expected growth rate. This is both an art and a science and encompasses both qualitative and quantitative issues. Earnings growth is driven by two principle factors: growth from the core portfolio and investment activity.

Growth from the Core Portfolio

The first, and most important, element is the expected growth from the existing portfolio. Here, the growth is driven by the lease terms but, more importantly, the supply and demand for space in each of a company's markets. Investors need to focus on both the employment growth and the resulting demand for space and the amount of new constriction being completed. New construction not only consists of similar space but also alternative space. For example, a tenant's construction of a new corporate headquarters or distribution facility frequently creates a major vacancy in the building it just vacated. The construction of a new factory outlet center could draw customers from a regional mall or community center 20 miles away. New construction does not always hurt a market and can generate earnings growth for companies that can develop. But supply becomes a problem when an economy slows and the space is completed as demand is falling. That subsequently causes occupancy rates to fall and rents to decline.

Myriad other factors can affect supply and demand, which can influence portfolio growth rates. First is the amount of available land for new development. The more land available, the more likely rents will remain at levels making development marginally profitable. As a result, rents will likely track development costs and the cost of capital. Second, the state and local regulatory environment has a major impact on both supply and demand. If a state or city has low taxes and minimal regulatory requirements to new construction, such as Houston does, companies can expand rather quickly, and demand for space can be high. Unfortunately, as Houston demonstrated, supply can form even faster and depress rents when too much space is built in a short period. Conversely, Austin, which benefits from Texas's low state taxes, has a difficult regulatory environment, which acts to limit growth and maintain a high quality of life. Despite historically high job growth and popularity with new employers, new supply has not kept up with demand because of Austin's hilly terrain and stiff local opposition to haphazard growth.

The following are other factors affecting core portfolio growth:

- Timing of lease expirations and the rents on the leases expiring relative to market rates.
- Contractual rent increases from existing leases.

- Increased operating expenses that are not passed on to tenants either through contractual agreements or due to lower vacancy rates.
- Higher interest expenses due to increased interest rates on floating-rate debt.

Investment Activity

The second major source of growth is from investment activity. Investment activity is comprised of three different growth components: so-called "positive spread investing," portfolio management, and the investment of internally generated cash flow.

Positive Spread Investing

Virtually every company can manage some element of risk so that it can earn a rate of return that exceeds its cost of capital. This is commonly referred to as *positive spread investing.* From an earnings standpoint, the contribution to growth is determined by three factors: investment yield, cost of capital, and rate of activity, as discussed below and illustrated in Table 14–3.

Investment Yield Investment yield is simply how much return a company can earn on an investment. The benchmark figure is the return on cost or return on assets. For acquisitions, the cost is essentially the cap rate adjusted for necessary capital improvements. Properties with high re-leasing costs typically trade at higher cap rates than those with lower ongoing re-leasing costs. The yield is also a function of the expected growth in the property's cash flow. For development projects, it is the stabilized yield after the project is completed and leased. Frequently, development yields are higher than acquisition yields due to the risk involved. Generally, the more risk a company can manage, the higher the expected yield. Of course, companies have to weigh the risk-adjusted return. Sometimes an extra 50 basis points in return on a development project is not worth the added risk when there are ample acquisition opportunities around. In the case of the example shown in Table 14–3, we assumed the company could earn 11 percent, unleveraged, on its investments.

Cost of Capital To create the spread, capital has to cost less than the investment yield. This cost is a function of the credit markets, the equity

TABLE 14–3

FFO Impact of Positive Spread Investing

		Purchase $200 of Property at an 11% Yield	Borrow $100 of Long-Term Debt at 8%	Issue $100 of New Stock at $14 per Share	Post Acquisition Financial Condition
Real estate	$2,000	$200			$2,200
Debt	$600		$100		$700
Equity	$1,400			$100	$1,500
Shares	100			7	107
Price per share	$14.00			$14.00	$14.59
Expected nominal FFO	$120	$22	($8)		$134
Expected FFO per square	$1.20				$1.2507
FFO Multiple	11.67				11.67
FFO/yield	8.57%				

Note: Example assumes that the FFO multiple remains unchanged so the higher FFO results in a higher share price.

markets, and the company's balance sheet. Companies with low debt levels and access to rated corporate debt will have a lower debt cost than those with below-investment-grade ratings. Companies with higher growth rates tend to have higher earnings multiples and lower equity costs. A frequent topic of debate is the cost of that equity capital. Over the long term, it is the expected return on the shares. For the purpose of determining whether an acquisition financed with common equity is additive or dilutive to earnings, the measure is FFO yield, not the dividend yield, on the shares. In our example, we assumed an equal amount of new debt and equity capital. With a long-term debt cost of 8 percent and a FFO yield of 8.57 percent, the company's weighted cost of capital would be 8.28 percent compared to an investment yield of 11 percent. For simplicity's sake, we assumed that the growth rate on the existing portfolio and new acquisition is identical in order to focus on the yield differentials.

Rate of Activity The third component is the rate of activity, how many investments the company can make over the next one, three, and five years. This is primarily a function of the capital markets, but since they are unpredictable, the easiest short-term indicator is the existing balance sheet. While industry practices will evolve over time, rating agencies and nervous shareholders are likely to pressure companies to keep debt levels below 50 percent debt-to-market capitalization. That means companies with debt levels below 30 percent have room to add leverage to their balance sheets, and the resulting investments can add to earnings. At higher debt levels, capital may be more difficult to obtain, and the investment pace could be much lower. Of course, the company can use proceeds from asset sales as a capital source, which we discuss further below.

To complete the example shown in Table 14–3, we assumed the company made investments that grew its asset base by 10 percent and financed its investments with an equal combination of debt and equity. As a result of the investments, funds from operations grew from $1.20 per share to $1.25 per share. Assuming no change in FFO multiple, the share price should increase to $14.59 as a result of the acquisitions to reflect higher funds from operations.

Portfolio Management

Portfolio management is another form of investment activity, but in this case, it is the sale of assets with below-average growth rates. By selling these assets, companies can enhance their core portfolio growth. Portfolio management also includes selling those assets that can be sold at low cap rates because the associated risk is lower. A company can then reinvest the proceeds into other assets where it feels it can effectively manage the risk and earn a higher return. In some respects, proceeds from assets sales are another form of capital. But the important element is the rate of sale and the amount of capital that can be redeployed without having to increase debt levels or issue more common equity. This component has important growth aspects but also important psychological benefits, which we discuss below in further detail.

Internally Generated Cash Flow

The last source of capital is internally generated cash flow, that is, operating cash flow after all capital expenditures, principal amortization of debt, and dividends to common shareholders. It is a company's cheapest form of capital. As companies move to lower their dividend payout ratios over time into the 50 to 60 percent range, internal cash flow can have a greater impact on earnings than most acquisitions. It has become an important valuation component because it not only adds to earnings growth, it creates stability for the dividend. This can act to lower the required discount rate on the stock.

DETERMINING THE APPROPRIATE DISCOUNT RATE

Historical Perspective

Historically, unleveraged cash flows from real estate have been discounted at 11 to 12 percent to determine present value. Investors traditionally have taken a long-term view and have used a 10-year holding period with a residual cap rate 50 to 100 basis points above the initial cap rate. There have been periods when discount rates have fallen outside the band, but this is the most frequent range. Depending on an investor's view of the cash flow growth, it frequently results in a cap rate between 8 and 10 percent. There are, of course, exceptions.

This discount rate is consistent with the long-term (1945–1993) annualized return of the Standard & Poor's 500 Stock Index. (Source: Standard & Poor's.) More recently, (over the past 5 to 10 years), the annualized return has been between 13 and 15 percent. Because growth rates in equities have been higher than real estate, the resulting "cap rate" or earnings multiple has been lower. A 12 to 14 earnings multiple equates to an 8.5 percent to 7.1 percent cap rate. But in this case, the cap rate is after taxes and depreciation as opposed to net operating income. Real estate valuations have reacted to these higher alternative returns with discount rates at the higher end of the historical range.

Dividend Discount Model Is the Basis for Valuation

Stocks are bought and sold according to a wide variety of valuation models, but the most comparable to the traditional 10-year discounted cash flow model used by institutional real estate investors is a dividend discount model. Investors receive a current dividend and assume it grows at a certain rate for three to five years and "cap" the residual earnings with a multiple that is equal to or slightly below the initial multiple. The resulting cash flow stream is then discounted back at some rate to derive a present value. The present value is compared to an investor's alternative, and the decision to buy, sell, or hold the stock is made.

However, since most equity investors are attempting to beat the Standard & Poor's 500 benchmark, they look to acquire stocks with higher rates of return. As a result, the implied discount rate for both real estate investment trusts and many other stocks is frequently at the higher end or above the historical rate of 13 to 15 percent.

The question, of course, is how much higher? Since the valuation is the mean valuation of the entire marketplace, we cannot quantify each component that goes into the higher discount rate. We can only highlight the factors, with each investor assigning his or her own individual weighting.

Factors Going into the Discount

A long list of items is factored into determining an appropriate discount rate. Some of these factors are highlighted in Table 14–4. The list is by no means all-inclusive, but it covers the major areas. The five main categories—management credibility, supply and demand, the balance sheet, and portfolio stability—are discussed below.

Management Credibility

In determining the discount, credibility with investors is the most critical factor and it can have a major impact on a company's cost of capital.

TABLE 14–4

Factors Influencing the Discount Rate

Management Credibility	Supply and Demand	Balance Sheet	Portfolio Volatility
Business plan	Barriers to entry	Floating-rate debt	Lease structures
Experience in property type and markets	Capital availability	Debt-maturity schedule	Lease-expiration schedule
Organizational depth	Employment base and growth potential	Interest-rate caps and swaps	Major tenants
Compensation structure	Regulatory environment	Interest rates on near-term debt maturities	Portfolio diversification
Ownership stake			Contractual rent increases
Conflicts of interest			
Attitude toward risk			
Accounting policies			

Institutional investors and analysts with access to management spend a considerable amount of time getting comfortable with the management team's experience, operating strategy, and business plan. Companies that have been able to create that comfort level, usually through extensive time as a public company, trade at multiples that are 20 to 50 percent above the group averages. This gives them major cost-of-capital advantages over other companies. The lower cost equity allows these companies to build a larger equity base, which pleases the rating agencies and results in favorable debt ratings. The ability to access the unsecured debt market quickly when rates are favorable is also an important advantage.

Credibility can be both lost and gained. Investors generally give companies the benefit of the doubt until the companies fail to meet earnings expectations. In attempting to create credibility, companies need to work extremely hard to manage expectations. That means having a firm handle on the business and being prepared for unforeseen events. If companies don't meet earnings expectations because of actual or perceived lack of control over their business, credibility is lost almost immediately. It can be very difficult to get back.

In establishing credibility, management needs a clear and concise business plan and an honest assessment of its opportunities and risks. It needs to demonstrate an expertise in a property type or in a market, or if it is new to an area, it needs to demonstrate it is making prudent investments and is assigning risk to other parties. Then the company must execute the plan as communicated without exception.

Supply and Demand

Investors prefer to get into markets early. They like to see ample upside and limited downside risk. The recognition that the apartment market was recovering in 1992 triggered a wave of capital into the industry. During this time, share prices soared as investors anticipated the higher earnings to come. In mid-1993, the real estate stocks were trading at 12 to 15 times earnings. Some multiples were near 20 times earnings. However, by mid-1995, the multiples had dropped to 10 to 11 times, as earnings increased but the share prices remained stagnant.

When construction began, investors cooled on the segment since the risk/return dynamics had changed. Potential returns were not as high, and investors perceived that the segment presented some risk that the apartment markets would become overbuilt. The stocks declined during this period as investors sought other property types or industries that had a more favorable balance of risk and return.

This view of the group exemplifies the fundamental dynamic of the real estate industry. It is a cyclical business that suffers from excessive inventory, not so much due to supply, but to a drop in demand when local, regional, or national economies slow. In this scenario, the projects under construction are completed during a period of slack demand, and it takes time for the economy to improve and for the new space to be ultimately absorbed. In short, it suffers a classic inventory problem, except demand is inelastic and the inventory cannot be liquidated quickly. However, prices typically plummet, and those inventory/property owners who have to liquidate their inventory under duress create great opportunities for companies with the capital and resources to acquire the inventory.

Investors try to anticipate the cycle and look to invest when there is limited downside risk and much potential appreciation. By doing so, the shares of real estate companies are likely to perform best when the industry fundamentals are just beginning to show some recovery. The real estate markets themselves may be terrible, but if they are not deteriorating further and are likely to improve over time, investors tend to bid up the shares. The net result are share prices that could precede the real estate cycle by as much as two years.

These dynamics make a real estate market's stage in its cycle a major factor determining the discount rate. The discount rate may be high very early in the cycle or low very late in the cycle. But, as we discuss in our example, it is likely to change as economic conditions change and the cycle moves.

Balance Sheet

The balance sheet is another critical area. As was discussed earlier, an assessment of floating-rate debt risk and refinancing risk is critical. It can also yield positive results. A balance sheet with low debt levels has consistently resulted in a lower discount rate on the company's shares. Companies with lower debt levels can generate higher growth rates but, more importantly, a reduction in overall leverage can, when the cycle turns down, result in lower earnings volatility. Such companies generally have the resources to acquire properties from distressed owners when the time is right.

The second benefit is psychological. Because investors typically fear highly leveraged situations, they realize that when a company's debt level exceeds 40 percent of total capitalization, it is likely to issue more common equity. As a result, because there is the potential for more shares being offered and a corresponding drop in the share price, investors avoid the stock. In doing so, they are implicitly applying a higher discount to the shares.

However, at lower debt levels, investors perceive that a company does not need to come back for more common equity for some time. Thus, there is a reduced risk that the company would issue more stock and the share price would suffer. With lower risk comes a lower discount rate. This dynamic, along with the growth prospects, allows companies with lower debt levels to typically have lower discount rates.

Portfolio Volatility

From the cash flow and growth analysis will come an assessment of the volatility of the cash flows. This will depend on property and geographic diversification, lease expirations, tenant mix, financial and operating leverage, and necessary capital improvements.

Dividend Stability

Finally, having looked at management credibility, supply and demand, the balance sheet, and portfolio volatility, an assessment will be made about dividend stability. This often involves a calculation of *a financial coverage ratio,* which measures a company's ratio of earnings before interest, taxes, depreciation, and amortization taxes (EBITDA after capital expenditures) to all the financial costs, including interest, preferred dividends, and common dividends. This measures how far earnings can fall before the common dividend is at risk. The higher the ratio, the lower the potential risk and, presumably, the lower the discount rate.

EXAMPLES

In the examples below, five companies specializing in different property types are evaluated using data contained in Tables 14–5 through 14–9.

To illustrate the valuation methodology, Table 14–5 compares their relative valuation to a market benchmark, in this case, the S&P Mid-Cap Index. Real estate investment trusts are primarily mid-cap stocks, so that benchmark is more appropriate than the Dow Industrial or S&P 500 Index, which include much larger companies.

TABLE 14–5

Comparable Company Analysis

Company	S&P Mid-Cap Index	A	B	C	D	E
Property type		Apartment	Neighborhood retail	Regional mall	Office	Industrial
Total assets		$1,630,000	$867,000	$2,160,000	$478,000	$735,000
Total debt		$415,000	$266,000	$960,000	$146,000	$400,000
Market value of shareholder equity		$1,368,000	$927,500	$1,250,000	$594,000	$420,000
Debt: market capitalization		21.51%	21.23%	41.45%	19.07%	47.17%
Market conditions		Demand is slightly ahead of supply	Stable	Demand is weak	Demand exceeds supply	Demand is slightly ahead of supply
Management credibility		Good but still evolving	High	Mixed	Being estab-lished	Being estab-lished
Accounting policies		Conser-vative	Conser-vative	Conser-vative	Conser-vative	Aggres-sive
Asset sales as a percent of total assets		5.00%	1.00%	0.00%	0.00%	5.00%
Share price	$225	$19.00	$35.00	$10.00	$33.00	$21.00
Estimated 5-year FFO growth rate	13.80%	14.39%	6.99%	4.15%	13.83%	7.70%
Estimated 5-year dividend growth rate	5.00%	8.00%	4.00%	2.00%	6.00%	4.00%
Dividend yield	1.90%	6.58%	6.86%	8.00%	5.15%	9.29%
Price: FFO	15.7	11.5	12.1	10.0	15.0	9.1
5-year Treasury yield	6.00%	6.00%	6.00%	6.00%	6.00%	6.00%
20-day average trading volume	NA	1,500,000	1,000,000	1,000,000	1,500,000	800,000
Trading volume as a percent of shares outstanding	NA	2.08%	3.77%	0.80%	8.33%	4.00%
Implied discount rate	13.35%	18.50%	11.75%	11.25%	12.50%	15.00%
Investment rating	NA	BUY	HOLD/ SELL	SELL	HOLD	BUY/ HOLD

As the table indicates, the S&P Mid-Cap Index has an expected earnings growth rate of 13.8 percent. It has a nominal dividend yield of 1.9 percent, and trades at 15.7 times the current year's earnings. Assuming the growth rate can be sustained and the dividend grows at a modest 5 percent, the implied discount rate to arrive at the current 225 value is 13.35 percent. This represents a 765 basis-point yield over five-year Treasuries (the risk-free alternative for the five-year holding period) that is consistent with the returns of the past 5 to 10 years.

Company A

The first real estate company is company A, and it has a "buy" investment rating. It has an expected five-year growth rate of 14.4 percent (see Table 14–5) yet trades at only 11.5 times earnings. The growth comes from both the core portfolio and investment activity. It can effectively manage risk, so it can earn an estimated 300 basis points over its long-term debt costs (see Table 14–6). With its expected dividend growth rate of 8 percent, the implied discount at current prices is 18.5 percent. This is 515 basis points above the Mid-Cap Index.

Demand is running slightly ahead of supply, so the fundamentals are good. Management's credibility is still being established but is considered good. The balance sheet has a low debt-to-market capitalization, and there is minimal floating-rate debt. The amount of debt maturing in the next five years is insignificant. With this balance sheet and planned asset sales of 5 percent of total assets each year, there is minimal risk of a new equity offering (see Tables 14–7 and 14–8 for more details). Capital expenditures for apartments are generally low although lease expirations are high due to the short lease terms. General and administrative costs are relatively high due to the conservative accounting policies, which expenses all development and acquisition personnel.

Since the equity markets are relatively efficient, other factors could be causing this buying opportunity. These factors may be concerned about construction or a recent change in strategy that the market may be skeptical about. On a quantitative basis, the shares certainly look attractive, but the markets may be waiting for an event to occur before bidding up the shares. In the meantime, it represents an opportunity for Company A's investors, who have a greater comfort with the outlook and disagree with the market's consensus.

TABLE 14–6

Comparative Growth Rates

Company	A	B	C	D	E	S&P Mid-Cap Index
Property type	Apartment	Neighborhood retail	Regional mall	Office	Industrial	
Supply/demand	Demand slightly ahead of supply	Stable	Weak demand	Demand exceeds supply	Demand exceeds supply	
Revenue change	4.00%	3.00%	2.00%	5.00%	0.03	
Expense change	3.00%	3.00%	3.00%	3.00%	0.02	
Change in EBITDA	5.22%	2.88%	1.46%	5.79%	3.37%	
Change in FFO	7.54%	3.48%	2.16%	7.55%	5.35%	
Growth from investments						
Potential volume[1]	$200,000	$60,000	$50,000	$50,000	$25,000	
Spread	3.00%	3.00%	3.50%	3.50%	3.00%	
Nominal FFO impact	$0.08	$0.07	$0.01	$0.10	$0.04	
Change in FFO	5.03%	2.34%	1.40%	4.42%	1.63%	
Growth from internal CF						
Internal cash flow	$19,375	$9,700	$8,000	$7,000	$3,000	
Reinvestment rate	11.25%	9.25%	9.25%	10.50%	11.00%	
Nominal FFO impact	$0.03	$0.03	$0.01	$0.04	$0.02	
Change in FFO	1.83%	1.17%	0.59%	1.86%	0.72%	
Total FFO growth	14.39%	6.99%	4.15%	13.83%	7.70%	13.80%
Estimated dividend growth[2]	8.00%	4.00%	2.00%	6.00%	4.00%	5.00%
Current share price	$19.00	$35.00	$10.00	$33.00	$21.00	$225.00
Implied discount rate[3]	18.50%	11.75%	11.25%	12.50%	15.00%	13.35%
Price: FFO: earnings multiple	11.46	12.08	10.00	15.00	9.13	15.70
Debt to market capitalization	21.51%	21.23%	41.45%	19.07%	47.17%	NA
Dividend yield	6.58%	6.86%	8.00%	5.15%	9.29%	1.90%
Conclusion	BUY	HOLD/ SELL	SELL	HOLD	BUY/ HOLD	

[1] Acquisition of existing property or completion of new development.
[2] Typically based on historical increases.
[3] Equates to an IRR or estimated average annual return if the shares were purchased at their current price.

TABLE 14–7

Comparable Balance Sheets

Company	A	B	C	D	E
Property type	Apartment	Neighborhood retail	Regional mall	Office	Industrial
Real estate	$1,600,000	$800,000	$2,088,000	$450,000	$700,000
Cash	$10,000	$55,000	$7,000	$8,000	$10,000
Current assets	$20,000	$12,000	$65,000	$20,000	$25,000
Total assets	$1,630,000	$867,000	$2,160,000	$478,000	$735,000
Current liabilities	$40,000	$16,000	$75,000	$6,000	$25,000
Floating-rate debt	$25,000	$100,000	$200,000	$10,000	$375,000
Mortgage debt	$150,000	$150,000	$185,000	$130,000	$0
Corporate unsecured debt	$200,000	$0	$500,000	$0	$0
Total liabilities	$415,000	$266,000	$960,000	$146,000	$400,000
Preferred stock	$300,000	$0	$0	$0	$0
Common stock	$905,000	$586,000	$1,200,000	$327,000	$330,000
Retained earnings	$10,000	$15,000	$0	$5,000	$5,000
Total equity	$1,215,000	$601,000	$1,200,000	$332,000	$335,000
Total liabilities and equity	$1,630,000	$867,000	$2,160,000	$478,000	$735,000
Shares outstanding[1]	72,000	26,500	125,000	18,000	20,000
Share price	$19	$35	$10	$33	$21
Market value of common equity	$1,368,000	$927,500	$1,250,000	$594,000	$420,000
Debt-to-market capitalization	21.51%	21.23%	41.45%	19.07%	47.17%
Debt maturing in next five years	$25,000	$80,000	$600,000	$20,000	$375,000
Percent of debt maturing in five years (excluding floating-rate debt)	6.67%	32.00%	67.80%	14.29%	100.00%
Floating-rate debt to capitalization	6.67%	40.00%	22.60%	7.14%	100.00%

[1] Includes operating partnership units.

TABLE 14–8

Comparable Income Statements

Company	A	B	C	D	E
Property type	Apartment	Neighborhood retail	Regional mall	Office	Industrial
Rental income	$330,000	$127,000	$255,000	$70,000	$100,000
Management income	$0		$5,000	$0	
Other income	$500	$9,000	$25,000	$600	$3,000
Total Revenue	$330,500	$136,000	$285,000	$70,600	$103,000
Operating expenses	$140,000	$38,000	$80,000	$17,000	$27,000
General administrative	$18,000	$5,200	$20,000	$2,000	$3,000
Total Expenses	$158,000	$43,200	$100,000	$19,000	$30,000
EBITDA	$172,500	$92,800	$185,000	$51,600	$73,000
Interest expense	$28,125	$16,000	$60,000	$12,000	$27,000
Preferred dividends	$25,000	$0	$0	$0	$0
Funds from operation	$119,375	$76,800	$125,000	$39,600	$46,000
Principal amortization	$2,000	$500	$2,000	$0	$0
Capital expenditures	$8,000	$3,000	$15,000	$2,000	$4,000
Funds for distribution	$109,375	$73,300	$108,000	$37,600	$42,000
Funds from operations (FFO) PS	$1.66	$2.90	$1.00	$2.20	$2.30
Funds for distribution (FFD) PS	$1.52	$2.77	$0.86	$2.09	$2.10
Dividend rate	$1.25	$2.40	$0.80	$1.70	$1.95
Dividend paid	$90,000	$63,600	$100,000	$30,600	$39,000
Remaining cash flow	$19,375	$9,700	$8,000	$7,000	$3,000
Shares outstanding	72,000	26,500	125,000	18,000	20,000
Operating margin	57.58%	70.08%	68.63%	75.71%	73.00%
G&A revenue	5.45%	4.09%	7.84%	2.86%	3.00%
Financial coverage	1.13	1.12	1.05	1.16	1.04
Payout ratio on FFO	75.4%	82.8%	80.0%	77.3%	84.8%
Payout ratio on FFD	82.29%	86.77%	92.59%	81.38%	92.86%
Capital expenditures per share	$0.11	$0.11	$0.12	$0.11	$0.20
Capital expenditures: revenue	2.42%	2.36%	5.88%	2.86%	4.00%
Weighted average debt cost	7.50%	6.40%	6.78%	8.57%	7.20%
Share price	$19	$35	$10	$33	$21
Price to FFO multiple	11.5	12.1	10.0	15.0	9.1
Price to FFD multiple	12.5	12.7	11.6	15.8	10.0
Percentage of leases expiring in next three years	100.00%	30.00%	30.00%	60.00%	45.00%

Company B

Company B owns neighborhood shopping centers. These are typically grocery- and drug-anchored shopping centers that total 100,000 to 200,000 square feet. The company appears to warrant a "hold" or possibly "sell" rating. The expected growth rate is modest, and the implied discount rate of 11.75 percent is below the market discount rate.

The apparently premium pricing may come from management's credibility with investors. Investors may feel comfortable with the company's track record and be willing to take a lower return because they may feel there is lower risk than the overall market. The business conditions are stable, and the balance sheet has low debt levels. However, 32 percent of the debt matures in the next five years, and 40 percent of the debt is floating-rate. Those investors looking for a higher return should probably sell their positions.

Company C

Company C is a regional mall company that appears to warrant a "sell" rating. The implied discount rate is 11.25 percent, again below the market rate, but it does not have the apparent elements that would lower the expected risk that existed in Company B. Demand for the space is considered weak, and management's credibility with investors is mixed. Expected growth is a very modest 4.15 percent, and the balance sheet is weak. The debt-to-market capitalization is 41.45 percent, and 67.8 percent of the debt matures in the next five years. With an average interest rate of 6.78 percent, and a five-year Treasury rate of 6.0 percent, there is a risk that interest rates upon refinancing could be higher. Finally, the financial coverage ratio is a weak 1.05. This means that if there is a downturn in the business, the dividend could be at risk.

The share price may be at its level for several reasons. First, institutional real estate investors have favored the apparent stability of regional malls and have historically been long-term holders. They may have expectations for higher growth in the future due to a pickup in demand. The other possible reason is a potential lack of liquidity. The stock's trading volume as a percentage of shares outstanding is the lowest of the five, and large shareholders may be unable to liquidate their positions at prices they find acceptable.

Company D

Company D is an office company whose shares are rated "hold" because they seem to reflect much of the expected growth in the company. At this time, the office market is in the earlier stage of recovery, so its core portfolio growth exceeds the other property types. The investment climate remains favorable, and given its low debt level, the company has leverage potential. Company D also has 60 percent of its leases expiring in the next three years, and with higher rents likely, rents on new leases are likely to be higher. The weighted average cost of debt of 8.57 percent is well above the current five-year rate so that debt maturing, while modest, might be able to be refinanced at lower rates. As a result of these factors, its expected growth is a relatively high 13.8 percent.

However, the shares have reached a level where the implied discount rate of 12.5 percent is slightly below the market level. Investors will most likely hold the shares because the company has a lower risk profile than the overall equity markets because of the company's stage in the real estate cycle. Since management is still establishing itself with investors, there may be some downside risk if management has a bad quarter or fails to achieve expectations. The most desirable time to acquire these shares would have been 6 or 12 months earlier, before the market realized the office recovery was about to start.

Company E

Company E owns industrial properties and warrants a weak "buy" or possibly "hold" rating. Its implied discount rate of 15 percent is above the market benchmark, but there appears to be risks, which may not make the excess return adequate.

Demand is slightly ahead of supply, so market conditions, while good, are not as strong as in the office market. The balance sheet is weak, with a debt-to-market capitalization of 47.17 percent. In addition, the financial coverage ratio is a low 1.04, which, given the lease expirations in the next three years, could create downside risk if the economy weakens. There is also interest-rate risk, as 100 percent of the debt is floating-rate and below the interest-rate caps. Finally, the debt all matures within five years.

Despite these apparent weaknesses, the dividend yield is 9.29 percent, which is 329 basis points above the five-year Treasury. If the economic outlook were stable or strong, there would be the opportunity to earn a very high yield for two or three years while the economy is good. For yield-oriented buyers who want as much of a front-end return as possible, the risk-adjusted return may look favorable.

RECONCILIATION WITH REAL ESTATE VALUES

In analyzing real estate investment trusts, it is always useful to compare the company valuation with the valuation of the individual assets without any franchise value for the company. Using some loose cap-rate estimates, the five companies trade at some premium to the underlying value of the assets (see Table 14–9). However, there are distinctions worth noting.

With Company A, there is clearly some value attributable to its value-added investment capabilities that typical risk-averse, institutional buyers do not have. Because of these capabilities, it could sell recently developed assets at 9 percent cap rates and reinvest the proceeds into higher-yielding development at a 10.5 percent or 11 percent return. This allows the company to turn a hypothetical $1.0 million of cash flow into $1.2 million of cash flow through the sale and redeployment. To illustrate, a property generating $1.0 million could be sold at a 9 percent cap rate to generate $11.1 million in capital. This capital can be reinvested in a hypothetical new development to earn 11 percent, thus generating $1.2 million in cash flow upon completion of construction. In addition, its long-term, fixed-rate debt at low rates

TABLE 14–9

Comparison to Real Estate Valuation

Company	A	B	C	D	E
Property type	Apartment	Neighborhood retail	Regional mall	Office	Industrial
NOI	$172,000	$83,800	$155,000	$51,000	$70,000
Cap rate	9.00%	9.25%	7.50%	8.50%	9.00%
Real estate value	$1,911,111	$905,946	$2,066,667	$600,000	$777,778
Other assets	$30,000	$67,000	$72,000	$28,000	$35,000
Liabilities and preferred stock	$715,000	$266,000	$960,000	$146,000	$400,000
Net value	$1,226,111	$706,946	$1,178,667	$482,000	$412,778
Value per share	$17.03	$26.68	$9.43	$26.78	$20.64
Stock price	$19.00	$35.00	$10.00	$33.00	$21.00
Premium (discount)	11.57%	31.20%	6.05%	23.24%	1.75%

also has some value. A valuation of the company with the debt in place could add as much as 5 percent, depending on the maturity. So although a premium may exist, it may be justified.

The premium in Company B does not appear justified. There is not much growth other than that associated with the core portfolio. It appears some investors have become very comfortable with the stock and are not maximizing near-term value. In deciding to either hold or sell this stock, the real estate valuation may push the decision into a sell rather than a hold.

The premium for Company D's stock is also high but may be more justified. Equity markets anticipate events faster than real estate markets, so cap rates have probably not caught up with share price multiples. Actually, the equity market may be pricing the stock more aggressively since it feels the company, with its strong balance sheet, may acquire properties from distressed sellers at very attractive prices. Investors may simply be using the company as a conduit to play a recovery in a market it could not access otherwise. This happened with the apartment stocks in 1992 and 1993 when multiples reached 18 to 20 times current earnings because the companies had good balance sheets and the Resolution Trust Corporation was liquidating properties from failed lending institutions. Many of the stocks showed little appreciation from that point on, as the earnings in 1994 and 1995 eventually caught and brought the multiples into more reasonable territory.

The valuations on Companies C and E are consistent with the real estate values. Because the private real estate market valuation is an art rather than a science, a variation within 5 to 7 percent is not considered significant.

CHANGES IN VALUATION

Any valuation of a real estate company is done in the context of alternatives, and the appeal of those alternatives changes constantly. The real estate cycle moves along, and interest rates move up and down. Other industries rise and fall in price, as do real estate stocks.

Before concluding, we will touch on two macro forces that arguably have the greatest impact on share prices. The first is the real estate cycle that we discussed earlier. As it moves, understandably, it will affect investors' perceptions of the group and the implied discount rate. As supply increases, so does the discount rate on the shares, even though growth may be positive. Investors fear that the economy may slow and an inventory problem may develop. When the economy shows signs of slowing, it is probably wise to reduce positions in the group. Conversely, when the economy improves, there is limited risk and plenty of opportunity for increased occupancy rates and rental increases. This is the time when exposure in the group should be increased.

The other factor is interest rates. Rising interest rates generally hurt these stocks, for fairly obvious reasons. Interest costs for the debt being financed will go up. And of course, the value of risk-free bonds becomes more attractive.

The interest rate sensitivity is higher in real estate stocks, not only because of the yield, but also because of the high predictability of earnings. Because markets are generally efficient and the predictability of real estate earnings is high relative to other industries, the share prices reflect most, if not all, the known information. That makes interest rates the determinant of price in the near term.

As Figure 14–1 illustrates, real estate yields tend to move with interest rates, but there are lag periods as the market becomes convinced that a trend reflects a true change in sentiment rather than just a trading period.

FIGURE 14–1

REIT Yields versus Five-Year Treasury Yields Since 1988

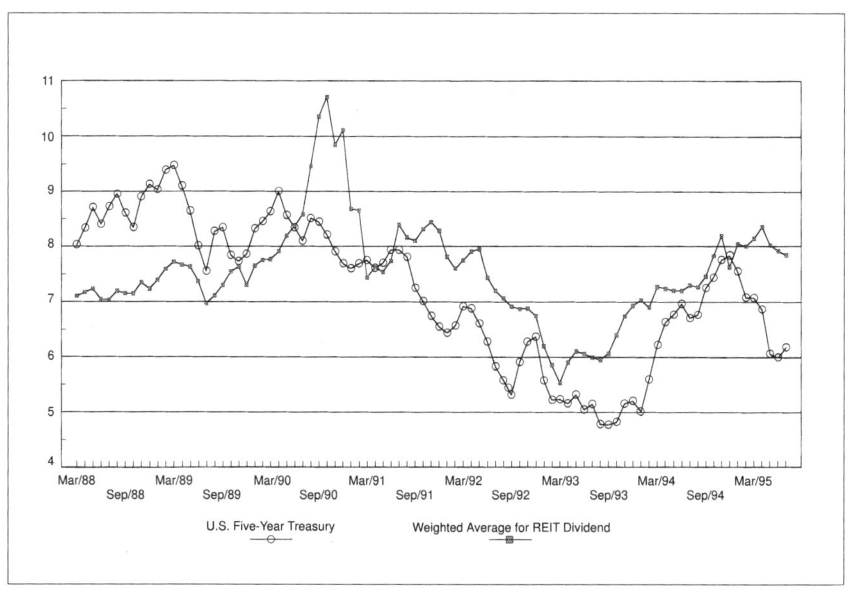

Despite individual company analysis, it will be difficult for companies to escape the strong influence of these two forces. Knowing and respecting these forces is likely to make for a much more pleasant and profitable investment in real estate investment trusts.

CONCLUSION

Real estate investment trusts are valued like other publicly traded companies and like individual properties. The fundamental analysis and methodology is identical. With more real estate companies publicly traded, the valuation has become much more dynamic and fluid. However, relative to other industries, real estate stocks are stable. But, relative to cap rates and private real estate valuations, the values of real estate investment trusts are more volatile in the short term. Over the long term, whether real estate or real estate companies are valued publicly or privately, the value is based on the discounted present value of its cash flows. The major difference is that public real estate companies will be affected by management and the financial structure. The shares will reflect these influences in a fluid and dynamic equity market.

CHAPTER

15

PUBLIC AND PRIVATE REAL ESTATE

Performance Implications for Asset Allocation

David Geltner, *Professor of Real Estate, College of Business Administration, University of Cincinnati*

Joe V. Rodriguez, *Director of Securities Management, INVESCO Realty Advisors*

1. BACKGROUND AND OBJECTIVES OF THIS CHAPTER

1.1 What is "Public" and "Private" Real Estate?

Pension funds and other institutional investors have long invested most of their capital in domestic stocks and bonds, the dominant asset classes in the public capital markets in the United States. The stock and bond markets are referred to as "public" markets because stocks and bonds are generally traded on public exchanges, such as the New York Stock Exchange (NYSE), American Stock Exchange (AMEX), or NASDAQ, which provide easy and inexpensive access to all investors, large and small. Public markets are characterized by the trading of small homogeneous units, or shares, of the underlying assets and by a high degree of oversight by both government agencies and the securities industry to insure fairness and openness in trading procedures, information revelation, and corporate governance.

The public capital markets are noted for generally high levels of *liquidity* and *informational efficiency*. "Liquidity" refers to the ability of the investor/owner of the asset to quickly and inexpensively convert the asset into cash at or very near the current full-market value of the asset. "Informational efficiency" refers to the propensity of the market prices of the assets to rapidly incorporate and reflect all publicly available news and information relevant to the value of the assets. The combination of liquidity and informational efficiency means that investors in publicly traded assets can generally expect to be able to quickly "cash out" any investment at a "fair" price, given the currently available information.

Although stocks and bonds represent over $14 trillion worth of assets by market value, they do not include all of the tradable capital assets in the Unites States. For the past two decades (particularly since the passage of the Federal ERISA legislation in 1974), a third major asset class, commercial real estate equity, has been seriously considered by many pension funds as a candidate for a significant share of their total portfolio investment. As can be seen in Figure 15–1, commercial real estate equity represents over $3 trillion in market value, or almost one-fifth of the investable, U.S. domestic "asset pie" (that is, excluding owner-occupied housing equity and other privately held assets in which it is often difficult for outsiders to invest).

Most, but not all, commercial real estate is traded *privately*. That is, most commercial properties are not traded on the public stock exchanges but, rather, trade directly in the private property markets in "deals" negotiated privately between individual buyers and sellers. In this chapter, we will refer to such real estate as "private" real estate. Only the publicly traded real estate investment trusts (REITs) and real estate operating companies (REOCs), whose market value totals around $100 billion, will be considered "public" real estate assets. In general, in comparison to the public capital markets, private asset markets tend to exhibit high transactions costs and a relative lack of liquidity and informational efficiency in asset pricing.

While the vast majority of commercial properties are held directly by owner-users and individual real estate investor/entrepreneurs who actively manage the properties they hold, it is also possible for investors who do not have the expertise or time to devote to active property management, such as most pension funds, to invest in commercial real estate equity. Broadly speaking, two approaches are available to such investors. They can invest in *public* real estate by means of the REITs or REOCs, or they can invest in *private* real estate by way of property "pools" and "syndications," such as commingled funds (CREFs) or separate accounts (SAs) managed by

FIGURE 15-1

U.S. Domestic Investable Assets by Market Value as of Mid-1990s

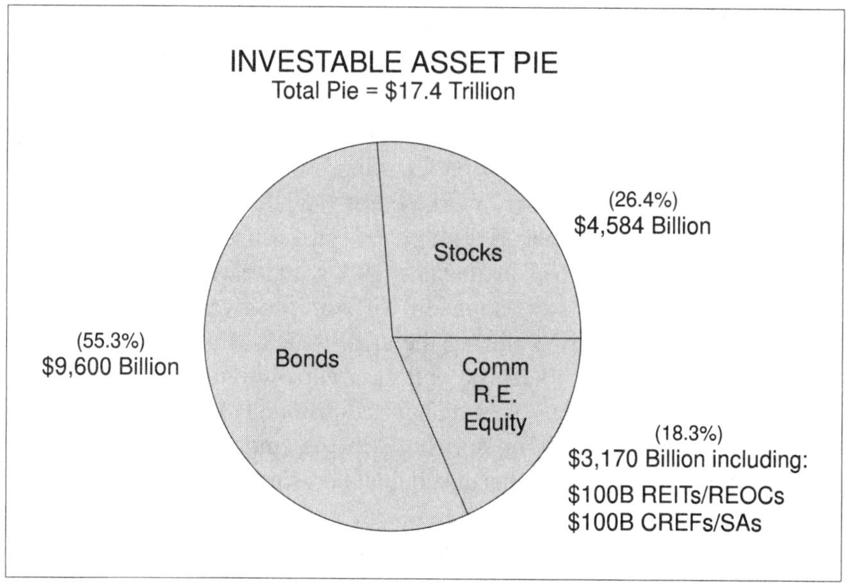

Source: Miles et al, *Real Estate Finance* 11(1), Spring 1994.
Excludes owner-occupied housing equity and non-real estate private assets.

specialized real estate investment advisers. By the mid-1990s, there were roughly $100 billion of pension fund assets invested in private real estate equity by these means, a value approximately equal to the total market value of the public real estate assets traded indirectly in the stocks of REITs and REOCs.

1.2 Why Should Pension Funds Care About Private and Public Real Estate?

From the beginning of pension fund interest in real estate as an investment asset class back in the 1970s, a major motivation was the belief that real estate presents risk-and-return characteristics that are different from those of the stock and bond markets. This would make real estate attractive as a *diversifier* of the stock-and-bond-dominated pension fund portfolios. At least since the development of modern portfolio theory (MPT) in the 1950s and 1960s, investors have understood how the overall risk in a portfolio can be reduced and the expected returns measured on a risk-adjusted basis can be enhanced by diversifying the assets held in the portfolio. Assets, or classes of assets, are particularly valuable as diversifiers if they provide returns that tend *not* to be highly correlated with those of the other asset classes in the portfolio. Such assets tend to dampen out the "ups" and "downs" of the portfolio, reducing the overall portfolio's volatility.

While the investments pension funds made in private real estate during the 1970s and 1980s generally worked pretty well as a diversifier, many investors became disenchanted with private real estate when commercial property market prices fell in the late 1980s and early 1990s. Lack of liquidity in the private markets made it difficult for investors to "bail out" of their real estate holdings during the crash. Lack of informational efficiency in the private markets as well as a narrowly defined concept of "institutional-grade" real estate may have contributed to prices of commercial properties "bubbling" up too high in the mid-1980s (when much investment was made) and then subsequently crashing to levels below what seemed reasonable in the long run.[1]

As a result of this experience with private real estate investment, especially CREFs, many institutional investors began asking whether public real estate investment vehicles, such as REITs, were not a better way to make their real estate investment. This question became all the more appropriate by the mid-1990s as a result of developments in the REIT industry. The Tax Reform Act of 1986 had removed the major tax advantages of private real estate for taxable investors while giving REITs greater flexibility and allowing them to be self-administered. This change allowed for the removal of a major source of agency problems associated with advised REITs and promoted better management of REITs. The Tax Act of 1993 then facilitated REIT investment by tax-exempt institutions as a result of the "look-through" provisions in the law (that is, relaxation of the 5/50 Rule for pension funds). The development of the UPREIT structure in late 1992 also contributed to a veritable explosion of REIT capitalization. This increase in capitalization brought REIT assets up to a critical mass, which for the first time enabled large institutional investors to seriously consider investing in real estate equity by way of publicly traded REITs.

A key question about the appropriateness of REITs as a vehicle for pension fund real estate investment has to do with the original motivation for such investment, namely, the concern for *diversification* of the overall portfolio. As REITs are stocks, and trade in the public exchanges, does the REIT investor not sacrifice much of the unique real estate characteristics of the investment? Would not public real estate investment (in the form of REITs) tend to be much more positively correlated with the stock and bond markets (which are also public) than is the case for private real estate investment? How much of the diversification benefit of real estate in the typical stock-and-bond-dominated pension fund portfolio derives from the fact that the assets are traded in private as opposed to public markets? Furthermore, while REIT share prices no doubt reflect greater informational efficiency than private property market prices, the stock market is often criticized for overreaction and excess volatility, at least in the short run. To what extent do these problems in the stock market reduce the desirability of REITs as a vehicle for real estate investment in institutional portfolios?

1.3 Main Objectives

This chapter sheds light on the answers to the preceding portfolio strategy questions, based on an analysis of the historical performance record of commercial property in both the private and public asset markets. This objective requires a careful treatment of the empirical data available on the investment risk-and-return performance of private and public real estate so as not to misleadingly compare apples and oranges. Consistently defined risk-and-return data (in particular, across public and private asset markets) is vital for accurate analysis of mixed-asset portfolios. Thus, we have made a major effort in compiling this chapter to develop historical risk/return performance data for private and public real estate that is appropriate for mixed-asset portfolio analysis for institutional investors.

Two main data problems need to be attended to in any careful analysis of the questions we seek to address. Because of thin trading in the property markets, return data for private real estate has been based on appraised values. This causes "smoothing" of the returns over time in such widely used indexes of private real estate returns as the Russell-NCREIF Index. On the other hand, indexes of REIT historical returns (such as the NAREIT Index), while based on liquid market transaction prices and therefore not smoothed, reflect the effect of *leverage,* which may distort the returns provided by the underlying property assets held by the REITs. Thus, in this chapter we attempt to adjust and correct the historical returns data to remove the effects of smoothing in the appraisal-based private real estate returns and of leverage in the REIT-based public real estate returns. In addition, as pension funds typically make their real estate investments with the expectation of a medium- to long-term holding horizon, we attempt to define returns in a manner more relevant to investors with such horizons. In particular, we shall define risk-and-return statistics based on a five-year holding period rather than the quarterly or annual holding period that has generally been considered in past studies.

The remainder of this chapter is divided into three major parts. Part 2 will describe the historical return data we are using, including a description of the methods we employ to "unsmooth" private real estate returns and to "unlever" public returns. We believe we can substantially correct these problems in the empirical data, to allow a more accurate examination of optimal mean-variance portfolios for medium-term investors. Such a portfolio analysis will be presented in Part 3, including a description of our method of modeling the five-year holding returns that are more relevant for many pension funds. Finally, Part 4 will summarize and conclude the analysis, with a particular focus on the strategic and tactical investment policy implications for pension funds.

2. HISTORICAL RISKS AND RETURNS OF PRIVATE AND PUBLIC REAL ESTATE

2.1 The Record of Private Real Estate

We will base our analysis of the historical investment risk-and-return performance of private real estate on the Russell-NCREIF Index (hereafter, RNI) and the Evaluation Associates Index (EAI).[2] Both of these indexes are based on appraised values and represent institutional-grade commercial properties typical of those held by pension funds. They depict period-by-period total returns (including income and capital appreciation) on a before-tax, "free-and-clear" unlevered basis, gross of asset management fees. In this section, we present a brief description of the indexes and discuss our treatment of appraisal smoothing.

The RNI is the most widely cited benchmark of commercial property investment performance in the private markets in the United States. This index currently contains over 1,500 individual properties, with an aggregate market value in excess of $23 billion. A shortcoming in the RNI is that it begins only in 1978. The EAI goes back to 1969, reporting the total return to the major commingled property funds held in institutional portfolios in the United States. There is much duplication and similarity in the properties included in the EAI and Russell-NCREIF indexes.[3] In order to obtain a longer time series, we have spliced these two return series. Our private real estate is thus based on the EAI returns from 1969 to 1978 and on the Russell-NCREIF from 1978 through 1993.[4]

Both the RNI and EAI are reported quarterly, but most of the properties are effectively reappraised only annually, at different times staggered throughout the year. As a result, these indexes are not really quarterly indexes so much as they are annual indexes partially updated each quarter. For this reason, it makes more sense to work with the annual frequency return data.

As noted, appraisal-based indexes are inevitably subject to lagging and smoothing across time. That is to say, the returns on the index itself present a smoothed and lagged picture of what was actually happening at each point in historical time in the underlying commercial property market. This problem is caused by two phenomena: (1) The appraisal process at the level of individual property valuation is essentially "backward looking," as it relies on transaction prices of past sales of comparable properties, and (2) the index construction process requires temporal aggregation of appraised values, as the index is constructed each period by averaging across the most recent appraised values of all the individual properties (even those that were not reappraised during the current quarter). This data problem causes the returns of appraisal-based indexes *to appear to have less volatility than is really the case and to have less correlation with other returns series that are not similarly smoothed and lagged.* This distorts any direct comparison of the risk-adjusted investment performance of private and public real estate (or of private real estate and liquid securities such as stocks and bonds) and biases the results of any mixed-asset portfolio optimization analysis based on the index returns data.

In this chapter, we address this data problem by using the unsmoothing procedure described by Geltner (1993).[5] While no unsmoothing procedure is perfect, this approach has the advantage of avoiding the assumption that the private property markets are informationally efficient.[6] Mathematically, the unsmoothing procedure works by applying a "reverse filter" to recover the true underlying private property market returns from the appraisal-based index:

$$g_t = (g_t^* - (0.6)g_{t-1}^*)/(0.4) \quad (1)$$

where: g_t is the unobservable underlying market appreciation return (growth, or capital gain) in the private property market in calendar year t, and g_t^* is the observable appraisal-based index appreciation return in calendar year t. This equation is based on a structural analysis of the sources and nature of smoothing in the appraisal-based index. It is argued in Geltner (1993) that this procedure can largely correct for both the disaggregate-level smoothing induced by the appraisal process as well as the aggregate-level smoothing caused by index construction.

Figure 15–2 displays the historical profile of private real estate nominal value levels (accumulated capital returns) implied by both the appraisal-based index and the unsmoothed index based on Equation (1). The graph provides a "reality check" for the path of commercial property prices over the past two decades. The historical value profile in Figure 15–2 appears plausible for institutional commercial property holdings. In comparison to

FIGURE 15–2

Smoothed and Unsmoothed Private Market Commercial Real Estate Nominal Value Levels (set to 1982–1992 avg = 100), Based on Appreciation Returns

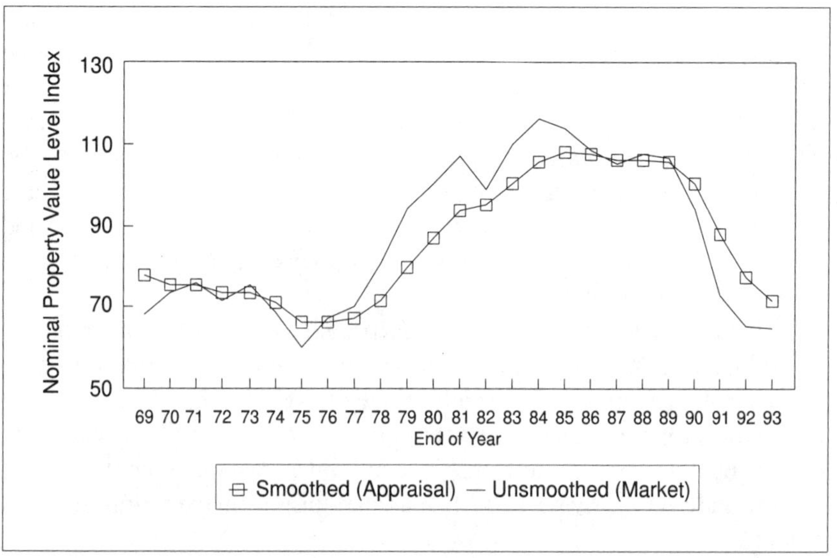

the unadjusted appraisal-based index, the graph shows the unsmoothed index peaking one year earlier (in 1984), and falling more sharply in 1987 and 1990. By 1993, the unsmoothed index suggests that the commercial property markets had largely "found bottom," even though the appraisal-based index was still falling rapidly that year.[7]

Equation (1) corrects the appreciation return in the appraisal-based index, which is the source of almost all of the volatility (and therefore of the risk and correlation statistics) in the historical returns data. However, it is still necessary to correct the total return, which consists of the appreciation component plus the current income component. While the income component of the appraisal-based index is presumably based on accurate and timely observation of the actual net operating incomes (NOI) of the properties included in the index, the income return is nevertheless distorted by the smoothing in the asset-value level across time (which is the denominator in the income return component). This distortion is easily corrected, however, once the unsmoothed asset value level series depicted in Figure 15–2 has been constructed.

The procedure for constructing the corrected, or unsmoothed, total return series is as follows. First, an index of the implied NOI value-level series is constructed from the appraisal-based appreciation and income-return components.[8] This series gives an accurate depiction of the profile of NOI over time, up to a constant multiple. This NOI level index is then divided by the preceding end of year *unsmoothed* value-level index (as depicted in Figure 15–2, computed from the unsmoothed accumulated appreciation returns). This unsmoothed value-level index is also an accurate depiction of the historical profile of property values, up to a constant multiple. Thus, the ratio we have just constructed of the NOI level index divided by the unsmoothed asset value-level index gives an accurate representation of the unsmoothed income-return component, up to a constant multiple.[9]

This constant multiple is now determined based on the criterion that the mean total return of the appraisal-based index is theoretically unbiased, taken over a complete real estate "cycle." That is, although the time-series second moments of the returns of the appraisal-based index (for example, volatility, correlations) are biased by the smoothing and lagging phenomena, the first moment (mean return across time) is not biased by these phenomena, provided we incorporate exactly one (or more *whole)* complete real estate cycles in the time series sample period. Examination of Figure

15–2 suggests that the period 1975–1993 included exactly one complete cycle. Thus, in theory, the appraisal-based mean total return over the 1975–1993 period should equal the true (unsmoothed) total return over that period. The unsmoothed income return component is thus multiplied by a constant multiple so that the unsmoothed total return and the appraisal-based total return will equal during the 1975–1993 sample period. The total return in any period, of course, equals the income return component plus the appreciation return component: $r_t=y_t+g_t$. We will label this constructed unsmoothed index of private real estate total returns, NCREIF(UNS), or unsmoothed RNI.

2.2 The Record of Public Real Estate

We will base our analysis of the historical investment risk-and-return performance of public real estate on the NAREIT All-REIT Index (hereafter, NAREIT).[10] We will incorporate the 1975–1993 period so as to coincide with the full cycle in the private real estate market, noted previously.[11] Based on the actual market transaction share prices in the relatively liquid stock market, the NAREIT Index does not suffer from the smoothing or lagging problems described previously for the private real estate index. However, it is necessary to address another data problem associated with using the NAREIT Index for the purpose of comparing the public market versus private market investment performance of real commercial property assets. This is the fact that REITs are typically levered (especially in the early years of the industry and, to a much lesser extent, currently) and we must remove the effect of this gearing on the REIT returns in order to obtain a return history for public real estate that is directly comparable to that for private real estate represented by the unsmoothed RNI Index described in the previous section, which is an index of unlevered, free-and-clear property values. This is in line with our objective in this chapter of considering REITs as essentially a vehicle for pension funds to invest in real estate, only through the public capital markets rather than through the private property markets. REIT investments could be effectively "unleveraged" by simultaneously investing in bonds.

In fact, REITs in general contain debt on both the asset and liability sides of their balance sheets. On the asset side, some REITs hold mortgages as well as property equity; and on the liability side, both mortgages and bonds or bank debt (backed, in effect, by property assets) are used as capital sources by REITs. In the aggregate across all REITs, the debt on the asset side typically roughly offsets the debt on the liability side, leaving REIT returns as a reasonable reflection of changes in the value of the properties held by the REITs as a whole. However, this offsetting relationship may not be exact at all points in time. Therefore, we have attempted to unlever the NAREIT returns by using a simple weighted-average cost of capital (WACC) model that corrects for the debt on both the asset and liability sides of the balance sheet.

The WACC model we use is based on the accounting identity

$$P_t + M_t = D_t + E_t \tag{2a}$$

where: P_t = value of property assets held at time "t"; M_t = value of other assets held at time "t" (mostly mortgages, with some other debt-like assets); D_t = value of liabilities as of time "t" (mostly mortgages and other debt backed by property assets); and E_t = value of shareholders' equity at time "t." From this identity, the return relationship directly follows:

$$r_{E,t} = (P/E)_t r_{P,t} + (M/E)_t r_{M,t} - (D/E)_t r_{D,t} \tag{2b}$$

where $r_{X,t}$ $\Delta DX/X$ refers to the percent change in item "X." Assuming that the return to all the REIT debt-like instruments is approximately the same (on either side of the balance sheet)

$$r_{M,t} \approx r_{D,t} \ \forall \ t$$

(2b) becomes

$$\begin{aligned} r_{E,t} &\approx (P/E)_t r_{P,t} + [(M/E)_t - (D/E)_t] r_{D,t} \\ &= (P/E)_t r_{P,t} + [1 - (P/E)_t] r_{D,t} \end{aligned} \tag{2c}$$

Thus, at least as a usable approximation, we can derive the property (unlevered) returns implied by REIT share market values as

$$r_{P,t} = \{r_{E,t} - [1 - (P/E)_t] r_{D,t}\}/(P/E)_t \tag{2d}$$

To quantify (2d) in practice, we have used the annual book values of property assets (P) and shareholders equity (E) reported by NAREIT for the REIT industry each year. To quantify the returns, the debt return ($r_{D,t}$) is represented by the Ibbotson Associates Long-Term Government Bond Index, while the REIT equity return ($r_{E,t}$) is represented by the NAREIT All-REIT Index annual return.

FIGURE 15–3

NAREIT Levered and Unlevered Accumulated Total Capital Index with Reinvestment (1974 = 100), Based on Total Returns

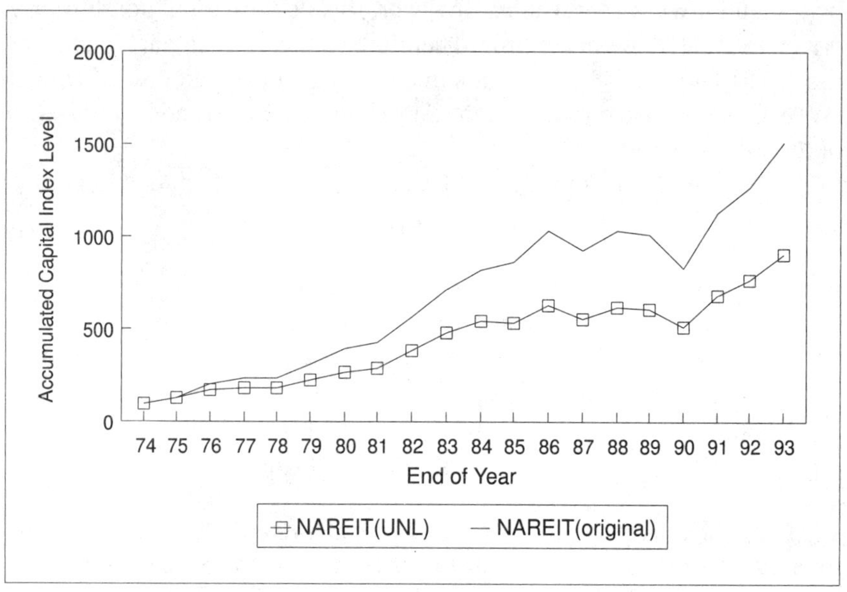

The original (levered) and unlevered NAREIT total returns have been compounded (or "chain-linked") and are presented for comparison purposes as accumulated total capital indexes (including reinvestment of cash flow), in Figure 15–3. As there has generally been more debt on the liability side than the asset side of most REITs (positive gearing), it is not surprising that the unlevered index shows a lower overall growth trend and less volatility, though with the timing of upticks, downticks, and turning points it is generally unaffected by the unlevering.

2.3 Comparing the Historical Performance of Public and Private Real Estate

The unleveraging procedure described above has been applied both to the total return and to the capital appreciation component separately. This allows us to perform the same kind of reality check we did before for the unsmoothed RNI Index, by examining the implied historical free-and-clear

FIGURE 15–4

Public (Unlevered) and Private (Unsmoothed) Real Estate Nominal Value Levels (Set to 1982–1992 avg = 100), Based on Appreciation Returns

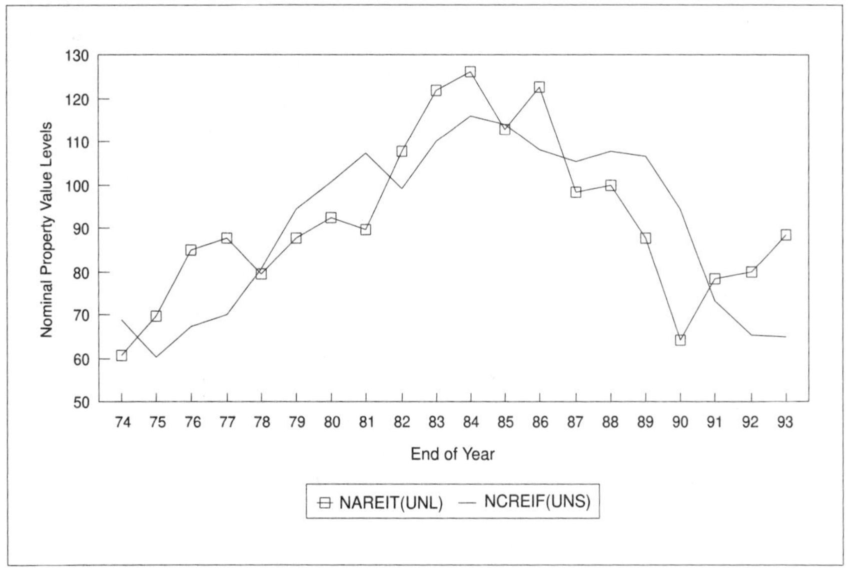

property values traced out over time by the corrected NAREIT capital gains returns. The unlevered appreciation returns have been accumulated to produce the unlevered NAREIT nominal property value index displayed in Figure 15–4, labeled NAREIT(UNL). Figure 15–4 also shows the corresponding unsmoothed RNI values, labeled NCREIF(UNS).

Again, as with any index, the absolute level is arbitrary; it is the relative change in value across time within each index that is meaningful. In Figure 15–4, we have scaled both indexes so that they have average 1982–1992 values equal to 100.[12] This facilitates comparison of what the two indexes are saying was happening at each point in time to commercial real estate values and reveals graphically the differences and similarities between private and public real estate over the historical period in question.

Examination of Figure 15–4 calls attention to some important similarities and differences between public and private real estate during the 1975–1993 period. The most striking feature in Figure 15–4 is the broad overall similarity in the two indexes. This is seen in the generally parallel pattern traced out by the two indexes. Both public and private real estate exhibited a notable "rise-and-fall" pattern during the 1975–1993 period, with peaks and troughs at similar (though not identical) points in time and relative magnitudes of rise and fall also similar across the two indexes. Viewed as a cycle, the broad-brush indication from Figure 15–4 is that both the period and amplitude of the public and private real estate cycles are very similar, but the two cycles are slightly out of phase with one another. In particular, it appears that public real estate *leads* private real estate, typically by about *one or two years.* That is, public real estate, as represented by the NAREIT(UNL) Index, experiences the major turning points in the cycle one or two years before private real estate, as represented by the NCREIF(UNS) Index. This pattern is broadly consistent with the hypothesis that public and private real estate are essentially the same thing (in that they both represent the same type of underlying assets) but with public real estate reflecting the greater informational efficiency of the public securities markets, while price changes in private real estate reflect the inertia and sluggishness of the less efficient private markets.

More careful analysis of Figure 15–4 reveals additional information about the differences between private and public real estate and the relation between these two ways of investing in real estate. Although public real estate generally leads private real estate, the length of the lead is variable. Both series peaked in the same year, 1984, while public real estate bottomed out three years ahead of private real estate (1990 versus 1993). Major downturns in public real estate in 1981, 1985, and 1989 were echoed one year later by major downturns in private real estate in 1982, 1986, and 1990. Major upturns in public real estate in 1975–1976 and 1982–1983 were followed one to two years later by major upturns in private real estate in 1976–1978 and 1983–1984.

Also intriguing is the evidence presented in Figure 15–4 regarding volatility. Even though we are working with an unsmoothed private index and an unlevered public index, public real estate seems to display greater short-run volatility than private real estate. However, it is important to note that most, if not all, of the "extra" volatility in public real estate prices appears to be transient in nature. That is, the public real estate prices bounce around a bit more in the short run, but *show a strong tendency to revert back toward the same long-run underlying trend and cycle.* The fact that long-run volatility is similar is revealed in the fact that the relative magnitude of the rise and fall (or amplitude of the overall cycle) appears to be *about the same* between the public and private value indexes. The relatively high short-run volatility in the public index may reflect stock market noise or overreaction of the type noted in Section 1. Highly liquid markets such as the public stock exchanges appear to be subject to transient bearish and bullish sentiments, which may cause excess volatility. There is some evidence in the academic literature that this phenomenon is particularly strong among small-capitalization stocks whose trading is heavily influenced by small individual investors. REITs have been in this category throughout much of the historical period covered in this analysis. One might anticipate that as institutional involvement in REITs becomes more pronounced, the volatility of REITs associated with market noise may decline over time.

Another important difference between the historical performance pattern of public versus private real estate is revealed in Figure 15–5, which displays the accumulated total returns of the unsmoothed RNI and unlevered NAREIT index (as opposed to the accumulated appreciation returns depicted in Figure 15–4). In Figure 15–5, it is apparent that over the

FIGURE 15–5

Public (Unlevered) and Private (Unsmoothed) Real Estate Accumulated Total Capital Index with Reinvestment (1974 = 100), Based on Total Returns

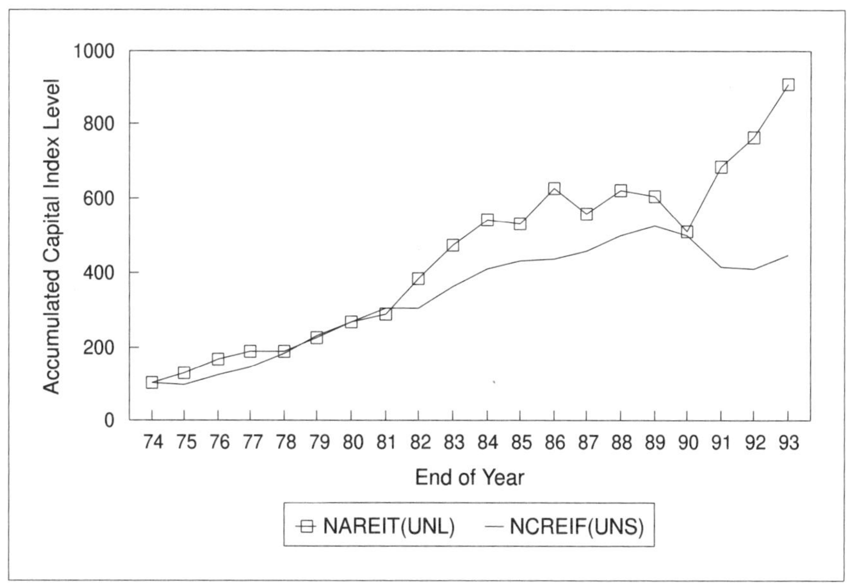

1975–1993 period public real estate has outperformed private real estate as far as the overall average total return is concerned. Although the two types of real estate investment tracked generally parallel to one another for much of the historical period covered in Figure 15–5, public real estate tended to outperform private real estate in the early 1980s and again in the early 1990s, to give public real estate the overall performance edge. Comparison of Figures 15–4 and 15–5 suggests, somewhat surprisingly, that the superior public real estate performance is due to generally higher income, rather than greater capital growth. As the NAREIT Index is composed of all publicly traded REITs at each point in time (including those that subsequently failed), this performance difference cannot be attributed to "survivor bias" in the public real estate index.

The historical investment performance of public and private real estate during the 1975–1993 period is summarized statistically in Table 15–1. The performance of stocks (represented by the S&P 500), long-term bonds (represented by the Ibbotson Long-Term Government Bond Index), Treasury bills, and inflation are also reported for comparison purposes in the table. The superior performance of public real estate over private real estate during this period is also apparent in the statistics of Table 15–1. The mean return was nearly 400 basis points higher. The performance of private real estate was barely above that of Treasury bills during this period. Examining the Sharpe ratio (the risk premium per unit of risk, as measured by the excess return over T-bills divided by the volatility), we see that public real estate had the second best risk-adjusted return performance, after the S&P 500, while private real estate had the worst performance. The 1975–1993 period was a particularly good one for the stock market, as reflected in the very high Sharpe ratio for the S&P 500.

One possible explanation for the superior total return performance of public real estate is that the greater liquidity and informational efficiency of the public capital markets puts greater pressure for performance onto the managers of public real estate (the REIT managers), which leads to a more effective weeding out of poor managers. The result would be that properties managed by publicly traded entities would tend on average over the long run to perform better than the average property held in the private real estate market. However, in the long run in equilibrium in the capital markets, such superior management should result in investors bidding up the price of REIT shares, providing the successful REITs with a lower cost of capital and a ready source of capital for expansion, but should not result in higher-than-normal risk-adjusted returns for the investors, on average. It is

TABLE 15–1

Historical Total Return Performance Statistics 1975–1993
(Annual Nominal Return Statistics)

	Private* Real Est.	Public** Real Est.	Stocks: S&P 500	Bonds: LTGovt	T-Bills	Inflation
Mean	7.88%	11.62%	16.09%	11.03%	7.40%	5.64%
Std.dev.	10.98%	13.54%	13.59%	12.34%	2.93%	3.25%
Sharpe***	0.04	0.31	0.64	0.29	NA	NA

* Unsmoothed RNI
** Unlevered NAREIT
*** Sharpe ratio, a measure of risk-adjusted return, equals mean total return in excess of T-bills divided by standard deviation.

possible that the historical period studied here does not represent the long-run equilibrium return relationships. Within the context of long-term equilibrium, it is probably more logical to expect a higher return for equivalent assets that are held privately to generate higher expected returns due to their lack of liquidity and greater management burden for investors. Over the subject period measured, this was not the case.

Apart from the superior management theory, there are other possible explanations for the superior performance of public real estate during the 1975–1993 period. For one thing, the types of properties held by REITs has historically not been exactly the same as what has been represented in the NCREIF Index. In particular, REITs have traditionally tended to hold smaller properties in smaller cities and to hold a greater variety of different types of properties (such as hotels and health care facilities). It may be that these types of properties tend to be more risky than the property types more strongly represented in the NCREIF Index. This greater risk would, in equilibrium, be expected to generally command a higher return premium, which would be reflected in higher long-term historical average total returns. Also, public real estate would be expected to have relatively more "systematic risk," or covariance with stocks and bonds, the main components of most investment portfolios. This could cause public real estate to command a greater risk premium in equilibrium, which could explain the greater Sharpe ratio noted in Table 15–1. Risk-and-return considerations such as these are often most effectively viewed from the perspective of modern portfolio theory, a perspective to which we now turn our attention.

3. PORTFOLIO CONSIDERATIONS

Since its development in the 1950s and 1960s by Harry Markowitz, William Sharpe, and others, so-called "modern portfolio theory" (MPT) has provided the basis for rational, quantitative investment analysis and planning. The basic idea in MPT is to minimize the overall portfolio risk, or volatility in the portfolio, associated with a given target total return objective for an investor's portfolio. As noted in Section 1 of this chapter, MPT has provided much of the underlying motivation for including real estate in the pension fund portfolio, as real estate has been seen as a potential diversifier of the stocks and bonds that dominate most pension funds' portfolios. Indeed, the ERISA law, which stimulated much pension fund investment in real estate beginning in the mid-1970s, was inspired by MPT when it urged prudent portfolio diversification to reduce overall risk.

Portfolio considerations are particularly important to the central question we are examining in this chapter, the role of public versus private real estate for pension investors. Viewed in isolation from portfolio considerations, the superior investment performance of public real estate, noted in the preceding section, would appear to make public real estate a "slam dunk." Why would anyone want to invest in private real estate when one can apparently do at least as well if not better in public real estate and with much more liquidity and lower management and transactions costs? But the point of MPT is that investment decision makers should not view each asset class in isolation but examine them from the perspective of how they affect the risk-and-return performance of the overall portfolio. As noted in Section 1, it is possible that public real estate, because it is traded in the liquid public capital markets where stocks and bonds trade, may have much greater covariance with these other dominant asset classes and therefore not provide as much diversification benefit as private real estate within the typical pension fund overall portfolio. This is therefore the question to which we now turn our attention.

3.1 MPT, Long-Horizon Investors, and Private Real Estate

In applying MPT, the main focus is to identify optimally diversified portfolios, that is, mixtures of asset classes that lie on the so-called "efficient frontier" of portfolios that minimize the overall portfolio volatility (return standard deviation over time) for any given total return target. Higher return targets will, of course, have higher portfolio volatility, so in choosing a return target the investors are, in effect, deciding or expressing how risk-averse or risk-tolerant (that is, how conservative or aggressive) they wish to be. But in any case, they should never, in theory, want to invest in a mixture of assets that is more risky than necessary to provide the given expected return target. (In other words, investors should never invest in a portfolio that is not "on the frontier.") Portfolios on the efficient frontier are known as "mean-variance efficient" portfolios because they minimize the variance in the return for any given mean return or, equivalently, maximize the mean return for any given variance.

To determine the frontier of efficient portfolios is a simple mathematical exercise with modern computers, given the risk-and-return expectations regarding each of the classes of assets that may comprise the portfolio. The necessary inputs include, for each asset class, the mean return, the standard deviation of that return (or square root of the variance), and the correlation coefficient between the returns to each pair of asset classes (a "correlation matrix").

Traditionally, MPT has been applied using quarterly or annual historical return performance statistics as the required inputs. By using such relatively short-interval returns, one obtains more data points from a given historical period. This enables one to obtain statistically more accurate and reliable estimates of the risk/return performance of the various asset classes. This is particularly useful for real estate, which does not have a very long history of good data availability. For example, the 1975–1993 period considered in the previous section provides us with 76 quarterly or 19 annual return data points, but it would not even provide us with four half-decade return periods.

The use of quarterly or annual return statistics should not imply that investors have such short horizons when they make portfolio policy and investment decisions. Indeed, most pension funds have a medium- to long-term investment horizon that would probably be better represented by a five-year period than a quarterly or annual period. But the use of short-period return statistics to apply MPT to longer-horizon investors does not matter *when asset markets are informationally efficient*. It is a mathematical fact that when returns are uncorrelated across time and unpredictable (that is, there are no lagged linkages between the returns to different asset classes), the return statistical inputs required by MPT will be effectively identical no matter what the length of the return time interval. This is because, with efficient markets, the mean, variance, and all covariances of the returns among all the asset classes will all be exactly proportional to the return time interval (for example, the variance in the five-year return will be exactly five times the variance in the annual return, and the covariance between any two assets in the five-year return will be exactly five times the covariancc in the annual return). The result is that one will obtain the same optimal portfolio no matter what return frequency is used for the input statistics. So why not use the shorter-horizon return frequencies that provide more historical data points?

The problem is that *private real estate is not informationally efficient.* Therefore, to properly conduct portfolio analysis for medium- to long-horizon investors, *if such investors wish to include consideration of private real estate as a potential asset class in the portfolio, one cannot simply use the short-interval return statistics as the inputs to the portfolio analysis.* To examine optimal portfolios for investors with five-year horizons, for example, one needs to use five-year return expectations regarding the mean, standard deviation, and correlations among the asset classes.

This distinction matters a lot when considering the role of private and public real estate in pension portfolios. Recall from our historical comparison of private and public real estate in Section 2.3 that, over the *long-run* (in the "big picture" of Figure 15–4, for example), public and private real estate seemed to perform rather similarly, at least as far as the "second moments" of the returns were concerned. (That is, the *deviation* over time of asset values around their long-run trends seemed to be similar between private and public real estate, as evidenced by the parallel patterns and similar magnitude of rise and fall apparent in Figure 15–4). Thus, in long-run returns such as five-year returns, we would expect to see relatively high positive correlation between public and private real estate. On the other hand, the lag of a year or more between public and private real estate returns means that short-run returns, such as annual returns, will show little or no correlation between public and private real estate. Thus, from a portfolio perspective, using annual return statistics will make public and private real estate appear much more different than they would appear using, say, five-year returns. This difference (which is not realistic for a long-horizon investor) will distort the roles that the two forms of real estate would play in optimally diversified portfolios.

Thus, to be more accurate and relevant to long-horizon investors such as pension funds, MPT should be applied using five-year return statistics rather than annual return statistics as the inputs for the optimization analysis. The five-year statistics will be, in effect, the same as the annual statistics for the efficient asset classes (public real estate, stocks, bonds).[13]

The five-year statistics will be different from the annual statistics for the inefficient asset class, private real estate.

It is important to understand the nature of the differences in moving from short-interval to long-interval return statistics for private real estate. In general, the volatility and correlation statistics will increase for private real estate relative to those for public real estate and the other efficient asset classes. The sluggishness and inertia in private real estate imparts positive serial correlation into its returns, which causes the return variance to increase more than proportionately with the return time interval. In other words, the five-year return volatility for private real estate will be more than $\sqrt{5}$ times the annual volatility. Intuitively, this can be understood as follows. With private real estate, the rise up the cycle is relatively smooth, and the fall down the other side of the cycle is relatively smooth. However, the amplitude of the cycle, the magnitude of the rise and fall, is quite large. With longer-interval returns, it is this amplitude of the cycle that dominates the standard deviation of the return. *With short-interval returns, it is the smoothness of the rise up and fall down that dominates the standard deviation. Similarly, in the longer-interval returns, the correlation should be greater between private real estate and other asset classes that are linked to private real estate by economic fundamentals, such as public real estate and the stock market.* This is because, in the longer run, the fundamental economic linkages come through, reflecting the "big picture" of the return histories.

As a result of these differences between short- and long-interval return statistics for private real estate, portfolio analysis using short-interval return statistics will be biased toward showing a larger role for private real estate than is actually appropriate for a long-horizon investor. We avoid this bias in the present analysis by applying MPT using five-year return statistics rather than annual or quarterly statistics. Our method of determining the five-year return statistics for private real estate is described in the Technical Appendix to this report, the results of which are summarized in the following section.

3.2 Five-Year Return Statistics for Private Real Estate

As described in great detail in the Technical Appendix, five-year-interval return statistics can be derived for private real estate using the 19-year history of annual returns for the unsmoothed NCREIF Index developed in Section 2. This is done by building statistical models of the annual returns, which include the lagged effects.[14]

For example, based on regression analysis, we can model the annual private real estate return as a function of (1) a "stock market factor," (2) a "bond market factor," and (3) a pure "real estate factor." In order to allow for the lack of informational efficiency in the private real estate market, a regression model can be developed, which allows for lagged relationships and serial correlation, based on the annual returns to private real estate and stocks and bonds. Such a model [Technical Appendix (3e)] has been calibrated as follows:

$$r_t = 0.005 + (0.11)m_t + (0.265)m_{t-1} - (0.123)b_t \\ - (0.093)b_{t-1} + (0.527)R_{t-1} + \upsilon_t$$

where: r_t is the true (that is, unsmoothed) real annual total return to private real estate in year t; m_t is the similarly defined return to the stock market (S&P 500); and b_t is the bond market (long-term treasuries). The R_{t-1} term is the lagged residual from the regression of private real estate on to contemporaneous and lagged stock and bond returns and represents the lagged component of the pure "real estate factor." The "real estate innovation," or new component of the pure real estate factor, is represented by the υ_t term, which is uncorrelated over time or with either stocks or bonds.

As can be seen from the coefficients on the stock market, this model suggests that, based on the 1975–1993 historical performance, private real estate has a "total beta" with respect to the S&P 500 of around +0.375. This is considerably higher than is typically reported in studies of historical private real estate returns because most previous studies have failed to correct for smoothing in the private real estate indexes and have failed to consider the lagged relationships and serial correlation implied by private real estate's lack of informational efficiency. These considerations are important for correctly applying MPT to include consideration of private real estate for medium- to long-term investors.

A similar regression-based model can be developed for the relationship between private and public real estate. As shown in the Technical Appendix (4d), the calibrated model is

$$r_t = 0.009 + (0.098)n_t + (0.257)n_{t-1} + (0.457)V_{t-1} + \varepsilon_t$$

where n_t is the public real estate return (unlevered NAREIT) in year t, and V_{t-1} is the lagged private-market effect. This model reflects the fact that public real estate leads private real estate, with most of the link between the two occurring after one year.

Using the above-described, historically based empirical models of private real estate returns, we can construct the implied five-year-interval risk-and-return statistics for private real estate. Along with the assumption that the public markets are essentially efficient, this results in the five-year-interval return statistics presented in Table 15–2. These statistics are the appropriate inputs for a five-year horizon portfolio optimization analysis based on MPT. The statistics in Table 15–2 represent the mean, standard deviation, and correlation coefficients in the five-year-interval, inflation-adjusted total returns to stocks (S&P 500), bonds (long-term U.S. government bonds), public real estate (unlevered NAREIT), and private real estate (unsmoothed NCREIF).

The five-year returns were calculated simply by multiplying the historical annual returns by five. The five-year standard deviations were calculated as the annual standard deviations multiplied by the square root of five (under the assumption that these asset classes, traded in efficient markets, have nearly zero autocorrelation), and by the same reasoning, the five-year correlations among the efficient assets were assumed to be the same as the annual correlations.

The correlation coefficients in Table 15–2 are not lagged, but contemporaneous within the five-year-interval return frequency and thus are the appropriate inputs for mean-variance portfolio optimization with a five-year investment horizon. In the case of the publicly traded asset classes, these correlations are the same as the historical annual frequency correlations, consistent with the assumption of informational efficiency in the public markets. The private real estate coefficients, however, are different, incorporating the lagged relationship at the annual frequency between private real estate and the other asset classes. For example, at the annual frequency, the contemporaneous correlation between the real total returns of private real estate and stocks during the 1975–1993 period was –23.9 percent, instead of the +25.2 percent obtained at the five-year frequency based on the market model described above. Similarly, the standard deviation indicated for private real estate in Table 15–4 is more than $\sqrt{5}$ times the annual standard deviation, due to the inertia in the private market annual returns.

3.3 Optimal Portfolios for Five-Year Horizon Investors

Based on the inputs in Table 15–2, the mean-variance efficient frontier of mixed-asset portfolios can be determined for five-year-horizon investors. This frontier and the efficient portfolios that compose it are shown in Table

TABLE 15–2

Risk-and-Return Expectations for Five-Year Horizon Optimal Portfolio Analysis

	S&P 500	LTG Bonds	NAREIT(UNL)	NCREIF(UNS)
Mean	52.28%	26.97%	29.90%	11.23%
Std. dev.	31.52%	32.64%	31.48%	28.30%
		Correlations:		
S&P 500	100.0%	49.6%	49.5%	25.2%
LTG bonds	49.6%	100.0%	42.3%	–6.1%
NAREIT(UNL)	49.5%	42.3%	100.0%	33.8%
NCREIF(UNS)	25.2%	–6.1%	33.8%	100.0%

Statistics are for five-year-interval real (inflation-adjusted) total returns based on 1975–1993 annual historical returns.

TABLE 15–3

Mean-Variance Efficient Frontier, Five-Year Horizon Investor

Portfolio:		*Shares (% of Portfolio Value):*			
Mean**	Std. Dev.**	Stocks	Bonds	Public Real Estate	Private Real Estate
22.50%	20.40 %	11.26	33.31	7.53	47.90
25.00	20.54	18.33	30.25	7.94	43.48
27.50	20.86	25.41	27.18	8.36	39.05
30.00	21.36	32.49	24.12	8.77	34.63
32.50	22.02	39.57	21.05	9.18	30.20
35.00	22.83	46.65	17.98	9.60	25.78
37.50	23.77	53.72	14.92	10.01	21.35
40.00	24.84	60.80	11.85	10.42	16.93
42.50	26.01	67.88	8.78	10.83	12.50
45.00	27.27	74.96	5.72	11.25	8.08
47.50	28.61	82.04	2.65	11.66	3.65
50.00	30.03	89.81	0.00	10.19	0.00

* Based on input statistics from Table 15–2.

** Inflation-adjusted five-year-interval total return statistics.

15–3 and Figures 15–6 and 15–7 for real five-year, mean-return targets ranging from 22.5 percent to 50 percent (equivalent to annual real-return targets of 4.5 percent to 10 percent).[15] The mixes of asset classes indicated in the table and figures represent the minimum variance portfolios for each of the mean-return targets, assuming no short sales are permitted.

As can be seen in the table and figures, both public and private real estate appear in the optimal portfolios in most of the target return range. As the return target becomes more aggressive, the optimal share of stocks and public real estate increases, while that of bonds and private real estate decreases. This is because the risk-adjusted performance of stock and public real estate is superior to that of bonds and private real estate. The large role of bonds and private real estate in the conservative portfolios is due to the very low correlation between private real estate and bonds, which enables the combination of these two asset classes to provide a low-risk element in the portfolio. In general, private real estate has as large a role as it does in the optimal portfolios despite its very poor risk-adjusted return performance because of its relatively low correlation with the other asset classes. Even so, private real estate drops completely out of the optimal portfolio at the most aggressive return target, while public real estate remains in the optimal portfolio at all target levels. In the midrange of target returns shown in the figures, which is typical of most pension funds, both private and public real estate have significant positions in the optimal portfolios.

4. CONCLUSIONS FOR INVESTMENT STRATEGY

Let us now return to the primary question that motivated this chapter, the role of public and private real estate in the typical pension fund portfolio. What light does the above-described, historically based portfolio analysis shed on this question? More broadly, what do our general findings in sections 2 and 3 about the nature of public and private real estate in a portfolio context tell us about the role these two ways of investing in real estate can play for pension funds?

Perhaps the single most important message to emerge from the foregoing analysis is that, after being as careful as possible to correct for statistical and data problems such as smoothing in private real estate returns, leverage in public real estate returns, and the implications of market inefficiency for long-horizon investors, *we find strong evidence that both public and private real estate should have significant positions*

FIGURE 15–6

Efficient Frontier of Portfolios of Stocks, Bonds, Public Real Estate, and Private Real Estate, Based on Five-Year Real Estate Return Statistics in Table 15–3

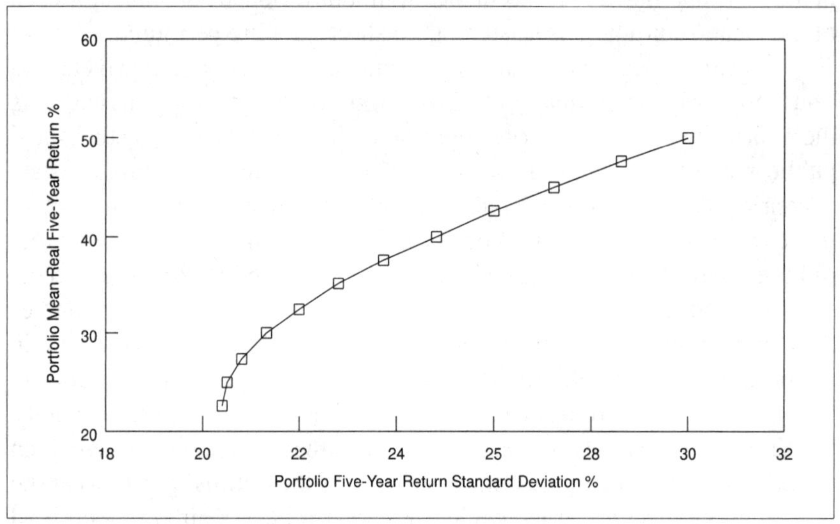

FIGURE 15–7

Asset-Class Shares of Optimal Portfolios, as a Function of Return Target

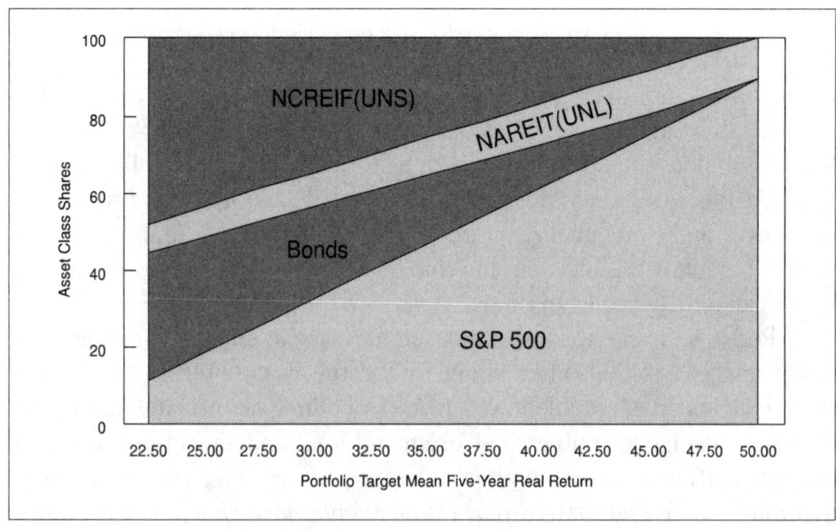

in the optimal overall portfolio of the typical pension fund. While the role of private real estate is more dependent on the particular portfolio return target the investor selects, the position of public real estate is more robust to the return target. More conservative investors would put relatively more into private real estate and bonds, while more aggressive investors would put more into public real estate and stocks. *Even the most conservative investors, however, would put some portion of their portfolio into public real estate*, according to the portfolio analysis described in the previous section.[16]

While we have not extended the analysis to more recent data than that for 1993 and prior years, we note that stocks, REITs, and direct real estate have all performed well since 1993. The turnaround in the direct market would likely appear stronger after correcting for appraisal smoothing than it appears in the published NCREIF returns, while both stocks and REITs have had strong performance in recent years. Furthermore, there is evidence that correlations between REITs and the S&P 500 have been lower since 1993 than prior to that time. Consequently, the usefulness of REITs in the mixed-asset portfolio may have increased, relative to what was the case in our analysis within this chapter.

In the broader picture, it should be noted that formal portfolio analysis based on MPT and the use of historically based return statistics as the inputs to such analysis should be taken with a grain of salt when making strategic investment decisions. Such analysis provides powerful and important insights, based on a more objective and quantitative approach than has hitherto been possible. But it cannot replace the common sense and broader perspective that is necessary in decision making.

With this in mind, it is often useful to think of two major considerations in strategic investment decision making, *diversification* and *timing.* Diversification responds to the common-sense argument against putting all your eggs in one basket. MPT has given diversification a more formal and quantitative framework to help direct investment decision making. The roots of MPT go back to the "classical" school of financial economics that flowered in the 1960s and 1970s, based heavily on the assumption that capital markets were essentially informationally efficient. Under this assumption, it is fruitless in the long run to attempt to "beat the market," and the efficiency of the market will tend to protect well-diversified investors from making serious "mistakes." This perspective tended to discredit or play down the importance of timing considerations in making investment strategy.

More recently, many financial economists have become convinced that even public capital markets are not *perfectly* efficient, although the efficient market assumption is probably close enough to the truth for most investors' purposes in the case of public market investments. Private real estate markets, however, are more indisputably and more seriously inefficient. While this does not mean that it is easy to "beat the market" in private real estate, it does mean that timing is a relatively more important consideration. Lack of informational efficiency brings both danger and opportunity. Particularly for long-horizon investors with relatively low need for liquidity, such as many pension funds, lack of informational efficiency in private real estate markets can provide opportunities to improve long-run investment performance. To take advantage of real estate investment timing opportunities, it is likely that a mixture of public and private real estate will be useful. Because of its greater informational efficiency and lower transaction costs, it may make sense to use public real estate as a "swing" element in the portfolio, *providing flexibility to the overall real estate position.* For example, during times when the private market appears overheated, additional real estate investments should be made using public real estate, and a rigorous "sell discipline" should be enforced for the private market holdings. For investors who do not wish to expose themselves to the dangers of market inefficiency (for example, buying "overvalued" assets), real estate investment should probably be confined to public real estate. One of the major points of the analysis in Section 2 is that, in the long run, public and private real estate are, to a considerable extent, the same thing.

TECHNICAL APPENDIX: DEVELOPING THE FIVE-YEAR RETURN STATISTICS FOR PRIVATE REAL ESTATE

With only 19 years of good return statistics, or less than four independent (nonoverlapping) five-year return intervals, how can we develop reliable five-year-interval return statistics for private real estate?[a] The answer is that we will use annual frequency data to develop a statistical model of private real estate returns, including the autocorrelation in those returns and the lagged relation between private real estate and public real estate and stocks and bonds. This statistical model can then be used to derive the implied five-year return statistics for private real estate.

Our statistical model of private real estate returns has two components: a "market model," relating private real estate returns to stock and bond returns, and a "real estate model," relating private and public real estate returns. Consider the market model first. We postulate that the private market real estate returns, as represented by the unsmoothed RNI described in Section 2, can be unbundled into a "stock market component," a "bond market component," and a "pure real estate component." The stock market factor exists because real estate is embedded in the overall economy, whose general health and direction is reflected in the stock market. The bond market factor exists because real estate has high-yield, low-growth characteristics, as well as in many cases a fixed-income component (based on preexisting leases) similar to bonds. The pure real estate factor then represents aspects that are unique to private real estate, not shared by either the stock or bond markets. This model can be represented as follows:

$$r_t = \alpha + S_t + B_t + R_t \quad (3)$$

where: r_t is the true private market total return to real estate in year t (that is, corrected for index smoothing); S_t is the stock component in year t; B_t is the bond component in year t; R_t is the year t pure real estate component from the private property market; and α is a constant reflecting a possible differential trend or "drift" rate for real estate as compared to stocks and bonds.

While the stock and bond markets are informationally efficient, the private real estate market is not, and so we would expect the stock and bond components within the private real estate return to possibly be lagged. Thus, we have

$$S_t = \beta_0 m_t + \beta_1 m_{t-1} \quad (3a)$$

and

$$B_t = \gamma_0 b_t + \gamma_1 b_{t-1} \tag{3b}$$

where m_t and b_t are the total return to, respectively, the stock and bond markets during year t. The pure real estate component is characteristic of the private real estate markets and thus also reflects the sluggishness or inertia of that market in responding to new information. Thus, we would expect the real estate factor to exhibit positive first-order serial correlation, well modeled in annual returns by a first-order autoregressive process:

$$R_t = \upsilon_t + \rho R_{t-1} \tag{3c}$$

where υ_t is the pure real estate "innovation" in year t, a serially uncorrelated ("white noise") element. This real estate innovation represents the "news," or *new* information that arrives in year t relevant uniquely to private real estate.

By definition, υ, and therefore R, are uncorrelated with either S or B (although S and B may be correlated with each other). Also, due to informational efficiency in the stock and bond markets, m and b are uncorrelated across time (white noise with drift) and unpredictable (no lagged cross-correlation). The lack of informational efficiency in the private real estate market is reflected in the lagged terms: the $\beta_1 m_{t-1}$ term in (3a), the $\gamma_1 b_{t-1}$ term in (3b), and the ρR_{t-1} term in (3c). It is possible that almost *all* of the relationship between real estate returns and stock and bond returns is lagged, that is, β_0 and γ_0 may be very small or nonexistent. In that case, the serial correlation in private real estate returns would derive entirely from the autoregressive pure real estate factor modeled in (3c).

Combining (3a), (3b), and (3c), we see that we can model the private real estate return for year t as a function of the stock and bond market returns in years t and t-1, and the autoregressive pure real estate residual:

$$r_t = \alpha + \beta_0 m_t + \beta_1 m_{t-1} + \gamma_0 b_t + \gamma_1 b_{t-1} + R_t \tag{3d}$$

While no model is perfect, this would seem to be a reasonable model for capturing the essence of what is going on in the annual-frequency private real estate market return. This model incorporates both the fundamental economic linkages between real estate markets and the economy and capital markets, as represented by the stock and bond markets. The model also reflects the possibility that there may be a unique real estate factor, and it allows for the lack of informational efficiency in the private real estate market.

In Section 2, we quantified the private real estate return series, $\{r_t\}$, by unsmoothing the RNI. As $\{m_t\}$ and $\{b_t\}$ are also empirically observable, it is clear that (3d) can be quantified empirically by regressing the unsmoothed private real estate returns onto contemporaneous and lagged stock and bond market returns. In so doing, we need to be sensitive to the fact that the residuals from such a regression, the pure real estate component $\{R_t\}$, would be expected to have positive first-order serial correlation. Thus, we need to account for this serial correlation in our regression estimation procedure. This can be done by using a generalized differencing procedure and an estimation procedure for the autoregressive coefficient r from (3c). We have used the Cochrane-Orcutt procedure for this purpose to obtain the following quantification of (3c) and (3d):[b]

$$r_t = 0.005 + (0.11)m_t + (0.265)m_{t-1} - (0.123)b_t - (0.093)b_{t-1} + (0.527)R_{t-1} + \upsilon_t \quad (3e)$$

Table 15A–1 presents more details of the regression estimation results for the private real estate annual return market model. While the fit of the regression is low by classical econometric standards, this is not surprising

TABLE 15–A1

Regression Results for the Market Model

Variable	Coefficient	Std. Error	T-Statistic	Prob.
α (constant)	0.005	0.051	0.101	0.921
m_t (stock yr t)	0.110	0.147	0.747	0.468
m_{t-1} (stock yr t-1)	0.265	0.141	1.876	0.083
b_t (bond yr t)	–0.123	0.172	–0.717	0.486
b_{t-1} (bond yr t-1)	–0.093	0.176	–0.528	0.607
R_{t-1} (pure RE yr t-1)	0.527	0.251	2.098	0.056

R-squared: 0.358	Adjusted R-squared: 0.111
Durbin-Watson statistic: 1.555	

Regression based on annual real (inflation-adjusted) total returns during 1975–1993 (19 observations). Dependent variable is unsmoothed RNI. Stock and bond returns from Ibbotson Assoc., Inc., SBBI Yearbook. Stock returns represented by S&P 500. Bond returns represented by long-term U.S. government securities. Cochrane-Orcutt procedure used to estimate autoregressive coefficient.

given the scarcity of data points for estimating the regression (19 annual return observations). Furthermore, a good fit is not a particularly important criterion for a market model of this nature. More important is that the signs and magnitudes of the parameter coefficients should make economic and intuitive sense, which in this case they do. In particular, we note that the relationship between real estate and the stock market is modestly positive, as we would expect given the real economic links between real estate and the rest of the economy. The two estimated b coefficients suggest a total (contemporaneous and lagged) "beta" of just under +0.4. Most of the relationship is lagged one year, which is not surprising given the greater informational efficiency in the stock market. The relationship with bonds is negative, which makes sense based on real estate's inflation—hedging abilities—versus bonds' exposure to inflation. The weakness in the bond relationship also makes sense, as most of the value of real estate does not derive from the preexisting leases. Finally, the autoregressive coefficient on the pure real estate factor (the residuals from the regression) is a moderately positive 0.53, which is in agreement with conventional perceptions that the private real estate market is sluggish in its incorporation of new information relevant to property values.[c]

The other aspect of the annual private real estate returns that must be modeled in order to develop the five-year-interval return statistics that we need for our portfolio analysis is what may be called the "real estate model," relating private real estate returns to public real estate returns. In this case, we model the annual private real estate market returns as a bundle of two components: a "public real estate factor" and a "pure private market factor." The public real estate factor is represented by our unlevered REIT returns and consists theoretically of stock market, bond market, and unique real estate factors all together but with the informational efficiency characteristics of the liquid securities markets. Then the pure private market factor reflects elements that arise uniquely from the private market structure in which private real estate assets trade. As before, the lack of informational efficiency in the private real estate market is reflected both in a lag in the relationship with the public real estate factor and in an autoregressive structure in the pure private market factor.

The real estate model can be expressed algebraically as follows:

$$r_t = a + P_t + V_t \tag{4}$$

where: r_t is the true private market total return to real estate in year t (as before, corrected for index smoothing); P_t is the public real estate factor in year t; V_t is the pure private market factor in year t; and a is a constant. Expanding the two factors as before, we have

$$P_t = \delta_0 n_t + \delta_1 n_{t-1} \quad (4a)$$

$$V_t = \varepsilon_t + \varphi V_{t-1} \quad (4b)$$

where n_t is the unlevered REIT total return in year t (which has no serial correlation or predictability, due to the informational efficiency of the public capital market) and e_t is the pure private market innovation (white noise). Equation (4a) captures the contemporaneous and lagged relationship between private and public real estate, while (4b) reflects the residual pure private market element in the private real estate returns.

As with the market model, the real estate model can be estimated using observable empirical data by regressing the unsmoothed RNI returns onto the unlevered NAREIT returns and explicitly incorporating the serial correlation in the residuals from this regression (which represent the pure private market factor). The regression is[d]

$$r_t = a + \delta_0 n_t + \delta_1 n_{t-1} + V_t \quad (4c)$$

The estimated relation, based on the 1975–1993 historical real total returns (and using the Cochrane-Orcutt procedure to estimate the autoregressive relation in the residuals), is indicated below:[e]

$$r_t = 0.009 + (0.098)n_t + (0.257)n_{t-1} + (0.457)V_{t-1} + \varepsilon_t \quad (4d)$$

The details of the regression results are presented in Table 15–A2. Again, the signs and magnitudes of the estimated parameter values make economic and intuitive sense and appear consistent broadly with the findings in the market model, equation (3d), which is simply an alternative model of the same private real estate returns.

The models of private real estate annual frequency total returns contained in equations (3e) and (4d) can be used to estimate the five-year internal return statistics of private real estate necessary to apply modern portfolio theory for long-horizon investors, as discussed in Section 3.1. In particular, market model (3d) implies that the five-year private real estate returns are related to the annual stock and bond returns and to the pure real estate innovations by the following equation:[f]

$$r_t^5 = 5\alpha + \beta_0 \sum_{j=0}^{4} m_{t-j} + \beta_1 \sum_{j=1}^{5} m_{t-j} + \gamma_0 \sum_{j=0}^{4} b_{t-j} + \gamma_1 \sum_{j=1}^{5} b_{t-j} + \sum_{j=0}^{\infty} \left(\upsilon_{t-j} \sum_{k=X}^{j} \rho^k \right) \quad (5)$$

TABLE 15–A2

Regression Results for the Real Estate Model

Variable	Coefficient	Std. Error	T-Statistic	Prob.
a (constant)	0.009	0.038	0.234	0.818
n_t (NAREIT UNL yr t)	0.098	0.115	0.856	0.405
n_{t-1} (NAREIT UNL t-1)	0.257	0.098	2.619	0.019
V_{t-1} (pure priv. yr t-1)	0.457	0.218	2.100	0.053

R-squared: 0.411	Adjusted R-squared: 0.293237
Durbin-Watson stat 2.035	

Regression based on annual real (inflation-adjusted) total returns during 1975–1993 (19 observations). Dependent variable is unsmoothed RNI. Unlevered NAREIT Index is RHS variable. Cochrane-Orcutt procedure used to estimate autoregressive coefficient.

where r_t^5 represents the five-year-interval return to private real estate for the five-year interval ending at the end of year t; m_s, b_s, and υ_s are the annual innovations (for year s) as defined previously in equation (3); and X is the maximum of either zero or j-4. Similarly, the real estate model (4c) gives the following relation to annual public real estate returns and the pure private market innovations:

$$r_t^5 = 5a + \delta_0 \sum_{j=0}^{4} n_{t-j} + \delta_1 \sum_{j=1}^{5} n_{t-j} + \sum_{j=0}^{\infty} \left(\varepsilon_{t-j} \sum_{k=X}^{j} \varphi^k \right) \quad (6)$$

Given informational efficiency in the public markets (that is, assuming that m_t, b_t, and n_t are not serially correlated and are unpredictable), the five-year-interval return second moments for private real estate returns we need for portfolio analysis are obtained as follows from equations (5) and (6). We can calculate the five-year return variance for private real estate from either equation (5) or (6) (very similar results obtain). For example, from equation (6) we obtain the following:[g]

$$VAR[r_t^5] = \left((\delta_0)^2 + (\delta_1)^2 + 4\,(\delta_0 + \delta_1)^2 \right) VAR[n_t] + \left(\sum_{j=0}^{\infty} \left(\sum_{k=0}^{j} \varphi^k \right)^2 \right) VAR[\varepsilon_t] \quad (7)$$

From equation (5) and the efficient market assumption for stocks we obtain the covariance between the five-year-interval private real estate return and the five-year-interval stock market return as

$$COV\,[r_t^5, m_t^5] = (5\beta_0 + 4\beta_1)VAR\,[m_t] + (5\gamma_0 + 4\gamma_1)COV[b_t, m_t] \qquad (8)$$

where m_t^5 refers to the five-year-interval return to the stock market. The five-year covariance with the bond market is similarly derived from equation (5):

$$COV\,[r_t^5, b_t^5] = (5\beta_0 + 4\beta_1)COV\,[m_t, b_t] + (5\gamma_0 + 4\gamma_1)VAR[b_t] \qquad (9)$$

While the five-year-return-interval covariance between private and public real estate is derived from equation (6) as

$$COV\,[r_t^5, n_t^5] = (5\delta_0 + 4\delta_1)VAR\,[n_t] \qquad (10)$$

Finally, the correlation coefficients are obtained using the standard definition. For example, the correlation coefficient between private real estate and the stock market is

$$CORR[r_t^5, m_t^5] = \frac{COV\,[r_t^5, m_t^5]}{\sqrt{VAR\,[r_t^5]}\sqrt{VAR\,[m_t^5]}} \qquad (11)$$

where $VAR[m_t^5]=5VAR[m_t]$ under our assumption of efficient public markets.

Using the above definitions and the empirical relationships established in (3e) and (4d), we obtain the inputs for a five-year horizon portfolio optimization analysis indicated in Table 15–2 of Section 3.3 of the report.

ENDNOTES

1. The twin problems of illiquidity and informational inefficiency led some observers to compare the private commercial real estate market of the early 1990s to "Chinese water torture." The "crash" lasted several years, during which time it was possible for investors to foresee that prices would continue to slide, yet because of the lack of liquidity they could not get out of their real estate positions.
2. The RNI is produced by the National Council of Real Estate Fiduciaries (NCREIF) in Chicago. The EAI is produced by Evaluation Associates, Inc., in Norwalk, Connecticut.

3. During the period of overlap, the two indexes have a correlation coefficient of 93 percent in their returns.
4. As the EAI does not separate the total return into income and appreciation components, we have used the "cap rates" (defined as net operating income as a fraction of property value) reported for commercial properties by the American Council of Life Insurance (ACLI) to approximate the income return component prior to 1978.
5. See D. Geltner, "Estimating Market Values from Appraised Values Without Assuming an Efficient Market," *Journal of Real Estate Research* 8, no. 3 (Summer 1993), pp. 325–346.
6. Some prior studies, particularly in the academic literature, have relied on the efficient market assumption (i.e., assumed unpredictability, or a presumed lack of correlation across time in the real estate market returns) in order to unsmooth the appraisal-based returns. This may lead to inaccurate unsmoothing if, as is widely believed by practitioners, the private commercial property markets are in fact not informationally efficient (and therefore have returns that are somewhat predictable over time). This issue, and a comparison of a number of unsmoothing methods, is discussed more fully in J. Fisher, D. Geltner, and R.B. Webb, "Value Indexes of Commercial Real Estate: A Comparison of Index Construction Methods," in the *Journal of Real Estate Finance & Economics* 9, no. 2 (September 1994), pp. 137–164.
7. Note that the absolute value levels of the smoothed and unsmoothed indexes are not rigorously comparable. (Both indexes are set arbitrarily to have an average value of 100 during the 1982–1992 decade.) However, this relative calibration of the two indexes agrees with the conventional wisdom that market values were well below appraised values by the early 1990s and with the observation that the commercial property market suffered a severe lack of liquidity at that time. Periods of illiquidity are characterized by market values below appraised values. As most property owners try to avoid selling at less than appraised value, and lenders hesitate to finance property purchases when they do not have confidence in appraised values, the situation is akin to "bid price" falling below "ask price" in a double-auction market, resulting in no trades. Such a circumstance tends to be a regular cyclical occurrence in an informationally inefficient market where price changes have "inertia." Falling market values tend to be followed by more falling values, which given the "backward-looking" perspective of appraisal, tends to cause appraised values to exceed market values on the downswing of the cycle. This then adds to the illiquidity in the private market, which thereby exacerbates the cycle. Once the market "bottoms out" and turns up again, the same dynamics tend to propel the market too high.

8. Letting NOI_t be the NOI level in period t, an index of NOI level over time can be obtained from: $NOI_t = y_t^* V_{t-1}^*$, where: V_{t-1}^* is the appraisal-based property value level (accumulated compounded capital returns up through t-1), and y_t^* is the current income return component from the appraisal-based index for period t. Of course, like any index, this NOI level index will have an arbitrary starting value but will accurately show the relative changes over time in the NOI level. While the return formula definitions in the Russell-NCREIF Index do not permit this index construction method to be formally exact, tests using the (proprietary) actual NOI data in the Russell-NCREIF database have shown that this method produces an index that is virtually identical to an exact index of the actual NOI level (see J. Fisher, "Alternative Measures of Real Estate Performance," *Real Estate Finance* 11, no. 3 (Fall 1994), pp.79–87.
9. Letting y_t represent the true (unsmoothed) income return for calendar year t and V_{t-1} represent the true (unsmoothed) asset value level as of the end of calendar year t-1, we thus have: $y_t = NOI_t / V_{t-1}$. Of course, our constructed indexes actually give the true levels up to a constant multiple, say a NOI_t for the NOI index and bV_t for the asset value index. Thus, we are actually obtaining the series $(a/b)y_t$. We need to determine the constant multiple, (a/b), so we can recover the true y_t series.
10. The NAREIT Index is produced by the National Association of Real Estate Investment Trusts (NAREIT), in Washington, DC. The All-REIT Index is used rather than the Equity REIT Index for two reasons. First, the All-REIT index includes a larger sample of properties and is less distorted by the "health care REITs," which are prominent among the Equity REITs. Second, as we will be removing the "pure debt" (i.e., interest-rate risk-based as opposed to default-risk-based) return component from both sides of the balance sheet by means of the unlevering formula discussed below, there is no reason not to include the mortgage REITs in our sample.
11. The NAREIT Index actually begins in 1972, but its first three years appear anomalous. During the 1972–1974 period, the NAREIT Index was dominated by the bankruptcies of a few large mortgage REITs that were caught in an interest-rate squeeze. For a few years prior to 1972, there had been a frenzy of growth in REITs, with most REITs highly levered with short-term debt, investing the bulk of their assets in long-term mortgages. With the dramatic rise in inflation and short-term interest rates in the 1972–1973 period, a number of large REITs were wiped out, even though the properties that secured the mortgages they held, and indeed the mortgages themselves, were generally still sound. The dramatic impact that these failures and near failures had on the NAREIT Index would not seem to be indicative of the underlying property values that are the focus of the present study.

12. This scaling, accomplished by multiplying each index by a constant, does not affect the implied returns or relative changes in index values across time.
13. Under the efficient market assumption, the annual mean would simply be multiplied by 5, the annual standard deviation would be multiplied by $\sqrt{5}$, and the correlations (with other efficient assets) would remain the same.
14. Note that using rolling five-year moving averages of returns is an invalid way of developing the return statistics required for five-year-horizon investors. *Independent* (i.e., nonoverlapping) five-year interval return statistics are required.
15. Assuming inflation of 4 percent per year, this would be equivalent to nominal annual return targets in the range of 8.5 to 14 percent.
16. Although one hesitates to take the precise numbers from an MPT-based portfolio optimization too literally, the findings reported in Table 15–5 suggest that even investors with overall portfolio real total return targets as low as 4.5 percent per annum would place 7.5 percent of their portfolios in public real estate. This would actually imply a REIT investment slightly smaller, as the asset class we are defining as "public real estate" is "unleveraged REITs," and so in practice would consist of a combination of REIT equity plus bonds. Currently no pension funds have even anywhere near 5 percent of their overall portfolios in REIT shares, and practical considerations would caution against moving too rapidly to increase REIT holdings.

TECHNICAL ENDNOTES

a. Note that we need a historical period with good return statistics not only for private real estate but also for all the other asset classes that will potentially be included in the portfolio because we require the correlation statistics between private real estate and these other asset classes. Thus, we are limited by the 19 years of good available data on public real estate returns, beginning in 1975.

b. A good introductory discussion of serial correlation in regression models, and the procedure employed here, is found in Chapter 6 of R. Pindyck and D. Rubinfeld, *Econometric Models and Economic Forecasts*, 3rd ed. (New York: McGraw-Hill, 1991), pp. 137–147. The market model has been estimated using real (inflation-adjusted) total returns, as these are the types of returns for which our informational efficiency statistical assumptions are most relevant. It should also be noted that the authors tested several alternative specifications of the real estate market model, including the possibility of lags of more than one year. The model described here performed best, and there was no indication of significant further lags in the relationships.

c. The low t-statistics on some of the parameters is also not surprising given the few data points and likely small magnitudes of the true relationships. While the standard errors provided in Table 15–A1 could allow sensitivity analysis to be conducted in the subsequent portfolio analysis, it should be emphasized that the point estimates represented by the estimated parameter values are unbiased and are theoretically the best numbers upon which to base investment decisions.

d. The reader may ask why we do not combine the market model and the real estate model and estimate a single regression, the combination of (3d) and (4c). There are two reasons. First, at a conceptual level these really are two separate and complete models, representing two different perspectives of the same phenomenon (namely, private real estate market returns). The real estate model and regression (4c) is not an "omitted component" from the market model and regression (3d) but represents a different way of "slicing the pie." Second, at a practical level (and related to this conceptual point), if we did combine the two regressions we would expect to have our estimation results severely clouded by the collinearity between the stock market (S&P 500) returns and the public real estate (unleveraged NAREIT) returns, both of which would then be right-hand-side variables in the single regression. This would make it empirically difficult to obtain the information necessary to apply portfolio theory to the five-year return statistics.

e. Again, tests of alternative specifications revealed no additional lags beyond those incorporated in (4c).

f. This follows directly from the definition of return. Working with continuously compounded returns (arithmetic differences of log value levels), five-year-interval returns are just the sum of the five annual returns included in the five-year interval.

g. In practice, we have used the variance implied by equation (6) and the real estate model (4d), as this model produced a better fit to the historical return data, as seen by comparing the R^2s in Tables 15–A1 and 15–A2. However, the variance implied by equation (5) and the market model (3e) is virtually the same, and our portfolio conclusions are robust to this difference.

PART

V

INSTITUTIONAL INVESTOR STRATEGIES

CHAPTER

16

REITs AND INSTITUTIONAL INVESTORS

John F. C. Parsons, *Managing Director, MacGregor Associates*

The recent growth of the real estate investment trust industry has been fueled primarily by institutional investors who have embraced the concept of real estate securities as a complement to the traditional direct forms of property ownership. Real estate operating companies that cater to the needs of these institutional investors have several advantages over their competitors in the capital markets. These benefits include a lower overall cost of capital, full realization of the REIT's enterprise value, reduced pursuit time and cost for raising both debt and equity capital, an increased stability in share price valuation, and long-term relationships that can fulfill multiple objectives for arranging private placements, property venture coinvestments, and property for share exchanges.

THE BENEFITS OF SPONSORSHIP BY INSTITUTIONAL INVESTORS

Real estate operating companies enjoy multiple benefits from creating long-term strategic relationships with institutional investors. Companies that have strong institutional sponsorship receive a superior valuation and a long-term "following" which provide a competitive advantage in the capital market over those firms that lack institutional support.

Institutional sponsorship results in the following key benefits for a real estate operating company:

Lower Cost of Capital

All things considered, the real estate company that has a strong institutional following will benefit from a lower cost of capital than its competitors. Strong ongoing institutional demand for the REIT's common shares will result in a share price premium that reduces the dividend yield and the related cost of equity capital. The same is true for the REIT's cost of debt capital. Those REITs that have a strong following for their mortgage instruments and rated paper will benefit from reduced interest costs. By achieving a lower cost of both equity and debt capital, the REIT management team will also achieve a premium valuation on the corporate enterprise—which fulfills the primary objective for being public.

Share Price Stability

A broad following by institutional investors, especially by pension funds and foreign institutions, tends to lower share price volatility over time. This is because these investors are employing their positions with specific REITs to achieve *long-term* strategic real estate investment objectives rather than short-term trading goals. A REIT that establishes relationships with these long-term investors will benefit from consistent share valuation and avoid the dramatic swings in share price that may occur with those REITs that have a shareholder base comprised predominantly of short-term investors. Against this background, it must be noted that many institutional investors—particularly among the mutual fund peer group—may employ short- to mid-term strategies for REIT shareholdings. These "high rotation" investors must be treated with caution by REIT management teams desiring true long-term relationships with institutional investors.

Consistent Source of Expansion Capital

Once the real estate operating company achieves a following with a peer group of long-term institutional investors, these investors can generally be relied upon for future capital-raising events, provided the REIT fulfills its strategic objectives and meets investor expectations. The ability to consistently raise capital from the same peer group of long-term investors reduces both the time required and the costs incurred for future capital markets activities.

Multiple Transactions

A REIT that has a relationship with a large institutional investor is well positioned to complete several types of transactions with this investor. As indicated in Figure 16–1, these transactions can include having the institution participate in a direct placement of common shares, a spot secondary offering, a portfolio joint venture where the institution may share direct ownership in an individual asset or portfolio, or a transaction where the

FIGURE 16–1

Transaction Preferences for the Universe of REIT Institutional Investors

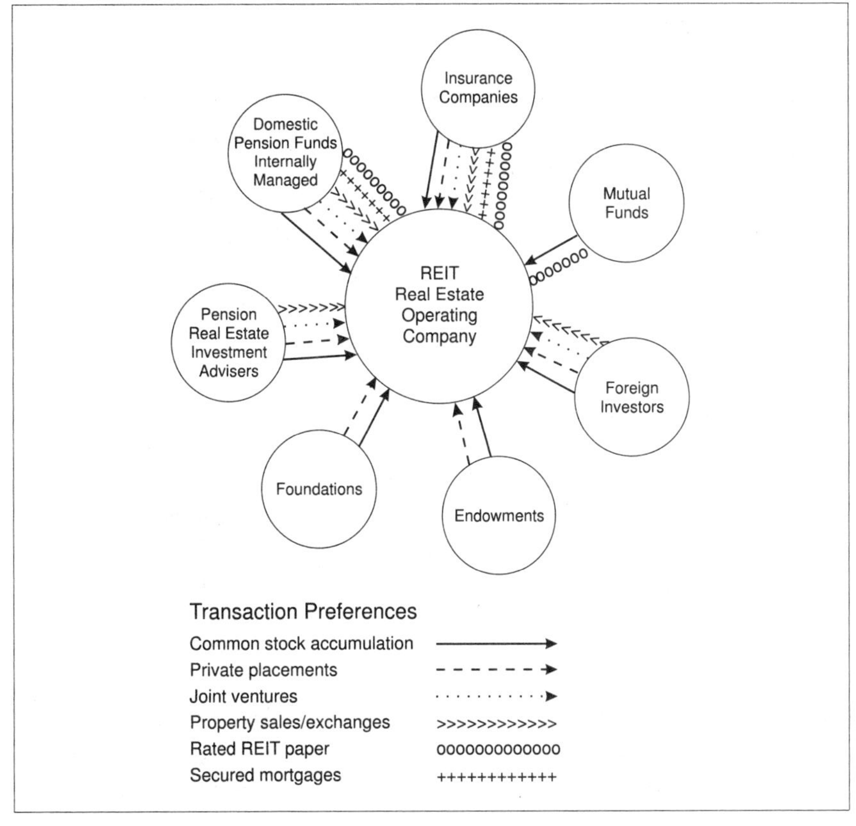

institution may exchange a direct property interest for shares. Additionally, many large institutions—particularly insurance companies—are candidates to invest in REIT debt offerings as well as equities. There is clearly a multiple payoff for REITs that are closely aligned with institutions capable of these transactions.

The "Lead Steer" Effect

REITs that can generate sponsorship from an initial select group of institutional investors often benefit from follow-on support from other institutions that are more comfortable following the lead of their institutional peers. Those REITs that commonly receive sponsorship from a few sophisticated investors usually benefit from additional investors who follow the lead of their institutional brethren. This process can occur quickly—within a few months—as institutional investors usually embrace a REIT as a group.

Source of Acquisitions

REITs that cater to the institutional community are also catering to a primary source of "investable" equity real estate for years to come. This is particularly true of those REITs that target large pension funds, life insurance companies, and foreign investors that are considering strategies for converting directly held real estate equities into securitized form. An important strategy for these large institutional investors is to exchange their directly held property interests into shares of those REITs that are appropriate buyers. A preexisting relationship between the REIT and the institution obviously facilitates the completion of these types of acquisitions.[1]

Long-Term Relationships

Generally speaking, the key senior decision makers at a large institution tend to remain in their roles for many years. This enables the REIT management team to develop close working relationships and personal ties with the key decision makers. Although these relationships take time to foster, the REITs that build these ties are rewarded with a long-term payoff through multiple transactions with the same executive team at the institution. These relationships also facilitate the speed of future transactions with the institution.

Peer Group Relationships

As the real estate operating company expands its universe of institutional investors, the peer group of investors also expands. Over time, these investors become part of the "team" of institutional followers, which lend long-term support to the REIT enterprise. This group of peers effectively become comarketers of the REIT's investment story and overall business plan, thereby encouraging additional investors to join the team.

INSTITUTIONAL TRANSACTIONS

REIT management teams pursue several objectives as they establish close relationships with institutional investors. These objectives include the accumulation of the REIT's common shares by institutional investors, the direct placement of common or preferred stock, and property joint ventures and acquisitions. Many of these transaction strategies are described elsewhere in this book, such as in Chapter 17 on pension fund REIT investing by John Imboden and Kevin Stahlman of Ohio Teachers, and Chapter 8 which describes insurance company REIT investments by Eugene Skaggs and Robert Ruess of Northwestern Mutual Life. Here we briefly summarize the types of transactions that fundamentally arise from close relationships with large institutional investors such as these.

Open Market Accumulation of Common Shares

The most fundamental transaction for an existing public real estate operating company is to have large institutional investors begin to accumulate sizable positions in the company's common shares through open market purchases. These purchases are generally made subsequent to one-on-one presentations by the REIT to the institutional investor and its team of decision makers responsible for real estate securities. Over time, through open market purchases, it is possible for a large institutional investor to accumulate sizable positions in a particular REIT, say 5 percent of the common stock. By regularly reviewing the 90-day SEC mandated 13-f institutional investor shareholding reports, a REIT management team can monitor its progress with these large institutional investors.

Private Placements

Once an institutional investor is familiar with a particular REIT, its strategy for growth and profitability, and its management team, the investor may consider the arrangement of a direct placement of common stock or preferred stock. Typically, these placements can be as large as $100 million[2] or as small as $3 million for investors who may participate in a placement syndicate. The advantages to the REIT in arranging this form of equity placement include the ability to raise capital relatively quickly and inexpensively vis-à-vis a secondary offering by Wall Street underwriters. The REIT typically avoids any negative announcement effect from a follow-on offering, and the investor commonly receives a meaningful discount in the price of the shares acquired, generally reflecting a share in the savings from a Wall Street offering—say in the range of 3 percent of the then-current share price quoted on the public exchange. In certain cases, the institutional investor may also commit to a so-called lockout period[3] whereby it agrees not to sell the stock acquired in the placement for a specified holding period. This lockout period is often in the range of one year subsequent to the closing.

REITs may employ several methods for completing variations of the private placement concept. For example, a private placement with one large investor can be undertaken concurrent with a broader public offering of the REIT's common stock. In this manner, the institutional investor can benefit from the preparation of the prospectus used in the secondary offering.

Finally, the REIT may elect to arrange a so-called *spot secondary* offering with an investment bank.[4] Under this arrangement, an investment bank acting as a principal will acquire a large block of common shares from a REIT and instantaneously sell these securities to a group of knowledgeable investors who are seeking to expand their current shareholdings in the REIT. The spot secondary enables the REIT to raise capital in a cost-effective manner and distribute the stock through its investment bankers to investors who are already committed to the REIT's long-term success. The spot secondary also enables institutional investors to acquire the shares of the REIT in reasonably large increments, say in the range of $3 million to $5 million.

Joint-Venture Transactions

Since the largest institutional investors continue to have capital for investing in direct forms of equity real estate—such as the ownership of regional malls and CBD office buildings—these investors maintain their appetite for direct property ownership. However, to access the typical high caliber of management that resides in most good real estate operating companies, many of these investors will consider transactions whereby direct ownership of a large asset or portfolio of properties is jointly held by the institution and by the REIT. This sharing of ownership can be accomplished on a 50/50 basis or some other mutually agreeable equity split.[5] There are several benefits to property joint ventures. The benefits to the REIT include the ability to avoid concentration risk in a particularly large asset or portfolio, the ability to generate a high return on equity through management fees on the nonowned portion, and the ability to compete for large acquisitions. The benefits to the joint-venture partner include the ability to work with the best management team available and the possible conversion at a future date into the real estate operating company stock as an exit strategy.

Many variants to the joint-venture tactic are surfacing as the REIT market grows. To date, joint ventures have been employed by REITs for development activities, for off balance sheet portfolios, and for a number of large property transactions—especially among REITs concentrating in regional mall investments.[6] Joint-venture activity is likely to expand in concert with the capitalization of the REIT industry, especially in the mall and office property categories, which represent the most capital-intensive sectors of the REIT market.

Property Acquisitions

The natural supply of investable real estate for REITs continues to be sourced from the pension funds, insurance companies, and foreign investors that are seeking an exit from their directly held equity positions. REITs that have preexisting relationships with the institutional community will benefit from an early knowledge of acquirable product and from close relationships with the key decision makers at each institutional seller.[7]

Debt Instruments/REIT Paper and Medium-Term Note Programs

Similar to equity financings, REITs with close relationships to institutional buyers of fixed-income instruments can benefit from cost savings and transaction speed of direct placements of REIT paper and medium-term notes. The typical purchaser of these instruments are the large insurance companies and mutual fund complexes that are investing in traditional fixed-income vehicles.[8]

THE BROAD SPECTRUM OF INSTITUTIONAL INVESTORS

With the tremendous growth in the REIT market, the term *institutional* has come to mean any large investor that manages equities and fixed-income investments for its own account or as a fiduciary for third parties. In the old days, the term *institutional real estate investor* connoted an investor that made direct investments in real estate assets and mortgages. Two worlds—the institutional stock and bond world and the institutional real estate world—have now overlapped, leading to a much broader definition of the so-called institutional market. Against this background, the most critical success factor in a REIT's institutional investor program is an appreciation for the differences among the various types of institutional investors and the nuances employed by each institution in its management of real estate securities.

For purposes of strategic planning by the REIT management team, it is critical to establish a distinction among the various types of institutional investors since they each have differing views about employing real estate securities in their investment portfolio and, consequently, have differences in investment management styles. Broadly speaking, the universe of REIT investors can be decomposed into the key groups found in Figure 16–2, which are evident on the quarterly SEC 13-F filings made by institutional investors.[9]

FIGURE 16–2

REIT Institutional Investors
Simon DeBartolo Group

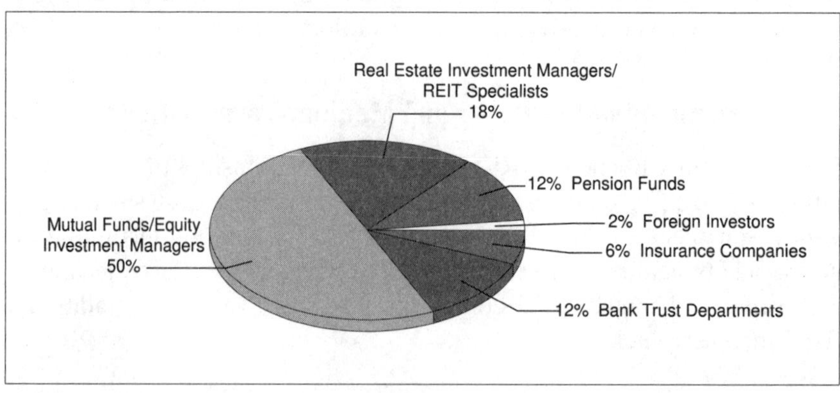

Source: Technemetrics/Bloomberg—January 14, 1997, MacGregor Associates

Mutual Funds

Mutual fund complexes are by far the largest category of REIT investors, having been active in real estate securities management for high growth and income objectives and for specialized portfolios managed for individual investors seeking exposure to the real estate industry. These mutual fund investors are notable for their rather rapid style of buy/sell decisions based on corporate fundamentals rather than specific insights developed from years of direct real estate equity investing. The decision-making framework and information flow at mutual funds tends to be focused on very concise presentations, and the dollars committed to a particular REIT are limited to the amount of capital available from an investor seeking prudent diversification. These investors require clear, concise presentations of a particular REIT's investment strategy, which is then viewed in the context of the REIT's industry peer group.

Among institutional real estate investors, the mutual fund complexes tend to have relatively high levels of stock rotation within their respective portfolios. Commonly, 30 to 50 percent of the REIT portfolio can be traded within a year. For REIT management teams, this suggests there is a reasonable probability that current shares held by a mutual fund complex today may be sold in one of the next three years. The reasons for the relatively high rotation by the mutual fund is to reap gains made from intelligent stock selection and continually post strong performance for the clients of the mutual fund.

Unlike other institutional REIT investors, mutual funds investing in REITs are not typically candidates for large, direct private placements due to their need for diversification. And since mutual funds never were direct investors in real estate, they also lack the potential for property ventures and property-for-share exchanges. However, they are the most critical peer group for establishing daily valuation of REIT shares. REIT management teams must be cognizant of this role as they make strides to foster relationships with other long-term institutional investors—such as the pension funds and insurance companies—which have a much longer history of traditional real estate investing.

Real Estate Investment Advisers

The passage of the Employment Retirement Income Securities Act in 1974 spawned a large community of real estate investment advisers that have traditionally provided investment management services to public and corporate pension funds and foundations and endowments. Since 1991, the majority of these advisers have acquired or internally developed investment management capabilities for real estate securities. Today, virtually all of the large traditional real estate investment managers are providing specialized services for real estate securities. These services generally take the form of offering research-driven investment strategy using broad themes for investing across the various national geographic markets and the various core property types—office, industrial, retail, and apartments—plus specialty real estate such as hotels, self-storage, net lease, and health care.

In addition to providing traditional services for diversified portfolio management, these real estate advisers are also capable of and interested in acting for their pension clients to complete structured forms of private placements, property joint ventures, and property-for-share exchanges. Generally, a special team of executives is employed by the advisers to complete these types of large, complex transactions. These REIT teams ensure that the adviser maintains confidentiality through a high "Chinese Wall," which separates the information flow from its "direct" real estate practice, such that active trading by the real estate securities specialists is not restricted by the provision of inside information that commonly arises from the complex direct real estate transactions.

To date, the majority of large transactions involving traditional real estate investment managers have been of a value-added nature, whereby advisers have deployed their client capital in pursuit of high-yield special situations with REITs. Over time, we predict that these real estate advisers will advance into more traditional forms of private placements in common stock as their clients use REITs to fulfill core investment objectives.

Foreign Investors

Approximately 5 to 10 percent of the common shares of the largest institutionally favored U.S. REITs are held by foreign investors who are attracted to the companies for their solid holdings of real estate, their fine management, current dividend income, and growth prospects and liquidity. To date, the most active foreign investors in the U.S. REIT market have been Dutch institutions. Through a special tax treaty arranged between the U.S. and Dutch governments, investors in Holland are able to repatriate their quarterly dividend income without paying the typical withholding tax levied on income generated from holdings of direct equity real estate. This tax provision is extremely attractive to Dutch investors, who have been accumulating REIT shares during the recent IPOs and secondary offerings, and through large private placements.

In addition to Dutch investors, investors from Germany, the United Kingdom, and France are becoming more active in the U.S. market. Institutional investors from these western European countries are displaying an increasing appetite for U.S. real estate securities as a complement to their existing directly held portfolios. Investors from the Pacific Rim are also becoming increasingly active. Additionally, Canadian institutions have plans to enter the U.S. REIT market as a strategy to access American real estate far more simply than by acquiring properties directly.

REIT management teams that cater to the foreign community typically work with the largest investors directly—in locations such as Amsterdam—as well as with U.S.-based investment management representatives of the foreign entity. A comprehensive discussion of the global market for real estate securities is provided in Chapter 18 by Fiduciary Trust Company International.

Insurance Companies

REITs have become an integral part of the real estate investment strategy at most insurance companies. Domestic insurance companies have grown to become major participants in the real estate investment trust industry, second only to mutual funds. There are several ways in which an insurance company may participate with REITs. These activities are more fully described in Chapter 8 prepared by Eugene Skaggs and Robert Ruess of Northwestern Mutual Life.

Fundamentally, insurance companies invest in REITs through open market accumulation of shares and private equity placements, as well as through traditional first mortgage positions and rated REIT paper. Interestingly, those large insurance companies that are active have extremely large portfolios of REIT investments vis-à-vis the mutual funds. Additionally, most insurance companies in the United States are executing strategies to reduce their direct holdings of equity real estate in order to better comply with risk-based capital rules adopted by the insurance industry. Many insurance companies have been actively selling large portfolios of real estate to REITs. In certain cases, the insurance company has arranged mortgage financing for these portfolio sales or exchanged a partial interest for shares in the REIT.

For all REITs, insurance companies represent high-priority investor candidates because of their ability to accumulate common shares, participate in private placements of common and preferred stock, arrange mortgage financings, acquire rated REIT paper, and sell assets. Because these diverse activities generally involve several executives at the insurance company, it is critical for the REIT management team to maintain multiple contacts within the insurance company. For example, at a large insurance company, there will likely be several portfolio managers, one handling common shares, one handling preferred shares, and one handling fixed-income portfolio management. The management team of the REIT will benefit by fostering close relationships with each of these executives.

Pension Plan Sponsors

The community of domestic pension plan sponsors is an extremely important sector of the institutional REIT market since it has historically represented the lion's share of annual investment in direct real estate. Currently, the U.S. pension plan sponsors are estimated to own approximately $130 billion to $140 billion of direct real estate equities. In contrast, we estimate that the pension plan sponsor community currently owns approximately $5 billion of U.S. REITs, exclusive of any venture interests.

The majority of large pension plan sponsors have now entered the REIT market. At this writing, 28 of the top 50 pension funds in the United States have participated in programs to accumulate common shares in private placements, in property joint ventures, or in property-for-share exchanges with REITs.[10] Pension plan sponsors represent between 10 and 15 percent of the institutional market for REITs. This level of participation is expected to grow rapidly, however, as the pension funds build on their current portfolios, new funds enter the market, and the traditional real estate pension advisers expand their operations for REIT securities management.

The so-called pension fund market can be described as having four basic constituent groups: (1) public funds, which include the large state employee and teacher retirement systems, (2) corporate funds, (3) foundations, and (4) endowments. Public funds dominate the market: 32 of the top 50 pension funds are state or teacher retirement systems. The vast majority of the capital available for investment in real estate generally, and REITs specifically, reside with those pension funds that represent the states with the largest populations, including California, New York, Ohio, Michigan, Florida, and Pennsylvania. These funds have long histories of making investments in real estate, and many have led the way in entering the REIT market. The following chapter prepared by the State Teachers Retirement

System of Ohio fully describes how this $30 billion fund employs REITs in its investment strategy for real estate.

Corporate pension plans are also major participants in the market for real estate investment trusts. Historically, these funds have acquired direct real estate investments through internally managed programs, separate account advisers, and investments in commingled real estate vehicles. Recently, many of these corporate funds have initiated programs for REITs as a complement to their direct real estate portfolios. Commonly, a corporate plan will elect to use the services of an experienced real estate investment manager that has a REIT capability.

Foundations and endowments generally represent a much smaller segment of the institutional real estate market. These funds typically have total portfolios less than $5 billion, which although quite large, prevent the funds from acquiring major holdings in a particular individual property or individual REIT. However, many foundations and endowments have initiated programs to invest in real estate operating companies as an attractive alternative to their former strategy of direct real estate ownership through individual properties or commingled funds.

Perspectives of the Pension Fund Investor Toward REITs

Through our continual contacts with the largest pension real estate investors, we have identified several common perspectives about the use of real estate securities. These perspectives are as follows:

REITs Are an Important Member of the Family of Pension Investments

At this stage in the development of the pension real estate market, the large plan sponsors clearly view real estate securities as a complement to direct real estate investment programs. Essentially, REITs are the newest member of the family of available real estate investments—which has to date been dominated by directly held properties, separate accounts and commingled funds managed by traditional real estate investment managers, opportunity-style ventures, and mortgage investments. This perspective has extremely important ramifications for REITs seeking to establish new relationships with pension funds since the funds must be convinced that the new REIT relationship plays a complementary role to its existing real estate portfolio.

Magnitude of Real Estate Securities Program

Typically, a small but significant portion of each pension investor's total real estate portfolio is allocated for investments in real estate securities. The investor's REIT initiatives are commonly measured as a percentage of the overall real estate program. Against this background, many of the active pension plan sponsors are targeting for REITs to represent a future range of 5 to 30 percent of their total real estate investment portfolio.

Multiple Motivations

During the course of our continuous investor research, plan sponsors have stressed that they have five basic motivations for their REIT initiatives. These motivations include the desire to (i) acquire attractive real estate, (ii) achieve strong current returns, (iii) work with experienced management teams that can grow the income stream, (iv) use REITs to serve the traditional goals for diversification, and (v) act as a hedge against inflation in a fashion similar to direct real estate investments.

As REITs prepare their initiatives to build close relationships with the institutional community, it is important that they cater to these multiple motivations of the investors rather than overemphasize any one motivation. For example, many of the early attempts at forming relationships with pension funds by REITs were rather sophomoric since they overemphasized only the "growth" aspect of the investment story to the exclusion of other key attributes, such as current income and portfolio quality. Typically, the growth story was better suited for the mutual fund complexes, which based their investment decision on this key fundamental. This caused many REITs to give "mutual fund" presentations to the pension funds—with little success. The pension funds for years had been acquiring property for other reasons besides "growth," namely for location, management, and current income. For this reason, a balanced presentation to a pension fund that addresses all of the REIT's qualities works best with these savvy real estate investors.

Decision Making by Real Estate Staff

For large pension funds, the real estate staff typically handles decision making, not the equity desk, presumably because the investors hold the view that the performance of REITs is predominantly determined by real estate fundamentals. Among the top 50 pension plan sponsors, as of this writing, four out of five handle decision making for real estate securities within the framework of direct real estate equity investments; the balance of plan sponsors manage real estate securities through their equity operations.[11]

Trustee Support of the Use of Real Estate Securities

A key element for moving forward with an individual REIT initiative at the pension fund is the support of chief investment officers and trustees. In order to launch the REIT program, support from senior management is key. Increasingly, senior pension officers are encouraging the use of real estate securities. This is due in large measure to their general comfort with the securities instrument vis-à-vis direct real estate holdings, as well as favorable experiences with recently constructed REIT portfolios.

Performance Expectations

As the relative newcomer in the world of pension real estate investing, REITs are being watched carefully for their overall performance. Certainly, most pension fund investors are operating with the perspective that REITs must outperform or at least match the financial performance that is anticipated from each investor's large portfolio of direct real estate holdings. Generally speaking, as of this writing, pension fund investors are targeting REITs to achieve annual returns in the range of 12 percent, generated through a combination of current dividend yield and earnings growth.

Transferring Experience for Risk Management

As REIT programs get under way at each pension fund, there appears to be a benefit in transferring investing experience to the real estate department from other departments of the institution that have a history in capital markets behavior and long track records in special areas such as private placements with publicly traded companies. Many of the "new" issues of today's REIT world, such as structuring private placements, have been dealt with extensively in other fields of pension investing outside of real estate.

Use of Private Placements

Nearly two-thirds of the 28 large pension funds now active with real estate securities plan to participate in the market using private placements.[12] These pension funds will act directly or through advisers to use private placements as a vehicle to take positions in specific operating companies.

Use of Coinvestments

One-third of the large plan sponsors currently investing in real estate securities also have experience coinvesting in specific properties and portfolios alongside real estate operating company partners.[13] In certain cases, these coinvestments were inherited from previous development company partners that elected to go public. In other instances, the pension funds have made new investments in portfolios whereby the REIT acts as a coinvestor and management agent for the portfolio. These types of relationships provide the REIT with an ability to acquire larger portfolios as well as boost their return on equity through the management income generated from the institutionally controlled portion of the venture.

CHALLENGES FOR INSTITUTIONAL INVESTORS

While pension fund participation in the REIT industry has been growing rapidly, there remain a number of challenges for these investors. These challenges include:

Market Size

At $100 billion, the equity capital market for REITs remains relatively small for an immediate large-scale push by the major pension funds into the REIT format. For this reason, over the short term, real estate securities are not likely to replace the role played by direct format real estate investments. As the market grows, however, these institutions are poised to commit additional capital to the REIT community provided their expectations for investment performance are met by the industry participants. For this reason, REIT executives are well served by remaining patient and consistent in their programs to foster long-term relationships with the pension community.[14]

Liquidity

The large pension investors are sanguine about the prospects for liquidity of REITs. Currently, the vast majority of REITs are relatively thinly traded. Against this background, pension real estate professionals are concerned that large positions in REITs are not as liquid as might have been originally believed. A decision to rebalance a REIT portfolio by selling shares needs to be weighed against the effect a sale of a large block of shares may have on price. Upon reflection, there is a sense among some members of the pension community that the liquidity of a large block of REIT shares may be comparable to the liquidity of a direct real estate investment—all things considered. However, it is interesting that this viewpoint does not appear to diminish the pension investor's appetite for real estate securities. Rather, the benefit of liquidity appears to rank behind the benefits of investing in solid real estate, aligning with a strong management team, earning excellent yields, and participating in the long-term growth of a real estate company.

Underwriting the Management Team

Pension fund investors have grown to appreciate the need for thoroughly evaluating the REIT management team prior to selecting a stock. A key lesson learned during the REIT IPO boom has been that companies that have apparently solid portfolios of real estate may falter due to management's inability to properly handle the operational aspects of running a public company. Going forward, the underwriting of REIT management teams by pension funds and their advisers will be much more rigorous, akin to the aggressive underwriting process now used in the selection of real estate pension investment advisers.

Measuring Performance

Pension investors appear to share a concern that there remains a need for broader acceptance of the NAREIT Index and other forms of performance measurement. As confidence grows in these measurement tools, the capital committed to real estate securities is projected to accelerate.

REITs in the Context of Pension Portfolio Management Techniques

In the current market environment, many pension professionals have expressed a need for additional research and analytical work that places REITs in the context of overall real estate investing and the business of stock and bond investment management. This future research will be instrumental in educating chief investment officers, trustees, and investment staff as to the appropriate role to be played by REITs. Currently, there does not appear to be a mutually agreed-upon paradigm for the role of REITs in the context of a large institutional investment portfolio, although recent research is building support for the implementation of REIT strategies.[15]

INSTITUTIONAL MARKETING STRATEGIES

As a REIT management team considers formulating its strategy for fostering and maintaining close working relationships within the pension plan sponsor community, two tenets guide the most successful institutional marketing programs:

- Institutional marketing strategy for the REIT must be driven by the unique real estate investment strategies of the target institutional investors.
- Institutional real estate investor strategies for REIT investments are a function of real estate portfolio size, yield requirements, staff levels for real estate, and the philosophy for internal versus external management.

REIT Investment Styles

For purposes of executing an institutional investor marketing strategy by a REIT, pension plan sponsors can be categorized as having five distinct investment styles as they advance with their individual programs for real estate securities. These styles are as follows: *strategic, diversified, value-oriented, sector-oriented,* and *index-oriented.* Additionally, it should be noted that multiple REIT investment styles may be pursued by the pension plan sponsor within the overall framework of the strategy for equity real estate investment. The current breakdown of the primary REIT investment styles of the 28 active U.S. pension funds is as follows:[16]

Strategic	46%
Diversified	35%
Value-oriented	11%
Sector-oriented	4%
Index-oriented	4%

Against this background, a convenient way to analyze the REIT investment styles of the universe of large pension funds is to compare their investment philosophy with their portfolio size and general type of organization for pension real estate investment management. The investment style chosen for real estate securities is normally a function of the size of the overall real estate portfolio, the number of internal real estate staff members, and the experience level of the plan sponsor's real estate department.

Internal versus External Management

Some pension investors are acting directly with internal staff for their REIT initiatives, while others are working in concert with members of the real estate advisory community. Also, some investors are approaching the

FIGURE 16–3

Pension Plan Sponsor

REIT Investment Styles Are a Function of Portfolio Size, Staffing, and Experience

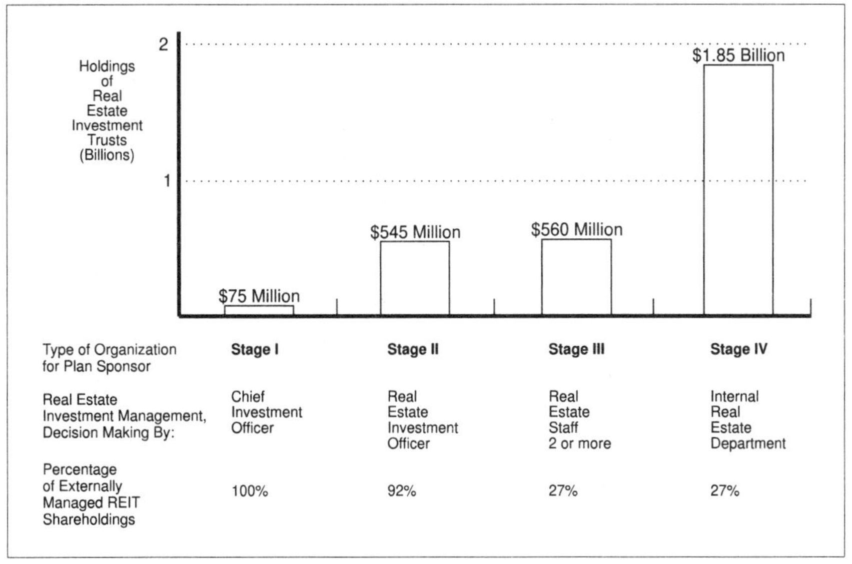

Type of Organization for Plan Sponsor	Stage I	Stage II	Stage III	Stage IV
Real Estate Investment Management, Decision Making By:	Chief Investment Officer	Real Estate Investment Officer	Real Estate Staff 2 or more	Internal Real Estate Department
Percentage of Externally Managed REIT Shareholdings	100%	92%	27%	27%

Source: MacGregor Associates

market by investing in a diverse basket of REIT names, while others prefer investing in a few names that can be closely monitored. Each investor appears to approach their REIT program slightly differently by tailoring the activities to fit within their general real estate program and overall portfolio management activities. Every institutional investor has special characteristics, a unique set of trustees and staff, and a slightly different perspective toward perceived risks of real estate and real estate securities. At this stage in the development of the REIT pension market, approximately 65 percent of the capital invested by the top 50 funds is internally managed.

At the largest strategically oriented public pension funds, the investment management function for real estate securities is commonly handled internally (see Figure 16–3). Plan sponsors pursuing a diversified approach for real estate securities typically engage the services of an experienced real estate securities manager. In select cases, a plan sponsor may invest using internal staff for strategic investments while also using an external adviser to execute a diversified strategy.

A complex set of strategic and organizational factors converge as each institution makes its own decision to press forward with the use of REITs. These factors must be well understood by the REIT management team in advance of proceeding with a program to form a relationship with a particular investor.

CHALLENGES FOR INSTITUTIONAL MARKETING

As the size of the REIT capital market expands, pension funds and other institutional investors are well positioned to expand their portfolios such that REITs may become as much as a third of their annual investment allocation toward real estate. However, several challenges remain to be addressed by all participants in the REIT industry, including the need for more aggressive underwriting strategies by investors, the need for broad acceptance of an industry performance measure, and the need for additional research to educate the investment community about the role of REITs in the context of broader portfolio management issues.

For the REIT management teams, the following challenges must be met to achieve success in the institutional marketing effort:

- Unique marketing strategies must be executed for each investor.
- Long lead times must be sustained. REITs will be required to make several contacts over many months to be rewarded with an investment commitment. In forming the relationship, lead times in excess of one year are not uncommon in the pension industry.
- The institutional marketing program must provide for both frequency and consistency in conveying the REIT's strategy to the investing organization.
- The institutional marketing process can be expensive due to the time and travel requirements for national marketing campaigns, supporting research, and for the one-on-one meetings necessary to generate a commitment from the institutional investor. These costs can be mitigated through the use of knowledgeable third-party advisers to facilitate investor targeting and regular contact.
- The REIT management team must be well organized to ensure the company maintains focus on the core business while simultaneously engaging in a continuing program to foster relationships with the institutional investor community.

Strategies for Forming Institutional Relationships

Those REITs that excel at catering to the institutional investor marketplace have adopted the following strategies:

Focused Investment Strategy

The fundamental attractiveness of any real estate operating company is the ability of the management team to develop, execute, and clearly describe its overall long-term investment strategy to investors.

Vision

The REIT's top management, particularly the chairman and CEO, frequently communicate their overall five-year vision for their sector of the industry.[18] Their corporate strategy for real estate investments is then presented to investors within an overall industry framework, not in isolation. This visionary ability truly distinguishes the leading REITs in the institutional real estate world.

Control of the Story

The best REIT management teams have control of their own investment story, rather than relying entirely on the investment banking community, real estate advisers, or other consultants to communicate their message. These parties are, however, critical in a supporting role.[17]

Frequent Contact

Every attempt is made to have regular, face-to-face contact with the largest investors to ensure they develop a personal bond with the REIT management team and are positioned for multiple transactions over time. This is accomplished by frequent visits to the investor's office, at least twice a year, complemented by conference participation and additional off-site meetings where industry knowledge and company strategy are discussed among the peer group of institutional investors.

Respect for Staff

The best institutional marketing programs are staff focused, such that the real estate professionals at the investing institution are treated with the utmost courtesy and respect and are provided with all of the information they need to generate their own internal reports to proceed with the investment decision. A common mistake among many senior real estate executives is to flaunt relationships with trustees or other senior officials to the exclusion of the real estate staff at the investing institution.

Institutional "Behavior"

As the REIT advances with its marketing program to the stage of actually meeting with the institutional investors, it is critical that the senior executives of the REIT come prepared with a comprehensive presentation, not just their business cards. These investors expect to receive a well-organized presentation. They also place a high value on their time, so the meetings must start promptly and be focused and to the point. Finally, the REIT team must be prepared to give all of its attention to the investor and its needs as the meeting progresses. The interruption of such meetings to receive an unrelated fax document or to make a cellular phone call can be fatal to the cause. These investors expect and deserve better treatment.[19]

Three-Pronged Approach

Fundamentally, a REIT's institutional marketing program should be comprised of three basic components: (1) a direct campaign targeted at pension funds that handle investment management internally, (2) an adviser/consultant-oriented campaign that is oriented toward the real estate investment management community, and (3) a continuing dialogue with the mutual funds and REIT analysts that drive day-to-day share price.

SUMMARY

Great rewards await those REIT management teams that adopt formal programs for fostering and maintaining relationships with institutional investors. The key aspects of a successful institutional strategy are a focused business philosophy, consistency and frequency in the contacts with each investor, a strategy to address the unique investment goals and organizational design of the target investors, and multiple activities to satisfy the nuances of the mutual funds, insurance companies, foreign investors, and the various types of pension funds and their advisers and consultants that comprise the complex world we refer to as the institutional market for real estate investment trusts.

ENDNOTES

1. Taubman Centers acquired the 75 percent interest in Fairlane Town Center previously held by a pension fund partner, leaving Taubman Realty Group with 100 percent ownership of the 1.5-million-square-foot regional shopping center. Company Announcement, July 19, 1996.
2. Simon Property Group completed a $100 million private equity placement with Algemeen Burgerlijk Pensioenfunds (ABP), the DFL $185 billion general pension fund for the public employees of the Netherlands. Company Announcement, October 30, 1995.
3. CenterPoint Properties Corporation completed a $50 million private placement with an institutional investor. The equity placement was initially structured as nonvoting preferred stock that automatically converted on a share-for-share basis to nonvoting common, upon shareholder approval at the company's next annual meeting. The dividend on the nonvoting shares was *parri passu* with, but equal to, 103 percent of the dividend paid to the voting common shares of the company. After three years, the shares are convertible to voting common shares on a share-for-share basis up to 4.9 percent of the company's then outstanding voting shares with all shares to fully convert within 10 years. As the shares convert to voting common, the dividend paid is the same as all other voting common shares. The new stock was issued at a price of $22 per share net to the company, which was the average closing price of the company's common stock over the 10-day period prior to pricing. Company Announcement, September 21, 1995.
4. Urban Shopping Centers, Inc., completed a $75 million offering of 3 million shares of common stock sold through Lehman Brothers. Company Announcement, November 25, 1996.
5. Simon DeBartolo Group acquired Smith Haven Mall, a major superregional mall in Long Island, NY. Simon DeBartolo Group manages the 1.4-million-square-foot Smith Haven Mall and owns 25 percent of the property, which was sold by Prudential Real Estate Investors Separate Account, known as PRISA. An institutional investor, represented by New York-based UBS Asset Management, owns the balance. Company Announcement, December 28, 1995.
6. General Growth Properties acquired Homart Development Co. from Sears, Roebuck and Co. for $1.85 billion. The acquisition of the Homart regional mall portfolio was made by a corporation formed by General Growth Properties, which invested approximately $200 million for a 38

percent ownership interest. The other investors in this corporation included the New York State Common Retirement Fund, through its investment adviser Jones Lang Wootton Realty Advisors, the Equitable Life Insurance Company of Iowa, USG Annuity & Life Company, and The Trustees of the University of Pennsylvania. In addition, General Growth Properties acquired Natick Mall for $265 million from Sears. Company Announcement, December 26, 1995.

7. Beacon Properties acquired Presidents Plaza, a 791,000-square-foot office complex located in Chicago, from Metropolitan Life Insurance Co. for $77 million. Dow Jones, January 6, 1997.
8. TriNet Corporate Realty Trust sold $150 million of notes in a two-part debt offering by J.P. Morgan Securities. Company Announcement, May 17, 1996.
9. Simon DeBartolo Group 13F Report. Technemetrics/Bloomberg, January 14, 1997.
10. MacGregor Associates Fourth Quarter 1996 Report—Pension Fund Trends with Real Estate Investment Trusts.
11. *Ibid.*
12. *Ibid.*
13. *Ibid.*
14. Please see Foreword by Sam Zell.
15. See Chapter 12—"Historical Performance of REIT Returns: A Capital Markets Perspective," Chapter 13—"The Historical Behavior of REIT Returns: A Real Estate Perspective," and Chapter 15—"Public and Private Real Estate: Performance Implications for Asset Allocation."
16. MacGregor Associates Fourth Quarter 1996 Report—Pension Fund Trends with Real Estate Investment Trusts.
17. See Chapter 11—"Investor Relations."
18. See Chapter 6—"CEO's Perspective."
19. Halpern, Philip, *Marketing Institutional Money Management Services.* (Burr Ridge, IL: Irwin Professional Publishing, 1995).

CHAPTER

17

REIT INVESTMENT STRATEGY

The Pension Fund Perspective

Ohio State Teachers Retirement System
John K. Imboden, *Director, Real Estate Assets*
Kevin E. Stahlman, *Director, Southern Region Real Estate Investments*

INTRODUCTION

The use of REIT stocks within a real estate portfolio is something that STRSO, (State Teachers Retirement System of Ohio) has been actively involved with since the fall of 1993. Our REIT investments exceed $300 million and currently represent 9 percent of our $3.4 billion real estate portfolio. This chapter consists of three major components. In the first section, we discuss several investment issues that set the stage for real estate and REIT investment decisions. In the second section, we discuss ways we have used REIT stocks to fulfill our investment objectives. In the third section, we explore additional ways we have considered using REIT stocks.

INVESTMENT ISSUES

In discussing the potential role(s) REITs might fill in a pension portfolio, the first point to understand is that the pension fund community is very diverse. Whether a fund is private or public, asset portfolio size, liability structure, funding status, and management experience all have an impact on the pension fund's investment objectives and strategy. This section will explore these differences and how they set the stage for real estate and REIT investment decisions.

Public pension fund investment policies are typically constrained to some extent by legislation from the applicable governmental entity. When the public fund's governing statutes most closely resemble a corporate fund, these restrictions are often patterned after ERISA's "prudent person" guidelines. In essence, prudent person rules view investments in a portfolio context that allow a reasonable risk exposure on individual investments so long as the overall portfolio risk level lies within acceptable limits. At the other end of the regulatory spectrum, some funds are restricted to securities that meet specific tests in terms of consecutive quarters of dividend payout. With the majority of current REIT market capitalization coming public in the last few years, some funds may actually be prohibited from buying several current issues until a longer track record has been established. Other restrictions limit private-market investments outside the governing jurisdiction or some other "nonmarket" parameter.

Beyond these legislative restrictions, public pension funds may have other significant differences from private funds on an individual sponsor basis. Typically, public funds have had more stable and predictable liability structures and a growing asset base. This point has been emphasized in recent years as many private corporate plans in mature industries have had to deal with the effect of downsizing in the workforce and early retirement programs on unfunded liabilities. Thus far, few public funds have had to go through this experience. There are important implications for asset allocation when liability duration is (or has the potential to become) significantly shortened. In general, shorter liability structures should be matched with assets with shorter duration. Real estate is generally considered a long-term, illiquid asset and therefore not an appropriate asset class for sponsors facing heavy near-term cash flow needs.

Whether the securitization of real estate has fundamentally changed this allocation issue remains to be seen. Exuberant promoters of this most recent wave of REITs would argue that sponsors in need of liquidity but attracted by the diversification and/or risk-return benefits of real estate can now have their cake and eat it too. While this is true to a certain extent, the majority of REITs are still small cap stocks. Individual investors can move into and out of a relatively small position in these companies with ease. Institutions, with their much larger transaction sizes, must be concerned with the average daily trading volume of the issues they are selecting. Many of the names in the REIT universe still have relatively small trading volumes. We must be careful not to overestimate the liquidity that has been gained for real estate through this latest wave of equity securitization. Furthermore, the issue of liquidity needs to be considered with the asset allocation in mind. If less than 10 percent of the portfolio is in real estate, the need for liquidity is most likely more psychological than investment driven.

One of the most important characteristics of pension funds relative to investment strategy is the total size of the asset base. Within the United States alone, there are thousands of plans, varying in size from well under $100 million to tens of billions of dollars. To our minds, portfolio size is probably *the* overriding factor in determining what role, if any, REITs can fill for a pension fund.

An example will help illustrate one aspect of this size effect. Let's assume a pension fund has $2 billion in total assets, not small by most individuals' definition but within the pension universe certainly not a "heavy hitter." Now, let's assume this fund has decided to allocate 7 percent of their assets to real estate, resulting in $140 million to invest. Two property types that institutions typically invest in are regional malls and downtown office buildings. Either of these property types could easily absorb the entire $140 million allocation. If the fund could only buy undivided interests in properties, they would be faced with the choice of (1) foregoing these major categories, (2) sinking their entire allocation into a few properties and having minimal diversification within the real estate allocation, or (3) leveraging their equity to obtain real estate diversification. None of these options are very attractive.

In the 1980s, smaller funds used commingled funds sponsored by a number of money managers to avoid this predicament. In effect, they pooled their allocation with other investors to achieve the diversification they could not attain by themselves. Smaller funds also had difficulty making investments in specialized real estate. If a plan wanted to allocate a small percentage of the real estate allocation to a special property type, timberland for example, simple arithmetic dictated a fairly small allocation in absolute size. Once again, commingled funds allowed these investors to make investments as small as $1 million in a variety of unique property type accounts. This is just one of the "size effects" that influences a fund's real estate investment strategy.

Another major plan characteristic to be considered is the liability structure of the fund. As discussed previously, liability duration and funding status are important considerations. Funds with relatively short liability duration must match this on the asset side. As noted above, real estate securities may allow a modest exposure to the asset class without a large sacrifice in liquidity. For larger investments, however, the liquidity issue is just as much a concern for a REIT position as for direct ownership of real estate. As an aside to this discussion, plans with long liability duration probably were overly vocal on the liquidity issue during the down cycle. Market timing is generally considered a loser's game in securities. It is that much harder to time the market with an illiquid asset such as real estate. In retrospect, what many were complaining about was the lack of control and ability to do anything about the loss in values across the industry. We were unable to sell our "dogs" and put the pain behind us. REITs will at least give us the ability to lock in our losses.

An issue related to the liability structure is the funding status of the plan. Other things being equal, an underfunded plan will be tempted to go with higher actuarial return assumptions than one that has a healthier funding status. Higher required returns generally argue for higher exposure to stocks. Real estate returns and risk are shown—by most studies—to be between those of stocks and bonds. In addition, a low correlation of returns between stocks and real estate makes real estate a good diversifier for heavy stock allocations without dropping all the way down to fixed-income returns. These asset-class risk and return characteristics are long-term historical averages, and even cycles as long as the recent one in real estate returns do not invalidate the historical picture. Funds requiring high stock exposure should consider adding real estate for diversification purposes.

Another variable in the "size effect" topic is the level of experience in real estate investing as well as the size and experience of the staff. Direct investing in real estate is not for the timid or inexperienced. Direct investors often assume the position of high-stakes negotiations and litigation. They deal with the daily real estate issues surrounding property and asset management, such as cash management and capital expenditures, which are similar to running a small business. These issues can be very time-consuming. In contrast, investing in REITs allows the plan to purchase the management expertise along with the asset base. Generally, only the larger funds can go beyond the commingled fund vehicle to the true separate account, and only the very largest can afford and justify the investment in experienced internal staff to directly invest. Staffing is not a static issue. Staffing starts with real estate "generalists." Specialty areas such as legal, accounting, construction, environmental, research, valuations, and engineering can be added as the size of the real estate investments grow and it makes economic sense to "in-source" these specialists.

The majority of investors were not happy with the results of their commingled investments at the beginning of the 1990s. It is unclear how much of their dissatisfaction stemmed from the vehicle versus the poor returns resulting from the depth and length of the industry depression. REITs represent a method of asset ownership, and the properties do not perform any differently as a result. While much wailing and gnashing of teeth occurred over the performance, perceived misalignment and conflicts of interests with the money managers, illiquidity, and lack of investor control in commingled funds, we believe that these same problems can (and in some cases do) exist in REITs.

Publicly traded REITs offer another form of financing and holding ownership of an asset. While capital market activities can cause an investment vehicle to perform better or worse than the real estate in the short term, we believe that in the long run, poor real estate performance cannot be hidden within an ownership structure (that is, a commingled fund, separate account, or public REIT) and that the underlying real estate performance will show through.

REITs can address a couple of these concerns for smaller pension plans but certainly not all of them. The interests of managers and investors are probably closer aligned, at least as long as a significant portion of the manager's wealth and income depends on the performance of the shares. The liquidity, at least at modest investment levels, is better than the actual liquidity available during the darkest days of the real estate capital crisis. However, REITs will not offer much help in performance during another serious downturn in real estate markets or on the issue of investor control. At the very least, smaller pension funds now have an alternative besides commingled funds to make investments in real estate.

It would be a mistake to assume that REIT's sole function for pension funds is to replace or supplement commingled accounts. Some characteristics of securitized real estate—lower transaction costs, increased liquidity, and protection from liability—give rise to other potential roles. Access to different sectors within real estate securities can be used as a tactical allocation tool and for investing in portfolios of unique properties, such as self-storage properties or franchise retail properties. In the next section, we explore how STRSO has capitalized on some of these characteristics.

STRSO USES OF REIT STOCKS

STRSO obtains its investment authority from Section 3307 of the Ohio Revised Code. In the fall of 1993, a legislative amendment that greatly expanded our investment alternatives became effective. Previously, we could invest in REITs only if they were public companies and met multiple tests on income coverage over fixed charges, market capitalization, and a history of dividend payments. These tests effectively prohibited us from making investments in REITs. The 1993 amendments broadened our investment authority in several areas and specifically granted authority to invest in public or private REITs.

STRSO's first REIT transaction occurred in August of 1993 when we were involved in bringing Excel (NYSE:XEL) public. We sold a portfolio of net leased properties to the company and received a combination of cash and convertible debentures. The debentures converted into XEL common stock as soon as the 1993 amendment that expanded our investment alternatives became effective. Although we ended up owning a minor portion of the company, we were prepared to own approximately 30 percent. Two critical events forced this change. First, as originally conceived in late 1992, XEL would finance the acquisition of our portfolio through a REMIC (real estate mortgage investment conduit) and then issue stock to the public at a later date. As the capital markets moved during the first part of the year and the IPO pipeline swelled, we (XEL, STRSO, and the investment bankers) decided to finance the acquisition with equity and then focus on the REMIC. Second, in early May, on the eve of filing the final S-11 registration statement, a tenant exercised their option to acquire their stores and the sale now involved 30 percent fewer stores and was $30 million smaller. As a result of these two factors, we owned in the neighborhood of 5 percent of the company when XEL went public. The decision to accelerate the IPO was well-timed because September of 1993 saw the IPO market hit the skids. We converted our debentures to common stock in November of 1993.

With our expanded investment authority in place, we developed a REIT strategy in late 1993 that complemented our direct real estate investments. Historically, we have focused our direct investments in the eastern half of the country. We also consciously avoided investments in malls because of pricing issues. Mall prices had come down by late 1993, and California's real estate markets had crashed. We felt strongly that this was the time to acquire malls and California property. Our REIT strategy focused on establishing positions in companies in the mall business or that had large property exposures in California. During this time, we were busy acquiring both California properties and mall properties so that by mid-1994, when our REIT portfolio approached $50 million, we had gained the portfolio balance we had set out to accomplish.

An interesting side note to the mall REITs is the rapid shift in ownership that took place as they came public, and their impact on pension fund investors such as STRSO. Before this last wave of equity securitization, owners regularly sold malls to raise liquidity or to redeploy capital into new projects. While we have not conducted a detailed count of malls, many of the better malls in the country are now in the public's hands via companies such as CBL, DeBartolo, General Growth, Mace-Rich, Rouse, Simon, Taubman, and Urban Shopping Centers. Other mall portfolios are controlled by companies that are private REITs (CPI, RPT). Clearly, we do not believe that all of the good malls are owned by REITs, but enough of them are to restrict the universe of mall investments on a direct basis more so than in any other property sector.

To supplement our real estate staff, we hired a stock analyst who would devote part of his time covering the REIT sector in the spring of 1994. From mid-1994 to mid-1995, our REIT investments increased to $150 million. Companies were selected on the basis of solid real estate portfolios, management, and stock market perceptions of the companies. Having been an active real estate investor since 1980 on a direct basis, we have acquired relationships with many of the REITs. We have known them as partners, competitors, property managers, and tenants. These relationships provide STRSO with a unique insight into a company, which we have used to complement our REIT investment decisions. For example, in early 1994 many apartment REITs were "printing money" by buying property at a reported 10 percent cap rate and then taking the portfolios public at an 8 percent dividend yield. On more than one occasion, we were competing bidders and felt that the 200-basis-point spread never existed because of the way in which the 10 percent cap rate was calculated. Accounting for management costs, meaningful replacement reserves, vacancy, and revenue loss to old leases can eat into the arbitrage quickly.

Private placements of REIT stock were the rage within the investment banking community before everyone started talking about mergers. In April of 1994, we reviewed a $25 million transaction with a retail company. Part of our due diligence on the company included a review of the real estate portfolio. We reviewed approximately 90 percent of the assets. When it finally came time to make the transaction, the stock price had slipped to a point where the company felt it could not issue additional stock. We reviewed a similar transaction in the fall of 1994 with an apartment REIT before the transaction was pulled for the same reason. Our experience with these two companies highlights the speed at which the capital markets can reprice a REIT when there's been no meaningful change in the company or the underlying assets; we will use this approach to REIT investments very sparingly in the future. This method of investing requires a sizable commitment of time and resources, and the ability to complete the transaction is subject to the whims of the stock market.

STRSO was involved in the recapitalization of the Meridian trusts in February 1996. Upon the consolidation, STRSO acquired $10 million of preferred stock in Meridian (NYSE: MDN). We viewed the MDN transaction as a way to expand into the industrial markets where properties are smaller and portfolios are often pricey as a result. In the Meridian transaction, we played a key role in the capital structure and assisted in bringing the company public (much like Excel); however, we did not participate as the "seed capital" in the initial recapitalization strategy that had a much higher risk profile. We believe we may find other opportunities such as Meridian attractive for new investments.

We also have completed a joint venture with a retail REIT. In this transaction, we view the REIT as a well-capitalized partner and we own the property in 50/50 partnership. We will continue to use this model of property ownership in future transactions. Variations on this theme include STRSO receiving stock or UPREIT units for half of the transaction rather than the partner-REIT investing cash.

On the direct-investment side, we watch the capital flows into public REITs because it affects what assets they buy and when they buy them. Beginning in late 1993 and continuing through the fall of 1994, we were outbid on multiple apartment projects by public REITs. In late 1994, we had a portfolio of apartments come back to us, at our price, after a REIT could not perform. It was the same issue as our private placement experience: The capital markets had shut off the REIT's acquisition activity due to a temporary price movement. The seller was more interested in selling his properties than in stock prices.

As a general rule, we like to keep our REIT shareholdings at less than 5 percent of a company. This eliminates most SEC filing and reporting related issues and limits the amount of risk we have in any single company. If we want to have a sizable enough investment to affect returns on a portfolio our size, we may be looking for $10 to $15 million investment positions. With the 5 percent ownership hurdle, this limits our REIT investments to companies with market capitalizations in the $200 to $300 million and larger range. Although the desired investment position and 5 percent limitation tend to limit the participation of larger institutional investors in smaller cap stocks, larger companies also facilitate sizable stock positions and benefit from broader coverage from the stock analyst community.

STRATEGIC USES OF REIT STOCKS

Pension investors can use REITs to gain access to different property sectors. STRSO, for example, does not directly invest in many small transactions because they are not a cost-effective use of our resources given our current investment objectives. Our size pushes us into larger transactions and by default limits the number of neighborhood, grocery-anchored strip centers that we own directly. Other property types (for example, mobile home parks, hotels) require specialized management, and REITs offer one way to obtain the requisite management expertise.

REITs in some cases own a portfolio of assets that will not be duplicated. If the investor wishes to own these unique assets, the REIT is the only way to own them. The mall REITs are good examples of portfolios that have been assembled over decades and will not be reproduced.

REITs can also be used to facilitate property dispositions given their ability to access debt and equity markets in a relatively short time frame. This provides REITs with an advantage over traditional noninstitutional buyers who must arrange financing on a deal-by-deal basis. A partial disposition to a REIT can also provide pension funds with the ability to liquidate a problem asset requiring specialized management (for example, leasing, marketing, development) and still allow the seller to receive some of the upside from the transaction.

Most pension funds that invest in real estate are concerned with diversifying their investments by property type and geographic location.

REITs do not fundamentally change this investment objective; however, they alter the speed at which a real estate portfolio can be reconfigured. A property usually takes months to acquire or dispose, so a large portfolio is not altered quickly. REITs, even with their small daily trading volumes, provide the investor with a greater ability to adjust their portfolio or to engage in active "sector allocation" strategies employed by several of the boutique REIT managers.

When exploring geographic diversification, REITs can be used as a replacement or a supplement to direct real estate ownership. It can take months to tap into the broker, developer, owner, adviser, and user markets to really know a market. Depending on the size of the market and its location, this investment may be worthwhile if the pension fund plans to invest there for some time. In this case, REITs can be used as an entry into the market and to rapidly establish the portfolio-structuring and allocation objectives. As assets are acquired on a direct basis over the ensuing months, the REIT allocation to the market can be lessened or eliminated. On the other hand, in a smaller market, or in a market in which the fund does not want to establish a direct ownership presence, REITs can be used as a permanent solution to the investment-structuring and allocation objectives.

REITs, because they have to meet dividend payout requirements to maintain their tax-exempt status, cannot retain large amounts of cash flow for future investment in the companies. Subsequently, REITs that have large internal reinvestment requirements or are growing quickly must frequently access the capital markets. This permits pension fund investors, with an appetite for direct real estate ownership, to acquire joint-venture interests in selected REIT properties. The capital raised through a partial disposition can be redeployed to other properties in the REIT's portfolio. For example, REIT A needs $50 million to repay debt lines or to buy new assets, and their stock price is at a level low enough to block them from raising new equity. Under this scenario, a pension fund could enter into a joint venture on some of the existing assets, thereby providing the REIT with the capital it needs.

CONCLUSION

STRSO has been an active REIT investor for nearly four years. We have invested in public, private, established, and start-up REITs. REITs, as we have discussed, can serve many investment objectives for the pension fund; however, REITs are not the cure for all real estate problems. REITs must be viewed as one of many avenues to make real estate investments.

CHAPTER

18

THE EMERGENCE OF U.S. REITs VIEWED FROM A GLOBAL PERSPECTIVE*

Fiduciary Trust Company International

David Harris ◆ John W. Foster ◆ Glenn U'ren

INTRODUCTION

This chapter, written by practitioners in the business of global, indirect property investing, aims to place United States real estate investment trusts (REITs) into a global context. How do these investments compare to listed property companies in other countries?

In the world of listed property shares, the United Kingdom has some of the best established stock exchange companies, and Hong Kong has companies and a property sector that in size dwarfs all others, but it is REITs that, since their rebirth in 1993–1994, have grown most rapidly and perhaps generated the most attention. Listed property companies in the United States as measured by Salomon Brothers in their World Equity Index–Property, have risen as a percentage of the index from 15 percent at the end of 1992 to 25 percent at the end of September 1996 (Figure 18–1).

*Authors' Note: The views expressed above represent the personal views of the authors and do not necessarily represent the views of Fiduciary Trust Company International.

FIGURE 18–1

The World's Property Share Markets

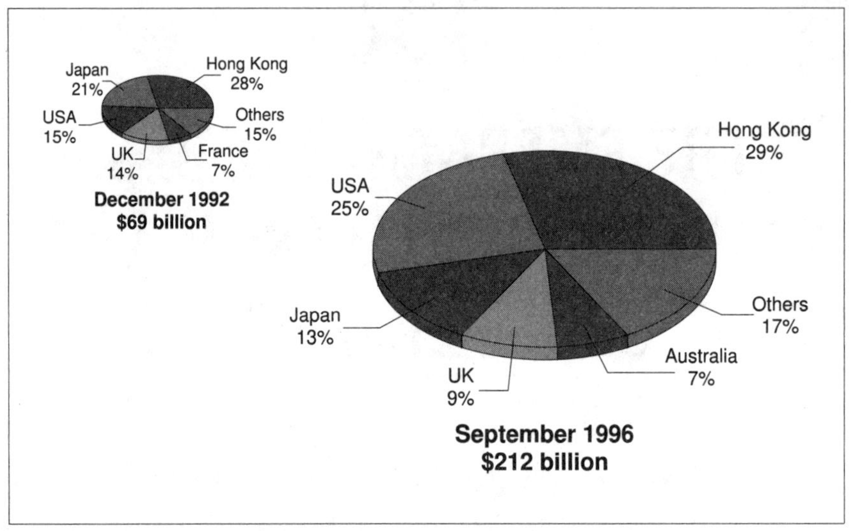

Source: Salomon Brothers

Significant though this is, the change in the value of this leading property share index from $69 billion* to $212 billion (as a sector now representing 1.9 percent of the total index) over the same period underlines the rise in importance of listed property companies on a global basis. Arguably, at the current level, the global listed property sector has reached a critical size, which has begun to command serious consideration by investors and, in practical terms, to provide a degree of investment choice and share liquidity.

The growth in cross-border global investment flows in recent years has been enormous, stimulated by the relaxation of capital controls and the desire by investors to seek higher returns and diversification benefits overseas. While cross-border direct property ownership has had a mixed record and presents considerable challenges, listed property shares represent a much easier way for investors to gain exposure to global property

*All dollars in U.S. dollars unless otherwise indicated.

markets. However, listed property companies are far from a homogeneous group. There are considerable differences in management styles, tax status, range of activities, and valuations. Certainly, to think of most listed property companies outside the United States as being very similar to "our REITs," or indeed likely to become so, would be a mistake.

THE GLOBAL PROPERTY MARKET

Property markets in most of the developed world experienced a notable boom-and-bust cycle in the late 1980s and early 1990s. This has been followed in recent years by economic recovery. Even by the standards of this highly cyclical industry, global property price changes over the last decade have been spectacular. From the mid-1980s, buoyant economic growth prompted occupational demand that, together with a plentiful supply of money, helped fuel a boom in property investment and development. Financial deregulation in a number of leading countries helped increase the oversupply of capital into property. The party abruptly ended in the late 1980s with the general raising of interest rates and the subsequent recession of many economies. Occupational and investment demand for property collapsed with a consequent and dramatic effect on commercial values, which in many instances fell by a third or more, in a couple of years. The crash in many countries took on the characteristics all too familiar to U.S. observers: tenants became scarce and investors even rarer, rents fell, vacancies rose, the lending institutions were forced to write down assets and to take back properties on default, and development projects were shelved.

Figure 18–2 provides a valuable indication of the trend of capital values for prime office buildings in the major cities, in the world's most economically significant countries. As can be observed, the trends over the long term have tended to show a degree of correlation and values in all three regions have begun at least to show signs of stabilization.

The recovery seen in many markets over the last few years, as in the United States, has been based on increased demand by occupiers and an absence of new supply. The severe downward price correction had brought income yields up to levels at or close to the cost of finance, thereby encouraging those contrarian investors with strong enough nerves back into property. The lenders with an uncomfortable level of property debt on their books have found ways to reduce their exposure, by writing

FIGURE 18–2

Capital Values for Prime Office Buildings

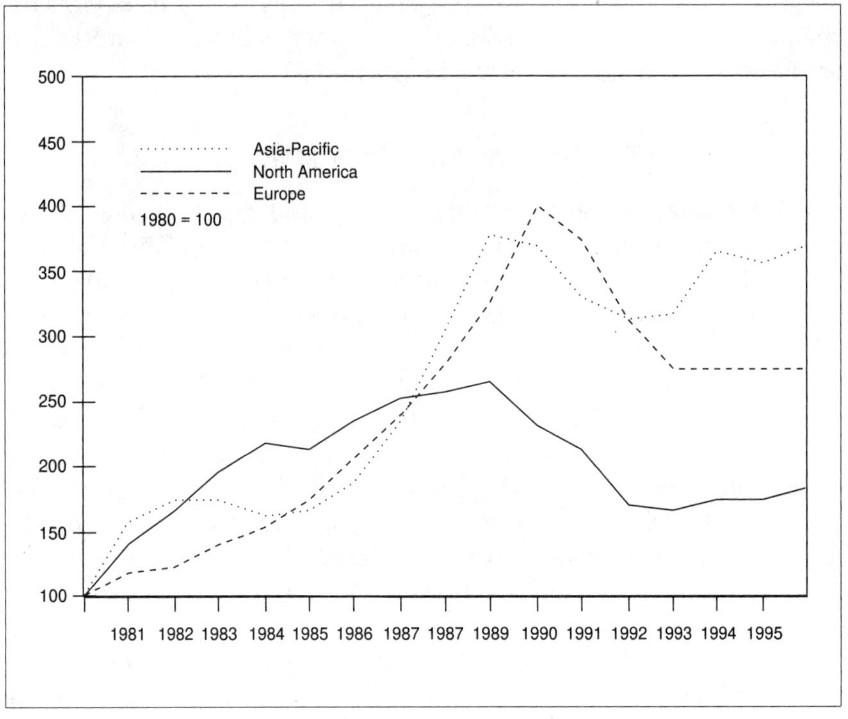

Source: Jones Lang Wootton

down these assets to a market-clearance level and selling them. This happened initially in the United States and United Kingdom, allowing the markets in these countries to recover first. Slower to act have been institutions in countries such as France, which now seems to have started a meaningful stock clearance, and in Japan, which may not yet have found a sustainable value level.

In the Asian-Pacific markets outside of Japan, the reversal was typically less pronounced and the recovery somewhat quicker. These markets generally can be said to experience much shorter cycles and to enjoy rather more positive demand fundamentals with significantly higher rates of economic and population growth, which quickly reasserted themselves.

In investment terms, many investors have remained understandably wary of new property commitments. Indeed, in a number of markets, a number of former big players have chosen to significantly reduce their role. A singular exception to these general trends in terms of direct investing has been the enormous growth experienced by the German open- and closed-end property funds, currently valued around $100 billion. These funds have been growing at over 10 percent per annum in recent years. Offering an attractive after-tax yield to German private investors, these funds have bought up virtually all the stock in the domestic market. The larger open-end funds have successfully moved offshore, buying central London offices and property in the Netherlands and Belgium.

The fortunes of the listed property companies in most markets has largely mirrored the trends in the direct market. They fell rapidly from being among the best share price performers during the heady late 1980s. Many companies during the early 1990s have felt the pain of asset write-downs, forced sales, dividend cuts, and prolonged poor share price performance. Now in the light of improved markets, property share prices and results performances have begun to pick up. Stock markets have anticipated the prospects for improved net asset valuations, earnings, and dividends with, in many cases, historically high stock ratings. This has triggered a spate of new equity fund-raisings in many markets, both by existing listed companies and through new company flotations (IPOs). The emergence of new listed companies has been a notable feature in the Australian Property Trust market and in Sweden, with the flotation of quite substantial companies formed around portfolios of properties taken in by the banks on default. In Hong Kong, the market has seen rights issues from the property companies principally to help fund the acquisition of development sites in the surging local residential market.

The surviving companies from the 1980s have in many cases been joined by new and reenergized existing companies with new management teams, often taking an active entrepreneurial approach to profitably working the property markets and providing shareholder returns.

The much discussed rise of a listed property sector in the United States, seemingly viewed by some as a singular phenomenon, is rather an occurrence with echoes in a number of other countries around the world. The main point of difference to the United States has been that the revival of interest elsewhere has been through an already well-established listed property share market.

THE INVESTOR PERSPECTIVE

Historically, property has often proven to be a troublesome investment for many institutional investors. Direct ownership of property has frequently experienced wide swings of favor over time. Commonly, institutions in any country have been of the same property mind-set at the same phase of the cycle. Direct institutional ownership of property in most markets has nearly always been restricted to the larger funds, usually with a long-term perspective. This has been determined by the large individual size of most single property investments, the need to maintain an element of diversification, and the high costs of maintaining management with the necessary specialized property skills. However, with the property market increasingly demanding a quick response and the need to maintain an entrepreneurial approach, many large institutions have often been found wanting. Direct property ownership has proven an easy target for criticism of these investing institutions. The failed and illiquid investments that the chairman of the investment fund's trustees can observe from his or her office window has perhaps added to the discontent.

Direct property's poor relative performance has coincided with a growing concern over liquidity and high management costs. Additionally, leading regulatory changes such as the introduction of the Minimum Funding Requirement for pension funds in the United Kingdom, has added to the unease many investors feel about meeting future liabilities while holding large amounts of an illiquid asset such as direct property.

Not surprisingly, in recent years many institutions have made the strategic choice to reduce their direct property holdings. This has often been achieved via asset sales, though frequently weak relative performance and inertia alone has been sufficient to substantially reduce property holdings as a percentage of the whole.[1]

However, the recent revival of interest in property as an investment media has been prompted not only by the improved prospects but also because numerous studies have shown its low correlation of returns to equities and bonds. Typically a late performer in the economic cycle, property can bring diversification benefits to investment funds. It follows that adding an international element will increase the diversification benefits further.[2]

The strength of the argument for investing in property shares over direct ownership has been most dramatically seen in the actions of the leading Dutch pension funds in recent years. ABP, Europe's largest pension fund, with around $130 billion, has made the strategic decision to withdraw from its direct property ownership and build up its position in listed property stocks on a worldwide basis. It has taken a substantial position in Rodamco, the world's largest international listed property company, at both the holding company level and in its regional/country subsidiaries in the Asia-Pacific region, the United States, and the United Kingdom. More dramatically from a United States viewpoint, ABP has emerged as a large and notable shareholder of a number of leading public REITs, including Simon, Taubman, and Equity Residential. Other large Dutch pension funds with similar property investment philosophies include PGGM and the Metalworkers Fund.

INDIRECT PROPERTY INVESTMENT OPTIONS AND THEIR PROXY STATUS

If investors are attracted by the arguments for including property in their portfolios but find the difficulties of direct ownership a major stumbling block, what other options are available to the investor and how good are they at capturing property returns?

In general, the indirect property investor has two options: the unlisted, commingled fund and listed property shares. In the United States, the commingled fund has been an established part of the market for some time, with investors being presented a wide choice of managers and varying fund objectives. Elsewhere in the world, the choice is much more limited, and the vehicles that exist often are closed to nondomestic investors. The debate on the merits of this type of investment is not part of this chapter, but suffice it to say that a common view is that the performance of these vehicles is closely aligned to the underlying performance of the direct market.

Currently offering rather more choice to international investors in most markets outside the United States are the shares of listed property companies. Listed property companies in a number of stock markets around the world have existed in their current form for a number of years and in a few cases represent a very sizable presence. Investors can look to a performance record of over 30 years from Land Securities, the United Kingdom's largest listed property company and a FTSE 100 stock. In Hong Kong, on the world's fifth biggest stock exchange, the residential developers Sun Hung Kai and Cheung Kong currently rank among the five largest companies on the Hang Seng Index, being capitalized at around $30 billion and $20 billion, respectively. Many companies and, most crucially, their managements have been known to investors over a period of time, and their performance record as publicly traded entities can be seen over at least one full cycle of the property market.

Do investors buy these companies as a means to capture property returns, or are they seen as just another sector of the equity market? Property company shares in the rest of the world outside the United States are almost always managed and viewed as part of general equity portfolios.

That said, some interesting work in the United Kingdom supports the view that, over the longer term, property share performance has had a correlation to the performance of the underlying direct property market, and that property does perform a role as proxy for direct ownership but with the added advantage of affording greater liquidity. In a study, SBC Warburg[3] looked at the total return performance of the four largest listed U.K. property stocks against the direct market over the past 27 years, which included three complete cycles of the property market (see Figure 18–3). Adding cash to negate the effects of company leverage, they concluded that returns have been closely correlated. This work is particularly of note given the quality and consistency of the back data on both the companies and the direct market and the long time period that usefully captures performance over this persistently cyclical market.

A study conducted by Lehman Brothers[4] arrived at similar conclusions for the United States, albeit over a shorter period of study.

Investors can use a number of established equity stock indexes that include global listed property stocks, such as those from Morgan Stanley, Salomon Brothers, and Datastream. However, while coverage of the direct market is well established in a number of individual countries and improving in others, little work has been produced on a global basis. Pioneering work has been done by the leading international firms of chartered surveyors, Jones Lang Wootton (with their International Office Index) and Richard Ellis (World Office Rent Index and their regional and country reports); however, further developments in this area face considerable challenges. Due to the heterogeneous nature of the direct property market and the lack of consistent data, it is much more difficult to construct global property indexes than for stocks and bonds.

F I G U R E 18–3

UK Property Returns—Direct and Shares
Rolling Ten-Year Cumulative Total Returns

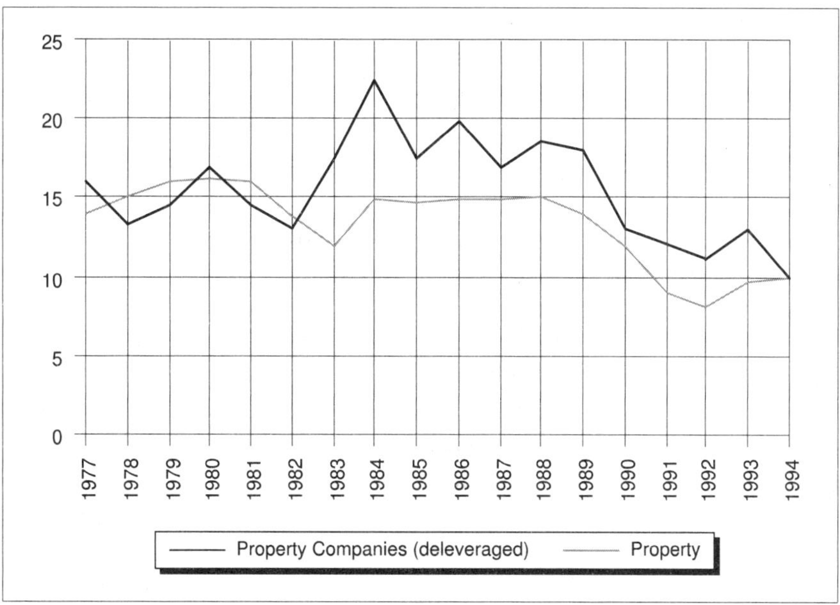

Source: SBC Warburg

THE ADVANTAGES AND DISADVANTAGES OF LISTED PROPERTY COMPANIES

As investments, listed property companies offer a number of advantages and disadvantages, which are discussed from a U.S. perspective elsewhere in this book. From a global perspective, we would briefly state that we see the principal advantages of listed property companies as being daily market pricing, greater liquidity (affording greater flexibility in positioning the portfolio over time), management cost savings, and lower transaction costs.

In a number of stock markets, there is a choice of large, well-established property companies with substantial free share floats. However, it is interesting to observe that in most markets the poor liquidity of smaller property stocks is as much an issue as it is for many REITs. In most mature property share markets with companies able to retain capital, the emphasis is on secondary market trading with occasional and substantial primary equity fund-raisings. This stands in contrast to the REITs, with their requirement to distribute most of their earnings and their frequent tapping of the market for new equity finance. U.S. investment banks have been notably aggressive in promoting the issuance of new equity by the REITs since 1993–1994.

An additional point of consideration regarding management in property companies versus direct ownership is that through an investment in a listed company, the investor is investing in local knowledge and skills that might be impossible or at least extremely costly and time-consuming to acquire in overseas markets.

Set against these advantages, listed property companies carry a number of disadvantages compared to direct ownership. Share ownership does not afford the same degree of control over the investment that direct ownership typically confers, even in an environment of open and responsive corporate governance. In some markets, shares provide either limited or no voting entitlement, and there can be restrictions on takeovers. One of the appeals of REITs has been the perception that there is an alignment of management interests alongside third-party investors. However, the commonly used UPREIT structure offers investors a less satisfactory investment than a company whose shares are of equal status. REITs with managers owning operating partnership units frequently have an entirely different perspective on the tax consequences of the actions of the REIT than a third-party investor, which might lead to future conflicts. Furthermore, as the battle for Chateau Properties highlighted, some REITs have an effective bar on takeovers. Of course, the liquidity of a listed investment usually allows the investor the exit option of readily selling his or her shares in the case of a difference of view over corporate direction.

A further specific disadvantage for investors in REITs compared to property companies elsewhere in the world is the alarming growth in executive remuneration packages in a number of companies. These packages often include large share options granted with modest or no performance hurdles that will potentially dilute the interests of third-party investors. We do not see rewards to executives outside the United States that come anywhere near the size of these packages, even for the best managed companies with superior performance records. In markets where executive options exist, they are commonly limited in size and are frequently attached to stated relative performance targets.

Taxes are the other substantive disadvantage to listed share ownership, in that many share investors receive taxable income in the form a dividend distribution after the listed company has itself paid corporate tax. Rental income from direct ownership, by contrast, is usually only taxable once, at the source. Many listed company investors are therefore at an income disadvantage through double taxation compared to investing in income-producing property directly. Furthermore, property companies in many markets are liable for capital gains tax if they dispose of assets in excess of costs. REITs, of course, have the advantage of offering distributions of income free of corporate tax, provided they comply with the REIT code.

Tax-favored listed property investment structures similar to U.S. REITs exist elsewhere in the world, including Australia and the Netherlands, together with new vehicles in Belgium and Canada. France in recent years has scrapped the REIT-like tax breaks once enjoyed by many of its listed property companies. Seeing the success of U.S. REITs, would-be sponsors in some other countries have been pressing governments for rule changes to allow the creation of REIT-style vehicles. Going against the grain of leveling the tax playing field, it is difficult to understand how the argument can be sustained in most countries for specifically giving the property industry a new tax break, unless it forms part of a larger reform of pensions and investments. This is especially so where listed property companies already exist. The conditions that frequently are attached to a tax-favored status, such as restricting development, trading, nonproperty investments, and debt levels, act as a fetter on the more entrepreneurial company managements and serve to limit the appeal.

With pension reform a pressing consideration for many countries, it appears likely that in the future we can anticipate a substantial build-up of pension funds around the world. Most of the new funds will almost certainly be invested in government bonds and general equities. It is almost as certain that property's strongest claim on a meaningful allocation of this future fund flow will be through indirect investments.

THE GLOBAL STOCK UNIVERSE

In recent years, there has been considerable growth in the investable universe of global listed property stocks in both number and size. This has been a function of the emergence of new companies, improved share performance, and the issuance of more stock from existing companies. The two largest global property share indexes, LIFE and Salomon Brothers, each include over 300 listed companies with a combined capitalization in excess of $200 billion. This compares to a sector with a capitalization of less than $20 billion in the mid-1980s.

There are presently four global listed property share indexes: the international property share index of the Datastream Global Indices, the LIFE Global Real Estate Securities Index, the Morgan Stanley Capital International property share index, and the Salomon Brothers World Equity Index–Property. All but LIFE form a sectoral part of an index of global equities, LIFE having been developed specifically as a dedicated property share index. All offer total return, price, and income return numbers. Salomon's and LIFE have the greatest depth, containing 340 and 367 companies in 18 and 33 countries, respectively. The indexes generally exclude the smaller companies below $50 million in equity capitalization/free float. The inclusion and exclusion of individual companies within these indexes can be idiosyncratic.

Listed property companies can be divided into developers and those with an investment orientation. The developers are primarily engaged in buying land, developing property, and selling it. This is a very different business in terms of the risk and reward from an investment company who holds a portfolio of usually commercial properties for rental and capital appreciation. Many companies are engaged to a degree in both activities. Over the property cycle, investors might expect the well-managed company to alter the balance of its activities to best suit market conditions.

Table 18–1 shows that the world's largest property companies are dominated by companies from Hong Kong, most notably the gigantic residential developers. Many of these companies in their core business have proved to be adept traders of a volatile market. Other developer/investor companies from the Asia-Pacific region also feature prominently. The mature markets of Europe are represented only by the three largest U.K. investment companies and by Rodamco, the largest truly international property investment company. Simon DeBartolo is the largest listed U.S. REIT. It will be interesting to observe in future years how many U.S. names break into the top 25. Much will depend on the relative pace of future securitization, corporate consolidation, and underlying property growth. The heavy presence of Hong Kong companies reflects a high degree of property

TABLE 18–1

The World's Largest Listed Property Companies
By Equity Market Capitalization as of December 1996

Company	Country	Activity	Market Capitalization (in billions)
1. Sun Hung Kai	Hong Kong	Residential developer	$30.1
2. Cheung Kong Holdings	Hong Kong	Residential developer	20.5
3. Henderson Land	Hong Kong	Residential developer	16.7
4. Mitsubishi Estate	Japan	Investor	15.8
5. New World Devmts.	Hong Kong	Residential developer	11.7
6. Wharf Holdings	Hong Kong	Investor	11.6
7. Mitsui Fudosan	Japan	Investor	9.4
8. City Devmts.	Singapore	Investor/developer	7.1
9. Hong Kong Land	Hong Kong	Investor	6.7
10. Land Securities	UK	Investor	6.4
11. Ayala Land	Philippines	Investor/developer	6.3
12. Wheelock	Hong Kong	Investor/developer	5.7
13. Rodamco	Netherlands	International investor	4.4
14. Hysan Devmts.	Hong Kong	Investor	4.0
15. Amoy Props.	Hong Kong	Investor	3.6
16. Simon DeBartolo Grp.	US	Investor	3.6
17. British Land	UK	Investor	3.5
18. Sino Land	Hong Kong	Developer	3.5
19. Henderson Investment	Hong Kong	Investor	3.5
20. DBS Land	Singapore	Investor/developer	3.2
21. MEPC	UK	Investor	3.2
22. Hang Lung	Hong Kong	Residential developer	3.1
23. Kerry Props.	Hong Kong	Investor	3.0
24. Hopewell Hldgs.	Hong Kong	Investor/developer	2.9
25. Sumitomo Realty	Japan	Investor	2.7

Source: Bloomberg, FTCI

securitization in Hong Kong, estimated to represent a third of the total property market. This compares to over 10 percent in Singapore, but only 2 percent in the United Kingdom and a mere 1 percent in the United States.

Aside from the "pure" property companies included in the property share indexes, a wide range of companies not classified as property stocks offer investors a property play. The land-rich Japanese railway companies stand out as a notable example of an asset story outside the property sector. In Germany, which has a very limited listed property sector, equity investors have bought the shares of the large construction companies that have significant land holdings as a way to gain exposure to German property. In addition, there are property companies in emerging markets, even including a recent offering of shares for a new company engaged in property redevelopment in Lebanon.

VALUATION CRITERIA

A company's share price expressed as a multiple of funds from operations is the most commonly applied valuation criteria used to value REITs and is a unique feature of the U.S. market.

Classic property company analysis, which is applied in most of the rest of the world, looks at the share price relationship to net asset value. The latter is therefore an exercise in analyzing a company's balance sheet and growth prospects as opposed to concentrating on the revenue account that REIT valuation pays most attention to. This is not to say that in the rest of the world a company's revenues are ignored, for in some markets and at different points in the cycle, a company's dividend-paying capacity is the principle focus of attention. Additionally, in some markets, property developers are valued principally by reference to the price-earnings ratio. However, what might be described as the British model of net asset value (NAV) is the standard method of valuation in the United Kingdom and notably in places such as Hong Kong, Singapore, Malaysia, and Australia, with a recent British influence and generally using the United Kingdom's accounting rules. Property companies in the Netherlands also include their properties at market value. It is significant that the most active property companies in countries such as Spain and France, notably those that have attracted the largest foreign interest, have moved to adopt the annual, externally assessed market valuation of their assets for inclusion on the balance sheet along British lines.

Company valuations based on NAV primarily give consideration to the market value of a company's assets. In the United Kingdom, this most importantly incorporates the inclusion on the audited balance sheet of a current market valuation of the company's investment properties. Development and trading properties are usually stated at the lower of cost or realizable value. The investment properties are valued by qualified external valuers according to the definition of open market value supplied by the Royal Institution of Chartered Surveyors:

> The best price at which the sale of an interest in the property would have been completed unconditionally for cash consideration on the date of valuation assuming: a) a willing seller; b) that, prior to the date of valuation, there had been a reasonable period (having regard to the state of the market) for the proper marketing of the interest, for the agreement of the price and terms and for the completion of the sale; c) that the state of the market, level of values and other circumstances were, on any assumed date of exchange of contracts, the same as on the date of valuation; d) that no account will be taken of any additional bid by a purchaser with a special interest; and e) that both parties to the transaction had acted knowledgeably, prudently and without compulsion.

No depreciation charge is set against a company's revenue account on the assumption that annually including properties at market valuation reasonably reflects depreciation on the properties held for investment. Periodically, this practice of not accounting specifically for depreciation through the profit and loss account has come under scrutiny by the accountants in the United Kingdom as being out of line with general accounting practice. As recently as October 1996, the Accounting Standards Board acknowledged that users did not wish to see change from the practice of annual valuations and that investment property companies should continue to be exempt from depreciation.

How does this NAV-based valuation methodology work in practice? Reliance on NAV as a measure of worth for listed property companies is principally predicated on the market's belief that it is a better tool to value those companies that typically hold low and no income-producing assets (such as reversionary investments, developments, and land) than to look at current income. There has been criticism of the use of NAV-based valuations, particularly at the bottom and top of the property price cycle; but, viewed over time, the practice has proved to be a good and well-tested guide to establishing the worth of these property companies.

FIGURE 18–4

Percentage Change in the UK Property Sector Relative to All Share Index and Capital Growth of Direct Property

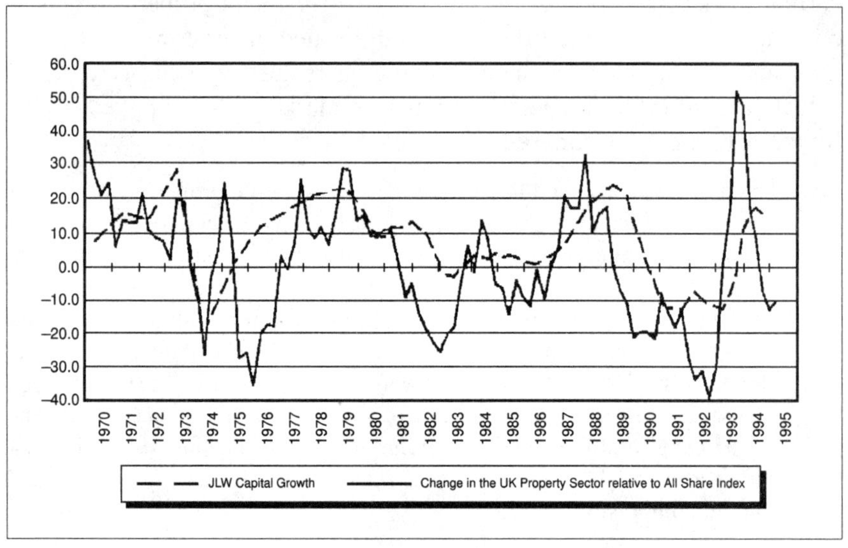

Source: SBC Warburg

On evidence from the United Kingdom, property share prices have proven good leading indicators of future performance of the direct market over the cycle, usually leading the underlying market by around 18 months (see Figure 18–4).

In other markets where property companies have been in existence for some time, market wisdom also supports the idea of property shares status as a leading indicator of the underlying property market.

Share prices have typically traded at discounts or premiums to estimates of future NAVs: on big discounts when the outlook for asset growth is poor; on low discounts/premiums when substantial growth is thought to lie ahead. In a similar manner to the price-earnings ratios used to value general equities, those companies with the best growth prospects stand at the highest ratings. Usually, these are the companies with the most highly regarded managements: for their transaction, development, and financing skills, and for the quality of the assets. At different points in the property cycle, investors have looked for different characteristics. During a bull phase, investors will often look for companies that offer the highest potential returns through deals, development, and leverage. By contrast, in a bear period, they will seek the defensive qualities of low leverage and dividend security.

Various manifestations of the net asset valuation approach to valuing property companies exist around the globe. Hong Kong, Singapore, Malaysia, and other Asia-Pacific developers are usually valued by estimating the net present value of their developments in terms of the NAV. In Japan, land prices movements and the associated effect on the value of a company's assets appear to be one of the chief drivers of property share prices, though in truth this remains one of the most difficult markets for outsiders to understand.

Why REITs should be usually valued on an entirely different basis than property companies in the rest of the world is perhaps due to the income orientation of the investment, the quarterly reporting requirements, short leases in the United States, and the low standing of the value of appraisals. As the REIT market matures, it would not be surprising if a NAV-based approach became more generally applied as the principal valuation criteria. Meanwhile, it remains a point of concern that the pursuit of short-term earnings growth by some REITs may not be compatible with longer-term property fundamentals.

A STRATEGY TO INVEST IN GLOBAL PROPERTY SHARES

Having decided on an allocation to global property shares, how might an investor develop an overall investment strategy? Indexation of the fund allocation against the desired benchmark would provide the simplest solution. However, given the misalignment of the indexes (most property share indexes are heavily weighted toward Asia), for many investors a combined top-down macro and bottom-up stock selection approach is appropriate in order to capture the greatest returns for the lowest risk.

The top-down approach weighs such macroeconomic/political issues as the outlook for GDP growth, interest rates, foreign exchange, and political stability to help form a view as to establishing an appropriate weighting for a specific country. Similar work can also be undertaken in reviewing a regional weighting.

For a property share investor, there is the need to research the underlying property market to form a view about the supply and demand factors at the national, city, and property level, and about the likely future trends in property rental and capital values.

The bottom-up stock selection process involves careful consideration of specific company investment opportunities. The investor will need to carefully review such factors as the company's activities, its performance record, management strengths and weaknesses, asset quality, finances, and dividend payments. This process typically involves meeting with senior management and reviewing corporate announcements, such as annual accounts and press releases. The investor will need to come to a conclusion about the outlook for growth potential—perhaps over a range of criteria such as net assets, earnings, and dividends and whether the stock market is valuing this growth appropriately. Stock market factors such as a share liquidity and analytical coverage will also need to be considered. For the global investor, market sentiment must be considered with a view to the broader market correlation of property shares to the overall stock market (see Figure 18–5).

The markets where property is a larger part of the equity market (in Hong Kong property shares are 30 percent of the Hang Seng), savvy investors will view the importance of this correlation as part of their overall strategy.

FIGURE 18–5

Property Stock Correlation

Correlation Country Indexes with Country Property Indexes

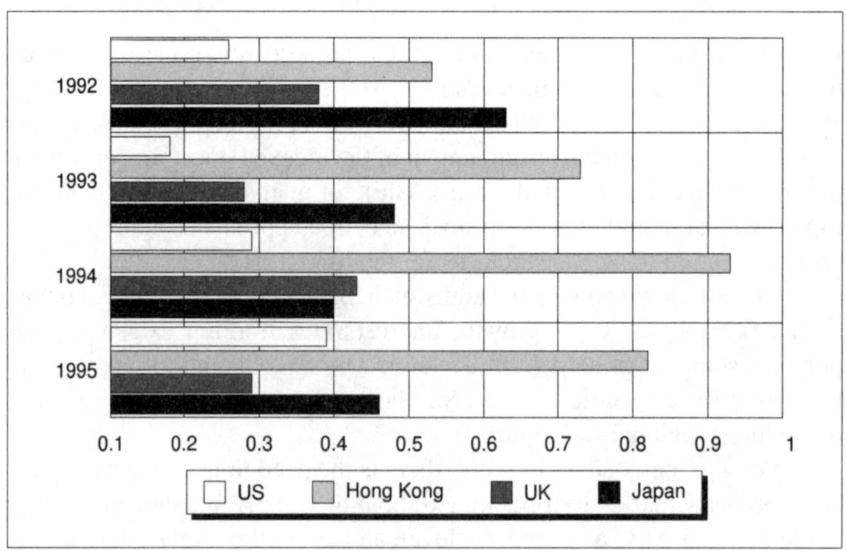

Source: Solomon Brothers World Equity Index—Property

Taking into account the conclusions on regional and country weightings together with the thoughts as to the desired balance of property type and yield, a portfolio can begin to be constructed of individual stock selections. The resultant portfolio can be viewed against a chosen benchmark over time to monitor relative performance. Many investors look for performance in terms of total return, combining both capital and income, though some focus on one or the other aspect. U.S. REITs, with their attractive yields and handsome price appreciation in recent years, would have provided a rewarding element to a global property share portfolio on any basis. Moreover, with a view, again, to a seemingly misaligned index, a perspective on the size of the U.S. GDP and total equity market capitalization combined with political stability would argue for a weighting of U.S. REITs well in excess of the current index weighting of approximately 25 percent.

Currency hedging considerations for any global equity portfolio are important. The currency risk can be managed, and the same is true for the property share sector of the equity market.

Ongoing management of the portfolio requires daily reviews of market pricing and consideration of announcements of a top-down macro nature as well as both property market and company-specific news. Regular contact with company management and stock market analysts are often key elements in this process.

Perhaps most important in the practical application of property share portfolio management, from an investor's perspective, is that the liquidity of listed property investments usually allows for timely adjustments in managed portfolios. A share portfolio can be adjusted quickly and inexpensively in response to a change in circumstance. Hence, a property share manager with a good perspective on the stock market and an eye on the underlying and less volatile property markets can add significant value by anticipating property market direction and placing clients in or away from those market directions within a property type, country, or region.

CONCLUSION

In the future, if property has investment appeal, the arguments in favor of indirect involvement for most investors, particularly for listed stocks, seem irresistible.

In a conservative environment that has been unfamiliar with securitized property, REITs appear to be gaining acceptance as a viable investment among investors in the United States. The growth of REITs in recent years is notable but not without parallels elsewhere in the world and indeed forms part of a significant increase in the size of the global listed property sector. Some international investors are well advanced in their thinking regarding global property share investing, and many more already own such shares as part of their equity portfolios. REITs have undoubtedly already proved to be an attractive and popular way by which non-U.S. investors can invest in U.S. property and form part of a global property share investing strategy.

The REITs themselves, "the new the kids on the block," have made an impressive start; the challenge for their management in the future is to add value over the full property cycle. As publicly traded entities, few have been tested over tough times. The positive spread-buying window of opportunity and recovery phase of the U.S. property market will not last forever. The other side of the next property bear market will be the time when investors can truly begin comparing the performance of the REITs and their managements with the more seasoned listed property companies the rest of the world has to offer.

ENDNOTES

1. The average Dutch pension fund holds 11 percent of its assets in direct property; in the United Kingdom the number is 5 percent, in Japan 3 percent, and in the United States 2 percent. Source: Pension Funds Indicators, UBS 1995.
2. Piet Eicholtz, "Does International Diversification Work Better for Real Estate than for Stocks and Bonds?" *Financial Analysts Journal*, January–February 1996.
3. SBC Warburg Property Briefing: "Achieving a Property Weighting through Property Shares," July–August, 1995.
4. Lehman Brothers, "REITs and Real Estate: Two Markets Reexamined," December 1995.

INDEX

ADDITIONAL COMMENTS ON REAL ESTATE INVESTMENT TRUSTS

"This book contains everything you would want to know about REITs—from launching an IPO to the nuances of corporate governance. It serves as a great road map to the future of the real estate industry."

Robert N. Jenkins
Vice President, Real Estate Investments
Metropolitan Life Insurance Company

"*Real Estate Investment Trusts: Structure, Analysis, and Strategy* provides informative and insightful perspectives from leading REIT experts. It is a superb resource on current industry issues and a highly valuable educational tool for investors and academia."

Steven A. Wechsler
President and CEO
The National Association of Real Estate Investment Trusts®

"John Parsons and Richard Garrigan have succeeded in compiling an exceedingly rich resource for participants in all facets of the REIT market. As we continue our attempts to take the Canadian REIT market out of its infancy, this guidebook on REITs will allow us to benefit from the experience of those who have walked the road before us."

Carolyn A. Blair
Vice President and Regional Director, DS Marcil Inc.
Vice President and Director, RBC Dominion Securities Inc.
Toronto, Ontario

"The size of the REIT industry has exploded both in terms of the number of companies and the total market capitalization since the early 1990s. Books such as this shed a great deal of light onto an industry of growing importance to us all."

Michael P. McCarty
Senior Vice President, Market Research
Simon DeBartolo Group, Inc.

"*Real Estate Investment Trusts: Structure, Analysis, and Strategy* is a comprehensive, thorough reference guide for all facets of REITs and REIT investing. This book is a must read for anyone having interest in real estate investment trusts."

Raymond H. Bottorf
Managing Director
ABN AMRD
ABP Stichting Pensioenfods